SEAWOLF 28

by Al Billings

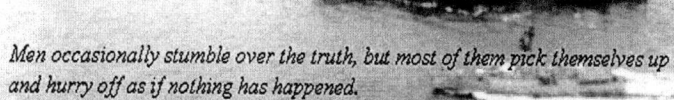

Men occasionally stumble over the truth, but most of them pick themselves up and hurry off as if nothing has happened.
--Winston Churchill

Copyright © 2004 by Alan J. Billings
All rights reserved
ISBN 1-59457-299-2

Library of Congress-in-Publication Data applied for
This work is collection of stories gathered over a 22 year career.
Many of the names have been changed to protect the identity
of those individuals that may wish to stay anonymous; however,
it is also based on factual events, persons and locations.

Cover Design by: Joe Kline
www.joekline.com
First edition
April 2004

To order additional copies, please contact us.
BookSurge, LLC
www.booksurge.com
1-866-308-6235
orders@booksurge.com

Seawolf 28

Al Billings

2004

Seawolf 28

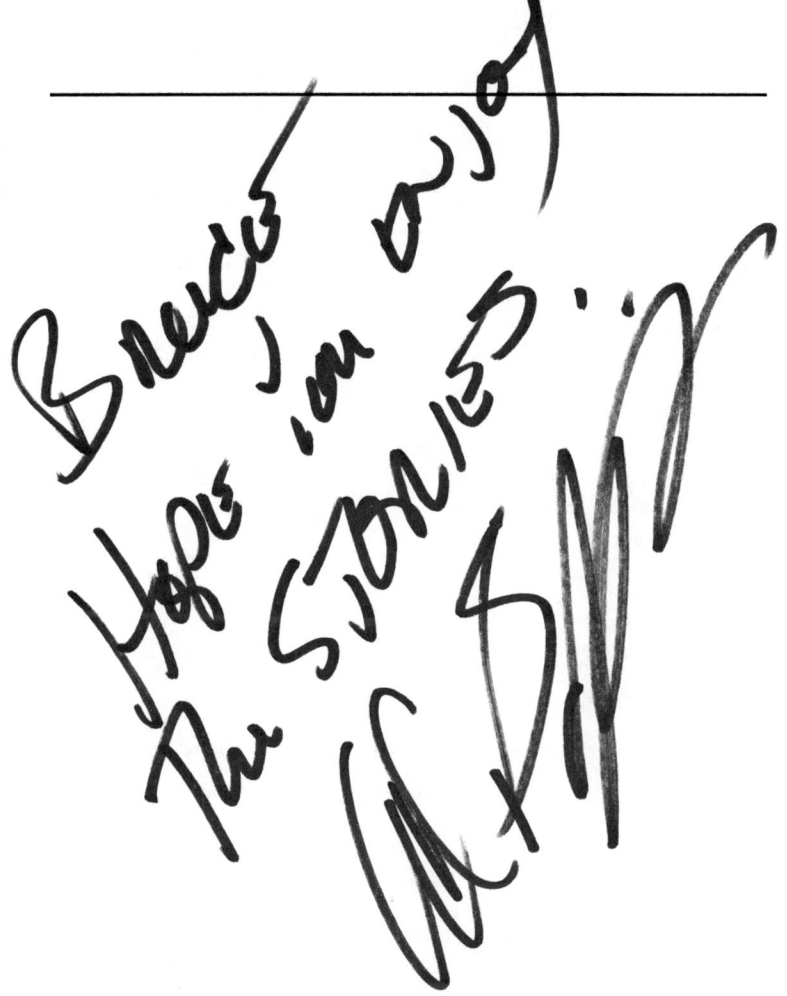

CONTENTS

PROLOGUE	xiii
Chapter One	1
"Wings of Gold"	1
Basic Flight Training	12
NAS Whiting Field and 6 1/2 G's without a "G" suit	16
Instrument training	22
Navigation and Cross Country Training	26
Carrier Qualifications	31
What the hell are helicopters?	39
First Engine Failure	44
Commissioning Day and Wings of Gold	47
Chapter Two	51
First Duty Assignment	51
Helicopter Combat Support Squadron One (HC-1), NALF Imperial Beach	51
Mr. Combat SAR	56
USS Bon Homme Richard, CV 31	63
Survival Escape Resistance and Evasion (SERE) Training	70
Chapter Three	83
Deployment to Southeast Asia	83
WESTPAC	83
Disaster aboard the USS FORESTALL	114
Chapter Four	121
Orders Back to Vietnam	121
Orders to HA(L)-3	121
Helicopter Aircraft Commander (HAC)	122
Fort Benning, GA Gunship Training	140

Chapter Five	145
The Seawolves	145
Helicopter Attack (Light) – 3	145
Detachment Two, Nha Be	150
Rush to become Aircraft Commander	156
Finally Fire Team Leader	162
Going against Squadron Policy	183
I'm going to see to it that you lose your wings for this.	199
Chapter SIX	217
Headed for Civilian Life	217
Navy Ferry Squadron	217
That's Our Motto, "You start it for us and we'll fly it."	229
Civilian life and college	232
Helicopter Training Squadron-Eight (HT-8)	233
Would I really lose my wing's wings this time?	240
Tactical Air Control Squadron Thirteen (TACRON 13)	247
Minesweeping in Hai Phong Harbor	253
Naval Postgraduate School, Monterey, CA	257
Chapter Seven	263
WESTPAC Trouble Shooter	263
USS Coral Sea and Detachment Four	264
USS Midway and Detachment Two	279
Chapter Eight	315
On the way to Command	315
I'm relieving you of your duties as Maintenance Officer, you're fired!	315
Operations Officer, "If you break out into a grin or laughter, I'll fire you again."	325
Executive Officer, the men and the squadron come first.	331
Commanding Officer, HC-1	342
Chapter Nine	355
USS Belleau Wood LHA-3	355

- Air Boss 355
- The games people play. 357
- Taking on the Commodore. 371

Chapter Ten 381
- A Matter of Trust. 381
- Not made for shore duty. 381
- You're not an asset any longer, you're a liability. 388
- Duty, Honor, Country 400

Epilogue 407

This Book Is Dedicated To My Grandsons
And
Those Dedicated Men And Women Who Serve
And To
Those Who Made The Ultimate Sacrifice In An Unpopular War.

PROLOGUE

Sometimes the most difficult challenge in life will be to stand up for what you believe in, no matter what the CONSEQUENCES.

While I was at the Naval Postgraduate School in 1974, I met a young lieutenant from the Citadel, in South Carolina. As we traded sea stories, he told me about a rescue made by a young Seawolf helicopter pilot in Vietnam. They read the story in the *Navy Times* and as part of a class project, they analyzed the events of the rescue. He was a little surprised to find out that he was talking to the pilot in the article. As I spoke, he seemed fascinated by some of the stories. Throughout the years people have always told me that I should write about some of my experiences, but I always thought it was the beer talking. Later in 2001 a retired Navy captain called me from Washington, DC. He said he had been given my name by a crew chief that had flown with me in Vietnam. The retired captain had been engaged to write a book for the Naval Historical Archives on the Navy Seawolves and their actions in Vietnam. The compliments the crewman bestowed on me were a little overwhelming. As we talked, I asked him if he wanted to know what truly happened or just the award version. To my surprise, he said he was only interested in the historical account and not what actually happened. This left me thinking. We owe it to our children and grandchildren to see that somehow the truth gets written down.

This book is an account of a man's career and his struggle to be true to what he believed. It describes the bond that was formed throughout the years with the men he served and how he would deal with each new situation. Some may refer to "Hollywood Al" as arrogant, and some will see him as a man who held steadfastly to his beliefs and was loyal to those men who believed in him. For without them, he was nothing. As you follow the journey you will have to make that determination for yourself. The documentation included in this book is to verify the actual events and to ensure the integrity of the stories being told, that they are not the products of the imagination or embellishment of an aging naval aviator. At the end of this introduction you will find statements from some of the individuals I served with in an effort to validate the authenticity. It is not my intent to judge anyone in this book.

People who have known me over the years would testify that I led a rather colorful naval career. Sometimes real life can be stranger than fiction. During the early years as a young Navy pilot I received many awards, medals and letters of commendation. I had nine engine failures, four of which were in single engine aircraft, a record that I would not boast about, other than the fact that I survived them all. Some may say at times I bit off more than I could chew, while others waited to see if I would fail. They could not understand that if men pull together and believe in each other, their accomplishments can be staggering. The record will show we took some hits, but in the end we proved to them all that we had what it takes. We fought for the things we truly believed in and trusted each other. What more can anyone ask? The successes we experienced, I can truly say, were the direct result of the sacrifices of those men who served with me and believed that what I was doing was right.

I can remember as a young cadet watching *Twelve O'clock High* in my military leadership class when they promoted it as an excellent example of good leadership. There have been other books and movies in the past like *Winds of War, In Harms Way*, and *Once an Eagle* that have chronicled the hazards and the politics of military life. But lately I've seen none. The world is in turmoil, and wars may be fought in different ways, but the values of the young men and women of today must not change. Strong leaders are made and some are born, but in the end they will owe their careers and successes to those sacrifices of the enlisted men and women that stand beside them.

As the years pass, some of the men I served with have called to remember those days. Some have been disappointed in civilian life, and some just wanted to talk about the times, both good and bad, and the brotherhood they shared with those men in some of the most memorable moments in their lives. I never understood why private corporations send their young executives away on weekends to play golf and bond "like they do in the military." This demonstrates a true lack of understanding of what it is really like to put your life completely in the hands of another and make sacrifices for the good of all. The feeling is difficult to put into words, and, unless you have experienced it, difficult to understand.

Ours is a great nation because of the sacrifices made by those in uniform. If this book can help bring some of this to light, and help those who have a passion to stand up for what they believe in, then it has succeeded.

(Bruce J. Boissey, Seawolf Door Gunner 67'-68')

I was a 20 year old door gunner returning from my first mission when I met LTJG Billings. We were both inspecting our two severely damaged helicopters on the airfield. It was his first week in country flying as the wing ship copilot.

Our pilots had made several tactical errors and the fact that everyone had come back alive was truly a matter of luck. As my tour of duty continued, I would learn that not all of the pilots were equally gifted.

Less than a month later LTJG Billings received his aircraft commander papers and I was flying as his door gunner when we had an engine failure while flying over a shipping channel. LTJG Billings remained completely calm and landed us safely on shore. Unfortunately it happened to be a minefield. That was the first of many missions that he proved to me that he was an extremely competent pilot in all circumstances, especially under fire. Like many of the other door gunners I flew with, I was always happy to see that I had been assigned to fly with Mr. Billings. Not only was LTJG Billings respected by the door gunners as a good pilot, his leadership style included a combination of confidence, skill, good humor and bravado in the best sense of the word. This made for a connection with the enlisted men that most other officers did not enjoy.

Al Billings was physically strong, a straight talker, a confident and extremely proficient Huey Gunship pilot. He is a man who under any circumstances had the courage and skill to get in and do the job. I met many men in Vietnam, both officers and fellow enlisted men. Although we shared an extremely intense time together, we were dropped in that foreign land from all walks of life to fight an unpopular war. Most of us had never met before and as our tours ended and we departed many of us would never see or hear from one another again. My tour of duty in Vietnam with LTJG Billings was only a small portion of his career. Therefore, I enjoyed reading about the entire career of this courageous and colorful officer and Naval Aviator in Seawolf 28.

(George "Ponch" Heady, Crew Chief and Door Gunner, 67 – 68.)

I was a 19 year old crew chief and door gunner transferred from Vin Long to Det Two in Nha Be shortly after the TET offensive. Det Two was the first time I had the pleasure of meeting LTJG Billings (or Mr. B, as I like to call him). I know some of the other pilots were envious of the connection that Mr. B had with the enlisted men. Just because you hold a rank, doesn't mean you've earned the respect and confidence of your men. Where another officer would put you on report Mr. B would go that extra mile to save your butt. Let me put it this way: I would follow John Wayne to hell and back and Mr. B was my John Wayne. A lot of men came home because of his skill and knowledge, yes and the balls to do what was right. I know first hand about this, because he saved my life. When we crashed in the water south of Nha Be and one man lost his life he did everything he could to put the safety of his crew first and for that I am thankful. His fast thinking, skill, and confidence made him not only a good pilot, it made him a great one.

Mr. B had the ability to make every member of the crew feel they were critical to the success of every mission, or as the saying goes today, "An Army of one." He had us all knowing that we could go anywhere with him and he would bring us home. Probably the best example of that was when we were scrambled to support a couple of PBR's that were under heavy fire (one dead, and the rest wounded, two seriously). Although Mr. B was sitting in the most junior seat on the Fire Team, he could not sit idly by. He had to do whatever he could to help those wounded sailors. That meant he had to get permission. He didn't get it. We knew what we had to do because we were a team and it was our job to do everything we could to ensure the safety of those we were there to support. Yes, he did have to disobey an order, but two men are alive today for it. As a member of that team I was awarded a Distinguished Flying Cross for the action.

My wife, children and now grandson's are grateful for you being there. I owe you fella.

(Dr. Robert E. May, MCPO, USN RET.)

When I first joined Commander Billings' command in

the Pacific, as the senior enlisted on board, I was not an early subscriber to his style of leadership. The command I was joining was just another helicopter-detachment that fit the old adage of "overworked and underfed" translated to navy terms "over fatigued aircraft and demoralized men". I had seen this to often in my 20 years of salt encrusted tours in navy helicopters. I had served under the best and worst leadership the United States Navy offered.

The helicopter is a virtual workhorse in naval aviation. Because of workload, in and out of port, there is little stand-down time to conduct gratuitous maintenance or appearance efforts on the aircraft (a source of unit pride) or to recharge the men's batteries. Low morale, under these conditions, is always a challenge and becomes magnified greatly by poor-leaders who pay only lip services to challenging and difficult circumstances.

Cdr. Billings' leadership style I soon discovered was not only charismatic but also systematic. It was reminiscent of Tom Smith the original "Horse Whisperer" and trainer of Seabiscuit fame. Cdr. Billings not only led by example but also by appealing to ones ability to reach inside and perform under difficult and dangerous circumstances using training and ingenuity to accomplish difficult tasks. He very seldom failed in challenging ones resourcefulness, taking self, and unit pride in their achievements.

In six months, under his leadership, I witnessed the men's morale go from the "bottom of the barrel" to "button busting pride" and aircraft metamorphosed from "tired and dirty" to "pride of the fleet". Leadership, example, and commitment in my opinion fill the void of to little time, to few assets, and too little appreciation. Al Billings' deep sense of responsibility to his country extended to his men. Duty, Honor, and Country were his credo. If Ralph Stogdill who published the standard text on Leadership were alive today he would say he liked Al's style. I know I sure as hell did!

Chapter One
"Wings of Gold"

Dr. Renzoni came into the room with a serious look on his face. As he approached the edge of the bed he paused for a moment and then started to explain what needed to happen. "I've reviewed the X-rays and have asked Dr. Shahhal to intervene in this case. The X-rays indicate extensive nerve damage. Dr. Shahhal is a neurosurgeon that specializes in this type of injury. I really wish we could have discovered this earlier, before all the damage was done. Dr. Shahhal is in surgery right now and will be in to see you this afternoon."

He asked if I had any questions, and I shook my head and replied," No." I already knew the extent of the damage. I just wanted to get the operation over with so I could start the recovery process. As Dr. Renzoni turned to leave, I took a deep breath, looked up at the ceiling and thought,. "After 22 years in the Navy, four tours in support of the Vietnam War, nine engine failures and God knows how many other emergencies and incidents, it comes to this?"

As I watched the doctor slowly walk out the door I tried to make sense out of what was happening. As a young man you form your beliefs and ideals through family, friends and from what's inside you. As you travel through life you will either follow those ideals and beliefs or bend to the pressures around you. You may even trade those beliefs for recognition, fame or money. To hold on to those beliefs will probably be one of the most difficult things you will ever have to do. So many times in life the full story never gets told. Young people make decisions, start careers and sometimes sacrifice their lives based on selected facts and not on reality.

Young men and women will continue to serve in the military, and go to war. The moments and the conflicts I experienced will be repeated generation after generation. Lives will be lost. How do we make the young leaders understand that there will be times when they will have self doubt? They will have to believe that our Commander in Chief has made the right decision. They will have to make a self-determination that what they see in the news, is either the truth, or that it is sensationalism for profit, or a "spin" on the truth to influence or persuade. They will have to believe that going to war is the best for the nation, and the people who are marching or protesting against them may not understand the consequences of their not going.

They will need to understand that when it is all said and done, it will come down to what's inside them and those standing beside them and the bonds that are formed through the good and the bad times. The years that follow may be some of the most significant in our history. This nation will always need good leaders with strong moral character, especially those that are willing to make the needed decisions and live with the consequences. Those leaders will need to have the ability to give the men and women that serve something they can accept as true. Words like duty, honor, country, and the individual moral choice that forms our character kept lingering in my head.

As I lay there my thoughts went back to the first day I arrived at the Naval Air Station in Pensacola, Florida and the long journey that brought me to this point.

Pensacola

It was a few minutes before 10 PM on a cold winter night in January when the Douglas DC-4 rolled to a stop and shut down its engines. My ears where still buzzing from the vibrations of the continuous roar of the four reciprocating engines and the long flight from California. It must have been close to freezing when I stepped off the plane. As I walked across the apron to the gate, I could feel the moisture in my lungs; it was something I had never experienced. California was very dry compared to Florida. There was a strong breeze and a deep penetrating cold in the air so I hurried inside. As I waited for my bag I looked at my watch. I had to report by midnight and didn't know how far it was to the base. When I saw my bag I didn't wait for the airline employee to pull it off the cart. As I reached for it, the agent glanced at me as if to say, "What's your hurry?" There was very little in it. The Navy told me I wouldn't need much, and any civilian attire would be stored or shipped back home. I hurried outside to look for the bus that would bring me closer to my dream of becoming a naval aviator.

As I went out the doors of the terminal I saw a bus at the end of the building. It was a large gray school bus, and I could see "U.S. Navy" printed on the side. When I reached the open door of the bus, I leaned forward and asked the driver if he was going to NAS Pensacola. The driver said "yes," and told me to get in.

I slowly walked down between the seats looking at the faces of each of the passengers. I wondered if they were all going to be Navy pilots. Most of them seemed much older; I had just turned twenty years old when I took my oath to serve in the Navy. I had no idea of what to expect. Becoming a naval aviator was what I wanted, and I was willing to make whatever sacrifices were necessary to achieve that goal. I didn't find college that challenging, and the naval aviation program was renowned for the demands it placed upon its pilots. The skills and concentration required to land a high-performance aircraft on board a pitching carrier deck in the black of night seemed to be the challenge I was looking for. I wanted to be part of a special breed that required a combination of talents and dedication that few people possessed.

I was one of the last Naval Aviation Cadets (NAVCADs).

They were in the process of phasing out the NAVCAD program. If it hadn't been for the Vietnam War, they might have already eliminated the program. Most of the candidates had college degrees and would have their commissions at the end of preflight training, which was a three month indoctrination program. Preflight included military training and leadership courses along with academic training in aerodynamics, engineering, air navigation, power plants, meteorology and plenty of physical training and marching, as well as water survival and flight physiology. They controlled your every moment from 0600 to taps everyday. If you were lucky, you might get a 48 hour pass one weekend during the last month.

As a NAVCAD I would have to complete all of the flight training, which was about 18 months as an enlisted man. If successful, I would get my wings and commission on the same day. If I washed out, I would be chipping paint and swabbing decks on some ship for four years. Everything rested on making it through the program. On the ride to the naval station I looked at each of the men in the bus and tried to determine where they were from and if they were officer candidates or NAVCAD's. I could feel the excitement building; I was about to embark on the journey of my life. The thought of being a carrier pilot was intense, and I had no one back home who understood what was driving me. These guys would know how I felt, they must. I was young with high ideals and strong beliefs. At 20 years old everything was pretty simple, and I hadn't as yet been exposed to a somewhat imperfect world.

After a short ride we were cleared through the main gate and one of the first stops was the cadet barracks. "Battalion II!" hollered the bus driver. I looked at my watch. It was 11: 13 PM. I thought to myself, "Just under the wire." Six of us got off the bus. As we approached the quarterdeck, I noticed several cadets in uniform and a drill instructor (DI) standing with his hands on his hips. He seemed to be glaring directly at me. He didn't have an ounce of fat on his entire body. From what I could see his head was completely shaved, his uniform was perfect. I wondered how he could wear it without putting a single wrinkle in it. It looked like they peeled him right off of a Marine Corps poster. The DI bellowed out, "Drop those bags and brace yourselves against that bulkhead!" pointing in the direction he wanted us to move. "Move! Move! Move! When I say something you don't think, you just react!" We all ran towards the wall. As he walked toward us, he bellowed out again, "When I say brace against the bulkhead, that means to freeze at attention with your eyes straight forward. Don't blink, don't move, don't breathe, is that clear?"

The DI walked up and down the line staring at each of us. For some reason he stopped right in front of me. I must have looked the youngest and most petrified. He got so close I could feel the rim of his DI hat, touching my forehead. In a loud voice he said, "Where are you from mister?"

I heard my voice crackle as I said, "L.A."

The DI bellowed out again, "L.A.!!! There's only two things in L.A., hot rods and queers, and I don't see any wheels on you."

About that time, I thought that just maybe, I made the wrong decision about joining the Navy. As the DI turned to move down the line, one of the cadets handed him a clipboard. He looked at the board and said, "Listen up. These are your room assignments. When I call your name, get to them, turn-in, and get some shut-eye. Reveille is 0500. Every minute you waste is one less minute of sleep."

As he read off the names, I looked at my watch. It was already 11:42 PM.

The next morning reveille came with a vengeance. The first ten days were called Hell Week. It was referred to as "Indoctrination," or "INDOC," and it was designed to eliminate quickly those candidates that didn't have the determination to make it through the program. To train a naval aviator cost almost $350,000 dollars in the 60's. The Navy didn't want anyone that was not willing to stay the course. The earlier they got them out of the program, the better it was for the Navy. There were many stories of candidates breaking and dropping out of the program. How many were true, I would never know, but they sure caught your attention. The first morning was like trying to herd a bunch of chickens. After several minutes of complete disorganization we were able to get into some semblance of a formation. They marched us down to breakfast, or at least tried to march us. I was amazed at the fact that a group of college graduates found it such a challenge to march in formation together. After breakfast it was off to turn us into naval officers and aviators.

They had the program down to a science. The first thing they wanted to do was take away your identity and anything that related to the civilian past. They marched us over to uniform issue, where we were given our uniforms and something they called a "Poopy suit." They were large sets of coveralls. I wore a size 42, and they gave me a size 54. We were going to live in it for the next ten days. Everything was accomplished by shouting orders and screaming in your face. Everywhere we went, we either marched or ran. By the end of the day we managed not to step on the guy in front.

Next was the barber shop, where they cut all our hair off. If you don't think that is a humbling experience, just try it. The entire ten days was filled with running, marching, inspections, the obstacle course and plenty of yelling. We would be up before dawn and have our running and physical training out of the way before the sun came up. I had always been into fitness and everyone I knew played some type of sport. I was a little taken aback when I saw that some of the cadets had trouble doing even one pull-up, or just ten push-ups. I looked forward to the physical training; it meant I didn't have to march around staring at the guy's head in front of me. As far as the yelling, I was used to the coaches always getting on my case, but when it happened all day long, it did tend to wear on me a little.

INDOC is where I learned for the first time that I had a temper. Up to that point I had always thought I was pretty easy going. There is a difference between trying to turn a civilian into an officer and harassment. It was one of the last days of INDOC, just before taps. One of the cadet officers happened to be an individual that enjoyed exercising his control over others, and he had been riding me all day long. I had no idea why he seemed to have it in for me. I was braced against the wall, or "bulkhead," and he was in my face. He had pushed me to a point that I didn't know I had, and I wanted to clean up the passageway with him. Even back then, I had trouble with people abusing their authority. He must have seen it in my face, because, just before I decided to go through with it, he said, "Mister you have a temper, and if you can't control your temper, you'll never make it through this program." That stopped me dead in my tracks. Nothing was going to stop me from becoming a naval aviator. I had never failed at anything, and I was not about to start.

We lost two people during INDOC. They didn't belong in the military anyway. It was difficult for me to understand at such a young age that people would give up everything over a little discomfort. Now it was on to the academics, and we got out of the "Poopy suits" and into uniforms. The days were filled with academics and all types of drills that the military had refined over the years to build character, teach us to follow procedures, and pay attention to detail. Spiffy questions, room inspections, formations and military exercises, and of course marching off demerits. We were making $65 a month, and a good part of that went to the laundry for our highly starched uniforms. Over the years, I've remembered it as some of the best times of my life. Testing, physical fitness, academics, marching, inspections, and more testing. The days passed by quickly. There wasn't much time to make friends, but the friends you did make were friends for life. Three of my closest friends are now dead, but I can remember them as if it were yesterday. They were the finest that this country had to offer. They were willing to do whatever it took to see that this country remained strong and safe. In Preflight everyone was in a survival mode. You learned early on to pull together.

I did seem to get more than my share of demerits. Back then I was full of life and everyday was an adventure. I even smiled a lot, sometimes too much. You weren't supposed to smile. I can remember one time during a room inspection I got put on report for breaking out in uncontrolled laughter. As a cadet, everything had to be perfect. They even used white gloves and rulers to make sure everything was exact. They did not allow any room for error. There were four of us in each room, and when the cadet officer came in for the room inspection, he started on the cadet across from me. His skivvies were folded wrong, so the cadet officer took out a pair and pulled them over his head. As the cadet officer continued to question the cadet, he had to shout answers out through the fly of his skivvies. It was funny, but I held back.

He went over to the cadet beside him and went through his things. He went to the medicine cabinet, where we all had an assigned shelf. He picked up the saving cream and inspected it. In order to teach us procedures, when we were done with the shaving cream, we had to take the top of the shaving cream off and turn it backwards so it couldn't be used. The cadet officer turned to the man across from me and asked him if it was secured properly. The cadet barked out, "Yes, sir!"

"Do you mean that if I take this shaving cream and stick it in your ear and push down on this button, nothing will happen?" the cadet officer asked.

"Yes, sir!" shouted the cadet. The cadet officer pushed the button down and emptied the can of shaving cream into the cadet's ear.

At that point I couldn't hold back. I broke out into a loud howl and couldn't stop. Luckily my physical conditioning always got me out of big trouble. Hit the deck mister and give me fifty push-ups. That was easy, but I always got the demerits along with it. It seemed like I spent half of Preflight doing push-ups and marching off demerits.

It got to the point where I had picked up a reputation for being able to do an exceptional numbers of push-ups, sit-ups, and whatever else they threw at me. They would trump things up just to see how many I could do. There was one incident where I was called down to the DI's office. After pounding on the pine, I was told to enter the room. "Cadet Billings reporting as ordered, sir!" There were DI's from all three battalions in the office; the room was full. I was asked a bogus question they knew I couldn't answer, and when I said I didn't know the answer, the DI told me, "Hit the deck and give me push-ups until I tell you to stop."

By this time I had caught on, and I knew how to play the game. As you completed each push-up, you had to holler out, "1 sir! 2 sir! 3 sir!"

By the time I got to 99, I made them think I couldn't do anymore, knowing full well that they would always ask for one more for the Corps. If you didn't give them one for the Corps, it was off to sit-ups, or the imaginary chair, or whatever they could dream up. When the DI looked down at me and asked for one more, I snapped it off as if it were the first one and jumped up to attention with a grin on my face. The DI glared at me for a second and hollered, "Get out of my office, cadet." I turned and left before he thought of something else for me to do.

Battalion II was always last in the regimental competition. They couldn't remember when they had won. The battalion commander was a Marine captain, and he was determined to win the regimental competition, and the boxing team would be the key. He asked for volunteers, and I jumped at the chance, boxing sounded like fun. 13 cadets out of 92 volunteered, and when the dust had settled, I was selected as the team captain. I was a little surprised since I was probably the youngest cadet in the battalion.

The boxing team had to get up an hour before the rest of the battalion and do their road work. Later in the day we would again have to go through the physical training with the rest of the class. My physical condition allowed me to lead the pack and set the example. The regimental competition gave me my first look at politics and how people tried to influence things to get the desired outcome. I was young and naive and at the time the manipulation didn't mean anything to me. But as time went on, I should have paid a little more attention to the devious ways of some individuals. The boxing tournament "Smoker" was the final event in the competition, and if it was close, everything usually depended on the outcome of the "Smoker." The DI's watched the boxing teams closely. They knew who could box and who couldn't. There would be six men out of the thirteen that would represent the battalion in the tournament. The DI's were in charge of the ranking. I was ranked number one, with the combination of boxing skills, experience, and PT score. Although I didn't have any boxing experience, they said it looked like I did, and ranked me accordingly.

To my surprise, the first man that was picked to represent BATT II, was our 5th ranked boxer. The other five were ranked 7, 9, 10, 11, and 12. When I protested the selection I was told it was too late. I couldn't believe we had been screwed like that. It was total bullshit! It did teach me a lesson. Men would manipulate events in order to ensure the proper outcome. In this case it didn't work. When the dust settled, BATT II won 5 of its 6 fights anyway, and we took the regimental competition. It was something I learned early in life and would carry throughout my naval career. If you worked hard things sometimes went your way.

Toward the end of Preflight I knew the system well. For kicks I used to see how alert the cadet officers were. During some of the morning inspections I would reverse my insignias or change something on my uniform and then stand there with a big grin like a Cheshire cat. It would distract them enough that I would get away with the obvious violation. Sometimes! It seemed I was always in trouble, but life was fun.

I earned three 48 hour passes, one for the boxing team, one for giving blood, and one for winning the regimental competition. When it came time to use the passes, I had so many demerits the battalion commander took all three 48's away, so I went on liberty in the trunk of a car. I spent the entire cadet officer week marching off demerits before I could graduate. George used to continually tell me that I needed to be more serious. George was from New Jersey and the oldest of the group of NAVCADS. He had been enlisted for several years before he qualified for the flight program, and he was totally focused on becoming a naval aviator. I was too, but at 20 years old, life had no limits, and I had a tendency to be a little reckless.

One weekend George and I were sitting in the chow hall when a couple of First Class Cadets came in. They were like gods to us. They had completed their carrier qualifications and were well on their way to their wings of gold and their commissions. Even today when I close my eyes I can remember the feeling I had when I first saw them. At that moment it seemed as though we would never get there. I remembered when the instructors used to tell us that only the top 5% of the men in the U.S. could become naval aviators and that many of us would not make it through the program. It wasn't that we were geniuses or something special, we were far from it, but between the physical requirements, academics, physical training, and flying ability you had to be extremely well-rounded and balanced to complete the training. I know of one cadet that was held back because he couldn't pass the swimming requirements, and they almost washed him out.

My Achilles heel was the leadership course. The math, physics, aerodynamics, Morse code, nothing gave me as much trouble as the final leadership exam. The first time I took it, I failed. I couldn't understand why it was happening;

it was one of the easiest courses we had. I knew the book backwards and forwards. It was the philosophy I disagreed with. If I didn't pass the retake, I was out of the program. I couldn't let that happen. I was the first of four brothers to graduate from high school, and I couldn't let this stop me. Fortunately the retake was an oral exam. As I went through the questions the instructor could see that I had the book memorized. He couldn't understand why I didn't pass it the first time around. He made the assumption that I got the answers out of sequence on the answer page. I told him I disagreed with many of the answers. They were vague. This assertion started a discussion about my philosophy of leading men. My philosophy totally centered around all the John Wayne movies I had seen. The instructor told me I was young and I would learn with time. He accepted my answers, and I passed the exam.

It was our last week. That Friday was graduation day. I was still marching off demerits right up to the night before graduation. I had never been exposed to anything that formal. The dress blues, the swords, everything was great. In a few days we would be off to Saufley Field and preparing for our first flight in the T-34B. The formal dance that night was something. It took a while to get used to all the protocol. I had to continually remind myself of the proper etiquette. It was something that was very new to me. The girls were all dressed in formals and looked fantastic. Life was good!

It was the beginning of the Vietnam War and out of our Preflight class, one quarter of them would never see their thirtieth birthdays and several would spend a number of years in the Hanoi Hilton. That weekend we celebrated like there was no tomorrow and moved to NAS Saufley Field for basic flight training.

Basic Flight Training

"There is an old aviators' saying that you start your flying career with a whole lot of luck and no experience. You hope to end your career with a whole lot of experience before you run out of luck."

Primary Flight Training at NAS Saufley Field would certainly test that philosophy. For some it would be the ultimate test.

As less of our day was controlled it allowed us time to develop friendships that would last throughout our lives. George, Mike, Rich and I started to run together. Rich was from Massachusetts and had his private pilot license and found the flying easy, but the academics would always give him a little trouble. Mike was from Half Moon bay in Northern California. He was a Marine cadet and probably one of the sharpest individuals I would ever know. He was also the only cadet that was younger than I was. He had one problem; he did not look like a Marine. He was just barely 5'6," with a baby face and a high-pitched voice. We always used to kid him about his transmission over the air when he was flying. He sounded like a female. Most of the officers lived off base and the cadets lived in the barracks. It seems as soon as the officers got their commissions, all cadets were second class citizens. You would have thought some of the ensigns' had just made admiral. Every time we turned around they wanted us to salute. These were some of the same guys we helped get through the obstacle course, swim quals, and academics. They continually used the cadets as "gofers." To be fair, not all of the officers were like that, just the ones that needed or demanded unearned respect from their subordinates.

Early on in the program we were continually reminded about the attrition rate. During our first indoctrination class at Saufley, an instructor stood in front of the class and said, "I want you to look to the right and look to the left. One of you will not be here at the end of primary training." He went through the statistics of the program and the losses they had from flying, academics, and even automobile accidents. I'm sure it was for effect, but it made you think and kept you focused.

We got flight skins, which meant our pay went up to $115 a month. We had so much money we didn't know what to do with it. I bought a used VW. Primary flight training was filled with plenty of academics. The T-34B was a very forgiving aircraft, and I found it fun to fly. I was surprised at some of the comments from the other cadets. George always gave me a hard time about being a natural pilot saying I didn't know how lucky I was. He had to work at it. I just knew it was fun. I couldn't wait to get in the cockpit. I was amazed at how disoriented some students got when they were in the air. There were stories of students flying right over the top of Saufley Field, not knowing where they were. I found that almost impossible to believe, but it did happen. It was obvious that some of them should not be in aviation; what drove them to stick it out was beyond my understanding. They were so tense in the cockpit they couldn't remember their procedures or to even think of lowering their landing gear before landing.

The initial flight training went by so fast it was a blur. Before I knew it, I was up for my first solo hope. Prior to Pensacola, I had only been in an airplane once, and that was on the flight out from California. On my first solo flight one of the cadets challenged me to a dog fight, so we set up our rendezvous point. All you had to do on your first solo flight was make a few landings at an outlying field and get the aircraft back in one piece. When I went out to the aircraft, I had to down it because of an oil leak. This delayed my getting off the ground and we never met in the air, which may have been good fortune. Unfortunately the other cadet found somebody else. He had a midair collision that day. The other aircraft chopped off the tail of his plane. When that happened he ended up in an inverted spin. To exacerbate the problem, he didn't have his harness locked. The negative G's pinned him against the canopy. He fell several thousand feet before he was able to work the canopy back and inch his way out of the aircraft. His chute deployed just before he hit the ground. The other aircraft landed in a field. When he returned from sick bay that night his eyes were blood red from the negative G's. You could tell he was shaken by his experience.

Although the cadet stuck it out for another five months, the nightmares got to him. He finally dropped out of the program. In those five months he went from 178 lbs. to 136 lbs. It was a shame; he would have made a good officer. You learned to accept the fact that some of those around you would not be at the finish line with you, but you never thought it would be you. Between the incidents in the air, academics and the car crashes while on liberty, we lost our share of students. It seemed the same character traits that drove you to be an aviator also drove some to be a little reckless on liberty. I have to admit I led the pack. The bet was I would never make it through flight training before I did something crazy that ended my flying career or worse. I laughed at the bet.

It's funny what stays with you over the years. Rare instances of kick thinking and bravado made life interesting. While I was out on a solo hop one day I overheard another student accidentally broadcast over the air. While he was on an instructional hop with an instructor the student inadvertently came up over the UHF and transmitted, "I'm sorry sir, I fucked up."

The tower immediately came back over the air and asked, "Who made that last transmission? Report your side number."

The air was silent for more than a minute. The tower came back over the air and demanded that the person who made that last transmission announce their name and side number. A few seconds later, another voice came over the air and said, "My student may be fucked up, but he's not that fucked up." The air was silent for a few minutes and everyone seemed to continue with what they were doing. To this day I still breakout in a smile when I think about it.

Saufley field was just plain fun. I got some of my highest grades in acrobatics; I couldn't get enough of it. I can remember one weekend when my brother came out to visit. He was going through Army helicopter training at the time.

We spent most the night drinking beer and talking about what was happening in our lives. That night I got about four hours sleep. The next morning I had two acrobatic hops back to back. When we landed the instructor walked up to my brother and told him that they were two of the smoothest acrobatic hops he had ever flown with a student. I had to be smooth; I didn't have any choice. I was so hung over I couldn't handle the exaggerated "G" forces that the acrobatic maneuvers required.

As the weekend came to a close my brother had to return to his duty station to complete his training. He was scheduled to head for Vietnam in a few months, and I wished him luck and hoped that I might see him in country in a year. In total we both completed three tours each, and I finished up a fourth minesweeping Hai Phong Harbor at the end of the war. Between flight training and Vietnam there would be enough memories to last a lifetime. And that was just the beginning.

I finished up with the T-34B. Then it was on to NAS Whiting field and the T-28B Trojan. Then, carrier qualifications!

NAS Whiting Field and 6 1/2 G's without a "G" suit

NAS Whiting Field was about 30 miles outside of Pensacola near a small town called Milton. I couldn't wait for my first flight in the T-28. I even went out the night before and sat in the cockpit for what most have been several hours. If they would have allowed me, I think I would have slept in the aircraft that night. The Trojan was equivalent in performance to some of the earlier WWII fighters, and I couldn't wait to get control of all that horsepower.

The routine had become pretty standard now. It was back to the academics, power plants, hydraulics, navigation, and aerodynamics, all just to get in the cockpit and do what I loved. Things went well in ground school. Many of the principles were the same; only the parameters and the names changed. I remember the discussions in the cafeteria with the other cadets. The talks we had about all the details of their flights and who was a good instructor and who was a prick. We used to listen to some of the advanced students talk about their instrument and acrobatic hops in the T-28 with their instructors. I couldn't wait to get my first solo hop; acrobatics were not authorized on your first solo flight, but it was too late. I already had it in my head that I was going to the acrobatics area. After all, the T-34 was a piece of cake -- why wait? I knew I was going to be just as good in the T-28.

Finally the day came. I was on my first solo hop. The sky was a deep blue, and it was a perfect day for flying. What could go wrong? As I climbed out of Whiting Field I turned south and headed straight to the acrobatics area. As at Saufley, all you were required to do was head to one of the outlying fields where you would practice touch-n-goes and return the aircraft back in one piece.

The exhilaration I felt as I climbed out of the field was incredible. I was young and invincible; I felt I could do anything in an aircraft. Little did I know my joy of flying and lack of fear was going to take me to the extreme limits of my ability. When I leveled off at 10,000 feet I looked around to see if there were any planes in the area. I didn't see any but remembered the talk about S-turns, or clearing turns. They were a safety maneuver to check to see if the area was clear before doing any acrobatic maneuvers. When I came out of the last clearing turn, I pushed the nose over and accelerated to 280 knots, pulled up on the nose and started into a loop. As the aircraft started up the front side of the loop the G forces started to pull the throttle off. I didn't realize that I hadn't adjusted the friction on the throttle quadrant properly. As I came to the top of the loop, I was inverted, and the aircraft shuttered and fell off to one side. The lack of power and airspeed at the top caused the aircraft to stall. Before I knew it, the aircraft went into a violent spin. The first thing that came into my head was the aerodynamics instructor telling the class that the T-28 doesn't come out of an inverted spin very well.

I didn't know if it was in an inverted spin or not. All I knew was I was in a very violent spin, and it was getting more violent with each revolution. I instinctively went into full left rudder and placed the control stick slightly forward of center, as I was taught by the flight instructor. The aircraft came out of the spin in a steep nose dive. I was accelerating through 340 knots. I had started the loop at 10,000 feet and the aircraft was recovering at 4,800 feet. In a matter of seconds I lost over 5,000 feet. I leveled my wings, pulled back on the stick, used the airspeed to start a climb, and added power to get back up to my original altitude. My heart was pounding, and it felt like it was up in my throat.

As I leveled off at 9,500 feet I gathered what I could of my composure and ran through the procedures in my head. It was a simple maneuver, what could I have done wrong? Now I was more determined than ever to complete the maneuver. I decided I didn't have enough airspeed, so I pushed the nose over and accelerated to 300 knots. This time I really pulled back on the stick. At the top of the loop I felt the aircraft shutter again. I was not about to let it go into another spin, so I rolled the aircraft over and did what some people might call a "half-assed" emullman, only I was 90 degrees off heading and the aircraft was shuttering at 85 knots, just above stall speed. While the aircraft slowly gained airspeed, I went through the procedures in my head. It couldn't be the airspeed; I had more airspeed than the NATOPS manual recommended. This couldn't be happening; I was an ace with the T-34B. What was going on? I decided a little more airspeed couldn't hurt.

This time I pushed the nose over and picked up 320 knots. When I pulled the stick back in my lap the G forces were tremendous. As I started up the front side of the loop, I felt the sensation they talked about in flight physiology. First there is a tingling sensation and then the outer edges of your peripheral vision start to get fuzzy. I tightened my stomach muscles; it didn't help. I held it off for a split second and the next thing I knew, I was looking down a very narrow tube or tunnel, as I looked at the instrument panel all I could only see one instrument at a time. I knew what was next -- I would blackout! The only thing I had left was to scream to try to keep the blood from draining out of my head. It worked, and I completed my first "Screaming Loop". If I hadn't been in such good physical condition I would have most likely blacked out. It finally dawned on me that perhaps I needed a little more training. I decided I would leave the rest of the acrobatics for another day and headed out to one of the outlying fields to do touch-n-goes.

The rest of the hop was pretty boring. Landing practice wasn't very challenging. After returning back to the field, I taxied into the line and shut down. Two plane captains met the plane, and as I shut down and climbed out of the cockpit one of the plane captains was in the backseat. As he looked at the G-meter in the back he said, "We're going to have to down this aircraft and get it inspected; it's reading 6 ½ G's back here." He glanced at me as I climbed off the wing. I looked back and shrugged my shoulders as I walked off. I waited to hear something but never did.

At times I think I aggravated the other cadets with my carefree approach to flying. George was always worried before every hop; I would come walking in a few minutes before the hop seemingly unprepared. It used to infuriate him. I stayed out of trouble until my first solo acrobatics hop. As I climbed out I was ready to do some serious acrobatics. I was going to make up for my first solo hop. I leveled off and then started into my clearing turns, once, twice, ... everywhere I turned, there was another aircraft. I tried it again, and there was another aircraft. I was never going to get any acrobatics out of the way at this rate. As I came out of another turn, I looked around, and it appeared to be clear. So, I pushed the nose over and started into the loop. At 280 knots I pulled the nose up, telling myself to pull the stick back smoothly until I saw 3 G's on the meter. I started up the backside, and everything was going well. As I reached the top of the loop I pulled my head back to look at the space below. I was looking straight down. Shit! Where the hell did they come from? As I looked down, directly below me was an instructor with his student. I could see them both looking up at me. I was close enough to see the expressions on their faces. As the instructor looked up at me, he watched as I continued all the way around them.

I pulled back on the stick, leveling off and starting a slow, climbing turn to the right. As I looked over my shoulder to see where they were, I could see the instructor turning towards me. Shit! My aviation career was looking a little shaky. I knew I was going to be hammered for not following proper safety procedures. I couldn't let the instructor get my side number. If they matched it up with the flight schedule they would know it was me. My career dissipation light started to flicker right in front of my eyes. I pulled the plane into a partial split S and tried to dive away from the instructor. As I looked back over my shoulder I saw the instructor coming after me. I turned away again; the instructor stayed after me. The climbing, diving, and a series of questionable maneuvers that I don't think they have in any book went on for what seemed like five minutes. The instructor didn't look like he was going to give up, and all I could do was compound the problem. I leveled my wings and kissed my wings of gold goodbye.

As the instructor pulled alongside and looked over at me, I smiled and threw him a salute, symbolically as anyone would do just before his execution. The instructor stared at me for a few seconds, returned a quick salute and peeled away. I slowly started a turn towards Whiting Field. I was in no hurry to end my last flight. As I returned to the field I remembered thinking what it would be like, spending the next three years swabbing decks. I told myself it couldn't be all that bad, maybe I could get into some "A" school and learn a skill.

As I entered the pattern, I slowly maneuvered the aircraft into a final approach on the duty runway. I wanted to remember everything about it, knowing it would be my last landing in a Navy aircraft. As I touched down and cut the throttle, I applied the brakes and pulled off the runway at the hub, halfway down the runway. As I taxied into the line, ground control came over the air and said that operations wanted to see the pilot of that aircraft in their office immediately. I continued beating myself up, "what a dumb-shit," as I shut down the aircraft.

The walk to the squadron operation office seemed like a death march. As I entered the operations office I saw a lieutenant sitting at the operations officer's desk. I had never seen anyone who looked as mean as this guy. As the lieutenant looked up he said, "Are you the pilot of Uniform Papa 126?"

"Yes, sir," I said in a low, barely audible tone.

The lieutenant shouted back, "Just who the hell do you think you are?"

"Sir?" I asked.

"What makes you think you can pull your aircraft off at the hub?"

I was stunned. I finally gained my composure and came back with, "What do you mean, sir?"

He came back at me with, "The operations manual clearly states that you will make a full rollout before departing the runway."

I felt myself starting to breath again. "I'm sorry sir. I must have missed it when I went through the manual."

The lieutenant grabbed the manual and started around his desk towards me. As he opened the manual to the proper page, he said, "You cadets piss me off. Everything you do is half-assed." As he put his finger on the procedure, he read it to me. "Upon completion of the landing, the pilot should complete the rollout and clear the runway as expeditiously as possible." He paused for a second and turned to walk back to his desk. As he sat at his desk for a minute, he looked up at me and said, "Cadet, I want you to sit down at that desk over there and go through the entire manual and underline anything you think is confusing, or you do not understand."

"Yes, sir! No problem." I was still alive. At that point I would have washed his car if it would have made him happy.

The lieutenant was wrong, but that didn't make any difference. He had me there; now he had to have me do something. I wasn't about to say anything. I was still waiting for the hammer to fall from my earlier escapade. After several hours of marking up the manual, I closed the book, got up and walked over to the operations officer's desk, placed the manual on the corner of the desk and stood there at attention waiting to be dismissed. After a few minutes the lieutenant looked up and dismissed me. I did an about face and walked out of the office. Almost three hours had passed since the incident in the air. That instructor had to be back on the deck. The first place he would have gone is to see that SOB in the operations office. I could not believe that I wasn't on my way to clean out my locker.

When I reached the cafeteria I saw Mike and Rich with a few other cadets sitting at a table eating lunch. As I sat down at the table I heard Roger telling them about his first acrobatic hop. Roger was a few weeks behind us in the training syllabus. He looked up me and said, "You wouldn't believe what I saw this morning while I was climbing out to the acrobatics training area. It must have been two instructors having a 'Dog Fight.', It was fantastic, and it looked like the real thing." I didn't say a word. I just wanted it to go away. The next couple of days were a little tense as I waited for the ax to fall.

Several weeks passed and nothing happened. I didn't know why, and I didn't care. I promised myself that I would walk the straight and narrow for the rest of my time at Whiting Field. Unfortunately it didn't work out that way. I didn't even make it through the next phase of training before I was in trouble, and this time it was for real.

Instrument training

I've always believed that you're in control of your own destiny, but life has a way of reminding you that fate sometimes plays an important roll in the path that you take. Since my arrival at Whiting Field, two students had died in a midair, and one more lost his life when he wrapped his sports car around a tree. The good thing about the aviation community is you never seem to lose focus on the mission. Death is accepted as a part of the risk of flying and being in the military. It's something most civilians do not understand. They always tried to determine the cause of the accidents so that it wouldn't happen again, but it didn't bring everything to a complete stop like it does in the civilian community. If it gets to you maybe you should look for another profession.

I ran into my first major obstacle since climbing into the cockpit. Instrument flying was not my strong point. I flew by the seat of my pants and loved it. Flying an aircraft with no reference to the outside was foreign to me. I felt every vibration and movement of the aircraft. In instrument conditions you had to ignore what your senses were telling you and completely rely on the instruments. It was a continuous battle between your senses and what the instruments were telling you. I had to accept that the instruments were always right no matter what my body told me. This was a continuous struggle for me throughout instrument training, especially in the T-28. It did not have the best instrument platform.

I think back to that memorable flight with that asshole Marine flight instructor, Captain Morgan. It was on my B-7, a basic instrument flight that almost ended my aviation career. I was in the backseat under the bag. The bag was a canvas device that attached to the windscreen so the student would not have any visual reference to the outside. As the flight progressed the Marine captain used every foul word known to man. To say the least, I was getting extremely frustrated. The instructor didn't let up. When he didn't seem to get enough satisfaction out of calling me names, he started slapping the stick around while I was trying to complete a maneuver or procedure. This lasted for what seemed like an eternity. Under the bag, it was sheer torture. The instructor hit the stick one more time using a few choice words and that pushed me over the edge. I took the stick firmly and proceeded to wipe out the cockpit by rapidly moving the control stick in a 360 degree circular motion throughout the cockpit, while keying the internal communications and expressing my frustration with the asshole.

To this day I can't remember exactly what I said, but I'm sure I taught the Marine a few new words. After several rotations the instructor was able to gain control of the stick. To my surprise he did not continue to use the foul language that had preceded this event. After about a minute of level flight the instructor came back over the intercom and said he was terminating the flight. I sat slumped in the backseat. When we returned, the instructor shut down the aircraft, got out and walked into the line shack. I remained in the backseat for awhile, then slowly got out of the aircraft and followed the instructor into the line shack. When I walked into the line shack the instructor had already gone. I took my gear and slowly walked back to the barracks and waited for the inevitable.

After several hours I couldn't stand the waiting any longer and headed down to the squadron. Some of the cadets were coming back from their flights and I asked them how things were going. They didn't mention anything. Stuff like that traveled like wild fire, especially when a cadet was getting washed out or a down on his hop. It was time for them to publish tomorrow's flight schedule. I knew George had the duty that day, so I decided to go in to see if I was on the schedule. Not knowing was killing me. I walked over and asked George if I was on the schedule for tomorrow. He shook his head and looked up at the names on the flight schedule board. My name was not there. I asked George if that was the complete schedule for tomorrow. He looked down at the paper in his hand, "Nope, you have a 1300, B-7 with Lieutenant Strock." I asked him if he had seen Captain Morgan. "Yes, he was in here earlier and went into the operations office to talk with Lieutenant York, then left for the day."

I didn't say anything and left for the gym. I was in bad need of a workout. At least I had another hop scheduled, it was a re-take of my B-7. That had to be a good sign, right? I couldn't believe that I pulled such a stupid stunt. I needed to learn to control my temper and keep my mouth shut.

The next day I was at the flight line an hour earlier than I needed to be. As I sat over by the wall in the line shack, I went over the procedures, again and again. I wanted to be prepared for anything. "Cadet Billings!" I turned to see who was shouting my name. When I saw Lieutenant Strock, I jumped to my feet, "Here, sir!"

Lieutenant Strock was a big man, about 6'2," 240 lbs. I wondered how he fit in the cockpit. His knees must have touched the instrument panel. Lieutenant Strock looked down at me, paused for a second, and then said, "So you're the student with the bad temper and foul mouth. You got a down on your B-7. You know what happens if you get a down on this hop." I didn't answer, but thought to myself, "Here it comes. My ass is grass and he's here to make it official."

Throughout the flight, Lieutenant Strock tried to rattle me. Every time the lieutenant chewed on my butt for something, I would reply, "You're absolutely right, sir. I'll try to do better the next time."

I made it through the flight without getting a down, but I don't think the grades could have been any lower. For the remainder of my instrument training I had a different instructor on almost every flight. Each instructor greeted me with the same phrase, "So you're the student with the bad temper!" Looking back on it, I probably benefited from it. No other instrument student had been put under that much pressure. My instrument flights had to be better than the average just to survive. Over the years that training would prove to be some of the most important training I had received.

I made it through the instrument training without another down and was headed for a new phase of training. During flight training you were so focused on getting through the syllabus, almost nothing else mattered. During this next phase I would start to learn a little about people and human nature, but again would pay very little attention to it. If it didn't have a set of wings on it, I wasn't interested.

Navigation and Cross Country Training

After instrument training, navigation and cross country flying was a piece of cake and a much needed rest from the risk of being eliminated from the program on every hop. Dead reckoning navigation was my cup of tea. Dead reckoning is the method of using a map and navigating using visual references on the ground. I never understood why some students had such difficulty recognizing things on the ground. They could be right over a major landmark and never see it.

I started to get a better understanding of the egos of men, especially when it related to cadets and officer candidates. I know some of the cadets referred to my confidence in the air as an ego, but I didn't look at it that way. I was young and just having fun; I couldn't believe I was getting paid to fly. To me an ego was self-importance, which was usually an obstacle to getting anything done. In the military it can easily get someone killed. Officer candidates got their commissions right after Preflight while the cadets had to complete the entire program. Some officer candidates felt that it was beneath them to listen to or even speak to the cadets. There were some good officers out there, but some of them hadn't changed since Preflight and continued to enjoy using their new found authority.

This type of superior attitude appeared on one of the cross country flights. The arrogance of some of the newly commissioned officers jeopardized the safety of the flight. We were on a cross country flight with six aircraft, a flight instructor and five students. As the flight progressed each student would rotate up into the lead position and navigate using dead reckoning navigation. I had already led the flight and was sitting in the third slot in a modified right echelon position. As the flight progressed I noticed there was a much stronger cross wind than what we were told to expect by the weatherman before take off. I came up over the flight's tactical frequency and told the lead aircraft what I had discovered. The lead aircraft, an officer candidate, didn't reply. A few minutes went by with no change in the direction of the aircraft.

At that rate, if we had continued on that heading we would have been real close on fuel when and if they finally discovered the error. If we continued too long we could all end up landing in a farmer's field. I came up over the air again, "Lead, this is 127, we are well south of our track, and if we don't make a correction soon we'll have to find an alternate field."

This time I got a reply, "Cadet, I don't think I need you to teach me how to navigate."

I sat back in my seat. I wasn't going to run out of fuel with this horse's ass. Where was the instructor? What were the other students doing? Was I wrong? I picked up my map and double checked my calculations and then started looking for an alternate field. I thought I would try one more time. "Lead, this is 127, I've double-checked, and I'm sure we are off course. We need to come 20 degrees starboard, to a heading of 280."

I did not get a reply. A minute went by, then a voice came up over the radio. "Lead, this is your flight instructor. I suggest you listen to what the cadet said and come right to a heading of 280." A few seconds later the lead reluctantly made a gradual turn to 280 and we followed.

Instead of gloating I sat there trying to understand what had just taken place. I didn't have an answer. Later in my career I would see this same ego centric type of mentality cost lives.

As the flight went on, I thought about the famous Flight

19. Five Navy Grumman Avengers were lost off the coast of Florida near the Bermuda Triangle. How easy it would be to get lost, especially over water with no visual ground references.. I decided I was going to pay more attention to the navigation lectures, especially when they talked about the ship steaming in one direction the flight going in another and two to three hours later you're supposed to rendezvous over the ship for a landing. We were lucky with the instruments we had in the 1960's. During the Second World War it was part skill and part luck.

Halfway into the flight the formation reached its refueling destination. I had the lead back and took the flight into the landing pattern. As I called for a downwind leg, the tower replied with, "Cleared to land. Beware of heavy turbulence from the Air Force tanker, on final." As I rolled onto final I could see the aircraft halfway down the runway. I continued my approach. At about 300 yards from the end of the runway the aircraft started to do a snap roll. As I fought to keep the aircraft upright, the bottom seemed to drop out, and the aircraft started a rapid descent toward the ground. Instinctively I applied full throttle as I continued to fight the aircraft to keep it upright. As I flew through the turbulence I regained control of the aircraft and touched down slightly past the end of the runway. Holy shit! That was something I didn't want to try again.

As I turned off the runway I felt the results of the adrenalin shooting through my body. Switching to ground control for taxi instructions I went over what had just happened. You can never relax when you're flying, especially on landings and take-offs. That was clear air turbulence, and I had no idea how severe it could be. The next time the tower warned me of turbulence I was going to pay attention. The old saying came back, "luck and experience, you hoped you got the experience before your luck ran out." Was it really luck? Did skill have a lot to do with the amount of luck you had? No one would ever really know.

While the aircraft refueled the flight got something to eat and we went back over to check the weather for the return flight. I went over what had happened with the instructor, and he shared some experiences with the rest of the group. Human nature was interesting. Instead of being appreciative of my trying to help him with the navigation, the officer instead held it against me. It was a new experience for me, and it would be repeated throughout my career.

Halfway back on the return flight I started smelling exhaust fumes. I felt a little flushed and seemed to have trouble focusing. I came up over the flights tactical frequency and told the instructor that I thought something was wrong. We discussed what it might be, and carbon monoxide poisoning was his guess. The instructor seemed concerned. I continued to get more confused and was really having trouble even focusing on what the instructor was saying. The instructor suggested that I go on oxygen, so I checked to see if there was any oxygen in the system. The gauge registered about half full, but I didn't have a mask. Oxygen masks were not required for this part of the training.

As we went over our options I reached under the seat and grabbed the oxygen tube and pulled it out. I turned on the oxygen, put the end of the tube in my mouth and checked to see if I had positive oxygen flow. It seemed to be working; it was hard to tell because I wasn't that familiar with the oxygen system, and there was no mask to form a tight fit around my mouth and nose. After a few minutes I seemed to be able to focus once again. The instructor came back over the air and told me to monitor the oxygen flow. We still had about a half hour left before we reached NAS Whiting, and he wanted me on the deck before the oxygen ran out.

I made it back to Whiting without incident and the instructor had me break off and head straight into the runway. After the debrief the instructor told me to head to sick bay and get checked out by the flight surgeon just to be safe. At sick bay one of the young doctors looked me over and said I would probably have flu-like symptoms for the next couple of days. The flight surgeon grounded me and told me to come back in two days. I was sick as a dog the following day.

When I returned to sick bay the flight surgeon gave me an up chit. Then I went down to the scheduling office to see if I could get back on the flight schedule. We had completed ground school, and I didn't want to get too far behind the other cadets. As I got closer to the line area I saw my flight instructor with a couple of students. The lieutenant called me over and said, "You're one lucky cadet. They found a cracked manifold on your aircraft. If you hadn't noticed what was happening, you could have just passed out and flown into the ground. We might have never known what happened."

Life is something you can't control if you're going to really live it. In aviation it was a matter of inches sometimes, or in this case, catching a slight whiff of engine fumes. I always took pride in knowing everything that was going on in the cockpit. I wondered if this situation had anything to do with the violent maneuver trying to keep the aircraft under control from the wake turbulence during the earlier landing.

I finished up the remainder of basic flight training and was preparing for the biggest event in naval aviation. My first carrier landing. Most of the cadets felt it was as important to them as getting their wings. But first, it was Christmas, and I hadn't been home in almost a year. I didn't have enough money to fly home so I decided to drive. I had two weeks of leave, and in those days I never knew any limits. I drove a beat up VW 38 hours straight through to L.A. by myself. I was eager to get home to my girlfriend, or so I thought. When I arrived she had a little surprise for me. She had met someone else while I was gone. The Navy has an old saying, "Absence makes the heart go wander." I took it in stride and in all fairness, I was too busy with the flight program and living life to have it make a big impact. She did the right thing.

I had a few days to spend with the guys I grew up with, but

it wasn't the same. I had already started to change and there was a whole new world out there left to discover. The guys had their bowling and poker nights, and working on their cars. Things seemed to be just as they were when we were in high school. I was bored and couldn't wait to get back to the excitement of flying. The trip back was as crazy as the trip out. I drove straight through to Dallas in about 23 hours, picked up a cadet that needed a ride, slept for two hours and then headed into Pensacola. It was something I seemed to be able to do without feeling any of the effects of fatigue. I think it was just the excitement of being alive.

Carrier Qualifications

The excitement was building. You could feel the electricity in the air. I was riding shotgun in Rich Graves' car. Gary, Pete and Travis were in the back. We were all NAVCAD's and started out in Preflight together. We were able to stay together up to this point. Travis was also a NAVCAD but had started two months ahead of us. We were from all over the United States. Rich was from Massachusetts, Gary was from New York, Pete was from Washington, Travis was from Georgia, and I was from California. We were on our way to "Bloody Baron Field." Baron Field was a small outlying field that was used specifically for Field Carrier Landing Practices (FCLP's). It was too small for anything else.

Nobody in the car knew why it was called "Bloody Baron," but we were sure it earned its name. The field consisted of just a few hangars and a short runway, a very short runway. We had to move from NAS Whiting back down to NAS Pensacola, and the second class cadet barracks. When we completed carrier quals we would be promoted to first class cadets. At Baron, we transitioned from the T-28B to the T-28C. The only real difference was the tail hook and some additional reinforcement on the undercarriage to take the impact of carrier landings.

As we walked into the training spaces we could see the flight schedule on the far wall. By flight three, I saw my name along with the rest of the NAVCADs. There was one other name that I didn't recognize. At the top of the list was Lieutenant Duckworth's name. He would be our flight instructor for the carrier qualifications training. Rich went up to the officer at the scheduling desk and said, "Cadet Graves reporting as ordered, sir!" The schedules officer looked at Rich and then at the flight schedule. "You're assigned to Lieutenant Duckworth. He's over at the table in the corner." Rich turned and walked toward the table and we followed.

Lieutenant Duckworth looked up at us and said, "So you're all NAVCAD's. This ought to be an interesting couple of weeks." He introduced himself and then took us into one of the small classrooms where the other pilot was waiting. For the remainder of the day we received briefings on field procedures at Baron and carrier procedures. In the afternoon we went out to the runway to watch another flight practice FCLP's. At the approach end of the runway was a landing signal system. The landing signal device was a set of horizontal yellow lights with a mirror in the center. When you were on glide path the mirror showed a yellow ball in the center. If you went high or low the ball turned orange then red the further off glide slop you got. If you got a wave off, the horizontal light would flash red. If you got a cut signal, the lights would flash green. That meant you cut the throttle and flew the aircraft into the deck. I looked around the field. There were huge pine trees surrounding the field. They looked to be at least 150 to 200 feet tall. The runway was one of the shortest I had ever seen.

On the return to NAS Pensacola after the first day of training all we could talk about was our first carrier landing. Rich couldn't believe that in two weeks we were actually going to land on a carrier. We were scheduled for a 0730 show the next morning with an 0830 launch for FCLP's. I had a little trouble sleeping that night. Everything to this point had built up to carrier qualifications. I had walked into Battalion II just a little over a year ago, and this was the biggest event of the entire year. I felt good about my flying skills, and I couldn't wait to land on the deck of a carrier. The two week training period would culminate in six landings and take-offs on the USS Lexington and then you would be sent to advanced training in your chosen pipeline. The pipelines consisted of jets, multi-engine planes, or helicopters.

The training went without incident with the exception of day five of the FCLP's. I felt great and as usual was "hot dogging" it up a little. The training was pretty easy, and I was getting a little bored and impatient. As our flight circled the field in a simulated carrier-landing pattern I had the Automatic Direction Finder (ADF) tuned into a local radio station. The ADF was a radio used in those days for navigation.

Carrier landings in the T-28 were made with the canopy open. The noise from the engine made it difficult to hear the radio at times, so I turned up the volume on the radio station. As I came around on final, I picked up the ball, and announced "ball" and my fuel state. When I got the cut signal I pulled the throttle back promptly and flew the aircraft into the deck. Piece of cake! The wheels chirped as they touched the runway. I applied full throttle, brought the speed brake up and started my roll down the runway.

As I accelerated down the runway I looked off to my left and saw the rest of the flight rolling down the taxi way. Oh shit! With my radio going and the cockpit open I must not have heard the instructor call the flight in. I cut the throttle and jumped on the brakes. With the power off it was quiet, very quiet. I could hear the instructor very clearly over the radio. "You're never going to make it!" Oh shit! Too much airspeed and not enough runway. I made a decision that a few seconds later I would regret. I pushed the throttle full forward with such force that I think I must have bent the throttle. The aircraft leaped forward again.

I began to accelerate down the runway again. Over the

radio came the same voice only a little lower, "You're ... never... going... to... make... it!"

I could see the end of the runway coming up quickly. I must have checked to see if the speed brake was up at least a dozen times. The speed brake adds drag on the aircraft and helps it to slow down. As the end of the runway came up I made another decision. Was it the right one? If I went off the runway with my landing gear still down the nose wheel would most likely collapse and the aircraft, if it had enough speed, might flip. I grabbed the landing gear handle and as the aircraft was about to leave the end of the runway, I raised the gear. The aircraft settled slightly but I was flying!!!

As I eased the nose up slightly I could feel the aircraft shutter. That meant I was right on the edge of a stall. The trees were very close to the end of the runway, and I couldn't get enough altitude. About that time I heard that haunting voice come over the radio, it was eerie, he seemed to be enjoying what was happening. "You're never... going.... to make... it!"

As I kept the aircraft flying I looked straight ahead. All I could see was pine trees, lots of tall pine trees. I had another decision to make. I remembered the stories in the briefings when they discussed going into the trees in a T-28. The discussion went something like this. The T-28 has a big, heavy engine. If you have to go in, stay down behind the engine, keep the wings level, keep your airspeed and aim between two trees and ride it out. With a bit of luck the trees will take the wings off and eliminate the fuel source, along with absorbing some of your forward airspeed. Hopefully, the engine would take out the rest.

The aircraft continued to accelerate. With the gear and speed brake up there was little drag on the aircraft and the T-28 could accelerate quickly. I saw a slight opening at the top of the trees but didn't think I would have enough altitude. Was there enough room for me to make it between the trees? I made a slight bank and headed for the opening. I had to be careful; so close to stall speed the vertical lift vector would be reduced with the increase in the angle of bank. The aircraft continued to climb. It looked like I wasn't going to make it. I could see the tops of the trees go past my canopy, and thought I had clipped one of the trees with the prop but wasn't sure. The aircraft was shuttering right on the edge of a stall, and it wouldn't take much to lose control and go into the trees uncontrolled. As I came out above the trees I rolled the aircraft level and continued my climb, scanning the engine instruments to see if there were any problems while I checked the aircraft for strange vibrations.

Everything seemed OK! I continued a slight climb to the landing pattern altitude, adjusted the power and turned downwind for a landing. Again I was lucky. If I would have over controlled the aircraft I would have easily spun in. Or was it luck? I had cornered the market on stupidity, but I knew that aircraft and always seemed to fly my way out of trouble.

As I brought the aircraft in for a landing the radios were silent. I didn't hear any chatter. I parked the aircraft on the line, got out and looked it over. There didn't appear to be any damage to the aircraft. I walked slowly into the line shack not wanting to hear all the jeers from my flight. Lieutenant Duckworth was in the line shack waiting for the rest of the flight to sign off their yellow sheets (maintenance and aircraft flight records). Duckworth looked over at me, with a grin on his face. "I would have lost money on you, Billings." I looked at the lieutenant not knowing how to respond. I didn't want to make a bad situation worse. I rolled my eyes back and wiped my brow. I waited to see if the issue was going to be carried any further; it wasn't.

As we returned to NAS Pensacola that afternoon we talked about the big day. Friday would be the actual carrier landings, no more practice. Gary mentioned that he heard a NAVCAD in one of the other flights had his nose gear collapse and the prop walked his aircraft right over the side of the flight deck and into the water. "That must have been hairy," he said. I wondered how the nose wheel would collapse like that. Did he dive for the deck? I'm sure it was just a mechanical failure. I had a tendency to always over analyze everything, it was my nature, that's how I learned. None of us got much sleep that night. The thought of being carrier aviators was just too electrifying.

The next morning everyone was at the chow hall early. You could smell the excitement in the air. MARCAD Faulkner came up to the table and handed me his silk scarf. Mike and I had started out in the program together and remained good friends. We got separated transitioning through the program when Mike's dad got sick and he had to go on thirty days leave to be with him. "Here's the scarf you wanted for the flight., Don't lose it." He handed it to me.

"Great, thanks," I said as I reached for the long, Marine green scarf. It always seemed like I did things with a flare. What could be better than making your first carrier landing with a silk scarf trailing out the cockpit like a World War I ace?

We arrived early that morning at "Bloody Baron," and did an extra thorough job on the pre-flight of our aircraft. As we reached the carrier, Lieutenant Duckworth passed the lead to me and said, "I'll join on the first aircraft at Angle's 2."

Duckworth would be circling above the carrier at 2,000 feet waiting to reform the flight and return to Baron field. I led the flight in and called abeam the ship. I was cleared by the air boss for a landing. As I rolled out on final, I called the ball and my fuel state. It was great. My radio blaring with the silk scarf trailing out of the cockpit, I lined up on the ball, adjusted my power and started down the glide slop. As I crossed the back of the ship, the landing signal officer (LSO) gave me the cut signal. I didn't plan on what happened next. When I cut the power it caused a vacuum effect around the cockpit. The end result was the long silk scarf was pulled back into the cockpit and swirled around in the turbulent air. As the air whirled around in the cockpit, it carried the scarf across and around my face. I frantically grabbed at the scarf, pulling it away from my face. Just at that instance the aircraft caught the wire and I came to an abrupt stop.

In my haste to get the scarf away from my face, I had pulled it from my neck. I remembered Mike's last words, "Don't lose it." I was looking at the Flight Deck Officer and getting a signal to raise my tail hook and taxi forward. I had to get out of the way, there was someone right behind me looking for a clear deck. I trapped the scarf by pinning it between my chin and shoulder; both hands were busy maneuvering the aircraft. I didn't have time to do anything else. As I taxied forward, the scarf was trailing out of the cockpit a good six feet. I had caught it right at the end and couldn't let it go. I don't know why the scarf was so important but I had promised Mike he would get it back.

I was passed to the Deck Launch Officer as I taxied forward he gave me the signal to run up the engine. The procedure was to run the engine up to 30" of manifold pressure to check the engine instruments before jumping off the front of the ship. I ran the engine up, checked the instruments, and was supposed to signal with a head nod that all the instruments were in the green. The launch officer waited for me to give him the signal. He watched me as I tried to give him the head nod with the scarf trapped between my chin and shoulder and the scarf trailing out of the cockpit whirling in the prop wash. He paused a moment, shook his head and pointed down the deck. I released the brakes, pushed the throttle full forward and the aircraft accelerated down the flight deck. As the aircraft rolled down the deck, I systematically tried to retrieve the scarf, methodically pulling it in a little at a time. By the time I reached 200 feet I had retrieved the scarf and stuffed it in the pocket on the leg of my flight suit. I decided "style" was not needed at this point.

The rest of the landings went without incident. As I completed my last landing, I made a 45 degree turn starboard off the ship's heading, cleaned everything up, landing gear and flaps, and checked the speed brake. I accelerated to 280 knots on the deck. I was supposed to make a gradual climb to 2,000 feet so the instructor could join me. As I reached 280 knots I pulled the nose up into a steep climb and did a victory roll as I climbed to the designated altitude. As I reach 2,000, I had traded most of my airspeed for altitude. When I pushed the nose over, the airspeed indicator read 90 knots, slightly above stall. Sometimes I think I pulled too many stunts, but when you accomplished something like carrier qualifications, you had to express it in some form. At least I did. The aircraft started to accelerate gradually to 180 knots. I looked over my shoulder and saw Lieutenant Duckworth. He was at my 8 o'clock, same altitude, lined up to join on my port side. I thought to myself, "Oh shit! I'm doing 90 knots and Duckworth is doing 180 knots or more. What a hell of a closer rate this was going to be!"

I couldn't do anything but hold my current heading and altitude and hope that Lieutenant Duckworth would see what was happening and wave it off. Just about that time I saw the lieutenant push the nose over and shoot under my aircraft. As Duckworth came around again I was at 180 knots. The lieutenant pulled slowly alongside, stared at me and shook his head. The lieutenant signaled for the lead and I fell in behind. I sat back, took a deep breath, and relished the thought that I was now a carrier pilot.

The rest of the flight joined up and we all returned to Baron field. I remembered the flight instructor saying that your landing after carrier quals was usually the worst landing you would ever make. The adrenaline and exhilaration of what you just accomplished would make you forget everything you learned about flying. Not to be out done, I made one that would definitely be remembered by several of the students on the ground.

On my final approach to the runway at Bloody Baron the adrenalin and euphoria were at a peak. I had the radio tuned in to one of my favorite local radio stations. I overshot the runway by a wide margin. I tried to save the approach, not wanting to have to go through the embarrassment of a wave-off and taking the aircraft around. That doesn't happen to a carrier pilot. I rapped the aircraft up into almost a 90 degree angle of bank and that immediately stopped the overshoot. In order to keep the end of the runway in sight I had to look directly out the top of the cockpit. I could see the students and flight instructor of one of the new flights on the ground near the landing signal mirror looking at me. I could see the surprised expressions on their faces as I rapidly started coming back toward the runway.

As the aircraft started to accelerate rapidly back toward the runway the students and the instructor ran for cover, diving behind the signal mirror and the pickup truck. It was the funniest sight I had seen in a long time. I didn't know what they were running for; I knew exactly what I was doing. As I got my lineup back I quickly wrapped the aircraft back to wings level and hit the numbers dead center with a nice sweet little chirp of the wheels touching the runway. I chuckled to myself as I rolled down the runway and thought, "I wonder what they thought I was going to do." It was a major milestone in our lives and it was over. We finished the debrief and returned to NAS Pensacola.

On the ride back in the car, it was deadly quiet. Finally Gary said, "That's it? That's all there is? It's over?" We worked for a whole year, and it was over in minutes. Everyone was a little introspective, each of us wrapped up in what we had just accomplished in our own personal ways. Every class, every formation, every flight had lead to that moment and it was over. Later that night the celebration would begin and now I was even old enough to drink legally. We couldn't wait to get back to NAS Pensacola.

What the hell are helicopters?

The following week, we got our new assignments. At the end of carrier quals, they totaled up your ground school and flight scores for the whole year and determined if you went jets, multi-engine, or helicopters. If you were in the top of your class and you selected jets, you got to go jets. The same for multi-engine and helicopters. There were a total of 14 of us in the flight pool that week. I sat patiently at the table waiting for the Scheduling Officer to read off the assignments. I couldn't wait to get into high performance jets. As the Scheduling Officer started to read off the names and assignments, he reminded us, "The needs of the Navy come first."

There was a critical need for helicopter pilots. Out of this class of 14 they needed 13 helicopter pilots. I thought, "Oh shit! I know I don't have the best grades in the group." The Scheduling Officer turned to Ensign Benson, "You have your choice of the one opening in the jet pipeline or helo's."

Benson said, "Sir, I want to go helicopters."

I held my breath. "Cadet Graves, jets or helo's?"

With Rich's previous flying experience he had accumulated several hundred flight hours before he even joined the Navy. He was able to stay at the top of the class and picked jets.

"That's it," said the Scheduling Officer, "the rest of you pick up your orders and report to base personnel at NAS Ellyson Field at 0800 Monday morning. Good luck on your next assignments."

I sat in the chair in disbelief. Helicopters! What the hell are helicopters? They still don't know how they get up in the air. In those days most of the aerodynamics for helicopters was prefaced by "theoretically this is what we believe is occurring." The joke was, they shake and shutter so bad, the ground rejects them. I was going to get hammered that weekend, but it wasn't to celebrate. That week Rich and I said our goodbyes and wished each other luck. Rich was on his way to jet training in Meridian, Mississippi.

NAS Ellyson Field was a small base halfway between Pensacola and Whiting Field. After checking in at base personnel, I had time to go out to the line to take a look at the helicopters I would be flying. As I walked over to the line I could see the Bell TH-13. It was a little two seat helicopter with a tiny glass bubble as the cockpit. I'd seen motorcycles bigger than that thing. Over on the other side of the hangars, I could see the Sikorsky, TH-34, it was what they used for advanced helicopter training. As I got closer to the TH-34 line, I was even more disappointed. The TH-34 looked like a dinosaur in deep depression; it was not meant to fly. It was ugly, something only a mother could love. The rotor blades drooped, bending towards the ground like it was asleep. How could anyone call that an aircraft?

After arriving at the squadron, we were given our flight assignments and briefings on what was expected of us. The flight instructors seemed professional and no different than the fixed wing pilots. In fact, at times they seemed even more organized. I knew what to expect. airframes, hydraulics, power plants, aerodynamics, operating procedures. Same song, different aircraft. I remember my first aerodynamics course when the instructor was going over retreating blade tip stall. Those famous words, "Theoretically, this is what we think is taking place when you get retreating blade tip stall."

I should have listened a little closer. It seems I was unable to get into any aircraft without taking it to its limits. There was a lot of new terminology. Cyclic stick, collective, tail rotor torque, fully articulated rotor head, you name it. The helo community had its own language.

My first flight in the TH-13 was an eye opener. I knew I was a good pilot; my friends always said I was a natural in anything that got off the ground. On the first flight the instructor showed me what it was like to hover, then gave me the controls. I took the controls and said to myself, this looks easy enough. Just about that time, I thought I had just strapped my ass to a bucking bronco. Something about gyroscopic precession, lead/lag, everything I did was wrong. Every control input did something different to the aircraft. The instructor took control of the aircraft. I gladly gave it back to him. The instructor told me not to let it bother me, nobody had ever hovered a helicopter on the first try, and it usually took about three hops to get a feel for hovering.

It was a real humbling experience. We spent most of the hop trying to hover, then the instructor got a clearance and took me around the pattern. In forward flight the helicopter was similar to a fixed wing. I felt a little better, but not much. After the hop the instructor debriefed me and told me what to expect on the next hop. I headed out to see if I could find another cadet to complain to about these flying machines. I was stuck in helicopters and to add insult to injury, they were hard to fly.

I caught up with George. We went over to get some chow. As first class cadets we were treated a little more like officers, but without the pay. We got to eat in the Ellyson Field officers' club. While we were inside, I noticed a couple of pilots that had different insignias on their flight suits. I asked one of the instructors eating lunch who they were. The lieutenant replied, "Oh, they're astronauts."

"Astronauts?" I replied. "What are they doing here?"

He explained that they take the jet jocks that qualify for astronaut training and send them through helicopter training. It seems the lunar landing module operated more like a helicopter than a fixed wing. I thought to myself, "That makes sense. Take a jet pilot, train him to be a helo pilot and them send him to the moon." I wondered if they would ever let a helo pilot go to the moon. In the early 60's Navy helicopter pilots were still the red headed step children of naval aviation.

On the first three flights we spent most of the time on the taxi way.

As the instructional hops went on, I quickly became quite proficient at flying the TH-13. By hop 13, my first solo hop, I was feeling good about myself again and was enjoying the challenges of helicopter aviation and reveling in the fact that I could fly anything. Those days we flew with a large sand bag in the other seat for balance on our solo hops. On hot summer days, if we had a large instructor, the engine was so under powered the RPMs would drop off when you picked the helicopter up in a hover. As I went out to one of the outlying fields on my first solo hop, I felt like I could lick the world and that usually meant trouble.

As I entered the field landing pattern I took the TH-13 to max forward speed, a blistering 85 knots. It was shaking all over the place. I split the field according to operating procedures and snapped the stick over to the side as a fighter pilot would in a break. As the helicopter rapidly tried to catch up with the abrupt stick movement, it rolled to the left and the nose pitched up. The helicopter started a violent thrashing up and down. If I hadn't been strapped in, it would have thrown me right out of the cockpit. The nose pitched up as if it was going to flip over on its back. I had no idea what was happening. Instinctively I lowered the collective to the bottom. This reduced the power setting on the aircraft and the angle of attack on the blades. The thrashing immediately stopped and the nose fell through. The aircraft started to fall out of the sky. I recovered the aircraft just above the trees, slightly descending into the tree tops. As I maneuvered the aircraft through the trees trying not to hit any, I pulled in the collective and started a positive climb back up to altitude. Climbing to 300 feet I started my downwind turn and reached the abeam position back at 500 feet. I made a precautionary landing at the field and sat there for a long time going over just what had happened. The outlying fields were nothing more than grass.

I decided that it must have been some type of retreating blade tip stall. I had max power and airspeed on the aircraft; it was hot with high humidity. The density altitude must have been way up there, which made the air thinner. When I snapped the cyclic over to the side it must have aggravated the blade position, resulting in the stall. I almost ended up on my back. I decided I needed to understand helicopters a little more before I started with the fancy stuff. Helicopters were much more versatile than fixed wing, but that also meant it was easier to get into trouble, especially when density altitude seemed to affect them so much.

I shut down and made a visual inspection of the aircraft, just in case there was some structural damage. The maneuver was pretty violent. A petty officer that was a field observer in the tower came over to ask me if I was having problems. The petty officer's job was to report any crashes or maintenance problems back to Ellyson Field. I told him I felt a vibration and just wanted to check it out. After the inspection I turned the helicopter up, completed my landings and then headed for Ellyson Field.

I spent the rest of helicopter primary training out of trouble. I really loved the full auto rotations all the way to the ground. Things happened fast and you needed to be right on or you could roll the helicopter up into a ball. It was challenging and that's what made it fun! I can't say flying the TH-13 was that exciting but it was the only way I was going to get into the air as far as the Navy was concerned. I completed primary helicopters and now it was off to advanced helicopter training and the TH-34.

First Engine Failure

As I finished up in the primary trainer I had picked up a reputation as a pretty good stick. The instructors were good; they treated you like a human being, and I enjoyed the environment. I did not want to go through anything like I had at Whiting Field during the instrument phase, so I kept my nose clean. I met my new flight instructor, 1st Lt. Wilson, U.S. Marine Corps. He was a very quiet and mild mannered individual, nothing like the previous Marines I had flown with. The first flight was interesting to say the least. It was like trying to fly a Mac truck with rotor blades on it. The TH-34 had more power than the T-28 and it needed every bit of it just to get off the ground. The aircraft didn't fly -- it beat itself into the air.

The first thing I was cautioned about was rotor engagement. It seems that the TH-34 can go into something they call "ground resonance" on rotor engagement. The way Sikorsky mounted the landing gear into the airframe allowed for an oscillation to build up between the rotor system and the ground, resonating up through the airframe. If it got severe enough the aircraft would disintegrate right where it sat. That sounded exciting! The nice thing about it was the pilots were sitting in the safest place, right under the rotor system. When a helicopter came apart, it was like a grenade. All the shrapnel went outward away from the center. If the remaining parts didn't fall on you, the crew usually survived. It all sounded a little exaggerated until I actually went through my first engagement. When the rotor blades started to engage nothing was in balance. The whole aircraft moved from side to side and backward and forward. I didn't know anything could move in that many directions all at once. It was a very enlightening moment. I couldn't believe the Navy actually bought these things.

The TH-34 was a challenge. To try to fly something that wasn't meant to fly would challenge anyone. I quickly picked up the idiosyncrasies and strange flight characteristics of the 34. The remainder of the training went without incident with the exception of one small engine failure, my first of many.

It was towards the end of my training. I was with another instructor, not 1st Lt. Wilson. The flight liked to rotate the instructors during training, hoping the students might pick up something from each of them. By this time I had earned a reputation for being able to handle the 34 better than most; my instructor even used the term "natural helo pilot," as if there were anything natural about flying a helicopter. I hoped it would go unnoticed. I didn't plan to be in helicopters that long.

It was toward the end of the hop. I had just finished a rough terrain landing and was climbing out to make my downwind leg. The instructor, Lieutenant Blanton, was sitting back in the seat with one leg propped against the instrument panel, relaxed. The landings and take-offs were a little repetitive and I was having no trouble with the maneuvers. It gave Lt. Blanton an opportunity to catch up on a little day dreaming.

As I was climbing to 300 feet to start my downwind turn there was a thunderous backfire from the engine compartment followed by continuous smaller backfires of the engine. We immediately started to lose power. As the backfiring continued, I looked over and saw the RPMs dropping off. I instinctively lowered the collective to maintain RPMs. My eyes scanned the engine instruments for any indication of what was happening. The manifold pressure dropped to almost zero. We were going in, so I rotated the nose to reduce forward airspeed and leveled the helicopter. All of this happened in the time it took the LT to get his leg down and hands on the controls. Out of the corner of my eye I saw the instructor reacting to the situation. We went into a corn field straight ahead of us. As I pulled the collective up I could feel the instructor on the controls. The aircraft rocked and settled into the soft earth.

There was no time for a may day, so the instructor got on the radio and called one of the squadron aircraft to relay our situation to home base. We shut down the aircraft and the electronics and climbed out to survey the damage. There was no physical damage to the airframe; it was a good landing, but we could see the oil pouring out of the engine compartment. When we opened the engine doors we could see the damage. It looked like there was a hole in the bottom of one of the engine cylinders and what was left of the oil was still pouring out.

The instructor told me that I had responded well to the emergency. Since we were climbing out from a rough terrain area, the aircraft was right on the edge of its flight envelope. The aircraft operating manual performance charts show there are areas in the flight transition where the airspeed and altitude do not allow for the safe recovery of the aircraft if anything goes wrong. It was a combination of reaction time and aircraft performance. All helicopters have these charts and conditions, some are just a little more restrictive than others. Since the TH-34 was not meant to fly, it had a very large envelope were you couldn't recover. There's an old aviator saying that in an emergency the sky above you and the runway behind you don't do you any good.

As the crash crew and recovery team arrived, Lieutenant Blanton and I got a ride back to NAS Ellyson Field in one of the trucks. The next morning Lieutenant Blanton and I were called into the CO's office. The CO complimented Blanton on saving the aircraft and the fine job he did in getting the aircraft on the ground safely. Lieutenant Blanton thanked the CO and both of us turned and left the Skipper's office. As we left, I thought to myself, 'He could have shared a little of the credit. At least I should get a 4.0 grade for that hop.'

I finished up with a few instrument training hops and then it was finally time to pin on those "Gold Wings."

Commissioning Day and Wings of Gold

I received my commission and Navy Gold Wings on June 17, 1966. I was a twenty-one year old ensign in the United States Navy. It felt good; I had the world by the balls. How could life get any better? I was still pretty young and stuck to my high ideals of right and wrong. Up until then I didn't have much time to think about anything accept the next aircraft or next phase of training. By the time I had completed Ellyson Field I had accepted the idea of being a helicopter pilot. It was challenging and very versatile, but it did not have the glamour of being a fighter pilot. I got an unrestricted designation, which gave me both a fixed and rotary winged qualification. It meant that if there was an opportunity to transition to a fixed winged squadron, I could. My first duty station would be Helicopter Combat Support Squadron One (HC-1) , at

Naval Auxiliary Landing Field (NALF) Imperial Beach, in San Diego, California.

That night I went through the traditional ceremony at the O'Club for new aviators. The tradition was all new aviators bought the drinks for the night. The evening would start with the young aviators sitting on the bar and placing their new gold wings in a concoction of one shot of everything in the bar that was drinkable. The Marines would have their drinks topped off with red food coloring and the Navy would have blue. When everyone received their drinks, one of the instructors would ring the large brass bell at the end of the bar and all new aviators would chug-a-lug their drinks, catching their new gold wings in their teeth. That ceremony usually led to a very short night for the new warriors.

As a result of one of the ceremonies, they had an X-ray on the wall of a student's chest. It has a nice wooden frame around it with a light behind it so you could see the X-ray clearly. Down on the left-hand side of the X-ray standing right side up, as if they were meant to be there, was a set of gold wings. It seems one of the graduating students was so eager to get his drink down, he forgot that he had a set of wings in the bottom of the glass and swallowed them. With a little bit of thorough searching, he finally got his wings back, although they were slightly tarnished.

The discipline the Navy taught me and what I learned about myself would be the foundation that I would build on throughout my adult life. I was about to embark on a career as a naval aviator that would encompass over 22 years of naval service. I had thirty days to report to my new duty station, and I was ready to see what life had to offer.

After my commissioning I was invited to spend a few days with some friends at a nursing school in Montgomery, Alabama. I was young and a little naïve. Some women seemed to find me attractive and they knew how to get what they wanted, which suited me just fine. When the partying ended I left and headed north to Michigan. I was already a day late from an extra day of celebration. I kept asking myself, could life get any better? I happened to know an airline stewardess from high school and she invited me to visit her after I completed flight training. I would also be able to see my aunt and uncle and hopefully renew an old relationship.

I arrived in Detroit about 2300 the following day. I was lost. I pulled off the freeway into a gas station to get directions. As I got out of the car, I saw two police cars pull up on the side streets. They jumped out of their cars and had their guns drawn. They were aimed directly at me. "Freeze or we'll shoot!"

I didn't move, except to put my hands in the air. The next thing I knew they arrested me and impounded my car, and I didn't have a clue why. On the way into the police station I was told that luckily my first move was to put my hands over my head. If I hadn't they were ready to shoot. Evidently someone in a bright red car had shot somebody standing on the corner a few blocks away. I was not in the best part of the city and back then the police didn't take any chances. I was driving a candy apple red Mustang that I had just bought with my new ensign pay.

When they cuffed me and searched my car, I had everything I owned in it. All my clothes, money and a loaded automatic under the seat. When they found the automatic you would have thought they just captured Al Capone. It was only a .22 caliber target pistol. On the way in, they told me that if I was innocent of the shooting, I would probably get only 3-5 years for having a loaded gun. I told myself this was all crazy and that it would soon be over. I spent that night in the jail and the only thing that went through my mind was, "If I was innocent, I would get only 3-5 years."

I couldn't believe this was happening. I went from the top of the world to total despair in less than five days. It was like a bad dream, sitting there in the jail watching my whole life pass by. Needless to say I didn't get much sleep that night. The minutes seemed like hours and all I had to do was stare at the floor and think about what was happening to me. The next day I finally got my one call and was able to reach my aunt. She knew a lawyer in that part of the state that was in the National Guard, and she was sure he would be able to help. By the end of the day, I was out of jail. It seemed the state law allowed an active duty officer to carry a weapon, to say nothing about the illegal search. They knew I had nothing to do with the shooting. I didn't ask any questions; I just wanted out. The battery on my car was dead. I had one of the first 8-track tape stereos in my car. The police spent most of the night listening to my stereo. It took another two hours to get the car started and get out of there.

Now I was over two days late. As soon as I could get to a phone, I called the stewardess. When she answered, I said, "You're never going to believe this!"

She said, "You're right; I have a flight" and hung up. At that point I almost didn't care. I just wanted to get to San Diego without anything else happening. I headed straight for California with a short stop by my aunt's house to thank her for the help. This was the first of many surprises that lay ahead.

Chapter Two
First Duty Assignment

Helicopter Combat Support Squadron One (HC-1), NALF Imperial Beach

I arrived in San Diego two weeks earlier than I had expected. It gave me enough time to find a couple of roommates and get settled before the training started. After checking into HC-1, I received the standard indoctrination including the UH-2B NATOPS instruction, which described UH-2B flight characteristics and base operating procedures. Naval Auxiliary Landing Field (NALF) Imperial Beach was a small auxiliary landing field just south of the North Island Naval Air Station in Coronado, CA. Imperial Beach was so close to the Mexican border you could see the lights of Tijuana at night. If you didn't pay attention you could accidentally fly across the border during an approach to the field. The runway was small; only helicopters and small planes could land.

The smallness of the base made for a tight knit community. I don't know what it is about war or armed conflicts, or being a naval aviator, but it seemed to make people live life a little fuller. I could never decide whether it was the type of personality that went into aviation, or the environment and risk that made them like they were. The Vietnam War (or police action to be politically correct), was building up. Men were going into combat, and there was always that ever present risk factor in the aviation community of losing a flight crew. I think this environment made the young pilots try to live everyday to the fullest. There were plenty of squadron parties and plenty of happy hours.

The UH-2B was not much to brag about. The Sea Sprite was made by KAMAN Aircraft. The squadron policy at that time was all UH-2B flights had to be escorted by a UH-34. The story was the UH-34 crew was there to pick up the UH-2 crew when the aircraft went in the water. This was a standing joke that was promoted because of the poor reliability of the Sea Sprite. It was a single engine helicopter that at times ran out of power. I remember our deployments to the South China Sea, where we had to hover to the edge of the deck with a full load and then dive for the water to get flying speed.

I was eager to show them how well I could handle a helicopter in hopes that it might get me a Combat Search and Rescue (CSAR) assignment on my first cruise. At that time the CSAR co-pilot assignments were usually kept for the more experienced co-pilots and aircraft commanders. The assignments were much higher risk, and it took pilots with some time under their belt to handle the challenging environment. They operated off destroyers and cruisers that were specially equipped to handle helicopters. Their assignment was to stay on Yankee Station and rescue any downed pilots off the coast of North Vietnam. This also included going inland if necessary to bring the pilots out.

The rescue helicopters were strategically placed up and down the coast of North Vietnam to support the carriers during strike operations. I knew that if I could show them how well I could fly, I would be a shoo-in for a co-pilot slot. In addition to looking very young, I had just turned 22 the week before and seemed to always be at least two or three years younger than the other pilots. I seemed to constantly be fighting against my age and even grew a mustache to try to add a few years. That mustache would stay with me for the rest of my Navy career and become part of that "Hollywood Al" image.

I was not a war monger. At that point in my life, I didn't know what type of a person I was, or would be and I wanted to know. I felt the combat experience would help me find out. It was worth the risk to find out the man I would be. I grew up watching John Wayne movies and probably didn't know it at the time, but what he seemed to stand for, set in motion many of my beliefs. I thought if you were honest and straightforward with people they would respect you for it and respond in kind. I believed that if you were strong and stood up for what was right, you would be admired. If you were to lead men you would have to win their respect and set the example. These core beliefs would at times be a stumbling block when it came to the intrusions and aggressions of people who did not have the same principles or values.

I had finished the UH-2B ground school and was eager to get started flying. As I sat in the ready room going over procedures for my first hop in the Sea Sprite, I overheard a group of lieutenants (LT's) and lieutenant commanders (LCDR's) talking about reverine force operations. They were trying to design a landing platform on a small watercraft that would be supporting the Navy forces on the rivers and off the coast of South Vietnam.

As I started toward the briefing room to meet my instructor, I stopped at the table to see what they were studying. They were trying to determine the best lighting arrangement for landing a helo on a small platform on top of a reverine troop carrier. There would be just enough room for the landing gear or skids and no room for error, especially at night. After a few minutes I piped up and said, "Why don't you just put a light at each corner and one in the middle? That way the helicopter can line up for the approach, depending on the wind conditions. Especially if the watercraft is not able to maneuver in restricted waters."

At this point, I was about to be reminded that an ensign is to be seen and not heard. Lt. Rainville turned around and said, "Son, things aren't always as simple as they look. When you get a little experience under your belt you'll understand." That condescending attitude irritated the hell out of me. I left wishing I had kept my mouth shut.

About three hours had gone by when I completed my flight and debriefing. On my way to the locker room, I passed through the ready room. The group of engineers and pilots were just finishing up the final design for the landing platform on the river craft. Curious, I looked over their shoulders again to see what the final design looked like. They had decided to put a light in each corner of the landing pad and one in the middle. This would allow the helicopter to make its approach from any direction. The light in the center would be red. I turned and walked out the door thinking to myself, "You learn something new everyday."

I was moving through the training syllabus quickly. HC-1 was a large squadron and there always seemed to be some new pilot that was sick, or had family matters that needed to be taken care of. That left an available slot open for me to pick up an extra flight. I was midway through training when I looked at the schedule board and saw I was flying with the skipper, Commander Jacobs. I knew this was my chance to shine. Not many people got to fly with the skipper, especially a new ensign. If I impressed the CO, I might get that Combat SAR assignment.

Commander Jacobs was an impressive individual, 6'2," 225 lbs., part American Indian with strong features and jet black hair. When he entered the room, people took notice.

Things did not go well on the hop. I was trying too hard. At best, I was an average pilot that day. When I completed the hop and walked back to the locker room, I was totally dejected. It was the worst hop I had ever flown. I flew better than that on my first hop in the Sea Sprite. I knew that any chance for a Combat SAR slot had vanished. Just to add insult to injury I was assigned a flight with Lt. McCormick the next day. Lt. McCormick was "Mr. Combat SAR," no other pilot even challenged him for the title. The tales of some of his aerial feats were hard to believe, even for someone as gullible as I was at that age. The stories about his antics off the coast of North Vietnam were even better. One of my favorite stories told of the time when Lt. McCormick was a new aircraft commander standing by to go into North Vietnam to pick up a downed pilot.

The survival rate for a rescue helicopter went down drastically if you took too much time to reach the downed pilot. The problem was a Commodore and his staff were in charge of all rescue operations on Yankee Station. When the pilots went down, the Combat SAR crew had to get permission to go in and pick up the pilot. For every five minute delay in sending the rescue crew inland, the survivability decreased significantly. Each delay would allow the North Vietnamese to set up around the downed pilot and wait for the rescue crew to come in, then ambush them. Decisions out of the command center were notoriously slow. Lt. McCormick had already experienced too many delays and knew that one day he would be put in a position where his flying skills would not get him out.

As the story goes, Lt. McCormick reported that he had the emergency signal from the downed pilot and a good fix on his position. He told them he was going in for the pick up. The command center reported back, "Wait one," while they analyzed the situation. Just like in the movies, Lt. McCormick said, "I'm sorry, you're... breaking up, ...say again." About that time McCormick reached over and turned down the volume on his radio, then went in for the rescue. After his successful pick up and what was to be the third rescue he participated in, the Lieutenant reported feet wet on his way back out over the water with the pilot aboard. Because of McCormick's quick action he was able to get in and out without endangering his crew anymore than they were already. Nothing was ever said about the radio communications problem.

They never seem to learn; this type of approach would be repeated again and again over the years. Once you've committed your troops, you need to give them authority to make the decisions. They're the ones that are on the scene. You cannot assess a combat situation from the wardroom or Oval Office. The Vietnam War was a political war not only at the executive level but within the military itself. The Johnson Administration and McNamara made a mess out of the Vietnam War with their silly little war room. Years later McNamara would declare the Vietnam War a mistake, but not once did I hear him admit to his complicity in the debacle that lost thousands of lives. The list is endless. Once the politicians make a decision to go to war, leave it to the professionals. All politicians do is get young men killed. The dedication and professionalism displayed by the military in contrast to some of the obviously incompetent politicians has amazed me throughout the years..

Mr. Combat SAR

I could not believe I was going to fly with Mr. Combat SAR. He was a legend when it came to flying the Sea Sprite. I had completed the pre-flight and was strapped in the co-pilot seat when McCormick arrived. I watched the LT climb into the aircraft; you could tell that McCormick was comfortable in the Sea Sprite. The way he strapped in was like putting on a glove. He became part of the aircraft. Some pilots can have thousands of hours and never look comfortable in an aircraft. To those pilots, it was a job from the time they took off to the time they landed. I loved being in the air. I was more relaxed in the air than on the ground. It didn't make any difference what I was flying.

We finished the checklist, called for take-off and headed

out toward the over water training area near San Clemente Island. I told McCormick I wanted to learn everything I could from him. I knew there were very few pilots around like the LT, and I wanted to be like him one day. McCormick said, "We'll see," and told me to head out to the assigned training area. McCormick was a low key, no BS type of officer. You could feel the confidence, yet he didn't try to impress you with his knowledge or skills. He was strictly business; I liked that.

McCormick told me, "This is a Combat SAR training hop so let's get as much out of it as we can. I'll take you through the maneuvers and then you do one."

I sat on the edge of my seat the whole time during the maneuvers. McCormick was able to explain the reasoning for the radical maneuvers and what the aircraft was going through aerodynamically. I had never met anyone that knew his job as well as McCormick. I couldn't wait to see what was next. The LT was part of the aircraft; he knew everything that was going to happen before it happened. Anticipating everything that happens to a helicopter was no easy task. There were too many outside factors that affected its flight characteristics. That is, if you did the same maneuver on a different day the helicopter may have responded differently.

Helicopters are very sensitive to density altitude (temperature, humidity, altitude) and each aircraft responded differently. Some engines had more power than others. Heck, the maneuver sometimes even changed toward the end of the hop. If you had ingested too much salt into the engine, you may not have the power you needed to recover if it was an extreme maneuver. When McCormick flew in a combat situation, you were on the edge of the flight envelope the whole time. That meant the slightest mistake or engine malfunction and you were in the water or down a mountainside.

While McCormick went through some low level maneuvers simulating avoidance of enemy fire, he went over the critical engine and RPM operating parameters and told me what to look for to avoid a catastrophe. In this type of flying the co-pilot was as busy as the pilot. McCormick was so close to the water, he had to keep his eyes outside the cockpit the whole time. That meant the co-pilot monitored the instruments, radios, called headings and altitude, and backed up the pilot whenever he needed it. McCormick told the two rescue crewman to setup for a simulated rescue over water under hostile fire. Petty Officers Jennings and Hayes were experienced aircrew men. Jennings had served with McCormick on his last tour off North Vietnam.

McCormick went over the importance of crew coordination. How everyone had to be thinking as one, anticipating each step. I had never seen anyone fly as close to the water as McCormick. He was everything I thought a pilot should be. We were so close, I kept looking outside instead of at the instruments. Jinking and zigzagging over the water, McCormick called out, "Simulated pilot in the water, mark, mark, mark!" The crewman tossed the smoke in the water and McCormick turned and left the area. He explained that you didn't want the enemy to get a solid fix on your position, or an idea of what direction you were going to make your approach for the rescue. The helicopter is very vulnerable in a hover, even with armor plating. They couldn't put armor plating everywhere; it made the aircraft too heavy. While this was going on, the whole time the crewman kept calling out the smoke and its relation to the aircraft.

McCormick started into a sharp 180 degree turn. We had been briefed on the surface winds, but McCormick said it was important to rely on the smoke if you could use one for your final approach because things change. As we came back into the smoke, I could see it was not a standard rescue pattern. Instead of heading into the wind, McCormick had maneuvered into a downwind track. As we came over the smoke we were as fast as the helicopter would go. McCormick pulled the nose straight up.

I saw out of the corner of my eye that the LT was rolling the throttle off. I had never seen that before in a turbine engine driven aircraft, other than a simulated engine failure. Unlike the old reciprocating engines, where you had to continuously marry the engine power to maintain rotor RPMs, the gas turbine engines had direct linkage to maintain the power settings and RPMs. Except when you were doing radical maneuvers like these.

These extreme maneuvers required drastic power changes, and the aircraft could not keep up with the power requirements without exceeding some of the performance characteristics. I watched the maneuver in amazement; I had never seen anything like that since I started flying helicopters. It was like a gymnast executing a tumbling routine and ending up on his feet, with a perfect score. The aircraft continued to climb. Lt. McCormick explained as calmly and relaxed as could be, "This is how you control the RPMs. If we pulled this without taking off power, we would over speed the rotor system for sure." As we reached the top of the climb we were at zero airspeed and the aircraft was slightly on its back. Helicopters were not designed for negative G's and could not go inverted, but at this point of the maneuver it seemed like we were weightless.

As we fell through the LT came back on the radio, "Now this is important; you want to apply the correct rudder pressure or you can deplete the rotor RPMs with the throttle turned back like it is now." As the nose came around we were looking straight down at the water. "If you back off slightly on the rudder the aircraft rotor torque will turn the aircraft for you." I watched and took in as much as I could. As the aircraft started to accelerate we headed almost straight down on top of the smoke. The LT was controlling the RPMs with the throttle and collective. Again the nose came up into a radical maneuver and all the forward airspeed dropped off.

As McCormick rotated the nose over into a hover, he brought the throttle full on, he seemed to know exactly how much rudder control would be needed. When you roll the throttle back on and pull all that power in at the bottom, there is a huge power surge. There was very little nose movement as we dropped into a stable 10 foot hover over the simulated pilot. I thought to myself, "This is what flying is all about."

Petty Officer Jennings had already let out the rescue hoist cable. As soon as we were in a stable hover he tossed it by the smoke, "Rescue harness away sir!" Jennings called out what was happening, "The pilot is getting into the harness. The pilot is in the harness. I have a thumbs up from the pilot. Weight coming on aircraft! The pilot is halfway up. The pilot is at the door. The pilot is in the aircraft!"

Almost simultaneously the nose pitched forward and we were on the move again, low level, jinking left and then right away from the shoreline.

I didn't say a word, I just took it all in. Lt. McCormick came on the radio, "You seemed to be enjoying this ensign. Most co-pilots get a little pale when they see it for the first time."

I responded with, "No sir! I think it was great, I can't wait to try one."

McCormick came back over the radio, "Now that was all to minimize our exposure to hostile fire. I had to do a similar rescue in Hi Phong Harbor. It got a little hairy, and I wished I had practiced it more. You can't practice too much."

Jennings came up over the radio, "No shit it was hairy, ...sir!"

McCormick continued with, "Now if the downed pilot were injured or had problems, it would have been a little different. We would have had to put a crewman in the water to assist the pilot and check his injuries. Here let me show you the difference."

As we came around on the first maneuver McCormick dropped the nose over into a hover and said over the radio, "Jump, jump, jump!"

A slight pause and then a voice came back over the air, "Simulated swimmer away and I have a thumbs up."

The nose of the aircraft went forward and we were off

again. The LT said, "The swimmer has things he has to do to get the pilot ready for the hoist. We're just sitting ducks hovering over the top of him. Our job is to get him out, not to get shot down right on top of him."

I thought to myself, "Holy shit! Those crewmen must have brass balls." Here you are in a hostile environment and you watch your pilot fly off. It takes a special type of person to focus on the task at hand and not worry about what might be. Out here, you become one, and think like one. Each person has his job to do or someone gets killed. You have to have complete trust in each other. Let's see them try to simulate that in a corporate boardroom, or on a golf course.

He completed the same maneuver on a slightly different heading, as he dropped the nose over and brought the power on, there we were in a stable 10-foot hover. It was amazing, most of the pilots I had flown with would still be making their first approach, or they would be drifting all over the place trying to recover from the extreme power changes. The crew chief went through his routine and finished with, "Pilot and swimmer in the aircraft," and we were off again.

Lt. McCormick came up over the radio and said, "Here take us up to 1500 feet, and I'll let you do a few coordination maneuvers. You have the aircraft," as he held both hands out in front, to signal he did not have control.

After demonstrating that I had no problems with controlling the aircraft, McCormick told the crewman to ready another smoke and they started down to the water for a simulated rescue. As we descended McCormick briefed me on a few things. "It's important to understand completely what the rescue crewman's duties are. You'll have to anticipate what he has to do to get prepared, and then give him enough time during your maneuvering to complete each task."

"Yes, sir," I replied. As I completed the maneuver and climbed out of the hover, I was totally disappointed in my performance.

McCormick came up over the radio, "That wasn't too

bad for the first try. They told me you were a pretty good stick. You just need to relax a little, and that will come with experience."

I was amazed at the freedom he allowed me during the maneuvers. Any other pilot would have been riding the controls along with me. We headed back into Imperial Beach.

As I headed back in, I thought to myself, "This is what I want to be. I want to be a pilot like Lt. McCormick." It was the first time I had not wanted to go fighters. The maneuvers we had just completed had to at least be what a fighter pilot would have to go through in a dog fight. What I had just seen, few pilots could do. I wanted to be one of them and would not settle for less. I knew that I had to get at least one more hop with the LT before I deployed. I asked McCormick what the differences were between a day and night rescue under hostile fire. McCormick replied, "Night and day. At night you don't have any depth perception; the majority of your maneuvering will be done on instruments and how much visual reference you have. It depends on the moon, stars and sea state. Of course the maneuvers will not be as radical, but you still want to expedite the rescue. Some nights you can hold your hand two inches in front of your face and you can't see it. Every rescue is different. Just remember, fly the aircraft and don't get caught in a canned scenario where one thing goes wrong and it disrupts the entire mission, or gets someone killed. It is a very dynamic situation and you may have to change as the situation develops."

It made sense, I had seen a lot of pilots that were strictly mechanical. They would apply the same technique to almost everything.

As we continued back into Imperial Beach, McCormick came up over the radio and told me to shut of the hydraulics and call for a simulated emergency to a run-on landing back at the field. I reached down and shut of the hydraulics and called the tower for a landing. The landing was a challenge;

the Sea Sprite was one of only a few helicopters that could be flown with the hydraulics off.

After the landing I turned the hydraulics back on and taxied back into the line and shut down the aircraft. During the debrief, Lt. McCormick emphasized the importance of practicing emergencies. "So many pilots practice them here in the syllabus and then go the whole cruise without doing another one, unless it's for real."

I was ready to call it a day, but first I had to get to the scheduling officer to see if I could get another hop with McCormick. To my surprise there was not a long waiting list to fly with Mr. Combat SAR. It seems not many of the co-pilots enjoyed that type of flying.

I got another hop with Lt. McCormick, unfortunately I was also assigned to Detachment Lima, aboard the *USS Bon Homme Richard*. Some bullshit about one of the co-pilot's having personal problems and he couldn't deploy with them. It seems I was my own worst enemy. If I hadn't been so aggressive in getting through the training syllabus I wouldn't have been eligible for this detachment and I may have been assigned to that CSAR detachment I wanted. I took it in stride and decided I would get as much experience and as many hours as possible. Maybe I would get that Combat SAR seat on my next cruise. It might even be as an aircraft commander.

USS Bon Homme Richard, CV 31

I didn't fit in with this detachment; the personalities were much different than mine. The Officer In Charge (OINC), LCDR Stuart was maybe 5'6" tall, with his shoes on, and 137 lbs. He must have needed a waiver; minimum height for a naval aviator was 5'6." He had a Napoleonic complex to go along with his size and didn't hesitate to let his officers know that this detachment was just the first step in making captain. I thought the first step should be to look after his men. At best he was a mediocre pilot. I was athletic, young and got along with all the enlisted men well. Day one started with the lectures on how to be an officer and what not to do with the enlisted men.

His assistant OINC was Lt. Sam Hunt, a former C-54 pilot. I had no idea how he got into helicopters. He was the worst helicopter pilot I had ever seen. From take-off to landing, he was totally out of control. They must have kicked him out of the fixed wing community and he ended up as a helicopter pilot. The worst thing about it was, he didn't understand how dangerous he was. I would watch and see. Who was I to say anything? I was a 22 year old ensign, and I knew nothing.

The detachment maintenance officer, a young LTJG was the best pilot in the detachment. There was one problem, he was the same height as LCDR Stuart and also had a Napoleonic complex. What is it with these little guys? It seems they are always compensating for their size and feel like they have to prove a point. To make things worse, the maintenance officer's wife happened to make a comment that she thought I was cute. I had never thought of myself as being cute, but never the less I was on the MO's shit list for the entire cruise. His insecurity was going to be my cross to bear.

The other aircraft commander was also a young LTJG. He was a good solid pilot, but was so introverted and quiet you could hardly hear him when he spoke. He was pure farm boy (from Minnesota); he looked like he just got off his tractor. The rest were co-pilots, LTJG Studameyer, LTJG Kent, and Ensign Clark. Clark was a piece of work. How he got in the Navy is beyond me. On his best day, he was a good 50 lbs over weight, and it bulged in all the wrong places. He could sleep more than any human I had ever seen. He slept so much, he even caught pneumonia while he was in his rack. I was going on a nine month cruise with these guys and knew I wouldn't have much in common with any of them. Since I was the youngest and most junior officer in the detachment, I was assigned every shitty little job in the detachment along with being the Line Division Officer. It was going to be a long cruise.

When I joined them Detachment Lima was finishing up a few months of work ups off the coast of Southern California. The work ups were in the company of the carrier air wing that we would deploy with. The exercises off the coast were to familiarize the AIRWING with shipboard operations aboard the *Bonnie Dick*. My first experience with the Assistant OINC was when we lost an A-4 during night operations in bad weather. It was towards the end of the week, and the AIRWING wanted to get the aircraft into the beach. They decided to launch the A-4 squadron first. It was at night, and the weather was so bad the decision was made to leave the rescue helo on the angle deck during the launch. We were turned up, with minimum tie downs on, so we could get airborne quickly in case an aircraft went in, or somebody got blown overboard.

As the A-4's started to launch I heard the pilot in the number 4 aircraft in the launch sequence. He was reporting his status after two pilots had already called in and said their aircraft were down (smart pilots). As he taxied forward for launch, I thought to myself, "Now there is a pilot that is in no hurry to get to the beach." I could tell from the sound of his voice that he didn't like the idea of getting hurled off the front of this ship on a moonless night, in the middle of a storm of this magnitude.

As the aircraft was catapulted off the front of the ship, I could see the lights rotate and the aircraft start to climb. Just then, the lights of the aircraft rotated back over and they disappeared below the flight deck. I came up over the intercom, "Shit! I think he just went in the water." About that time the ship's collision alarm sounded, and the ship started to maneuver to avoid running over the top of the aircraft in the water.

The next thing I heard was Lt. Hunt screaming over the radio for the air boss to launch the rescue helo. Lt. Hunt was signaling for the flight deck crew to remove the chains from the aircraft. This was not a good idea. The ship was still maneuvering to avoid the aircraft in the water, the winds were shifting and the flight deck was heeling and pitching as it turned into the waves. With the heavy rain we were sliding all over the place. My survival mode went to full alert. I knew that Hunt was a disaster waiting to happen, but was I good enough keep us both out of trouble. I was young and foolish, but I had good instincts and was about to be tested.

As the ship turned back into the wind, the helicopter continued to slide around on the deck. I could see the A-4 tail passing down the port side of the carrier. Just about that time the air boss cleared Lt. Hunt to launch. As we leaped off the deck, the LT maneuvered the helicopter with the grace of a gorilla at the controls. I started through my co-pilot duties. Gear up, lights on, all gauges are in the green. As my eyes came up over the instrument panel, all I could see was water. We were in a thirty degree nose down attitude in about a forty degree angle of bank passing below the flight deck and headed directly for the water. Lt. Hunt had done just about everything wrong that he could possibly do.

He had pulled an insane maneuver that nobody in their right mind would ever attempt, and I was not ready for it. The carrier was headed into the wind at a surface speed of about 12-15 knots. The surface winds were reported at 30 knots, gusts to 45 knots. The LT leaped off the deck and immediately did a 180 degree turn without gaining any forward airspeed. At night, in a high sea state, on instruments! This meant that the aircraft went from 42-60 knots of relative forward wind to a 42-60 knot relative tail wind. Fortunately as we passed below the flight deck the ship's superstructure blocked some of the surface winds.

I grabbed for the controls and to my surprise the LT did not fight me for them, which was my biggest fear. I quickly leveled the aircraft, pulling in all the collective I could, to stop our descent. As I fought to get the aircraft under control and start a positive climb, I saw the low RPM warning light come on, so I eased off on the collective just a little but kept the positive climb. I leveled off at about 1500 feet and swallowed my heart back down where it belonged. I could feel the LT still on the controls; I was not about to let go of the aircraft until I knew what he was going to do next. Just then the air boss came up over the radio and asked if everything was alright. The LT sat silent, with his hands resting on the controls. I suggested we start a standard search pattern behind the ship at 300 feet to see if we could locate the pilot and wreckage. This was standard squadron procedure and what we should have done initially. I started the aircraft into a gradual descent and could feel Hunt take control of the aircraft. Just then, he came up over the radio and told the air boss that we were going to start a search pattern astern of the ship, unless he had a better location to start.

I slowly took my hands of the controls, but kept my eyes glued to the flight and engine instruments to monitor what he was doing. At 300 feet with no visual reference it only took a split second to fly into the water. As the LT settled down I thought to myself how lucky we were. The Sea Sprite is an inherently under-powered helicopter. If it hadn't been December, off the coast of California where the air temperatures were pretty cold, we would have never had enough power to get out of the situation the LT had put us in. I knew we wouldn't have that luxury operating in the South China Sea. It was my aggressive personality and confidence in my flying ability that saved my butt. Most new co-pilots would have watched the pilot fly it right into the water. I wondered if I would be as lucky the next time.

After a few hours of searching with no luck, we landed to refuel and were relieved by LCDR Stuart and Studameyer. We searched through the night, rotating crews every three hours when they came in for fuel. We searched along with the destroyer escorts for the next two days and never found the pilot. I expressed my concern about the LT and his skills as an aircraft commander to the OINC. LCDR Stuart made a joke out of it, and replied by saying, "It isn't my problem I don't have to fly with him."

I failed to see the humor in his comment. As the LT continued his antics during the remainder of the work ups, his reputation as a bad pilot continued to grow. LTJG Studameyer and Ensign Clark had quietly refused to fly with him, and the OINC agreed to let it happen instead of taking it up the chain of command. I talked it over with LTJG Kent, my roommate. We both decided we could keep an eye on the LT and try to avoid trouble before it happened. This later proved to be a big mistake.

As the work ups progressed I had another incident with the LT during one of the night exercises a few weeks later. It was about 2300 hours, off the Southern California coast. We were in a starboard delta at 300 feet. The starboard delta was standard plan guard position during night recoveries. It was about as boring as it gets. I would challenge myself by flying instruments the whole time. As we were on our outbound leg the transmission chip warning light came on. It was very dark, and the yellow light stuck out like a beacon on the instrument panel. As I mentioned the chip light, the LT had simultaneously bottomed the collective and was heading for the water.

I grabbed the collective and started pulling up, "What are you doing?" I shouted into the intercom.

"I'm putting it in the water," he replied. (This may sound crazy to most helicopter pilots, but it will give you an idea of just how bad a pilot he really was.)

I was in a struggle with the LT.; it was just what I had feared. The LT was about 200 lbs and in pretty good shape. I pulled up on the collective with everything I had, while the LT was pushing down on the collective.

"Wait a minute," I exclaimed, I had to talk fast. "All the other instruments look good and the aircraft is still flying. Call for an emergency landing. Let's turn inbound and close on the ship." I felt him ease up on the collective. "Let's get closer to the water and slow our airspeed. If anything starts to happen we can flare the helicopter and put it in the water with little or no impact." Just about then I felt him bring the collective up a little further as the helicopter leveled off.

The LT called for an emergency landing and slowed the aircraft to about 60 knots at 150 feet. The carrier was in the process of recovering aircraft so the winds were right down the deck. As the air boss came up over the air, he asked what the emergency was and the LT told him we had a transmission chip warning light. The air boss waved off the remaining aircraft and put them in an over holding pattern. The nice thing about it was we were only 40 miles off Miramar, and if anyone was low on fuel they could bingo into the beach. I'm sure they wouldn't mind spending the night on the beach.

As the LT brought the helo across the stern of the ship we could see the landing signalman enlisted (LSE) come running up the flight deck with his wands over his head. He signaled for us to come up the centerline of the ship. I was always impressed with the professionalism of the enlisted personnel in the detachment. Of the 78 enlisted men, I had not met one that I didn't like. As Lt. Hunt landed the helicopter and shut it down, the crew was all over it, getting the yellow gear (tow tractor) and tow bar in place. The ground crew was up on the rotor head folding the blades, so they could get the helo parked back in the pack. They needed to do it as quickly as possible so they could continue to recover the fixed wing aircraft. The entire process took only a couple of minutes from the time the aircraft was shut down to getting the helo parked back in the pack. They were good. You would like to think it was because of the leadership the officers displayed, but you would have had to be there to understand. The two chiefs and a couple of the first class petty officers were some of the best the squadron had to offer. I looked forward to the cruise with them and planned to learn as much as I could. At that point in my life I was like a sponge, everything was interesting to me.

As the next few weeks went by, we continued to bring up our concerns about Lt. Hunt's flying ability. It was consistently ignored, and we were told that we didn't have enough experience to know a good pilot from a bad one. It would be just a matter of time.

Survival Escape Resistance and Evasion (SERE) Training

All that was left before deploying to the Western Pacific was a week of leave and Survival Escape Resistance and Evasion (SERE) training. I looked forward to the idea of finding out more about myself. Rumor had it that SERE training would bring out either the best or worst in you. SERE was a 5 day course that started in Coronado, California at the SERE school and ended up in a prisoner of war camp up in the high desert. The whole exercise deprived you of sleep, food, and creature comforts. If you were not in good physical condition that would also take its toll.

The exercise started out with the first night on the beach and lectures on survival, escape, and resistance. The night was spent trying to catch something to eat with just your survival gear, which was typically what you had in your survival vest when you departed your aircraft. It wasn't much. Small water bottle, water purification pills, signal mirror, strope light. They wanted you to have as little as possible so you could exercise your ingenuity. Early in the Vietnam Conflict they were still formulating the escape and evasion and survival techniques they had learned from the Korean War. After the first night of very little food and sleep the students were bused to Warner Springs to complete the escape and evasion and prisoner of war phases.

The second night was spent in the high desert near Warner Springs, California. There were a total of 82 students in the class. We were able to catch only two rabbits for all of us. My share was a rabbit's eyeball, only because nobody would eat it. The taste and the texture of it were indescribable. After surviving for a night out in the brush, the next day was the evasion phase. The instructors would be out in the field acting as the enemy, and we were to try to make it from point A to point B without getting caught.

We received a briefing of the area and what was expected of us. We were then led off into the hills. The instructors boasted that we would all be captured. Nobody had made it to freedom village under their watch. At this point it appeared that the entire SERE training phase was nothing more than an adult Boy Scout camp, minus the creature comforts. It always amazed me to see how small some people's discomfort thresholds were. As we broke up in groups, I decided to go off on my own to try to make it to Freedom Village. I felt I would have a better chance on my own than with a group of guys I didn't know.

I was about half of the way to Freedom Village when I saw two instructors dressed as enemy soldiers carrying weapons. I quickly got down and crawled into some nearby bushes to wait until they left the area. After about 20 minutes, it looked like they were going to leave.

Just about that time I heard some rumbling that sounded a little like a herd of buffalos. As I looked back over my shoulder, I saw part of the group I had left earlier that morning. There were five of them running through the brush like they were on a Sunday afternoon picnic. As they came upon the soldiers, they started diving everywhere. One dove into a bush about 15 yards from where I was, and another kept going until he landed in the bush right next to me. "What a bunch of putzes," I thought. Not only did they get themselves captured, they took me along with them. From that point on it was just a matter of the instructors walking over and capturing us, as they tried not to laugh. The rules required no resistance once we were spotted.

As we were escorted to the POW compound, I wondered what it would be like in a real situation with some of these egg heads. I hoped I would never have to find out. I was about to learn a little more about myself and a lot about human nature. As we entered the compound I immediately started to assess the area for potential escape routes. I was looking forward to this part and took the lectures seriously. If it was our job to try to escape, then I was going to see if there was a way to make it happen.

It turned out I had a different interpretation of escape than the majority of the prisoners. The senior officer in the compound was a Navy commander. He called for a meeting of all the officers and chiefs. I was a little disappointed in what came out of the meeting. There was no discussion about escape, all they really got sorted out was, if there were any problems we were to report them to the senior ranking officer or one of the three LCDR's that were also prisoners. It seemed we were just going to sit there for the next few days and wait it out. This didn't seem right,. I wanted to see if I could escape. It was a game; let's see how far we can take it.

I tried to get a few of the junior officers interested in making an escape and to my surprise, I could not develop enough interest to get anyone to try to make the attempt with me. I didn't understand their attitude. This was training, no risk of life, and no severe punishment if they got caught. What were they going to do, nothing? If that was the attitude this whole compound could be guarded by one individual.

Maybe I had seen too many movies. Maybe this was how the majority of the captives really reacted. I decided to see what I could do on my own. From what I could see, there were plenty of opportunities to get out of the compound. The rumor was, only the Navy SEALS had escaped from this compound more than once and that seemed to be a good goal to try and match. As the story goes, the SEALS turned the compound upside down and took over the camp when they escaped.

The compound was full of ways to escape. The hardest problem would be to distract the guard in each of the towers located at the opposite corners of the compound. Meanwhile I and one other ensign had been called out on a work detail, along with about 15 enlisted. As we were being lead out the gate, Roger the other junior officer came up to me all excited. He wanted to know what my lineal number was in order to determine who was ranking officer in charge of the work detail. I thought it was pretty dumb to try to determine who was the senior of the two ensigns. So I said, "Roger, don't worry, you're in charge." That seemed to make him happy and he ran up to one of the guards and told him that he was the senior officer on this work detail.

During the work detail, every time one of the enlisted men screwed up, or even if they didn't, Roger would get slapped, knocked down, kicked, or hit with a rifle butt. Towards the end of the detail I looked down at Roger on the ground, his face grimaced as he was kicked in the side by one of the guards. He glared up at me as if to say, "You bastard, you knew this was going to happen."

I shrugged my shoulders and continued on with my assigned work. The guards weren't allowed to seriously hurt us and a few bruises never hurt anyone, especially if it taught him not to volunteer to be in charge. As we returned to the compound, there was lots of talk about the interrogations that were taking place. Some more exaggerated than others.

I still couldn't understand the thinking of most of the class. Some of them were acting like they were really prisoners of war. I kept telling myself it was a training exercise! Everyone knew they couldn't do anything to really hurt you. Rumor had it that they already had a young sailor break during the interrogation. I found that hard to believe. What would make a person give in like that, knowing that they would be out in a couple of days? This was a new experience. I kept remembering the lectures about the Korean prisoners of war and their heroic efforts during their captivity. I didn't see any heroism here. Would it be different in a real situation? Would these guys rise to the occasion when it was really needed?

The first night was miserable. The guards would not let us sleep. Just as we started to doze off, they would call us out to stand in formation. Each one of these exercises would take about an hour, depending on how much shit they gave us. Some of the guards would come down the line and single out someone they particularly didn't like. I was one of the unlucky ones. It must have been the rolled up bill on my fatigue hat, with the extra large ensign bar from my raincoat pinned on it. It was straight out of the TV "MASH" program, only "MASH" had not been written yet. Thinking back, it was pretty dumb to call attention to myself like that. Back then, everything was a game to me. I was always good at calling attention to myself.

As I stood at attention in formation, the guard started riding me, calling me every name in the book and when that didn't seem to get my attention, I would get a rifle butt in the stomach or a hand across the face. This went on all night long during every formation. I was pleased with my response. I knew my temper and also knew how it showed in my face when I was pissed. Throughout the night I never let them know that they were getting to me.

A few hours before sunrise I decided to escape. If I didn't I was going to punch that guard right in the nose, and I knew that was the wrong thing to do. Earlier I had spotted a couple of areas the lights from the towers didn't completely cover, especially in the corners. Most of the guards were busy debriefing from each of the formations and planning what they were going to do on the next one. All I had to really deal with, were the guards in the towers.

I made it through the first set of barbed wire. I couldn't believe how easy it was. I crawled on my belly all the way down to a point where it was the shortest distance to the woods, and I was still in the shadows. When I reached that point, I rolled about six feet and under the second set of barbed wire. Just past the wire was a slight hill. I slid down the hill and was into the brush before anyone could see me. Freedom Village was at the top of a small hill near the compound.

As I reached the small shed at the top of the hill, I could see the sign on the door, "Freedom Village." I went inside. The small 10 by 10 foot building was empty with the exception of a wooden table and chair. There was a telephone on the table. During the briefing we were told that if we made it to Freedom Village, we would get some food and a few hours of rest. I wanted to make sure I got the food so I picked up the phone and called. After a few seconds, someone answered the phone. "This is Ensign Billings. I'm at Freedom Village." After a slight pause, the instructor responded. He didn't sound very happy as he said, "There will be someone up there in a few minutes."

Within a half hour, one of the instructors arrived at the door with a sandwich and a jug of milk. He asked me how I made it out. I gave him the name, rank, and serial number bit, the instructor looked at me and then tossed the sandwich on the table and handed me the milk. As he turned to leave he told me that he would be back at 0600 to take me back to the compound so I could complete the rest of my training.

I couldn't believe they left me alone up in the shed without a guard. I finished the milk and sandwich then decided to look around. I slipped down the back side of the hill and circled the entire compound far enough away as not to be seen. As I completed my exploration, I notice the electrical boxes that controlled the lighting for the entire camp. I knew I couldn't do anything on this time out, but if I escaped again, it would be great to shut down the lights in the entire complex. I wondered if the Navy SEALS had done something similar.

I got back to the shed and closed my eyes for a few minutes before the guard returned. It was a different guard; he wasn't as congenial as the last. In fact he seemed a little aggravated that I had escaped in the first place. The first thing the guard did was push me down as we stepped out the door of the shed. I picked myself up, brushed the dirt off and reminded myself that it was all a game, and it would be over soon.

It was daylight when we entered the compound with the rest of the prisoners. The guard that escorted me back shouted to the guards in the towers. "This is a special prisoner. I want you to see that he stays busy while he's in the compound." The guard pointed to a large bolder by one of the bunkers, it must have weighed 50 lbs. "See that rock? I want you to pick it up and carry it around the compound until the guards tell you to stop." I walked over and picked it up and started walking around the edge of the compound.

This went on for what seemed several hours. The guards in the towers seemed to enjoy it. The activities ranged from carrying the bolder do push ups and sit ups, to leaning against a post with your feet out away from it as far as you could get them. Your head would support the weight of your body until you couldn't hold the position any longer.

Just when it seemed they had run out of things to have me do, one of the guards came in the compound and hollered for Ensign Billings. I pushed myself away from the post and held up my arm. I knew it was my turn in the barrel for interrogation. At least I was going to get out of all the harassment from the guards, although I didn't know if that was going to be a good or bad thing. The guard escorted me out of the compound and into one of the buildings where they did the interrogations. As I entered the room I could see one of the instructors dressed in his version of an enemy uniform. He even made up an accent when he spoke. I thought to myself, "These guys really get into it."

As I was told to sit down, the guard that escorted me in tied my hands behind my back. As the interrogation progressed, the senior interrogator got more and more hostile. After about 30 minutes of slaps, yelling, and name calling the guard picked up the .38 revolver on the table and told me that if I didn't tell him what he wanted to hear, he was going to put the gun to my head and pull the trigger.

I didn't understand why he thought that was going to work. This was training. Was I supposed to be intimidated with the .38, knowing that they couldn't have live ammunition in the gun? I would find out later that the commander broke during the interrogation phase.

I did get a chance to reflect on some of the briefings of the treatment of the Korean War prisoners. In Korea, the prisoners had to dig their own graves and kneel in front of the grave. The North Korean guards would then put a gun to the prisoners head and pull the trigger. They would never know if the gun would be loaded or empty. Sometimes this process would go on every day of the week for months. I wondered how they kept from going insane, or just giving up. In some of the lectures they talked about the Korean prisoners just curling up into a fetal position and dying.

When I didn't respond with anything other than name, rank and serial number, the guard in the back of the room kicked my chair over and I went sprawling over the floor. As the guard got me in a choke hold the other one came around the table and grabbed me. They dragged me over to a plank in the corner of the room, put me on it, and tied me down. The plank was set at about a 30 degree angle with the base on the floor. One of the guards placed a cloth over my face. What came next was just another example of the unlimited way of finding a weakness that would push the individual past his personal limits. The guard took a cup of water and started to pour it over the cloth covering my nose and mouth. It made it very difficult to breathe, and as I opened my mouth to try to take in more air, the guard would pour more water causing me to choke.

This went on for what seemed an eternity. I'm sure it was only a few minutes, until they were satisfied that I was only going to give my name, rank and serial number. As they untied me the guard grabbed me by the hair, and I was shoved out the door of the interrogation building. Both guards took me over to a row of small boxes. For the life of me couldn't figure out what they were for, although I was sure I was about to find out. The wooden boxes were slightly larger than an orange crate. One of the guards picked up the lid and told me to get in., I just looked at him. How the hell was I supposed to fit in that box?

Both guards grabbed me and forced me down into the box. I knew I wouldn't fit, but somehow the guards were able to get me in and were even able to close and secure the lid. I was on my knees in the box with my hands and head shoved in one corner of the box. The guard had to stand on the box to get the lid closed and latched. I knew I was getting special treatment for escaping.

I found out very fast that I was a little claustrophobic. As I went through the mental process of trying to maintain my composure, I quickly realized that the enemy would be able to break anyone they wanted. It was just a matter of time until they found the right weakness. It was a good thing they were not allowed to use pain in the training environment or they would have broken half or all the people in the compound. I knew at this point that I never wanted to get captured. It seemed like several hours went by before they took me out of the box. I wasn't sure; all of my focus was on keeping control of myself and making sure I didn't let the situation get to me. It was one of the toughest personal struggles I had ever known. It wasn't physical pain, or physical exhaustion, it was the feeling of being trapped and having no control.

When I was taken out of the box I couldn't stand. I had no feeling in my legs, and the circulation had been cut off. The guards dragged me back to the compound and left me lying on the ground just inside the gates. LTJG John Grimes, one of the AIRWING's A-4 pilot's came over to help me up.

"You alright?" he asked.

"I'm okay, just lost the feeling in my legs. Give me a minute."

Grimes helped me over to one of the bunkers. As we walked over, Grimes told me, "At least you're better off than the commander. The commander and another airman broke. They've been sent back to North Island."

I couldn't believe what I was hearing. This was a fucking training camp. How the hell could they let them get to them like that? That commander could kiss his career goodbye, and he definitely wouldn't be going to Vietnam. Maybe that is what he wanted.

As we talked about what had gone on that day, I told Grimes about my escape and the electrical power boxes outside the compound. Grimes asked if I could shut off the power if I got out again. I told him it would be no problem, but we needed to wait until it got dark before I tried to escape again.

Tonight would be the last night in the compound, and if I didn't go now, it was all over. Grimes told me he knew a couple of good JO's that would probably help. Once I got out, they would try an escape as soon as the lights went out. I told Grimes not to tell them what the plan was until I was into the underbrush. They would have plenty of time to plan before the lights went out. After I rested, we went over to a couple of junior officers, and I told them what I needed. I wanted them to group over by the north fence to block me from the guards in the towers. I could slide under the barbed wire when they weren't looking.

Grimes, three other JO's, and I went waited for sunset then we went over to the north side of the compound. As I told them where to stand, one of the JO's said he didn't want anything to do with it and left. That was about all it took. The other two walked off with him. I was learning more about human nature than I cared to, and I didn't like what I saw. We both went back to the bunker. Grimes went off to see who was going to be the new ranking officer now that the commander was gone.

I sat there for awhile and then decided I would just have to chance it and go for another escape. When Grimes came back I asked him if he would distract the guard in the tower for a few seconds while I slipped through the fence. He agreed, and I told him that as soon as I got to the fence he should try to get the guards attention and have him look the other way.

I walked over and stood by the fence and watched Grimes walk up to the other side of the tower and holler up at the guard. As soon as the guard looked at him I dropped down and slid through the wire without any problem. I made my way down to where I crawled out the first time. Just when I was about to make my break for the second set of barbed wire, two of the JO's that I tried to get to help me earlier, came up to the fence where I was lying. With their backs to me, they told me I had to come back inside the compound. I couldn't believe what I was hearing. What the hell was going on? One of them said, "That's an order from the new officer in charge. Get back in here." They walked off.

I laid there for a minute. This whole thing didn't make any sense. It was riskier for me to try to get back through the first set of barbed wire than it was for me to continue with my escape. I made my way back to where I slipped through the fence and waited for the right opportunity. I almost didn't care if I got caught. I rolled through the wire and sat up against the post. It worked!

I sat there for a few minutes and then got up and started walking back to the bunker. I saw Grimes on the way back and asked him what the hell was going on. He looked at me with a puzzled look and said, "I thought you were going through the fence?" When I told him what had happened he said he didn't know anything about it. I walked off grumbling to myself. I was pissed.

I set out to find those two assholes that told me to get back in the compound. When I caught up with them, I asked them what was going on. They told me that the new ranking officer in the compound put out the word that there would be no more escapes. The guards told him they would kick over the food if there was another escape. That did it. I wouldn't be caught in a Boy Scout camp with these limp dicks.

The training ended the next day. The food they were going to kick over was one head of cabbage and a couple of potatoes in fifty gallons of water. They would be out tomorrow. Whatever happened to the fucking idea that it was our duty to try to escape? I couldn't control my rage. To my knowledge there had been no other attempts to escape during that entire exercise. I turned and walked off as my rage continued to build.

I was disgusted and went back and sat by the bunker. I didn't want to have anything to do with these spineless jerks. I decided to just stick it out and get through the night. I couldn't get it out of my head. This was a game, what would they do in a real situation?

Throughout the night we kept getting called into formation. It was about 0530 in the morning, and I had just dosed off for a couple of minutes. That was not good. I was never very pleasant when I first woke up, and with all the shit I had seen while I was in the compound, I was at a boiling point. I just wanted out.

As we made it into formation, I saw the same instructor coming down the line that had been slapping me around for the past two nights. For the first time, I was a little concerned. I knew the instructor was going to hit me again. If I got hit by that SOB one more time, I was going to clean up the compound with the little prick. It wasn't the hitting as much as it was the instructor seemed to enjoy it a little too much. I needed to take out my rage on someone. I was not a big man, but I was in the best physical condition of my life.

It was absolutely the wrong thing to do, and I knew it. As soon as I went after him, I would be jumped by the other guards. Everything they taught us up to that point was not to get hurt or injured. Injuries and infections drastically reduced your survival chances in a real situation. The guard came up to me like he did every other time and got in my face. I was sweating bullets; I wasn't sure how I was going to react. The guard just stared at me, his nose almost touching mine. I was rigid.

After what seemed like a couple of minutes the guard said, "The exercise is over." I didn't move. The guard said it again, "end of exercise." I still didn't move. The guard said, "You take this too serious Ensign."

It finally registered. I was not happy the exercise was over. I was disappointed in what I had seen and just wanted to leave.

I had learned a lot about human nature that week. I spent the entire time on the way back to Coronado trying to make sense out of what had happened. I always liked to understand the cause and effect of things. In this case, I could not find any answers for why some people acted the way they did. Maybe it was me; I was young and impetuous. Maybe they were the ones that were right and I was wrong. I did take one thing away from SERE school: never get captured!

I was about to embark on my first cruise. I would learn more about human nature and would lose a roommate and a very close friend. Burials at sea would become commonplace.

Chapter Three
Deployment to Southeast Asia

WESTPAC

We were headed for the Western Pacific. Our transit was slow and boring. We had very few flight ops on the way over, which meant the AIRWING had very little to do, except for maintenance on the aircraft. A typical day on the carrier was 12 hours on and 12 hours off, except for transits. Most of the squadron personnel were split into two crews (day shift and night shift). During normal carrier operations they operated around the clock. When they weren't flying, they performed maintenance on the aircraft. I often found a good poker game to help break up the boredom and spent plenty of time working out. During the transits the helicopter detachments were usually the busiest units in the AIRWING. We provided personnel and parts transfers between the units within the carrier group.

The ship's company was a different story. The majority of the ship's personnel were not in aviation; they were surface line. I had the opportunity to make friends with a few of the ship's company on the way over. I didn't completely understand them. They seemed to enjoy pain and discomfort, especially the junior officers. It seemed their goals were to get physically run down and have as little sleep as possible. It was part of their job description and considered some kind of badge of honor. I used to listen to them in the wardroom during meals. The conversations would go something like this:

"I haven't had any sleep in 24 hours."

"You think that's something? I haven't slept in almost 48 hours."

"That's nothing. I went so long without sleep I came down with pneumonia."

I thought this was a little crazy, but that's the way they lived aboard ship. I imagined their fitness reports read something like, "Ensign Smith gets a 4.0 rating because he had pneumonia twice while on deployment."

It was the last day before arriving in Hawaii, and the helo crews were rotating every 24 hours, unless we needed more than one crew to make transfers while we were underway. The standby crew would be dressed in flight gear and ready for launch, should there be a need, such as a man overboard or an unscheduled personnel transfer from one of the "Small Boys" for medical reasons.

The "Small Boys" were the destroyer escorts that accompanied the carrier on deployments. The smaller destroyers did not have medical officers aboard. They had senior corpsman, usually a chief or first class petty officer. If there was something they couldn't handle, they would transfer the person to the medical staff onboard the carrier. LTJG Jenkins and I were the ready duty pilots on that last day before arriving in Honolulu.

It was about 2200 in the evening, and I was up on the flight deck enjoying the warm tropical air as we approached the Hawaiian Islands. I wondered what it would be like to pull into Honolulu and actually see the sight where the Japanese launched the attack on December 7, 1941. Petty Officer Joyce came up to me on the port catwalk, "Sir, it looks like you're going to get some flight time. Mr. Jenkins and LCDR Stuart want you in the ready room ASAP."

A helicopter detachment ready room is not the grand room you see in the movies. It was more like a few chairs crammed in a small space along with the maintenance control, the hub for all the maintenance within the detachment. The communications within the detachment worked very well. Because of the cramped spaces, everyone spent a great deal of time hearing what was going on. Everyone knew everything that happened in the detachment within minutes. This was good and bad.

As I reached our ready room, I could see LCDR Stuart and LTJG Jenkins talking in the corner. The OINC had just returned from the Combat Information Center (CIC). It seems two destroyers had collided at sea off of Hawaii. They had three injured onboard one of the destroyers. Two were in critical condition, and one was in serious condition. The ship's corpsman wanted to get the men medical attention as quickly as possible. From their coordinates, they determined that the two ships were about 78 miles from the *Bon Homme Richard*. LTJG Jenkins and I went up to the CIC to get the radio frequencies and call signs for the ships that were involved in the collision. While we were in the CIC we got a weather briefing so we could determine fuel requirements and what effect the surfaces winds would have on our track from the carrier to the destroyer and into Honolulu. Our job was to make a hover transfer of the most seriously injured and take them to Tripler Army Hospital in Honolulu.

The Sea Sprite had about 3 hours of fuel onboard and fast cruise was about 125 knots. This made planning the fuel requirements of the entire sortie critical to the success of the mission. The outbound leg was an estimated 78 miles; the damaged destroyer was trying to make its way back to Pearl. That meant their position would be continuously changing, and it was a big ocean out there. Fortunately the ship's radio beacon was still working, and we would be under direct control of the carrier. The *Bonnie Dick* would vector us to the stricken ship. The destroyer was 125 miles out of Honolulu. The estimated time to make it to Pearl was a little over 60 minutes if everything went well. The surface winds were in our favor; the sea and winds were almost calm. In fact, that's what had contributed to the collision. The air was so calm, a thick haze, almost fog-like, had formed from the surface to about 300 feet. This reduced the surface visibility, which ultimately contributed in the collision of the two ships.

We figured 15 minutes for the transfer of personnel, 30 minutes at the outside, if the ship was not ready for the transfer, or there were problems. None of the crew had been into Tripler Army Hospital before, so we figured another 15 - 30 minutes to find it, land and transfer the personnel to the ambulance. Then ten minutes down to NAS Barbers Point to refuel. Total flight time was about two hours and 45 minutes. This cut into the standard 20 minutes of fuel reserve. Worst case scenario, we would have to shut down at Tripler and get fuel. The *Bonnie Dick* had changed direction and was closing on the destroyer to reduce the distance between the two ships.

As we launched from the carrier, I could feel the adrenalin building. Here we were in an aircraft that was built by the lowest bidder and notoriously known for mechanical problems and engine failures. We were going to launch off into the middle of the night on a 200 mile trip over water with no rescue vehicle as a backup. The plan was to make a hoist transfer of some injured sailors off of a damaged destroyer in the middle of the Pacific Ocean. This was going to be exciting. We were focused and headed out on our mission.

The flight to the destroyer went without incident. The night was dark, no moon. If you have ever been out at sea without any light from the moon or stars, you understand the absence of light. The only thing you had was the red glare of the instrument lights to tell you where you were and what the helicopter was doing.

As we made contact with the destroyer, the ship turned to get the best surface winds possible for the transfer. With the damage to the ship, the destroyer could only get about 8 knots across her superstructure, 15 degrees to port. This gave the pilot in command the best visibility during his approach and transfer. Unfortunately, the Sea Sprite didn't have enough power to take all three injured personnel the first time around. The UH-2B was a single engine aircraft and didn't have the power to make a 40 foot hover over the back of a ship's rolling deck to pick up three litter patients. We would have to return for the third patient.

I handled most of the communications; LTJG Jenkins was one of the quietest people I had ever met. It was almost impossible to get a conversation out of him, especially when he was flying. I could read most people, with LTJG Jenkins, I didn't have a clue. It was like he was happy to have someone else do the talking. He never hesitated to speak up if he thought something should be handled differently.

As we descended down through the haze, I adjusted the navigation lights to keep the reflection from distracting the pilot. The destroyer had lights all over the place, and with the flickering of the rotor blades off the thick haze, it was really disorienting. I had never seen a ship lit up like that before. As we came down through the haze, the light gave off a ghostly affect, making it difficult to distinguish reference points on the ship. I completed the checklist and looked up to see LTJG Jenkins transitioning to a hover over the aft gun mount of the destroyer. I was thinking, "It's a good thing Lt. Hunt isn't the aircraft commander on this mission." Bill was a good stick. I had complete confidence in him.

Just as the upper mast came into sight, I could see it moving rapidly back and forth from the roll caused by the large sea swells. I noticed a rapid drift to the right. As I tried to assess what was happening, I could see the angle of bank continue to increase. We headed across the deck of the ship rapidly picking up speed. I could see the water across the starboard side of the helicopter. I came up on the intercom, "What's happening?"

I grabbed for the controls. Just then Bill pulled up on the collective, and started a climb. As we leveled off at about 1500 feet, I asked him again, no answer. He started a slow turn to orbit the ship. I tried to get him to tell me what was wrong. He finally came up over the radio and responded to my last question. "I don't know what happened. With the reflection of the lights off the rotor system and the haze, I guess I got a little disoriented."

He told me to stay with him in case it happened again, and we contacted the destroyer for another approach. This time the transfer went without a hitch. We picked up the two most seriously injured and Petty Officer Joyce reported both patients secured and ready for departure. We headed for Pearl. As we departed the destroyer Joyce came up over the intercom and said, "Holy shit, sir! This guy has his foot lying next to his head. He's really fucked up!"

As we approached Pearl we switched from the *Bonnie Dick*'s control to NAS Barber's Point. The idea of having the *Bonnie Dick* track the majority of the flight made us feel a little better. At least if we went in, the carrier would have a good idea of where we were. As we got closer, NAS Barber's Point vectored the helicopter into Tripler Army Hospital. When we were handed off to Tripler, the hospital radio operator described the helicopter landing area used for medical emergency landings. We found the landing zone without any difficulty and setup for an approach. It was a small soccer field with no landing lights, but plenty of room for approach and take-off. As we set down in the middle of the field we could see the ambulance waiting in the distance.

I watched the ambulance heading towards the helicopter with its lights on. Without hesitation, the ambulance driver shot right up my side of the helicopter, directly under the rotor system. My initial reaction was to turn my head away from what appeared to be a collision between the ambulance and the rotor system. As I did, I instinctively pulled in a little collective causing the helicopter to raise up on its landing gear as the rotor blades pulled the helicopter slightly upward. As I turned back, I was happy to see that the van made it under the rotor arch. The Sea Sprite is not a very large helicopter; the rotor system not colliding with the van was a total surprise. As the ambulance crew got out to remove the patients I could see the reflection of the rotor system from the lights. There was less than a foot clearance between the roof of the van and the rotor blades. By increasing the collective the rotor system would create a little lift, thus raising the tips of the rotors slightly. We kept the collective in until they left.

As the ambulance drove out of sight I thought to myself, "You really need to stay ahead of the situation when you're flying these things." Helicopters are so versatile, things come at you from all directions. A fixed wing always needs a runway or carrier to land on; helicopters can go anywhere and the situations are unlimited. I was glad I was in helicopters. There was always something new.

As we departed Tripler we made contact with Barber's Point tower. We needed fuel for the return flight to the destroyer. As the Sea Sprite landed at Barber's, I switched us to ground control and we were directed into the line for refueling. LTJG Jenkins had just finished shutting down the aircraft when the fuel truck arrived.

After talking with the driver, Petty Officer Joyce came over to the helicopter and said, "We may have a little problem, sir. The guy running the fuel truck says we need some kind of form before he'll give us any fuel."

We climbed out and went over to talk with the driver. Bill tried to explain the situation to him. After a few minutes the driver told him that he would not be able to give us any fuel without the proper paperwork, it was base policy.

I had always tried to control my short fuse but had trouble dealing with stupid people. In my youthful fervor I felt my next step was justified. As I stepped toward him I reached up and put my hand on the handle of my .38 revolver and said, "There is still an injured sailor on that destroyer, and if we don't get back out there he might not make it. You see this .38? This .38 tells me that if you don't give us the fucking fuel, I'm going to take it, and you'll have nothing to say about it. You can explain what happened to your boss. If you give us the fuel, we'll sign any fucking piece of paper you want to show that we took the fuel."

My face was an inch from the driver's nose by this time, and the look on my face was total determination. Jenkins had his hand on my arm as if to try to impede my aggression. I think the fuel truck driver knew I was serious, as he stumbled backward, he said, "You can have the damn fuel." I turned and walked back to the helicopter without saying a word.

As I got back to the helicopter, Petty Officer Joyce was up on the rotor system doing an inspection. Joyce said, "Holy shit, sir! I thought you were going to actually pull that .38 out."

As I got in the co-pilot seat I replied, "So did he."

A few minutes later we were on our way back out to the destroyer. The *Bonnie Dick*'s control center had us under radar contact and vectored us to the destroyer. It was 0215 in the morning and the destroyer was a little over 100 miles out now. The *Bonnie Dick* had closed to within 43 miles.

I estimated the time to reach the destroyer and gave it to the Bill. "We should be overhead in about 50 minutes, all gauges are in the green."

I sat back a second and took a minute to relax. As I sat there, I thought, "It's nice to fly with Jenkins. He's so quiet I got to do a lot more of the communications than I normally would. Anyway, if it were anyone else, I would probably be getting a lecture about threatening base personnel right now." The *Bonnie Dick* and the destroyer were in constant contact. The *Bonnie Dick*'s CIC came up over the air and told us that the doctors aboard the carrier had talked with the corpsman aboard the destroyer and they were going to bring the last patient back to the *Bonnie Dick*. We acknowledged and said we would let them know when we had the ship in sight.

The remainder of the transfer went smoothly, and the Sea Sprite touched down aboard the *Bonnie Dick* at 0405 with the injured sailor. I didn't get any feedback about the incident on the beach. I figure LTJG Jenkins didn't even bring it up. I was starting to get a reputation in the enlisted ranks. I wasn't sure what it was or if I should even be concerned. To me, at that point in my life things were either right or they were wrong, and I usually acted on what I thought was right. My approach may have been a little unorthodox, but it got the job done.

After a short stay in Hawaii we arrived on the line (Yankee Station). The whole transit took about three weeks. I remember how young and naïve I was when it came to women back then. We were on liberty at Fort Derucy in the O'club in Hawaii when I noticed our waitress kept smiling at me. She had great, tall, long legs, and her eyes danced when she spoke. She had the prettiest smile that I had ever seen.

After two hours of drinking, I finally got up enough courage to ask her to dinner. She replied by saying, "Sailor, you need to know what you want and go after it. I've been trying to get you to ask me out for the past two hours, and five minutes after that lieutenant over there asks me to dinner, you finally ask me out."

At 22 years old, I wasn't that experienced with women and decided I needed to be as aggressive on the ground as I was with my flying.

The Navy was not conducive to teaching you good drinking habits. There is no alcohol allowed onboard U.S. military ships. That means a sailor may go 30, 45, 60 days without any alcohol, and then he gets 5 days in port, of which one or two days, he may have duty. On his liberty days, his mental attitude is to consume as much alcohol as he can and get as little sleep as possible before they go back to sea. Some of your best sailors partied a little too much while they were on liberty. This is why sailors get such a bad reputation while on liberty, but the women seem to love it.

Yankee Station

The first few months on the line gave me an appreciation for what the pilots and sailors had to endure during WW II and the Korean War. The *Bon Homme Richard*, CVA-31 (nicknamed "Bonnie Dick") was built during the end of WW II and arrived on station for duty in mid-1945. In 1946 it was mothballed and didn't return to duty until the Korean War.

The *Bonnie Dick* was taken out of preservation on January 15, 1951. Following a short training period and post-shakedown repair, she steamed for San Diego, California where she picked up her air wing and headed for the Western Pacific. The *Bonnie Dick* continued to serve throughout the Korean War.

With the advent of hostilities in Southeast Asia, the *Bon Homme Richard* once again was deployed to the Western Pacific. Following the North Vietnamese attack upon the U.S. destroyers in 1964, *Bon Homme Richard* entered her third war. About to return home after a routine deployment, she was extended in the Western Pacific for an additional 45 days to commence operations against North Vietnam. Detachment Lima was part of the crew that deployed on *Bonnie Dick*'s second cruise in support of the Vietnam War effort. The *Bonnie Dick* was an older 27 Charlie Class carrier that had her straight deck converted to an angled deck during overhaul after the Korean War. The living conditions although improved were still similar to the conditions the crews were exposed to during WW II.

Although the *Bonnie Dick* had been fitted with air conditioning, many of the compartments were cut off from the cool air depending on the location of the compartments. The ship's engineering department worked around the clock keeping the ship in operating condition. I remembered a call I made after being on the line for a couple of months. I noticed flooding on the O-2 level, in officers country just below the catapults. When I called engineering, I was surprised at the answer I got.

After I told them about the problem, engineering asked, "How deep is the water?"

I replied by stating that "The water is two to three inches deep."

Engineering acknowledged with, "We'll get to it later. We have higher priorities."

That was not the worst of it. After extended periods on the line in the heat and humidity of the South China Sea, the ship's crew had to take saltwater showers. It takes about 90 gallons of fresh water to catapult an A-3 off the front of the ship. With flight operations being conducted 12 hours a day, 7 days a week, the evaporators could not keep up with the fresh water requirements. When we did get to take a fresh water shower we smelled like jet fuel. It seems the evaporators would pick up some of the jet fuel along with the sea water and the fuel would get trapped in the fresh water system. It got so bad at times the joke was that you shouldn't smoke a cigarette right after you showered. The JP-5 in the drinking water also helped keep you regular. Needless to say when the ship headed for a liberty port, there was a high level of excitement throughout the ship.

I was used to living in an environment where you lost pilots and crews, but it was about to get up close and personal. I even accepted the students we lost in the training command, but I was not prepared for the loss of Ensign Graves. Richard and I had started out in Preflight together and became very good friends during flight training in Pensacola. After carrier quals he selected the jet pipeline and ended up in A-1's. We always tried to keep in touch and pull liberty together whenever possible. Rich was always down in my four man stateroom. There never was a day when he didn't have a positive attitude and a big grin on his face.

Rich was attached to an A-1 squadron. The A-1 was a single engine prop driven aircraft that came out in 1945 at the end of WW II. It carried a tremendous amount of ordinance and could stay on station far longer than the jet aircraft. Their mission was close air support and RESCAP (Rescue Close Air Support). It made me feel good knowing that if I had to go inland for a rescue, Rich would be overhead providing cover.

It was our second time on the line after a short liberty call in Subic Bay, in the Philippines. Rich was in my stateroom the night before telling me about the mission the next day. He was saying that the weather was expected to be so bad that he didn't see how the aircraft were going to see their targets.

It had happened before. The Task Force Commander would order a strike, and the aircraft would drop the ordinance in the water before coming back aboard the ship, because they couldn't see their targets. Then the Task Force Commander would send out a (SITREP) Situation Report, stating they had flown so many sorties that day and dropped so much ordnance (politics). On this particular day the ceiling was about 200 feet. Rich and his flight leader were flying below the overcast a few miles off the beach. Their mission was to fly RESCAP and provide cover for any of the jet pilots that got shot down. The flight leader told me that the weather was so bad, their wing tips were almost touching the water when they made a turn. The flight leader could not tell me exactly what happened. All he knew was, Rich had gone into the water when they were in a slow shallow turn. If he had engine problems he may not have had time to react. The tip of the wing caught the water and the aircraft cart wheeled across the top of the water as it broke up. The flight leader circled for about an hour and never saw Richard come to the surface.

This was hard to take. Rich was a great human being. God, country, and the American way was what he was all about. Rich did not have a mean bone in his body. He loved being in the Navy. Why did we lose people like this, on bullshit sorties? It didn't make any sense. The military had the best, the brightest, and the politicians are getting them killed. For what?

I knew why I was there, and it wasn't for God, country and

the American way. I was still searching for who I was and hoping to find out. I wanted to know what type of person I was and how I would react in a dangerous situation. Up until now I felt I had responded well, but they were reactionary types of responses. Ones that you really didn't have time to think about, you just reacted. The more I was exposed to danger, the more I wanted it.

Three days later, I participated in a ceremony to remember Ensign Graves and two other pilots lost that week. I, along with three of Rich's squadron mates, carried a wreath and placed it over the side at the end of the ceremony, to symbolize giving Rich's body to the sea. I was still struggling with the idea of good men dying for no apparent reason. I could only justify it in that Rich knew the risks involved and accepted them.

The stories about President Johnson and McNamara kept popping up since they were calling the shots in the war. Their little "war room," where they made the decisions and selected targets, drew a lot of flack from the junior officers in the AIRWING and was considered ridiculous bullshit, but nothing was said outside the ranks. Although President Johnson was the Commander-in-Chief he should have left the war fighting to the military and left politics out of it. McNamara was an automobile executive not a tactician.

Yet the pilots continued to do their job. I wondered what it was that drove them to do it. The damn politicians would not even let us bomb Hanoi. If we had bombed Hanoi, they would have come to the negotiation tables. This was 1966, and even as a young ensign I understood that. It wasn't rocket science. Everyone knew that a politician would fight to his last soldier's last drop of blood, but if you threatened the politician directly, they would negotiate immediately.

It was our third month out on the line. We were on a stand down. That meant the entire ship's crew got 24 hours to catch up on personal things such as writing letters back home. They would catch up on overlooked maintenance or repairs that were neglected during the heavy flight operations. I enjoyed working on the helicopters with the maintenance crew. I wanted to learn as much as I could. I had been told on many occasions by the OINC and some of the other pilots that I was too friendly with the enlisted men. They told me that the enlisted men would never respect my authority if I became one of their buddies. This was a constant battle. I felt what I was doing was right, but at 22 years old, I was always being told it was wrong, and I had self doubts.

I didn't think I was that friendly, but I did treat them with respect and didn't talk down to them. I would help them perform some of the maintenance on the aircraft, only to learn more about it. I had one incident where a young petty officer called me by my first name. After I pulled him aside and explained that it wasn't the way to address an officer, the petty officer said he understood, and it never happened again. Most of the men did address me as Mr. "B," and I enjoyed it. It showed respect yet made me feel I was accepted for who I was. Besides, it was a hell of a lot better than, "Hey Ensign," which meant you were at the bottom of the food chain.

During one of our stand downs, an airman came up to me while I was working out on the flight deck. "Sir, I heard you've done some boxing?"

I replied by saying, "I've done a little."

He told me some of the guys in the detachment would like to know if I would teach them a few boxing moves. I didn't see any harm in it, so we went down into the hangar bay with a few of the men from the detachment. I sparred with them, or basically played around for about 15 minutes with two of the men. It was like trying to teach two guys to dance that had two left feet. They were about as fluid as robots. Boxing was a sport I really enjoyed. Just you and the other guy. There was no bullshit; you knew who your opponent was. Either you kicked his butt, or he kicked yours. In real life that wasn't always the case. Just about that time Petty Officer Minor told me there was a guy from the ship's company that wanted to spar with me. I shrugged my shoulders as if to say, "I guess it's okay." I was just getting into it, and the men in the detachment had seemed to have lost their enthusiasm.

Just about then a tall, thin black sailor came out of the crowd with a set of boxing gloves on. I glanced around and was amazed how the crowd had grown. I was beginning to think this was not a good idea, and I was glad that I wasn't wearing anything with an officer's insignia on it. There was no ring and no three minute rounds. It was simple -- you stayed in until you had had enough. With the first two it was just playing around; this guy was a little more determined.

He was faster, but I had a solid punch, and he knew it after I connected with a couple. After about ten minutes he went over to the side and shook off his gloves, saying he'd had enough. Before I could get my gloves off, another sailor stepped out of the crowd. It was another black sailor, a little shorter than me, but his muscles were bulging out all over. I was caught in the middle; I had the feeling I shouldn't be sparring any longer. Yet I didn't know how to gracefully get out of it. The match didn't last long. He was always off balance and after he got knocked down several times, he got frustrated and threw the gloves off and walked off.

I was getting tired. As I looked around, I realized the crowd had almost doubled again, and much to my surprise there were quite a few men from the detachment there. I walked over to Petty Officer Minor and held out my gloves, "Get these things off of me," I said.

He said, "I think we have one more man over there that wants to give it a try."

I told him I was tired, and I'd had enough.

"Sir," Minor said, "Just one more. The guys are watching."

I looked around, then took a deep breath and turned to assess my opponent. It was another black sailor. I thought to myself, "Where the hell are all the white sailors, or don't they like to box?" This guy had a way about him; he'd been in the ring before. I thought I had taken on one opponent too many.

Was I going to end up flat on my back in the middle of the hangar bay?

It was a tough fight, but after a few minutes I could see he was breathing heavy. I got in a good solid right and rang the guy's bell. I could see his knees buckle a little. I moved around him staying away until I saw what the guy was going to do. He did just what I had hoped, he said he'd had enough.

I walked back to Minor with my gloves out, "Get these things off."

Just then someone shouted from the crowd, "Wait a minute! We got someone with some experience! They've gone down to the engine room to get him."

I looked over my shoulder and said, "Bullshit! Minor, get these things off of me, now."

Later on that night, I got another ass chewing and lecture from the OINC. I knew it was the wrong thing to do, but I was in a tee shirt and shorts, nobody got hurt and the guys in the detachment had fun. The next day I had to listen to yet another lecture from the OINC on how not to fraternize with the enlisted men.

It was back to flying support. My roommate and I continued to fly with Lt. Hunt and would tell the OINC about his aerial antics. The other two pilots would always find a way to avoid getting on the flight schedule with him. Up to this point Lt. Hunt had not had any major blunders since leaving California. The LT still handled the helicopter like a gorilla, which kept you on the edge of your seat the entire flight. The only time you could relax is when he turned the helicopter over to his co-pilot.

My roommate's luck was about to run out. Two days later the weather got so bad they cancelled flight ops. Now this makes no sense, but that's when they decided to do helo transfers to the small boys (destroyers). The weather was too rough for fixed wing ops, so they launched the helicopters on a mundane log run. In those days a lot of the fixed winged pilots didn't really understand helicopters, and didn't want to. You'd be surprised what they asked us to do back then.

A good example of their lack of understanding was one time when we returned to San Diego from one of our short cruises. The fog was so bad the ship couldn't see to navigate into San Diego Harbor. The air boss turned and asked me if they could launch the helo and have it go out and find the channel buoy. The helo could hover over the buoy and the ship could get a radar fix on the helicopter and work its way into port. Once they had a bearing and range on that one, the helo could go find the next buoy and they would do the same thing. I tried to tell him in the nicest way possible that he was crazy. Helicopters have just as many restrictions as the fixed wing aircraft.

Part of the helicopter mission aboard ship was to conduct administrative flights, where personnel, mail and parts were transferred to the ships in the task group. These missions were called "log runs." It was the OINC's job to tell them that we shouldn't be flying in that weather, but he wanted to make captain. The OINC and I were on the number one catapult forward on the port side. Lt. Hunt and my roommate had already launched to one of the destroyers, but couldn't get the mail to them. The ship was pitching so badly they couldn't make the transfer, and they were on their way back.

The surface winds were in excess of 40 knots with gusts up to 55 knots. The winds were so bad the ship had to steam downwind so we could engage the rotors and then they would have to turn back into the wind before we could launch. Before the ship turned to launch us, they wanted to recover the other helicopter on the number two catapult. That meant Lt. Hunt would have to make a bow on approach. The ship was doing about 20 knots through the water with the wind coming down the flight deck from aft, forward at about 20 to 35 knots. I knew this was an accident waiting to happen and told LCDR Stuart to tell the air boss to take him after the turn. The OINC condescendingly told me it would be okay. The LT could handle it. How the hell did he know? He never flew with him.

The LT would have to do a bow on approach with the ship heading directly at him, then match his ground speed with the ship's ground speed. That meant the helicopter would actually be moving backwards in relation to the water but would have a 20 plus knot headwind as it set down. He would have to match the ship's movement with the helicopter's movement as he touched down. Not an impossible maneuver for a good pilot, but I had my doubts that he could do it. I had seen too many of the LT's clumsy landings, and they were under ideal conditions. To compound things, if he crashed on the flight deck, he would most likely take us out along with him.

Needless to say it made for some tense moments. As we sat there turning on the number one catapult, we watched the helicopter approach. He was all over the sky. His approach was way too fast, and he didn't compensate for the ship's movement. I thought he would have to wave it off, but at the last minute the LT pulled the nose almost straight up to stop his forward speed. They lost complete sight of the flight deck. Then with no airspeed remaining, he slammed the nose over, and the helicopter plunged to the flight deck. It hit so hard it bounced back up in the air. After a couple of bounces, it finally settled on the deck. It was more like the helicopter had been dropped on the flight deck than landed.

I couldn't believe the LT got it on the deck. I wondered how much structural damage he had done to the helicopter. I could see my roommate's face; it was white as a sheet. He was holding onto anything he could get his hands on. Before the ground crew could get the tie down chains on the helicopter, the ship started a turn into the wind so we could launch. As we got halfway through the turn the ship started to heel in the rough seas. The flight deck must have had a 30 degree slant to starboard

By this time the winds were about 90 degrees to port. The LT's helicopter started to slide towards the catwalk. The ground crews were running to get out of the way of the helicopter. Just then the helicopter leaped up into the air and headed out over the water, downwind. As it passed over the side of the ship, the helicopter was about 50 to 100 feet above the flight deck. Lt. Hunt ran out of power at that time and lost control. The helicopter made a violent maneuver like it had lost its tail rotor and then went inverted and crashed in the water upside down.

We were already turning on the other catapult. The ship stopped its turn and asked Stuart if the winds were good enough to launch. Stuart said they needed to continue the turn until the winds were down the deck. When the ship stopped its turn we launched and headed for the debris in the water. As the helicopter passed behind the ship, Miller reported seeing something in the water and gave a distance and bearing. The sea swells were a minimum of 20 to 25 feet high; it was difficult to maintain contact with anything in the water.

As the OINC brought the helicopter into a hover over the wreckage, I could see my roommate. He was unconscious, and the entire seat had been ripped out of the helicopter. He was floating about a foot below the surface of the water. Stuart directed the rescue swimmer to stay attached to the rescue hoist. The seas were too rough, and it would be difficult to get the sling to him if he detached. I wanted to be in the right seat, I knew I could do a better job.

Stuart had to maintain a 30 foot hover in order to avoid the high swells. Every time the swimmer got within reach of the co-pilot, he would be jerked away by the helicopter. Seconds seemed like minutes; the frustration was building. I felt helpless; the OINC was all over the place in the high winds. I thought he was doing a lousy job, but couldn't say anything. That was my roommate and friend down there, and if we didn't get to him soon, he would be dead for sure.

Out of total frustration I unbuckled my seatbelt and said I was going in after him. I knew I was a good swimmer, and if the helo couldn't get me back in, they could pick us up with the destroyer.

Stuart was looking down at the swimmer. He responded by saying "It's too late. He's already dead."

I didn't want to believe it. We had to try. I knew he was probably right, but how would we ever know? I sat back in my seat knowing I let him down, but as co-pilot there was nothing I could do. I swore I would never let it happen when I was the aircraft commander.

The OINC was still looking out the door and maintaining a hover over the debris as the crew chief started to bring the swimmer back into the helicopter. Resigned to the fact that I had let down my roommate as I buckled my seatbelt, I looked back out the front of the cockpit. Just as I looked up a huge wave was heading right for us. We were hovering at about 30 feet, and the wave was well above the rotor mast. I was looking up at the wave and didn't have time to warn Stuart. I grabbed the collective and pulled in the power. We rose to about 60 feet and then settled back down again. The crew chief shouted, "What the hell was that?"

I replied, "How's the swimmer?"

"He's fine sir. Just got slapped in the face by that last wave."

LCDR Stuart was surprisingly quiet, usually he was very talkative and always ready to lecture me. I had an idea of what he was going through. Stuart knew Lt. Hunt was a bad pilot, but he always made a joke about it. This incident never had to happen if everyone had done their job, including the air boss. Now we had four people dead.

I could remember the air boss's statement when I was up in Pri-Fly. "Helicopters can do anything, can't they?" I replied by saying they were affected by the same laws of physics and aerodynamics as fixed wing aircraft.

In those days we usually had a helicopter pilot in the tower to answer questions or to prevent what had just happened. That day we didn't have anyone. LTJG Kent's body and the bodies of the rest of the crew were never recovered. I was not looking forward to another senseless funeral and four more wreaths delivered to the sea.

As I usually did, I went over the incident in my mind until I was certain I understood what really took place. I tried to decide what would have been the best response to what happened. This was always useful to me. When something actually happens, you don't have time to think it through, in most cases you have a split second to react. I made the assumption that the LT had no choice but to turn downwind. It was understandable; we were sitting on the other catapult so he turned away to avoid us. That meant he went from the deck to a 40 to 55 knot tailwind. He was about 150 feet above the water when he ran out of power. We were in the South China Sea in the middle of summer and not a cold December night off the California coast. The only way to save the crew and himself would be to lower the collective and head for the water to get his airspeed. Instead he held in the power until the RPMs slowed to a point where he lost control of the helicopter. Once that happened, the blades stalled out and the helicopter flipped upside down, and they impacted the water inverted. Worst case scenario, if he had lowered his collective, he would have pancaked into the water level, cushioning the landing with his collective. They would have been able to exit the aircraft. You always try to keep the aircraft under control.

Nobody talked about what happened. It was a wartime environment and everyone kept focused on the mission. The OINC sent a message to the squadron to tell them what had happened and to request a replacement crew. About ten days had passed when the replacement pilots arrived. I was glad to see them. Their personalities were completely different from the rest of the detachments pilots, and that was good for me. Now, maybe I would have someone to joke with. Three days after they arrived the ship was headed to Hong Kong; talk about timing. Since they just got there, Cyril and Bob volunteered for duty the first night in. The detachment was ready for Hong Kong; we had just passed the halfway mark on the cruise and the only liberty port we had seen to that point was Subic Bay. Hong Kong was special, and the detachment had made plans for a big detachment party the first night.

That night, I was about to get my first lesson in leadership from LCDR Stuart. The incident happened in the nightclub they had selected for the detachment party. With Cyril and Bob aboard ship as the standby crew, the rest of the detachment pilots went to the party along with all the off duty personnel. At the club the officers sat at one table and the enlisted dispersed throughout the club. I was the only officer that was mingling with the enlisted men. At 22 I had more in common with them and sat right in the middle of a long table of about 15 of the of the detachments crew. I enjoyed beer, and we just completed a 32 day line period with no alcohol. As the night progressed the officers sat at the table talking and watching the crew and I enjoy our liberty.

About 2300, one of the crew came running to the table, "Mr. B, Mr. B, you need to get over there. Things are getting out of hand!"

As I looked over at the officers table, I saw Sipes and Dugan grab Ensign Clark. I jumped up from the table and started in that direction. I could see the other officers backing away from the scuffle. As I made my way over I saw LCDR Stuart try to step in and stop the fracas and get knocked into a table and slide to the floor.

When I reached the disturbance, LCDR Stuart was picking himself up from the floor. I was able to get my hands on Sipes and Dugan before they could do anymore damage. Both of the airmen had quite a bit to drink, and I had plenty of experience dealing with drunks. I wanted to get them out of there before they ended up in the brig. As I grabbed the backs of their shirts, I shook both of them to get their attention. "If there is going to be a fight, it will be with me, and we'll do it outside." It was the beer talking, but it worked.

Sipes turned and looked at me, "No sir Mr. B. We don't want any trouble with you. It's that fucking Ensign Clark."

I pulled them both toward the door, trying to get them outside before anyone could continue with the hostilities. As we got out into the street, I asked them both what had happened.

Dugan started with, "We were coming out of the head and we overheard Ensign Clark say, 'Look at those animals.' No body calls me a fucking animal!"

I said, "You're both drunk. Get in that taxi over there and get your asses back to the ship before you spend the rest of the cruise in the brig."

I put them into the taxi and returned to the club. As I approached the table, Stuart and the other officers were picking up the chairs that had been knocked over. The expression on the OINC's face was menacing. He wanted blood.

I asked him what had happened. I could see that Ensign Clark's shirt was torn. Clark was over in the corner staying out of the way. From what I saw there were no punches thrown. The first thing out of Stuart's mouth was, "I told you, you would never get any respect from the enlisted men."

That stunned me, but I chose to ignore it. "Sir, they had just a little too much to drink. I sent them back to the ship. They won't give anyone anymore trouble tonight."

Ensign Clark was not talking, at least not at that point. LCDR Stuart told me he wanted to see both of them first thing in the morning. I wasn't happy to hear that; it meant my plans for my first night in Hong Kong were shot. I needed to get with Sipes and Dugan before they buried themselves with the OINC. Especially Dugan, he was a hot head, and if anything, I knew about being self-destructive.

The next morning I went to talk with Mr. Stuart before getting the two airmen. Even though the detachment OINC has the authority to give non-judicial punishment, LCDR Stuart wanted to kick it up to the CO of the carrier.

"Sir, if the Captain gets these guys, he's going to think it was a major incident, and he will throw the book at them. Why don't you just restrict them to the ship for the remainder of the in port period? They're some of the best mechanics we have."

I explained why they reacted the way they did when they heard Ensign Clark call them animals. Clark was disliked by all the enlisted men; his pompous attitude and the slovenly way he kept himself rubbed the men the wrong way.

"It was nothing more than a shoving match. Besides, if it goes to the ship's captain, it may get messy when it comes out that Ensign Clark may have initiated it with his derogatory comments." It was weak, but all I had.

The OINC understood the situation and knew the crew thought Ensign Clark was an asshole. That wasn't going to change. Stuart told me to tell the men that they had a choice, captain's mast or no liberty for the rest of the in port period. I never understood why he didn't want to take them to OINC mast. He could have even fined them if he wanted to make a bigger impact.

I went back to Sipes and Dugan and told them what the OINC was going to do, and that they were very lucky they had not taken a swing at Ensign Clark. The two airmen were bent out of shape. Their first reaction was let him take them to captain's mast, but with a little reflection on the potential consequences, they accepted the restriction. You usually get only one port call to Hong Kong during a cruise, and they were going to miss it. I learned at an early age, the biggest challenge in being an officer was keeping good men from self destruction. Now, if I could just learn that for myself.

I finally got off the ship and met up with two of the junior officers from the *Bonnie Dick* and pulled the remainder of my liberty with them. Hong Kong was truly a fascinating place. Anything you could think of you could find in Hong Kong. I had a lot to learn and was going to try to see as much as I could in three days of liberty.

Ensign Clark never said a word to the rest of the crew about the incident, but I'm sure he complained enough to the OINC about his treatment. He may have learned from the incident. He never talked down to the crew for the remainder of the deployment.

After a couple of weeks back on the line, the air wing was on its typical rotation of 12 hours of air ops and 12 hours of maintenance. On the evening of day 15, our air ops had been cut short, nobody really knew why. Everyone was in a stand down mode.

Bill and I got called into CIC. When we entered the space we saw LCDR Stuart over at one of the plotting tables talking with the CAG (Carrier Air Group) Commander. As we approached to report, Stuart turned and said, "You both volunteered as the back up Combat SAR (CSAR) pilots, right?"

LTJG Jenkins answered, "Yes, sir."

"Well, we have a little problem. We have a downed pilot in the jungle about sixty miles south of Hanoi. They attempted a rescue, and the rescue helo was shot up crossing the beach and had to turn back. The secondary CSAR helo is in the process of changing engines and will not be available until tomorrow at the earliest. The attempt was during the day, and we think we'll have a better chance going in at night. The problem is, there are no combat rescue assets available."

We listened to CAG and the OINC describe the situation. We volunteered to be replacement CSAR pilots if one of their pilots got sick or injured, not to use one of our unarmed helos to go inland. They knew none of the helo's had armor or guns on them. They couldn't do anything about the armor, but they had sent for the OINC of the Marine detachment.

They told us the "Marine detachment is rigging up an M-60 to put aboard the helo. They'll select one of their best Marines to go with you. This is strictly a volunteer mission, and you need to select two of the back up air crewman."

The DET had four volunteer air crew in case one of the

combat aircrew was hurt or pulled off the line for some reason. "The ship was headed in toward the beach and will be in position for launch in about 3 ½ hours. The A-1 squadron has been briefed and is ready to provide as much air cover as needed."

I listened intently. Even though it sounded like a good plan, I knew it was a suicide mission. Everything that Lt. McCormick taught me said this was a bad idea. Over eight hours would have elapsed from the time the pilot went down to the time of the rescue attempt. That meant Charlie could have a company surrounding the pilot waiting for the next rescue attempt unless the pilot was able to evade the NVA and get to a different location. We had not trained together as a combat rescue crew, and the crew coordination would be critical.

I didn't say anything. It was our job, and if there was a chance to get the pilot out, we had to try. I wanted to be aircraft commander but had no choice in the matter. Bill was a good pilot, but he was not very aggressive. He never took the aircraft to the edge of its envelope, and I knew we would need every trick that McCormick had taught me. We finished the briefing and got the radio frequencies and call signs. Then we headed for the DET ready room to brief the air crewmen.

After explaining the situation, all four air crew volunteered. These guys were great! I never understood human nature. Either these guys were all heroes or they didn't fully grasp what we were getting ourselves into. Either way I couldn't have asked for a better crew. We all agreed that Petty Officer Joyce and Airman Sipes would be the ones to go. Even after Sipes got his ass chewed by the OINC, restricted to the ship and threatened with captain's mast, he volunteered. That says it all about these men and what they're made of.

Bill broke in and said, "Let's get up and make the helo ready. The Marines are probably up there already. We need to go over everything with the gunner. It'll be live ordnance, and we've never done this before. It's going to be risky enough without us shooting ourselves down." We all headed for the flight deck.

At 2130 we had completed everything. All that was left was to sit and wait. We were leaning against the front of the helo. It was very quiet. Everyone was left to their thoughts. The night was calm with about 20 knots of wind coming over the bow as we steamed through the water. The air was warm, the type of night you'd like to be on the beach with your favorite girl. An hour went by and not a word was said. It was one of the longest hours I had ever known. The wait was unbearable, not knowing what would happen next made my imagination run wild.

I was ready to get on with it. I went through every scenario in my head. I thought we should be getting the word any minute. Another 30 minutes went by, no word. We could see some of the lights on the shore now. I had never seen the carrier this close before. I went over and over in my head everything I had learned from Lt. McCormick. Neither one of us had any combat experience. We had everything against us -- no armor, no fire power to speak of, and we were going to try to pull a pilot out of the jungle in the middle of the night. There was no moon; all we had was the light from the stars. I had plenty of time to do some soul searching. I didn't believe in luck, and I wasn't a very religious person. I believed in one thing: the training and the skill of the crew and the pilots. Bill would be calling the shots, that I had to accept. Even at 22 it was difficult for me to sit second seat to anyone. I kept telling myself, if the pilot could be rescued, we had to try.

As I turned around I saw someone come up on the flight deck from the direction of the DET ready room. It was Minor. As he came up to us, he looked over at LTJG Jenkins and said, "They passed the word to stand down."

LTJG Jenkins said, "Let's go down to the ready room to see if we can find out what's going on."

We waited in the ready room for about 30 minutes and then got a call from Mr. Stuart. They had lost the signal from the downed pilot. They weren't sure if he was captured or his radio went dead or he turned it off. Without the radio signal, it would be almost impossible to find him at night. They were going to wait to see if they made contact with the pilot again.

At 0230 the mission was called off. It took me the rest of the night to wind down. I sure could have used a couple of beers. I spent the rest of the night going over the mission in my head. What would the mission have been like? How would I have handled it? Would there have been heavy fire? How would I have reacted under fire? I would never know. In a strange way I felt almost cheated. They never heard from the pilot again and assumed he was a POW. Call it dumb luck, but I don't believe we would have had a chance. Eleven years later in a different country this same scenario would be repeated again, only with a different outcome.

The next day we were back to normal ops. I was feeling good about my flying, every chance I got, I would kick one of the systems off and try a simulated emergency. On one particular approach with LCDR Stuart, I made an ASE off approach. The landing was nice and smooth, but it was a little long in the hover as I struggled to grease it onto the flight deck. The ASE is the Automatic Stabilization Equipment that assists the pilot in flying the aircraft.

As I brought it over the deck, Stuart asked me what the hell I was doing. I replied with, "I'm practicing an emergency. Lt. McCormick said to practice simulated emergencies any time you get a chance. You never know when one is going to happen."

"That's bullshit," said Stuart, "you just handle the emergency when you get it. Any good pilot can handle the emergencies when they get them."

LCDR Stuart was always on my case. No matter what I did, it wasn't right, and this was another incident that would endear me to him. Stuart grabbed the controls from me, "I have the aircraft. I'll show you what I mean," as he called the air boss for a take-off and practice emergency landing.

As LCDR Stuart received the clearance, we lifted into the air and made a left-hand turnout for a downwind. While we were on the downwind leg Stuart kicked the ASE off. He immediately started to over control the aircraft. He started to settle down by the time he got abeam the carrier and called for a landing. "Roger, you're cleared into spot one for landing," the air boss replied. As Stuart approached the ship and started to transition into a hover, he realized he was too fast and overshot the spot. As he waved off to go around, I didn't say a word. I knew I was in a no win situation.

I thought to myself, "It's a perfect day, no weather and a calm sea state with plenty of wind down the deck, what would he do in bad weather?" As Stuart brought the helicopter around again, I could see the concentration on his face. He came over the deck and arrived in a very rough hover over the spot, dropped the collective rapidly, making a hard landing on spot one. LCDR Stuart did not say a word; he quickly shut the helicopter down, got out and went down to maintenance control to fill out the log book.

As Stuart was walking away, Airman Sipe's said, "That was one hell of a landing."

I turned around and said, "Knock it off." I stayed up with the crew on the flight deck knowing I did not want to be in the same room with the OINC. This was something that would follow me throughout my career. I always had a knack for unintentionally pissing off senior officers

The next few weeks passed without any incidents in the detachment. We lost two more pilots in the air wing, one was missing in action. The other was CDR Smith, the CO of one of the attack squadrons aboard the ship. CDR Smith was captured and presumed a POW, but they hadn't received any confirmation yet. Scuttlebutt had it that CDR Smith was pretty tough and that the North Vietnamese would have their hands full at the Hanoi Hilton when he arrived. Missing pilots and burials at sea were commonplace, and we learned to accept them as part of the job. You continued on with your daily routine rather than dwell on what may, or may not happen next. It was the mission that everyone stayed focused on.

I was beginning to think I would make the whole cruise without getting a rescue. We were in starboard delta boring holes in the sky. Nothing was more tiresome than the starboard delta. Just about that time, the Alpha Strike flight was inbound for landing. One of the A-4's had been hit and was losing power. The air boss handed us off to CIC, and they vectored us in the direction of the crippled aircraft. As I switched the radios we could hear the A-4 pilot talking to CIC. He was losing oil pressure and could not maintain his altitude. He had plenty of altitude and thought he might be able to nurse the crippled aircraft all the way to the ship. A few minutes later the pilot radioed that his engine had just quit. LTJG Jenkins pulled in all the power he could without over-heating the engine. CIC asked if we had copied the last transmission and Jenkins answered, "Roger, we're buster on a heading of 345."

Another minute or two of silence and then the pilot came up over the air and said he couldn't get a restart and was ejecting. About that time Jenkins reported we had a visual on the A-4. I could see the smoke trailing from the aircraft as it descended toward the water. Just about that time we saw a parachute. The level of excitement increased as we got closer. You could feel the adrenalin throughout the helo. The jet pilot was surprisingly calm right up to the ejection. I wanted to meet this guy when it was all over. Anyone that can remain calm while ejecting from a crippled aircraft was worth meeting.

We still had a couple of miles to go as the parachute descended to the water. The helo crew could see it slowly descend until it went out of sight. Would he be injured? Would he be able to get away from his parachute? If he didn't get away from his chute, it would fill with water and drag him down. We needed to find him as quickly as possible.

As we approached the area where we thought the pilot made impact, we immediately started a search pattern expanding as we completed each leg. It's a big ocean, even when you know the area where the pilot went down, you can still have a hard time spotting him. After a couple of minutes, the crew chief came up over the radio and said, "I have a survivor in the water at 4 o'clock."

Everyone started into their assigned duties. I was always impressed with the air crewmen, they all knew their jobs well. The rescue went without a hitch. The crew chief checked the pilot over and reported back. "Sir, the pilot looks alright. He says he smashed his knee up a little, but doesn't think anything is broken."

Jenkins reported his condition to the ship and said, "We're inbound with the pilot, minor injuries, and can we have someone from sick bay meet us at the helo?"

I was happy. At least I got to participate in a rescue on the cruise. It was a pretty standard rescue without any problems, but we did our job, and I'm sure the pilot was happy we were there when he needed us.

It seems that Bill and I were always on duty when something happened. It was less than a week later when we had a man get blown overboard during night flight ops about 0300 in the morning. It was another dark rainy night. This time we had a heavy overcast sky, which gives you about as much visibility as if you were in a sealed room with no lights. As we started the search astern of the ship, all we had was our search light to provide any illumination on the water. We had no idea what condition the sailor was in or if he had a signal light with him.

Within about 20 minutes one of the crewmen spotted something in the water. I was surprised when Bill turned and headed right for the survivor instead of setting up for a standard night approach. The winds and the sea state were pretty bad. As we headed into the hover, I was trying to get a good reading on what direction the wind was coming from. I think Bill had a little too much adrenalin going. As we came into a hover, he immediately started into a rapid right drift. As I looked at the attitude gyro to confirm what I thought was happening, I could see we were rolling rapidly into a right bank. We were too close to the water, and I didn't have time to ask questions. This time I grabbed the controls and pulled in the collective to get us some altitude. Bill didn't fight me. I climbed out and leveled off at about 1,000 feet circling to stay over the man in the water. I asked him if everything was all right and he said, "I think so. I guess I got a little vertigo." We talked about making a standard night rescue approach then started back in.

As we transitioned into a hover the crewmen called out our position in relation to the man in the water. Bill picked up the hover and did an outstanding job considering the weather conditions. We had no problem sending the swimmer down the hoist to make the rescue. About 45 minutes had passed when we brought the sailor back onboard the *Bonnie Dick*. He was okay and everyone was impressed with the fact that we were even able to find him with the weather as it was.

Bill was a good pilot; everyone is susceptible to vertigo. I may have had a tendency to get in there too quickly, but when you're in a 20 foot hover in bad weather, you don't have time to ask questions. You can be in the water in the blink of an eye. Bill never said a word about what had happened. If I hadn't been as aggressive as I was, I would have been in the water at least three times within my first year in the fleet. Later I was given a Medal for the two rescues. It was my first award and what made it so special was we had saved two lives. Nothing is more rewarding than that. Bill ended his flying career after his first tour and got out of the Navy.

Disaster aboard the *USS FORESTALL*

The next few weeks went without incident. Everything

went smoothly right up to the last four hours on the line. The OINC and I were getting ready to provide support for the last strike into the beach and then we were on our way home. We were going over the checklist when we got word the *USS Forestall* was on fire. The air boss came up over the 1MC and said, "Let's get the helo in the air and get the back-up helo ready to recover the aircraft."

The flight crew wasted no time in getting the helo engaged. I was looking up the radio frequencies as the OINC gave a signal to break us down (take the tie down chains off and remove the chocks in preparation for flight). We got a briefing over the radio from the air boss along with an initial heading to the *Forestall*. As we left the deck, primary instructed us to provide whatever assistance the *Forestall* needed, and we were cleared to switch frequencies to get vectors on the stricken ship. As CIC gave us updates on the distance and bearing to the *Forestall*, they also brought us up to speed on what had happened. It seems there were several explosions on the flight deck, and some of the bombs were still going off. The fire was out of control, and there was a possibility they could lose the ship.

As we got closer to the *Forestall*, we could see the large column of smoke coming from the ship. When we made contact with the ship they told us there were survivors in the water. They didn't know what condition they were in or how many. Some had been blown over the side from the explosions.

All available assets had been assigned to provide assistance. Several Air Force helicopters from Da Nang had been deployed to assist. The *USS Repose*, a hospital ship, was in route to the *Forestall* and all available surface ships were closing on the stricken vessel. About 10 miles out, Petty Officer Joyce spotted the first survivor in the water. As we passed over him, he seemed to be alright, so we put a smoke in the water to check the surface winds. We came around and made a standard approach and then had the swimmer go down the hoist to check the condition of the survivor. The rescue went without a hitch. The crew chief reported that the survivor was in good condition, and we were cleared to depart. As we broke our hover we continued to look for additional survivors as we approached the *Forestall*. After about 15 minutes we were told to contact the *USS Oriskany*. When we reported in they told us they wanted to transfer some medical personnel and supplies to the stricken ship.

We headed directly to the *USS Oriskany* to drop off the sailor and pick up some medical personnel and equipment. As we headed toward the *Forestall*, we could see the dark, black smoke billowing out from the flight deck. It looked like half the ship was on fire. As we orbited the ship waiting for a clearance to land we could see the huge holes in the flight deck. They were so big you could almost fly in one and out the other.

The smoke made it difficult to make the approach to the ship. If we headed into the prevailing winds, the smoke would block our approach. We had to make a cross deck approach to the forward part of the flight deck. We were lucky we didn't have any bad weather to complicate the transfers. We were one of the first, if not the first, helicopters to land on the flight deck. They were still fighting fires that were out of control below decks. Once we got on deck, the ship told us they were in desperate need of additional fire fighting equipment and wanted us to return to the *Oriskany*. After the second trip we were directed to return and search for additional survivors.

By this time there were several helicopters in the area. As we spotted our second survivor we setup for an approach. When we came around on final into the wind and started the transition into a hover, we saw an Air Force Jolly Green make an accelerated approach downwind. They looked like they were going to set down right on top of us. Stuart made a right hand turn away from the Jolly Green and climbed back up to 300 feet. He said, "This is not a contest to see who can get the most rescues. If he wants to run his rescue count up, he can have them. I'm not going to risk a mid air." The Jolly Green was a CH-53 and about 3 ½ times the size of a Sea Sprite and had all the power in the world to make an approach from any direction he wanted. We had no communications with the other aircraft. There was no time to coordinate radio frequencies or call signs.

After a few minutes went by we spotted another survivor in the water. As we headed inbound we saw an SH-3, which passed us on the starboard side and raced in for the rescue. It was getting ridiculous; the OINC was flying like an old lady, and all I could do was sit there and watch them make all the rescues. The OINC finally told me to broadcast over the guard channel and suggest all rescue aircraft come up on our frequency. We spent the next 90 minutes looking for additional survivors and avoiding mid airs.

With the arrival of additional rescue vehicles, the OINC decided to return to the *Forestall* where he felt we could do more good than we were doing out there. The *Bonnie Dick* had recovered the aircraft and was closing on the *Forestall* so we returned to refuel. When we arrived back overhead the *Forestall*, they were still fighting the fires below decks, but had cleared the flight deck enough to start transferring the injured personnel to the hospital ship.

As the news came in, it seemed that a ZUNI rocket was fired accidentally from an aircraft being readied for launch. The rocket sailed across the flight deck, struck another aircraft and ignited an external fuel tank. The initial fire could have been contained, but seconds after the fire started, the first bomb detonated, killing or seriously wounding most of the fire fighters. The detonation ruptured the flight deck, and burning fuel spilled into the lower levels of the ship. Bombs, warheads, and rocket motors exploded with varying degrees of intensity in the fire, killing an estimated 134 and wounding more than 160 men. Twenty-one aircraft were destroyed, and some were pushed over the side to clear the flight deck.

We had received fire fighting training before we left the states. The squadron had lost all eight helicopter pilots in the fire aboard the *USS Oriskany* on their previous cruise. A shipboard fire is one of the most dangerous things you'll ever see. We continued throughout the day transferring injured personnel to the hospital ship. Later that day and into the next, we started transferring the body bags to the hospital ship. Even with the closed body bags, you could still smell the burnt flesh of some of the dead. It is a smell that would stay with me for many years. I can't remember how many we transferred, but we spent most of the next day transferring the dead. As we returned to the ship that evening we learned that we were extended indefinitely.

From the support we gave to the *Forestall* we received a letter of commendation from commander carrier division two. As in most citations, what actually happened was slightly different from the actual events. Of course we couldn't state that every time we went in for a rescue we were almost run down by a larger helicopter. What we ended up doing for the *Forestall* was probably more critical to the support of the ship than the individuals in the water, although I'm sure the sailors in the water would have contested that.

Four days later we finally received word the *Bonnie Dick* was going home. On our return home we learned that the *Forestall* was still fighting fires below decks when they pulled into the Philippines three days later. The three week trip seemed like three months. Again I was able to find a few good poker games to pass some of the time. I did have to endure several lectures from the OINC on the way back. He was convinced that I would never be able to lead men if I didn't distance myself from the enlisted men. To this day I still disagree with him; I had seen these men perform. They were dedicated, and I believed in them. All they asked for was fair treatment and respect for their individual contributions. They certainly were not in it for the pay, and the recognition they got for a job well done made it all worth it. It was simple, but the OINC didn't seem to catch on. He was more interested in what CAG thought of his performance. In the last few weeks of the cruise I must have had a dozen of the men come up to me and tell me they enjoyed serving with me and wouldn't mind deploying with me again. Some may think I was wrong, but that meant more to me than anything the OINC could have said.

I had just spent almost ten months at sea and had visited Hong Kong, Bangkok, Sasebo Japan, and Subic Bay, in the Philippines. I had learned a little more about myself and could not wait to see what was over the next horizon. The next years would continue to increase in intensity and test my beliefs and my trust in people.

Chapter Four
Orders Back to Vietnam

Orders to HA(L)-3

It was seventeen days since we had left the line. The detachment was preparing to fly into NALF Imperial Beach. I had mixed emotions. I didn't have anyone back in San Diego to go home to, but it was still good to get back to the States. I never thought I would miss *the Bonnie Dick*; it was rusty, leaky, and noisy, but it had been home all those months. According to HC-1 tradition, the detachment helicopters would fly into the field in formation, make one circle around the field and then land and taxi into the line together. LTJG Jenkins and I were pilots in the number three aircraft.

As we taxied into the line and shut down the aircraft, some of the squadron personnel were out on the line to meet us. When I climbed out of the helicopter the Executive Officer (XO) came up to me and held out his hand. I reached out to shake his hand and the XO said, "Congratulations, you have orders to Vietnam."

"HA(L)-3," I asked.

The XO replied, "Yes."

I had heard about Helicopter Attack (Light) Squadron-Three and volunteered to go in country to fly gun ships while on cruise. I was surprised to hear that I was the only one of the three, including the OINC that was selected.

The XO told me that I was to report to Fort Benning, Georgia in February for gun ship training. I was excited, gun ships, that's great!

HC-1 was one of the largest squadrons in the Navy, with over 300 officers at the beginning of the Vietnam War. The original Game Warden detachments came from HC-1 before they made it a squadron. I took a week of leave and went up to Los Angeles to tell my parents I would be returning to Vietnam. I was not one to handle time off very well. I always liked to stay busy, and there wasn't much to do while I was home on leave. I had been away for too long and didn't really know how to relate to the guys I went to school with anymore. Time seemed to have stood still for them. I wanted to get back to the squadron and build up as much flight time a possible. I didn't realize that in a few short months of flying back in the States, I would have plenty of new sea stories to add to the list of in-flight emergencies and engine failures. Back then life was exciting, and I couldn't get enough of it.

Helicopter Aircraft Commander (HAC) Designation

I was amazed at how easy it was to get flight time. With all the officers in the squadron I thought I would have to fight to be put on the flight schedule. I was one of the more junior officers in the squadron and I already had orders out. Within a month I had qualified as Helicopter Aircraft Commander (HAC) in the UH-2A/B and the new twin engine UH-2C. To my surprise I was asked to take one of the older UH-2B's to the KAMAN Factory in Connecticut and pick up a new twin engine Sea Sprite. I was eager; I had just made LTJG and now I was going to take a helicopter from San Diego to Connecticut and return in a new twin engine version. I would be aircraft commander and in charge of my own fate. I'd already had enough close calls flying with other pilots and didn't need anymore. I was amazed to find out that with all those pilots in the squadron, there were only two pilots on the beach that were qualified in the new twin engine version, and I was one of them.

My co-pilot would be LTJG Thomas (Sandy) Sands. He was more than a year senior to me but wasn't qualified in the UH-2. Sandy was a great guy -- low key, easy-going. He was good-looking and could really draw the women. That I liked. It came in handy on the road. Sandy had a reputation of partying hard. The crew chief would be Petty Officer Spears. I laughed. The first thing that came to mind was I thought Spears was a little young. He was only twenty-one. Then I remembered I had just turned twenty-three a week earlier. Sandy was the oldest at twenty-six and would prove to be the most trouble. The first day went without incident, but on the second day, things started to change.

As each day passed we were adding gripes to the yellow sheets on each turnaround. We had many more than I was used to, but the helicopter was just going to the factory to be converted to the new twin engine version. I briefed the XO each night on our progress and expressed my concerns about two of the major gripes. The tail rotor started to pick up vibrations, and that meant the bearings were starting to fail. We also had a hydraulic leak and a list as long as my arm of minor gripes. If the hydraulics failed I could still get the helicopter on the ground, but it wasn't the easiest thing to do. You had to find a place to make a run-on landing; it was difficult to make a hover landing in the Sea Sprite helicopter with the hydraulics off, but it could be done. I had tried it with Lt. McCormick, and the run-on landing was the only way to go.

The XO told me to monitor the tail rotor vibrations and if they got too severe, land the helicopter and they would send out new bearings and parts. The XO emphasized that they needed that helicopter at the factory as soon as possible. I paused and thought to myself, what is *too* severe?

The next day we made it most of the way through Texas and were headed into Longview at the eastern edge of Texas. The weather was lousy, ceiling 200 feet, in and out of rain showers. We were about 75 miles out trying to stay under Visual Flight Rules (VFR) when we lost our hydraulics. The rain kept increasing in intensity, and we were in and out of heavy thunderstorms. I had to fight the aircraft the whole time. When the hydraulics fail, the Automatic Stabilization Equipment (ASE) fails along with it. This meant you had to fight the feedback from the controls to keep the helicopter stable without any assistance from mechanical devices. The thing that was bothering me most was our low altitude. I knew there were tall radio towers around, and I couldn't see them very well because the windshield wipers also worked off the hydraulics.

There was nothing Sandy could do to help. I was glad I was in good shape because I was really getting a workout. I slowed the helicopter a little to give myself some reaction time if we saw something up ahead. I couldn't slow the helicopter too much; the slower you got the harder it was to control the helicopter. We were about 50 miles out now and had just picked up another problem. The vibration in the tail rotor had almost doubled. The vibration was so bad we couldn't read the instruments. I was ready to set it down anywhere I could find a field. I knew I was going to bust the aircraft up. It was tough enough to get it on the runway let along make a rough terrain landing in a farmer's field with no hydraulics.

I ran the emergency procedures through my head. I knew how the helicopter would react if I lost the tail rotor. I'd practiced run-on landings plenty of times, simulating a tail rotor failure. I would take it down controlling the nose with the power and airspeed. I decided it wouldn't make much difference if I tried it now or when the tail rotor stopped. The results would most likely be the same. A good landing would be if we all walked away from the helicopter. I didn't know what would happen if we completely lost the tail gear box.

That would change the center of gravity and no one had ever landed one in that condition that I knew of. The gear box had a chip detector, and it would give us a warning before it started coming apart. By this time we were about 25 miles out with no change in the vibrations.

I looked over at Sandy; he seemed to be handling it well. I was glad I was the aircraft commander. I was tired of my fate always being in someone else's hands. All Sandy could do was sit on his hands and switch the radios when needed. We were flying at 150 feet staying below the overcast. I had the radios on the Longview Tower frequency but was unable to get them. At 22 miles we finally made contact. I told the tower our situation and asked for a bearing and distance from their navigational aid. The tower replied by saying the field was closed but to bring it on in and they would have the crash crew standing by, then gave me distance and bearing from the radio beacon. At 15 miles I had Sandy go through the landing check list. When he got to the gear down item, Sandy reached for the handle and dropped the gear. They didn't come down.

"Shit!" I said. The landing gear works off the hydraulics. I thought they would free fall with no pressure on them. "Spears!"

"Yes, sir!"

"Can you see why they're not coming down?"

"Sir, I pushed on them and nothing moved. Let me see if I can find something to pry them down."

"Make it fast, Spears. I don't want to keep this thing in the air any longer than I have to."

Spears took apart the troop seat and pulled the metal bar out. He was able to get the landing gear to drop in place by forcing the metal bar behind the wheel and airframe, using the leverage to get it down. I told him that he had to somehow get the pins in the landing gear. I had to make a run-on landing, and with no pressure to hold the gear in place, it could collapse.

He replied, "Yes, sir. I think I can reach out and set the pins in place."

I was getting to like this kid more each second. "Make sure your harness is secure. Be safe, but let's get it done. I have the field in sight."

A few moments later he said, "The pins are in, and the gear is locked in place, sir."

I called the tower and told them Navy 128 was on final for emergency landing. "Tell your crash crew we'll be making a run-on landing."

The tower acknowledged and said, "They're ready."

I lined the helicopter up with the runway and maintained 60 knots right down to a few feet from the runway. I slowly lowered the collective, gradually coming back on the airspeed until I came in contact with the runway. Perfect, just like I had practiced. The last few months I had almost spent more time practicing emergencies than flying in normal flight. Flying the simulated emergencies gave me more of a challenge and it paid off. I was glad I never listened to LCDR Stuart's advice about waiting to handle the emergency when you got one.

I brought the helicopter to a stop on the runway and then had the crash crew tow us into the line. I reported to the squadron later that day and told them what was wrong with the helicopter. The XO said he would have the parts flown out the next day and again re-emphasized that they needed that helicopter at the factory. Now it was Sandy's time to go to work. We were going to be in Longview for at least two nights. It was his job to find some entertainment that would keep us busy evenings while we repaired the helicopter. Let's put it this way, Sandy drew women like bees to honey.

The next day only some of the parts arrived that we needed to fix the aircraft. I couldn't believe we didn't get what we needed. I sent a message with a detailed list of parts that were needed to get the helicopter back in the air. Using his own initiative, Petty Officer Spears found a machine shop at the airport and was able to make a new hydraulic line. He was one of the sharpest mechanics I had seen. There wasn't much he couldn't do to get a helicopter up and flying. I bet he could figure out how to change an engine on his own if he had to.

After taking apart the tail rotor Spears handed me the bearings; they were nothing but broken bits of metal. "How is the gearbox?" I asked.

"Fine, sir. I checked it out thoroughly. The chip detector in the gearbox had no metal on it. If it starts coming apart, it'll let us know."

We turned up the aircraft and ran it for about 30 minutes and then drained the gear box again. We didn't find any metal particles in the oil and decided it was good to go.

By the morning of the third day we were on our way to the East Coast and then up the Atlantic seaboard. We were inbound to Hunter Army Air Base in Savannah, Georgia when the engine oil pressure suddenly started to drop. I had Spears check for any oil leaks. He reported back, "We have a large oil leak down the starboard side of the aircraft all the way back to the tail pylon."

We were only a few minutes out of Hunter, so I made a decision to continue into the air field. I had done plenty of auto rotations in the Sea Sprite and felt it would be no problem to set it down. Sandy kept his eye on the oil pressure gauge and monitored the rest of the instruments.

It gave him something to do. I kept an eye out for a field to land in if we lost power. If it dropped to zero, we were setting down immediately. It was a race to the field to see if the oil pressure would hold. Although I felt I could handle anything the Sea Sprite threw at me, even I was beginning to lose confidence in this particular helicopter. I know we had to be breaking some kind of record for the most downing gripes on a Sea Sprite at one time.

We were able to make it to Hunter and I made another run-on landing, not knowing what the engine would do if I pulled in full power to make a hover landing. The landing went well and as we turned off the runway ground control cleared us to taxi into the line.

I was almost embarrassed to park the Navy helicopter on the Army's nice clean line. The sun bleached cement was pure white, and the helicopter was leaking engine oil and hydraulic fluid all over their nice white apron. After we shut down a couple of Army NCO's came over to look at the Navy helicopter. They didn't say a word. They just looked at the silhouette of oil and hydraulic fluid on the ground. I looked at them and said, "We always fly them this way. The oil helps to cut down on the wind resistance. Where can I send a message out?"

"Base Ops," replied one of the men.

Later that day I sent a two page message out to the XO. The entire message was a list of gripes and mechanical problems that were wrong with the helicopter, including a hole worn in the bottom of the engine oil sump tank from all the vibrations. I later followed up with a phone call to the XO. The XO wanted me to stay there until the helicopter was repaired. If they could get the major downing gripes fixed, he wanted me to take it the rest of the way to the factory. He actually said he didn't think he could get anyone else to fly it. It was either a compliment, or I was the only one stupid enough to fly the damn thing.

We tried for two days to weld the hole in the sump tank with no luck. It was a special lightweight alloy, and we didn't have the proper equipment to do the welding. It was going to be awhile before they could get a sump tank out to the aircraft. It wasn't something that usually failed and they didn't have any spares. The XO finally gave in and told us to come on home.

The next day we caught a commercial flight out of Savannah with a stop in Dallas. Unfortunately the trip must have taken a toll on Sandy. As soon as he got aboard the airliner he started tipping a few drinks. At first the stewardesses thought he was cute, women always thought Sandy was cute, it was his boyish charm. They even let him serve some of the meals. As he was going up and down the aisle, I could overhear Sandy telling the passengers about his hair-raising cross country and how he saved his crew. The stewardesses were all smiles and couldn't seem to get enough of his help, or his stories.

Sandy had called a buddy of his in Dallas. We had a two hour lay over, and his buddy was going to meet him for a few drinks. When the plane landed he took off on his own for a few hours. Sandy made it back just as they were closing the doors and when he got onboard, he was tanked. He was back aboard the plane, but Sandy was way past cute and well on his way to obnoxious. About 30 minutes into the flight I overheard the stewardess telling Sandy that if he didn't sit down they were going to turn back to Dallas and put him off the airplane. Sandy was not listening. We were all three sitting in separate seats, so I talked the stewardess into putting Spears next to Sandy so he could keep an eye on him. That seemed to work; Spears was a good kid, and he had his head screwed on straight.

I know! Why didn't I go back and sit with Sandy? Who wants to sit next to a drunk for almost three hours?

I was back in San Diego less than a week when the XO called me in and told me they needed me to go back and pick up the helicopter. The XO said, "We tried to get VRF-31 to ferry it the rest of the way, but they didn't want anything to do with the helicopter. Evidently one of their pilots went down and took a look at it."

I also found out from some of the maintenance department personnel that they had taken everything out of the helicopter that was any good and replaced it with what they had left. This didn't give me a tremendous sense of confidence that the helicopter would make it the rest of the way, but I was too young, or too stupid to say anything.

I asked, "When do I leave and who will be my crew?"

"LTJG DeFry and Petty Officer Spears will be your crew."

"Good, Spears is a genius at keeping that thing in the air."

"You leave tomorrow out of Lindberg at 0615."

I said, "Yes, sir," and turned to walk out the door. I needed to talk with Spears to make sure we'd have enough parts and everything we needed to get us to Connecticut. I liked LTJG DeFry; he was also a NAVCAD. He wouldn't be as good as Sandy on liberty, but he was a good stick.

When we got back to Hunter Army Air Base, one of the Army NCO's said he was glad to see someone come and take ownership of the helicopter. They were thinking about having it towed to the local junkyard. The Navy ground crew had replaced the sump tank and checked out the engine and that was about all they did. The remainder of the two pages of gripes were still there. Spears had anticipated some of it, and he told me that he needed a day to clean up some of the major gripes with the parts he brought with him. I was always amazed at how self-sufficient these guys were. How does the Navy find them? They don't pay them shit, their living conditions at times are less than desirable, and yet they stay in for the love of the job and the Navy.

We made it to Connecticut without anymore incidents. I was eager to get back to San Diego. I had met someone and wanted to spend some time with her before going to Fort Benning for gunship training. The next morning, bright and early, we were ready for an acceptance check flight. After we looked over the aircraft I gave the acceptance check list to Lenny to mark off the items as we went through them. I taxied out to the runway, pulled in a bunch of power and we jumped into the air. It was nice to have two engines. The UH-2C had plenty of power.

We were out about twenty minutes when the starboard engine's RPMs started fluctuating. I looked over the gauges and everything was fine except for the surging of the engine. I brought back the #2 engine to flight idle to see if I could get the engine to stop cycling. It didn't do any good, so I brought it back up to full power. We turned back toward the field and headed inbound. Just about that time the engine dropped off the line. I called the tower and told them we had just lost an engine and would be returning to the field. If I lost the other engine, I didn't have much practice auto rotating with the twin engine version. The autorotation characteristics were a lot different than the single engine.

I made another run-on landing. The twin engine was much heavier and didn't hover on one engine. We taxied back into the line, shut down the helicopter, got out and briefed the ground crew. When I got back into the maintenance office the KAMAN test pilot met me and asked what the problem was.

"I don't know," I said, "the engine started surging all over the place and then dropped off the line."

"I'm sure it's just a minor adjustment. They'll have it fixed in no time and you'll be on your way," replied the test pilot.

Later that day they told me the helicopter was ready for another acceptance flight. This time the KAMAN test pilot went with me instead of Lenny. As I rolled out on the runway we got a clearance to take off, and I made a high performance take-off and climb. At about 200 feet the test pilot put his hands on the controls and started to lower the collective, "We don't need to keep all that power," he said. I put it over into a steep bank and the test pilot again pulled it back to about a 15 degree bank.

"LT, this isn't a fighter. See there's nothing wrong with the aircraft." The test pilot wanted to go back to the field. "You already completed most of the checks on the last flight. You can see there's nothing wrong. Why don't we get back and you can get started on your way to San Diego?" I liked that idea, but was not sure about the helicopter.

After a few more minutes the test pilot finally talked me into landing. I knew what the game was. KAMAN didn't get paid until I signed off on the acceptance of the aircraft. I taxied back into the line and started to shut down the helicopter. Just as I brought both of the throttles back to ground idle, they both went berserk. Smoke started coming out everywhere. As I tried to get the rotor system shutdown I saw some of the ground crew running over with fire extinguishers. Out of the corner of my eye I caught the backside of the test pilot as he jumped out of the seat onto the ground and took off running. I thought to myself, "Holy shit! He knows something I don't." I grabbed everything and shut it down as quickly as I could, starting with the fuel.

When I got out of the helicopter I went over to the test pilot and asked him, "What the hell was that all about?"

The test pilot replied, "Nothing, I just wanted to help the ground crew."

He was obviously agitated but not as much as I was. I knew it was bullshit when the test pilot hit the ground he was headed for the hangar. The test pilot told me they had another aircraft coming off the line and it would be ready for an acceptance flight first thing in the morning. I said "Fine." I was eager to get out of there.

The next morning we went over the new helicopter and completed the acceptance flight without any problems. After signing the paperwork we headed west. The trip was uneventful right up to Texas. We had taken the southern route because of the weather. It seemed that Texas was just too big of a state to get through without anything going wrong. About 50 miles outside of Lubbock, we got an engine chip warning light. The Charlie model came with small electronic devices in the engine sump that would transmit a signal if they detected enough metal particles to set off the detector. The theory was that if the metal was detected in the engine oil that meant the engine might be coming apart, and it would give the pilot enough time to get the aircraft down before there was a catastrophic failure.

As soon as the warning light came on I started monitoring the engine instruments to see if there were any other indications that would confirm the engine was failing. At the same time I was looking for a landing sight. I knew I could make it to the Air Force base in Lubbock on one engine but didn't know if the engine would come apart. I continued looking at possible landing areas as we approached the air field. About five minutes passed when the decision to land was made for me. We got another chip warning light in the combining gearbox. This was not good! The combining gearbox drove the rotor system from the input of the two engines and had a completely separate oil system. There was a good chance something was coming apart up there and that was enough to cause me to set it down in a cane field in the middle of Texas on New Year's Day.

We were headed for the Dyess Air Force base in Lubbock. I shut down the helicopter and walked over to the closest farm house and introduced myself to the local farmer and asked to use his phone. I was really impressed with the Air Force. They were very professional and said they would dispatch a security team and transportation immediately. I was happy to hear that. If it were Navy, I would most likely be camping out inside the helicopter with my crew. I heard the January nights in Texas got real cold. The farmer and his wife were extremely hospitable, while we were waiting she came out with more food than we could possibly eat and we watched football games until the security team arrived.

When the security team arrived they briefed me on their procedures and said they would take care of everything, so we set off for Dyess AFB. When we reached the base I contacted the Squadron Duty Officer and told him to let the XO know what had happened. We needed a maintenance team out here to go over the aircraft. The next day, two Navy mechanics came up from NAS Dallas to look the helicopter over. Spears already had the plugs out and was looking at them when they arrived. A first class engine mechanic helped him drain all the oil out of the two systems, clean the chip detector plugs, and look over the entire helicopter for any signs of a catastrophic failure. It took another two days but the Mechanics wanted to replace the engine just to be safe. After replacing the engine we all agreed that I should turn the aircraft up and give it a hover check for about thirty minutes.

Hovering the aircraft would pull maximum power and place stress on any parts that may be close to failing. I completed the hover and shut down the helicopter. We finished up about 2100, and I decided it was not a good idea to take an unpredictable aircraft in bad weather at night into the air base. The ceiling had dropped to less than 400 feet and we would have to stay VFR all the way in, which meant we would be flying at the same altitude as the water towers and radio antennas. I wasn't familiar with the area and wasn't about to try it. I briefed the Air Force security team and told them we would be back out first thing in the morning. "No problem, sir, we'll look after the aircraft for you." Boy! I liked the way the Air Force did business.

The next morning we were at the helicopter, had it inspected and were ready to get airborne by 0830. The weather had gone from bad to worse. It was that freezing mist that so often rolls through the open plains in the Midwest during the winter months. The temperature was about one degree above freezing and there was lots of moisture in the air. After we finished the check list I pulled the aircraft up into a hover. As I brought the helicopter up into a hover the rotor downwash of 80 to 100 knots drastically dropped the air temperature around the helicopter. In less than a second all the windows in the helicopter were frozen over. I had no visual reference to the outside. There I sat in a ten foot hover completely on instruments.

I pulled it up into a little higher hover to get better ground clearance and hollered to Lenny to increase the window defrost to maximum. Unfortunately I had my door closed because of the cold weather. That meant I had no reference to the side either. Caught off guard I was all over the place. I told Spears to get my door open. Immediately, Spears had the door open and I finally had some visual reference to the ground. I set it back down on the ground and relaxed for a few minutes trying to let the adrenaline wear off. Within a few minutes the windows started to clear and we were ready to try it again. After hovering for a few minutes and regaining my composure, I cleared the area and passed close to the farm house waiving goodbye to the couple that opened their home to us. We were headed for Dyess AFB.

The weather was really bad. We were less than 100 feet above the ground all the way into Dyess. We were actually looking up at the water tower as we passed the edge of town. We reached the air field without any further incidents. It never ceased to amaze me, no matter what you planned for, there were was always something unexpected. Especially in helicopters, every landing zone, every situation seems to be different. As we reached the air base, I landed and shut down the helicopter. We went into base operations to check the weather. I wasn't about to spend anymore time flying in that shit than I had to. I couldn't get above it, the tops were too high, and I couldn't fly in it, the icing conditions were too severe, and I sure as hell couldn't fly under it.

I decided to wait it out. It was time to see what Lubbock had to offer. It took two days for the weather to clear. At this point I had been on the road three out of the last four weeks. I was starting to understand what "get home itis" was all about. "Get home itis" was a condition that killed pilots. In order to get home, they would take chances that were not in their favor. I was not going to be one of those pilots, or was I?

On the third day the weather had cleared a little but the ceiling was still about 300 feet. Visibility was good. I got a briefing from the Air Force meteorologist. He described the front as passing through and about 30 miles to the west it was clear with no clouds. It would be my first of many inaccurate weather briefings. I decided to take a chance and leave beautiful downtown Lubbock and its memories behind. We got our gear together, did a pre-flight on the helicopter and headed west. About fifteen miles out I handed the aircraft over to Lenny and started going over the map. The visibility was not as good as it was at Dyess. We were cruising at 200 feet and about 125 knots trying to make up some time.

As I looked up from the map I started to suggest that we reduce the forward airspeed a little because of the visibility. I didn't and looked back down at the map. As I came up from the map a second time, I looked out and all I saw was the ground going up into the overcast. Holy Shit! I grabbed the controls just as Lenny pulled the nose up. I said, "I got it!" I had no idea how high the hill was, but we kept a steep climbing right hand turn to about 3,000 feet where I was sure there were no obstructions. We were completely on instruments now. Trying to do a rotor over on instruments was a feat in itself. Now I was trying to complete a climb out to get above the obstructions without getting disoriented. I had Lenny quickly switch to Dyess tower and make sure we still had their radio beacon dialed in. We were alive and not all over the side of a hill. We got a clearance back into Dyess.

As Dyess picked us up on radar, we were vectored direct to the field. I didn't want to spend anymore time in icing conditions than I had to. The ice was already building up on the edges of the wind screen and I had no idea of the build-up on the rotor blades. We should require meteorologists to be pilots. They would have a better appreciation for what pilots have to go through when they screw up. I made a mental note not to trust any meteorologist again. If we ever survived these cross countries, I would have a hell of a lot of experience crammed into a very short period of time. That old saying I learned in Saufley about luck running out before you gain the experience you need kept popping into my head. I got the feeling that getting this assignment during this time of year was not an honor. The XO couldn't find anyone else crazy enough to go. At 23 I was still invincible and never thought about failing.

We remained in Dyess for another night and the weather finally cleared up the next day. We made it the rest of the way to NALF Imperial Beach without any further problems. That night I was in my apartment when the phone rang. It was the XO.

"Al, I'm glad you made it back okay." The XO said he had a problem. The only other qualified pilot had cut his hand and was grounded. He needed me to go back and get another helicopter. I was pissed and let the XO know it. It was my self-destruct mode that I sometimes slipped into when I wasn't prepared.

"That's bullshit XO. You have 300 fucking pilots in that squadron and only two of us are qualified in the Charlie model?" It was not a good conversation, and it ended when the XO said he wanted to see me in his office first thing in the morning.

As hung up the phone I realized I didn't make any friends that night and decided to go get the helicopter from the factory. I knew it was that piece of shit on which I did the initial acceptance flight and had all the engine problems. Up to this point I had not made it all the way across without major problems. I hoped they got all the bugs out of it before I got there. As I walked into the XO's office that morning, I said, "When do I leave and who is my crew?"

"LTJG DeFry and Petty Officer Smith. You leave tomorrow morning. Your tickets are over in Admin."

I hoped this would be my last trip for awhile. Only I could end up on the XO's shit list by helping the squadron out. The smart ones were sitting in the O'Club at happy hour, telling the XO what a great guy he was.

We got into Connecticut that same day and arrived at the KAMAN facility the following morning. I wanted to get out of there as quickly as possible, but had reservations about the helicopter I was going to have to ferry to San Diego. I told the crew to look the helicopter over and we would run a thorough acceptance check. The flight was uneventful and everything seemed to checkout fine. The weather was starting to worsen and I wanted to get out of there that afternoon. We filed the flight plan over the telephone and jumped in the helicopter. The snow flurries started just as I lifted into a hover. It was well below freezing so I didn't have to be as concerned about icing. The ceiling was about 1500 feet. We wouldn't have any problem staying under the overcast. I wasn't familiar with flying in snow and wasn't ready for the effects of the snow falling.

As we departed the field the snow fall increased. The meteorologist played a key roll in my decision, again. The weather was supposed to clear as we headed southwest. The squadron policy on all ferry flights out of the factory was to stay VFR. It was also mine, since I didn't have much confidence in the Charlie model. As we turned southwest and headed out over the water the snow continued to fall. They were still calling the ceiling at 1500 feet but with the heavy snow we were in, we had no visual reference to anything. It was what they called a white out. We were well below the overcast but IFR. I had not heard of this type of weather condition and it was not the time to learn about it for the first time.

I was glad I had Lenny make a backup flight plan using the NAVAIDS on the IFR map. I did it for good reason; I did not completely trust meteorologists anymore. I knew he had a 50/50 chance of being wrong and I don't believe in luck. We called into the air traffic control center and filed in the air. We stayed IFR for the next hour before the weather started to clear. I was exhausted and cold. The floor heater wasn't working and my toes were numb. I passed the controls over to Lenny so I could get my bearings and take a look at the map. I did not want to go through that type of weather again. As I sat back, I hoped the rest of the squadron personnel were having a nice holiday season. At least Lenny would be qualified in the twin engine when we got back to San Diego.

The rest of the flight went without incident until we got over Alamogordo, New Mexico. I had decided to try to cut some time off the flight so I headed diagonally across the United States. The standard flight plan for that time of year was to get south as quickly as possible before you ran into bad weather and then head west. The new flight path took us right over the Continental Divide. The sky was clear with a full moon and millions of stars. We were cruising at 9500 feet. We couldn't go above 10,000 feet legally without oxygen, so we were navigating through some of the lower passes. It was 2130 at night and we had already put in a long day. I was letting Lenny get as much stick time as possible.

Lenny had the aircraft trimmed out at about 115 knots and the air was calm with the exception of a little turbulence coming over the mountains. I sat back in my seat, closed my eyes and said to myself, tomorrow night we'll be in San Diego. I didn't know how much time had gone by, but the next thing I knew, the helicopter start bucking like we were on the back of a wild bull. I reached for the controls out of instinct and looked over at Lenny. I then came down to the instruments. It hit me instantly. Lenny had the collective pulled in for maximum power. We were doing almost 125 knots at 9500 feet. I knew what it was. I immediately pushed the collective to the bottom. As soon as that happened the violent thrashing stopped.

We had gone into retreating blade tip stall. I had seen it at Ellyson Field when I snapped the TH-13 over on its side. I almost ended up on my back. Lenny was trying to cut off a few minutes of flight time and was pushing the envelope a little. As a helicopter goes up in altitude the air gets finer so you need to reduce forward airspeed. If you don't the blades will need to increase their angle of attack to try to maintain the airspeed until they stall out. We discussed it a little. Lenny had never seen anything like that before and had no idea what was going on. I told him about my screw up at Ellyson field. If you live through your screw-ups, you become an experienced aviator.

We arrived in San Diego the next day and I decided to put in for a week of leave before I headed out to Fort Benning. I had already had enough emergencies to last a life time, and

I had only been in the fleet for a little over one year. What would be next?

Fort Benning, GA Gunship Training

I was impressed with the training the Army provided. The ground school was a piece of cake, but thorough. The UH-1 was much simpler than the Sea Sprite. It was a good reliable helicopter, and I liked the flight characteristics. We started our initial flight training in the UH-1D and finished up with the UH-1C. The D model was the slick version or troop carrier and the C model was the gunship version. The Seawolves would fly the UH-1B. The Army had traded the Navy some old beat up UH-1B's for a few P-2V's for a special operation along the DMZ in Vietnam. I don't know who got the worst of the deal. After flying the H-2, I liked the idea of flying a reliable rugged helicopter.

We were in the initial part of our training. A lieutenant and I had been assigned to an Army warrant officer for the flight basics. We were on our third flight when the warrant officer commented on the fact that it was nice to have experienced pilots to train; it made his job a lot easier. The new Army helicopter pilots kept him on his toes. The warrant was sitting in the co-pilot seat, and I was flying the helicopter. The other student was in back, so we could swap out halfway through the flight and not have to return to the air field. We were making rough terrain landings. When the Army did rough terrain practice they literally did it anywhere they could find a landing zone, as long as the Army owned the land. I liked that idea; most of my experience with the Navy up to then was in small prepared outlying fields.

I was on my fourth approach and the warrant was looking out the side window completely relaxed with his foot propped up on the instrument panel. As I adjusted the attitude for the approach, the controls jammed. I pulled on them to see if I could free them but nothing worked; they were frozen. Fortunately the attitude was already set for the landing before they jammed. I didn't want to alarm the warrant, he might overreact. We were on short final, so I keyed the intercom and said. "Now, I don't want you to get excited but, the controls are jammed."

Before I could say anything else the warrant jumped out of his skin and grabbed for the controls. Two seconds later the helicopter came in contact with the ground. It was a bumpy ride but after a few hundred feet the helicopter came to rest, rocking for and aft on its skids. We were on the ground.

I came up over the intercom, "We were lucky they froze when they did." If the controls jammed in another flight condition we would have had to fly around until we could figure out a way to get the aircraft safely down and we had less than an hour of fuel onboard. The warrant tried to free the controls with no luck and decided to shut the helicopter down after calling for maintenance support. When the maintenance personnel arrived they took the floor of the helicopter out and discovered the heater duct had come loose and had fallen into the control linkages, jamming them. The maintenance crew finished fixing the helicopter at about 1930 and we flew the aircraft back to the line. We finished the basic flight training and by the end of the week we were in the gunships.

I loved the guns and the rockets. I was meant to do this. While others seemed to be happy with just having the rockets hit in the general vicinity, I was ready to bet on hitting the targets. What firepower they had for that day! Anyone that stuck their head up while all that furry was coming at them had to be crazy. The Army gunships carried four M-60 machine guns, two on each side. The co-pilot controlled them. Each door gunner had an M-60, and the helicopter also carried 14 rockets, seven on each side. It was something to see when everything was going off at the same time. Flying gunships was the ultimate in flying helicopters; there was nothing better. I finished the training in less than four weeks and headed back to the Naval Amphibious Base in Coronado, California for Vietnamese language school.

The school was only two weeks and I ended up the top in my class, whatever that was worth. Two weeks of language school didn't teach you that much, but it seemed to come easy to me. The last night in the O'Club before departing I met a young Navy SEAL at the bar. We got along great. I told him that I was a helicopter pilot and that we might see each other in country. As the beer continued to flow the SEAL looked over at me with a serious look on his face and said. "Tell me, how bad were your grades?"

In those days helicopter pilots in the Navy were treated like third class citizens. The jet pilots were at the top and supposedly, the pilots that couldn't hack it got helicopters. I tried to explain that I was in a class of 14 students and they needed 13 helicopter pilots to meet the quota for that quarter. It made no difference. At the same time I had mixed emotions. After seeing some of the pilots on my first tour, I wasn't so sure the SEAL wasn't right. I liked this guy. He was young, straight-forward, full of confidence and didn't bullshit. I thought it must be challenging to be a SEAL. I knew I had the physical conditioning, but hated the idea of cold weather and cold water.

We parted by shaking hands and said we would meet again in country. I headed up to Los Angeles to say goodbye to my parents and catch a plane to San Francisco. The Tet Offensive had been all over the news for the past couple of weeks. My parents expressed very little emotion, and there were no discussions about Vietnam. At the end of the week they took me to the airport in Los Angeles. My father pulled the car up to the curb and opened the trunk. I pulled my bag out, and we shook hands. My mother waived goodbye through the side window as they pulled away from the curb.

I stood there a minute watching them drive off and reflecting on what just took place. I was headed back for my second tour and going to land right in the middle of the Tet Offensive. I knew my parents were a little distant, but that departure was a little lacking even by their standards. I was the least favorite of four sons, and I always tried to please them. I was the only one to play sports and graduate from high school. I even scored six touchdowns in one game and my father never even acknowledged that he went to the game or told me it was a good game.

The nicest thing they ever said to me was, "Why don't you stay in school, maybe your younger brother will see you graduate and do the same." They made a few other comments but the one that probably cut the deepest is when my older brother died in a construction accident. After the funeral my father got drunk and stood there in the middle of the kitchen and said, "Why couldn't it be you? I never liked you. Why did it have to be Paul?" Even after that I still tried to do everything I could to make him proud of me. I shrugged it off as I usually did, turned and walked inside to check my bag at the counter.

The flight over was gruesome, a short flight up to San Francisco, bus over to Travis AFB and then Flying Tigers all the way into Saigon, with stops in Alaska and Japan. As the bus entered Travis AFB, I saw protestors for the first time not on TV. It was difficult for those who were going to Vietnam to fight for God, country, and mom's apple pie. Seeing those assholes out there holding signs, jeering and flipping the bird as we drove by was a little disheartening. I could give a shit. I was on a journey and prepared to endure the risks in order to find out who was waiting on the other side. All I knew was, I was a damn good helicopter pilot and could handle the H-1 better than anyone I knew.

I had been watching the news, I thought my flight might be delayed because of the Tet Offensive. It was all they talked about on the news. Thousands of Viet Cong had infiltrated Saigon and the outlying provinces. They had no idea what their real strengths were; everything was mass confusion. The news was reporting the airfield at Tan Son Nhut was under attack and there was fighting all around the airfield. They had even seized part of the U.S. Embassy in Saigon. I wondered how they would get me out to my squadron, if the airfield was under attack. I wouldn't be any good to anyone if I didn't have a gunship strapped to me.

I had plenty of time to sit on an airplane and imagine what might be in store for us when we landed in Saigon. I was luckier than most. The life and death realities of fear, pain, excitement and doubt that most people feel seemed to be distant to me. I was so driven to find out who I was, it outweighed everything else.

Chapter Five
The Seawolves

Helicopter Attack (Light) – 3

    I was beat. We were on final approach to Tan Son Nhut. The Flying Tigers Boeing 707 had us packed like sardines. The trip from L.A. to Saigon took 27 hours. I didn't know they could cram so many seats in an aircraft of that size and still take off. As I sat by the window I could see the countryside as we came out of the clouds. The landscape was beautiful with the exception of the bomb craters. All of the tropical vegetation reminded me of the Philippines. As we approached the airfield I noticed the steep descent. It was something I had never seen a commercial airliner do before. I learned later that Charlie still had control of some of the ground at both ends of the runway. The rate of descent and approach angle continued to get most of my attention.
    As the pilot flared, we hit the runway and the 707 became airborne again. We hit hard; the pilot flew the aircraft right into the runway. As the aircraft climbed back into the air you could feel the pilot fighting to maintain control. I was sitting by the window, and as I looked out I saw the aircraft

rolling to the left. It was like it was in slow motion, the only thing that went through my mind was, shit! I didn't even make it in country before I bought it! The wing looked like it scraped the ground as the aircraft rolled back the other way and hit the runway again. The airplane gyrated wildly for the next couple of seconds while the pilot continued to fight for control. As the airplane finally settled onto the runway I could feel the pilot engage the reverse thrusters to slow us down. The landing sure made me forget about how tired I was.

As we taxied in and got off the plane, people were scurrying in every direction. They weren't running but they were certainly moving a lot faster than normal. Jeeps and trucks were going in all directions and you could hear gunfire in the distance. The first building we were directed into looked like an old hangar. As I looked up I could see the larges hole in the roof from what I assumed were mortar rounds. I was eager to try out my Vietnamese on one of the locals.

I walked up to a small thin man that was stacking bags from the flight on a rack across the room. I pointed at my bag and spoke a few words in Vietnamese. The elderly man turned and looked at me as though I had just stepped off the moon. This was not going to be easy. The Vietnamese language is a monosyllable, bi-tonal language. The meaning changed depending on what inflection you used when you spoke the words. I would learn that the instructors back in Coronado would understand me a hell of a lot better than the Vietnamese. I also found out from the military police assigned to guard the airport that we were only the second commercial airliner to land since the Tet Offensive started.

As we were loaded into an Air Force bus I could see the gunships overhead. Off in the distance some jets were periodically making low passes over the city. They were just far enough away to where I couldn't see the results of their strikes. As we headed to the hotel I could see the motorcycles and small cabs going in all directions. There was nothing uniform about driving in Vietnam. Everyone seemed to be going somewhere but it certainly was not like the States. Anywhere there was an opening it was fair game for anyone who had a vehicle small enough to fit into the opening. The smells were distinct and unlike anything I had ever experienced, even in Bangkok and the Philippines. The city was fascinating, most of the architecture was from the French prior to WW II. I couldn't absorb it all fast enough.

I was scheduled to fly out to my squadron in Vung Tao the following day. That night I would stay in a hotel in Saigon. As I checked in, I saw a lieutenant that I recognized from the training command, and I went over to say hello. Ron was attached to NAVFORV, the unit that would be flying me out to Vung Tao. After a few minutes of small talk he suggested I get some rest and we would meet for dinner, have a few drinks and catch up on the past 18 months.

I checked in and went up to my room. The hotel room was fascinating. Everything was right out of the movie *Casablanca*, from the old plantation shutters on the windows to the fan in the middle of the room, slowly turning one revolution every couple of seconds. The water in the shower only trickled out; it was barely enough to get you wet. I loved what I was seeing. I felt like I was in an old Errol Flynn movie. After resting for a few hours I headed down to meet Ron and his co-pilot in the bar. During dinner Ron went over what had taken place during the Tet Offensive and what they expected from Charlie over the next couple of weeks.

Charlie still held a large section of the city. As soon as we started putting in an air strike to take him out, Charlie would leave that section of the city and come up someplace else. By the time they completed the air strike the entire area was leveled, which didn't endear us to the local population. After dinner Ron suggested we go up to his room to watch the fireworks. He was on the top floor and had a good view of he city. As we entered the room Ron went over to the window and pulled open the shutters. "Grab some chairs and I'll get some drinks." Ron handed out some glasses and poured each of us a glass of bourbon, no ice. Ice was a little hard to get.

As the night went on we gazed out the window with our feet propped up on the ledge and watched the gunships and attack aircraft putting in strikes in suspected enemy locations. With the tracers from the guns and bomb blasts going off against the night sky, it was like we were watching a huge fireworks show. You were in a war zone, but not part of the battle. We watched the fighting for several hours and traded sea stories until the bottle of Jim Beam was gone. I decided to call it quits. Ron said we would be leaving early in the morning on his standard log run, and he would drop me off in Vung Tao half way through his run. I headed for my room to get some rest.

We met in the lobby the next morning and headed for the air field. By 0800 we were airborne and flying over the city in an old UH-34. I hadn't been in one since the training command. Ron gave me a set of headphones so he could tell me what was going on during our flight over the city. As we passed over certain areas of the city he would explain, "We can't fly over that area. Charlie still owns it and we might get shot down."

We could see pockets of gunfire, clouds of smoke from previous attacks and the gunships rolling in off in the distance. As we circumnavigated the hot areas in the city we would periodically watch another air strike being put in by the jets. This is not what I expected; they seemed to be street fighting door to door in downtown Saigon. There were no battle lines. You didn't know where the next shot was coming from.

As we cleared the city and headed south, I could see the tropical landscape with bomb craters scattered throughout the countryside. We made a couple of stops along the way to drop off mail, parts and supplies to a couple of the outposts and then headed on to Vung Tao. If anything could be described as a Vietnamese beach resort, it was Vung Tao. Located on the coast looking out into the South China Sea, the French used it as a resort before they were chased out by the Viet Cong. It was nothing like Saigon. Fishing was the predominant industry along with a few restaurants and bars. The Seawolves shared part of the air field with the Army. As he landed, Ron pointed out of the cockpit window in the direction of the Seawolf hangar and told me he had three months left in country. If I made it back to Saigon, we'd have dinner. I waived and headed out to see where I was to report.

After checking in with the squadron admin officer, I was told that I would be in Vung Tao only a couple of days for indoctrination before they sent me out to one of the detachments. The detachments usually consisted of two helicopters, and were generally assigned to a small base near a hamlet or strategic point with a small airstrip or a helo pad. Some were aboard the LST's (Landing Ship Transports). The airstrip was typically made of PSP and about the length of a football field. The PSP was a series of metal plates with holes in them linked together that allowed the engineers to come in and establish an airstrip in a matter of days. In fact the entire runway at Vung Tao was made up of the PSP although it was long enough to land much larger aircraft. After delivering my orders a young Petty Officer was assigned to take me downtown to the squadron BOQ.

I checked in at the BOQ, headed for my room and started to unpack. After I was done, I went downstairs to the Seawolf bar. There were a couple of officers sitting there drinking a beer. I went up and introduced myself. Everyone seemed to be upbeat and very positive, even with what was happening in the midst of the current offensive. As I ordered a beer, LCDR Price introduced himself. He was an older man, a Limited Duty Officer (LDO), a mustang that had worked his way up through the ranks. He was the squadron Maintenance Officer (MO). As he spoke he added that the Seawolves had more purple hearts than any unit in the Navy. For some reason I did not find that statistic very appealing. A purple heart, as I saw it, was a sharp shooter's medal for the other side and that was the last thing I wanted.

As the other pilots came in from the airfield the night was filled with rounds of beers and plenty of stories of the exploits of the Seawolves. As sea stories go, if it doesn't sound exciting enough the first time, it usually got better the third, fourth, and fifth times it was told. I did find out that I should make Helicopter Aircraft Commander (HAC) in a very short time. I was considered second tour and had over 800 hours under my belt. They had plenty of nuggets coming right out of the training command that would be co-pilot for a good part of their tours. I was happy to hear that; I wanted to make HAC in the shortest time possible. I had gotten used to being the pilot in command and didn't want to sit second seat for very long.

The indoctrination consisted of a few lectures on tactics, flight characteristics of the UH-1B, and a briefing of the detachments with an overview of what to expect out in the field. The tactics were a little thin; there wasn't much written about helicopter tactics. Back in those days they had just put guns on the medical evacuation helicopters and found out how effective they were. They were sort of writing the tactics manual as they went. After a few mail and parts runs out to the detachments, I was ready to be assigned. The afternoon of the fourth day I was told that I was to report to Detachment Two, in Nha Be. The detachment was to protect the shipping traffic in and out of Saigon as well as support the Riverine Forces in and around the Rung Sat Special Zone and T-ten area.

Detachment Two, Nha Be

The Rung Sat Special Zone was a large area of thick jungle, triple canopy. It was believed that there were heavy concentrations of Viet Cong and NVA in that area. The jungle was so thick that no army could get through it, which made it just about impossible to sweep the area. Almost everything had to be done by water. Above the Rung Sat was the T-ten area. Another bad news area with heavy jungle growth, but it was a little more accessible. There was also believed to be a heavy concentration of enemy forces in the area. Later in the year I would discover a complete Viet Cong city concealed by the heavy jungle.

The next morning I was at the airfield early. The flight took only about 40 minutes. Nha Be was half way between Saigon and Vung Tao, right on the shipping channel. As we approached Nha Be, I could see the small base and the air strip sitting right out on the point of two large rivers. Nha Be was home to the Seawolves of HAL-3, Detachment Two. The small base was located at the intersection of the Long Tau shipping channel to Saigon and the large Soi Rap River. The entire base couldn't have been larger than 900 yards by 1,500 yards at the widest points. That included a small 200 foot PSP runway with four revetments for the helicopters to park. The revetments were areas of pilled sandbags and 50 gallon drums filled with sand to protect the helicopters from mortar attacks. The other two revetments were for transient aircraft that came in and out of there on temporary assignments.

After checking in and getting settled in my room in the barracks where the officers stayed, I returned to the detachment spaces. It was a small building with eight bunks for the duty crew. There were also tables and chairs for the duty crew and a few desks for the OINC, Operations and Maintenance. Everything happened in this one building. They fondly referred to as the Seawolf Hooch. As I entered, Lt. McKenzie, the Operations Officer looked up and said, "Welcome aboard. I already have you on the flight schedule for tomorrow."

"Boy, they don't waste time," I thought. "That's great. I'm here to fly not sit around and play cards."

"You'll be LCDR Beard's co-pilot and LCDR Aldridge will

be the Fire Team Leader (FTL)." After a few introductions, I walked outside to take a look at the two Navy UH-1B's sitting in the revetments.

The flight crews were on a 24 hour shift. The shift was from 0800 in the morning to 0800 the following morning. There were two crews, give or take an extra pilot or door gunner. That meant we had duty every other day. That was fine with me; there was absolutely nothing to do on the base except watch a movie, workout, go to the chow hall, or drink. I arrived at the Seawolf Hooch at 0700 the next morning. The crew briefing started at 0730 and they switched crews 30 minutes later. Part of the brief was to go to the base command center to get an update of what was happening in the area. The FTL and the pilot in command of the wing ship usually went to the brief, depending on the OINC's policy the co-pilots would also go. I was invited along to see what took place in the command center.

Two LCDR's in one detachment; I had heard that the LCDR's rotated through the detachments often. It seems every helicopter LCDR that had aspirations of higher rank had to get time as an OINC of a combat unit. The Seawolves were a 100% all volunteer unit. Most of the JO's were there for various reasons, and some were not career minded, including me. I was too busy living in the moment to plan for the future. There was an obvious difference between the thinking of the LCDR's who were there for their careers and the JO's, at least those who didn't plan to make the Navy a career. For me, this was an adventure.

My childhood hero was John Wayne. At 5'10" I was too small to fill his shoes, so I started smoking cigars to make up for the height difference. As the newest pilot in the detachment I was assigned the call sign of Seawolf 28. To get the boot pilot some experience, two Harassment and Interdiction (H&I) flights were scheduled for that day. H&I flights were sorties flown over known or possible areas of VC activity. They would usually scout the area first for any enemy movement and if none was discovered a rocket and machine gun attack was placed in a strategic area. This helped with crew coordination and kept Charlie hiding and guessing. Every once in awhile you would get a secondary explosion. The triple canopy jungle made it almost impossible to spot anything on the ground in those areas where there was heavy jungle. Our best missions were flown at night when Charlie made most of his moves.

Later that night the crew ate chow and went to the movie, which was pretty standard on a duty night. The movie was shown in a small building about 100 yards from the runway. The helicopters were all readied for a quick launch in case of a mortar attack, or a scramble. In 1968, Nha Be at times was getting hit a couple of times a week. Charlie would set up and drop two or three mortar rounds on the compound. If the helicopters didn't get airborne right away, Charlie would adjust and drop in a couple more rounds. If the helos could get airborne quickly enough, they could sometimes catch the flashes from the mortar tubes, so Charlie wouldn't chance a second attack. The last thing Charlie wanted was two fully armed gunships rolling in on his position.

As luck would have it, at about 2115, the first round came in and the base siren sounded almost simultaneously. The first round hit pretty close to the runway. Charlie's favorite targets were the helicopters. That meant when the rounds came in, your job was to run directly toward the area they were targeting. You had anywhere from 3 to 5 minutes to get airborne before Charlie adjusted and sent the next mortars in, if he had them. One reason for the time delay was the forward spotter had to radio corrections to the mortar crew. That meant the VC spotter could be in the Vietnamese village adjacent to the air strip.

As the siren sounded the whole Seawolf crew jumped from their seats in the movie and headed for the door. It was a dark, overcast night with very little lighting on the base. As we reached the door I took off on a dead sprint. All this took a matter of seconds. Halfway to the runway the second mortar came in, and the next thing I knew I was on the ground with the wind knocked out of me. I was sure the second mortar landed right on my chest. As I struggled for air, I tried to pull myself up. Another mortar hit at the other end of the runway. As my vision and head cleared I could see I wasn't hurt. I was in a fucking ditch! In the dark I had run full speed into a large ditch, hit the other side and it had knocked all the wind out of me. Once I realized that I wasn't hurt, I pulled myself out of the ditch and made it to the helicopter as quickly as I could. I didn't tell a soul what had happened, and hoped that nobody saw the incident.

We immediately got airborne and patrolled the area with reports coming in from the command center as to where they thought the rounds came from. We flew around checking out all the reports with no success. We put in a strike in the suspected area and returned to base, refueled and prepared the helos for a quick launch. After the adrenaline slowed down we each turned into one of the eight bunks in the ready room. The mortar attacks became a common event. It was amazing what you got used to. Before the first week of combat action was completed I would get a lesson in combat tactics from the two LCDR's that almost ended my tour prematurely.

It was duty day number three at Nha Be. I was still teamed up with the two LCDR's. We had flown one patrol early that morning and were on standby. About 1420 that afternoon we were scrambled in support of a rocket attack on one of the large oil tankers coming up the channel into Saigon. The area of the attack was directly across the river, only a few minutes away by air. Nha Be had been strategically placed on the main shipping channel to quickly respond to the attacks on the shipping traffic. As we came into the area the FTL descended to 200 feet and slowed to 60 knots.

I was the new kid on the block, but I knew this was not a good idea. Even with the couple of days of training I received in Vung Tao, flying in this envelope was just asking for trouble. I reached down and rested my hand on the armament switch. I had not been told to go hot yet, which should have been automatic and I knew if anything happened the first thing would be to return fire. At that altitude we wouldn't have much time to react. I watched the lead ship slowly crisscross back and forth. I felt like a sitting duck, and there was nothing I could do about it without looking like a chicken shit! It was the *Bon Homme Richard* all over again. I was sitting there as co-pilot, and my fate was in the hands of someone else who didn't seem to know what he was doing. I wanted my HAC designation.

We spent about 15 minutes flying back and forth over the suspected area of the rocket launches. All of a sudden LCDR Aldridge came over the radio in an excited voice, "We're hit! We're hit! We're going in!"

I immediately said, "You're hot" as I pushed the arming switch forward. What happened next I would not have expected from an experienced pilot. LCDR Beard pushed the nose over from 200 feet and dove directly at the area beneath the lead helicopter. I started shooting up the place with the flex guns in the suspected area of the enemy fire hoping to keep their heads down. As we passed through 100 feet Beard fired all 14 rockets into the area. By this time we were headed right for the tops of the trees. He had just blown up everything in front of us, trees, stumps, and rocks, anything that was in the area. The helicopter continued on its descent toward the jungle and the tops of the trees. We then flew right through all the debris.

As the debris hit the helicopter it cracked the windscreen and shattered the chin bubble. There was so much debris that for a second it looked like we had just flown into the ground. At that point the helicopter felt like it was coming apart. We were still flying as we skimmed across the tops of the trees, but for how long, I didn't know. As the pilot tried to maintain control of the aircraft and gain a little altitude the FTL came back over the radio, "I think I can make it back to base."

Beard didn't say a word, the helicopter was shaking so bad it took everything he had to keep it level. I knew we couldn't set it down there, it was all jungle and Charlie would probably be waiting for us. Beard turned in the direction of the lead helicopter. The closest and safest landing sight was Nha Be, directly across the shipping channel. It was only about four kilometers away, but it was the longest four kilometers I had ever flown.

As we reached the end of the runway LCDR Beard set it down right there and shut down the helicopter. I said to myself as I unbuckled and climbed out. "I am going to make aircraft commander as soon as humanly possible." I didn't need someone else killing me with stupid stunts. Charlie was already trying to do that. In the past year and a half I had seen enough stupid stunts to last me a lifetime. I promised myself that I would never put my crew in a situation like that, unless there was no other way. This was a crap shoot. If I went in for an attack, I wanted everything in my favor, as much as possible.

As we inspected the helicopter it looked like it was a total loss., I didn't see how we could make it flyable again. There wasn't one piece of the helicopter that didn't have a dent or crack in it. Even the drive shaft leading to the tail rotor had a huge dent in it, over half the diameter of the shaft was caved in. It was a testament to the durability of the Huey. How the engine intake escaped ingesting some of the debris was nothing more than a miracle. If the engine would have taken some of the rocks and stumps it would have come apart immediately, and we would have crashed right where the last rocket hit. The only thing I could think of was we were nose down and everything had to pass through the rotor system to get to the engine. The Army came in and towed the helicopter off. I don't know what became of it.

Rush to become Aircraft Commander

The next day I asked LCDR Aldridge what I had to do to

get my HAC papers. I wanted to be on the fast track. The OINC told me to talk with the Ops Officer, Lt. McKenzie. Lt. McKenzie was a sharp naval officer, a good stick with plenty of common sense. He knew why I wanted to know about HAC qualifications without asking. The one thing I had going for me was that both of the LCDR's would be rotating soon, and they were not that eager to get back into the air. Also, several of the experienced pilots were due to rotate back to the States over the next couple of months including the lieutenant. Less than a week later the OINC got orders back down to Vung Tao. I had my HAC papers in just over a month from the time I arrived in country. At 23 years old I was confident and always pushed the flight envelope of the UH-1B. LTJG Stanley and I were rotating in and out of the HAC slot until Rick rotated back to the States, which was about a month away. He was a good pilot and would be missed. He was going to head down to Vung Tao the last two weeks of his tour. Nobody liked to fly right up to the last day, something about bad karma and buying it on your last week in country.

I made HAC just as the rainy season started, and it could really rain in Vietnam. At times, the rain came down horizontally and in buckets. Charlie was using the opportunity to make a few moves. Close air support during this type of weather was difficult if not impossible at times. We had just finished a flight before the rain started and had switched seats. I was now in the co-pilot for the next flight. As luck would have it we got scrambled in support of an Army outpost that was being overrun. Army support was not available. The Army didn't give their aircrew much instrument training when they turned out their pilots. They were great sticks in VFR conditions but some of them were a little uncomfortable in bad weather under IFR conditions. Rick was sitting in the right seat and had signed for the aircraft. We were flying wing on Lt. McKenzie as the FTL. The ceiling was less than 200 feet and it was raining harder than a cow pissing on a flat rock.

As we switched radio frequencies we could hear the shooting and explosions. They were in a bad situation; the Army had several advisors in a compound with a bunch of ARVN soldiers. When the Seawolves arrived Charlie was climbing the fences that surrounded the small compound. The fighting was intense and my adrenalin really got going when I heard the Army advisor on the radio. You could hear him shooting the VC with his pistol as he keyed the mike asking for support. It's difficult not to get worked up when you hear someone in a combat situation say, "Tell my wife and kids, I love them." Yes, it really happens and not just in the movies. The advisor told us the VC were inside the compound and they were being overrun. As we approached we could see small explosions throughout the compound. To attack the compound during the daylight hours was crazy, even during a heavy thunderstorm.

As we rolled in we were sitting ducks at such a low altitude but there was no other way. It was worth taking the chance and I had complete confidence in Lt. McKenzie and Rick. We came in hot with guns blazing at about 125 feet in order to stay below the thunderstorms and heavy clouds. We caught Charlie by surprise. They did not expect to see the Seawolves as we strafed the fences. The complexion of the battle changed almost immediately as the helicopters unleashed all their fire power. Charlie had taken over the pagoda at the far end of the compound and opened up on the lead helicopter. Rick immediately turned toward the pagoda and the two door gunners and I opened up on it. Rick pickled off a whole salvo of rockets and most of them hit in and around the pagoda. An M-60 will put out about 550 rounds per minute; I had four of them on the flex guns and one door gunner had one. The crew chief usually manned the twin 30 CAL's in the wing ship. That made it close to 3,000 rounds a minute going into the pagoda. It wasn't long before the VC in the pagoda were silenced. The weather was really hampering our attack and we kept losing visual contact with the lead ship as we went in and out of the base of the clouds. At times we were down below 100 feet to stay under the clouds.

After a few more passes, Charlie had decided that it wasn't an even trade with them out in the open and two gun ships overhead. They turned and tried to make their way back into the jungle. As they retreated we stayed after them until we were out of rockets and almost out of ammo. Needless to say the Army was more than ecstatic to see Charlie turn and run. We stayed in the area for awhile to make sure Charlie wouldn't return. The compound had surprisingly few wounded due to the rapid response from the Seawolves. When it was all over the senior advisor asked if the Seawolves would be available the rest of the night in case they came back after dark. Lt. McKenzie assured him we would be on call all night.

Later that week the senior member of the Army team got a ride into Nha Be just to meet the Seawolf crew and shake their hands. This is what I thought the war should be all about. If nothing happened the rest of my tour, I felt that I had helped to save the lives of some U.S. soldiers that had to have some brass balls to be stuck way out in the middle of nowhere with nothing but ARVN soldiers to support them. What drives these guys to do something like that? I was glad I was in helicopters.

Timing is everything in life. For switching seats with Rick just before we got scrambled, I received a Single Action Air Medal and he received a well-deserved Distinguished Flying Cross.

About a week later, it was my turn in the pilot seat. Rick had less than two duty days before he headed down to Vung Tao. We were coming back from a patrol when the engine oil pressure went to zero. I informed the lead helicopter and started a slow descent down from 1500 feet. We were over the water so I wanted to make sure we could make it to dry land before the engine froze up, which was just a matter of time. As we crossed the beach I made a slight turn to where it looked like a good landing area and made my approach.

As I came in, I planned for a no hover landing, which ended up being a good idea. When I pulled in the power there was nothing there. The engine just unwound and the inertia from the rotor system cushioned the landing. Rick stayed with the helicopter while we set up a perimeter. Petty Officer Boyd and Airman Smith grabbed their M-60's and set up at the 4 and 8 o'clock positions about 20 yards from the helicopter. I took the M-79 grenade launcher and headed for the 12 o'clock position and Rick handled the radios.

Rick was on the radio with the lead ship while they circled overhead. I could see a group of Vietnamese approaching about a quarter of a mile away, when they came to a stop on the edge of a rice paddy dike. They didn't seem to want to come any closer and that was fine with me. Just about that time, I heard Rick yelling and turned to see him waving his arm outside the cockpit. I headed back to the helicopter when he signaled for me to stop. He pulled off his helmet, leaned out the cockpit door and yelled "They said we're in some kind of a minefield." No wonder the Vietnamese stopped at the edge of the rice paddy. I told the crewmen to stay where they were, while I slowly made my way back to the helicopter.

As I approached the helicopter I saw a large mortar round laying in the mud about 15 feet in front of the helicopter just off to the left. I put on my helmet and was brought up to speed on what was taking place. The lead ship was relaying information from the command center. It seems Charlie had rigged some booby traps in the area and it had not been cleared. Not knowing what to call what we were in, they called it a minefield. As much as they knew they were not conventional land mines, they were makeshift booby traps made up of anything Charlie could get his hands on. There was no intelligence on how many or what to look for. I hollered out to the crewmen and told them to slowly make their way back to the helicopter and not to deviate from their original steps that got them there. We didn't have to worry about being overrun by Charlie, but needless to say we were walking on eggshells until help came.

We got word that the Army was going to crane the UH-1B out using an Army Chinook helicopter. The Army came in and marked the mortar round that I had seen and found one other in the area, only clearing an area big enough to get the Army maintenance crew in to rig the helicopter for an external hoist. We stood there watching the Chinook lift and fly off with the UH-1B helicopter, and then climbed in the Army Huey that landed right behind it.

In less than two days I was sent down to Vung Tao to pick up the helicopter after they replaced the engine. LCDR Rice met me in the hangar, "You guys were lucky that engine was just about ready to quit. LTJG Stanley did a good job of getting it down in time. I remember when I was a crewman on a P-2V. We lost an engine. It's good training."

I thought to myself, a P-2V has four engines, two recips and two jets. I had one. He must have been in a real scary situation. I didn't say anything about who was flying the helicopter. It didn't make any difference. Rick had arrived in Vung Tao the day before and evidently the MO had assumed he made the landing. If I had rolled it up into a ball, I can guarantee you, I would have gotten full credit for it. What I couldn't understand is how little people understood about the characteristics of a turbine engine.

If an engine has no oil and isn't running at full power, it's an engine failure. I remembered when an Army pilot went into the water off the end of our runway. The accident investigation team tried to say the engine was still turning when it impacted the water. They lost two people that day. If an engine is turning at 30% power upon impact, that is an engine failure. I couldn't believe where these guys got some of their ideas. Some of those guys that were on accident investigation teams came up with some real strange theories.

While we completed a pre-flight on the helicopter, Lt. McKenzie picked up the new OINC, LCDR Martin and flew him back to Nha Be. They were eager to get the wing ship back; we had been down as a fire team for two days and were unable to support any of the operations that were going on. When we arrived back in Nha Be the men had the helicopter ready for action in less than an hour. The old OINC was leaving at the end of the week and he would be returning to the States a couple of weeks later. That meant that our new OINC would take over the detachment by the end of the week, which was fine with me. LCDR Martin seemed a little more gung-ho than the other two. We could use a little more positive re-enforcement around the detachment. I never understood some of the thinking. Some of the senior officers volunteered for this duty and then seemed to hold their breath until it was time to leave Vietnam.

Lt. McKenzie was gone that same week, and that was a real loss. He was an exceptional officer and good pilot. He always made sure the crews had what they needed. He had recommended me for the detachment Maintenance Officer (MO) and I was looking forward to it. I loved being in the aircraft. The men had confidence in me and told me when I flew, it was like the helicopter was a part of me. My cigars became a symbol of good luck. They always carried an extra one in case I didn't have time to get one before the launch. When we got in a tight situation I always had a lit cigar in my mouth. I loved playing the part. I was moving up the ladder quicker than I thought. It seems all the senior people would be leaving the detachment in a very short time span and I would get my FTL papers. I was ready. I had studied the tactics of the other pilots and I had gone over many different scenarios in my head. I knew the best ways in and off the targets and would always try to use them to my advantage.

Finally Fire Team Leader

I was gung-ho but we were a team out there. Everyone in the crew played a critical roll. If one man didn't do his part, someone could get hurt or killed. Again I was impressed with the caliber of the enlisted personnel I served with, maybe I expected too much from some of the officers, I always pushed myself to fly better and thought the rest should do the same. Less than one week after I turned 24 and slightly less than three months from the time I arrived in country I had finally made Fire Team Leader (FTL). It was a great feeling. I finally had total control over what happened in the fire fights. I was determined not to repeat any of the mistakes I had already seen. I would be aggressive, but I wouldn't endanger my crew unless there was no other way to get the job done. When we rolled in we were always ready to kick ass and take names. The crewmen placed their trust in me and I was not about to lose that trust. Whenever we got into a fire fight I used what I had learned to minimize the risk for taking hits. Of course there was always the unknown. It worked out well. We all enjoyed flying together and looked forward to each duty day. I was in my element and loving it.

The weeks started to pass by; the mortar attacks were further apart but still commonplace. The small skirmishes kept life interesting. It's amazing what you start to consider as commonplace. A few new pilots came into the detachment; they were nuggets right out of the training command. They were wet behind the ears and lacking in confidence. LTJG Bill Davies had arrived a few weeks behind me. He was a good stick and I liked him. We worked well together. I was a little hot headed and Bill was always calm. We were good when we flew together.

I can remember an incident back when LCDR Aldridge was still at Nha Be and I was impressed with how well Bill handled himself. Aldridge was leading a flight and Bill was his co-pilot and I flew wing. They had the doors off the helicopter for better visibility and were dropping tear gas into a suspected enemy bunker area. One of the crewmen hit the skid with the canister and it bounced into the chin bubble of the lead helicopter. All I could hear over the radio, was "We're going to crash, we're going to crash," as I saw the white smoke come out from the lead ship cockpit.

When the tear gas started coming up into the cockpit

LCDR Aldridge gave up trying to fly the helicopter. His next reaction was to come over the radio and holler "We're going to crash," as he let go of the controls. Bill didn't think that was such a good idea, so he took control of the helicopter, kicked in full right rudder keeping the tear gas away from him and landed the helicopter in a field so the crewman could get the canister out. I circled overhead providing cover until they got airborne again. When we returned to base, LCDR Aldridge never mentioned a word about the incident.

I had the duty and Bill was my wingman. We prepared the helicopters and as was standard operating procedure called the command center and told them the flight crew would be in the movie if we were needed. As luck would have it the command center dropped the ball. Two of the river patrol boats (PBR's) started receiving heavy fire and the command center didn't call us at the movie. Instead they called the Seawolf Hooch where LCDR Martin happened to be. The OINC, knowing where we were, grabbed the men that were there and launched the helicopters to support the PBR's. The operation went nowhere. By the time the OINC got airborne the PBR's had pulled out of the area and the OINC didn't fire a round.

I was a little aggravated with the command center. Our team took a great deal of pride in how we performed. I think the new co-pilots enjoyed flying with me. They all got plenty of stick time and I tried to pass on as much as I could. That may sound a little egotistical at the early age of 24, but I could fly that Huey. Bill and I met the OINC as he returned from the flight. The OINC started toward me yelling at the top of his voice. "What the hell do you think you're doing? I had to take the flight 'cause you weren't around. If you can't do your job, maybe I should take your Fire Team Lead designation away."

I tried to explain what had happened, but the OINC had had a little too much to drink to listen to what I had to say. I finally had heard enough and said, "Do you think we can have this conversation in the morning when you're sober?"

The OINC blew up, "That's it you arrogant son-of-a-bitch! You're relieved of your duties."

I looked at him and said, "I think I should finish my duty day first unless you have a better idea," and I turned and walked away disgusted.

The next morning Bill and I were talking outside the Seawolf Hooch when the OINC approached us. The OINC was a little more composed than he was the night before. He said, "Al, I know I took your Fire Team Lead away last night, but we're a little short of experienced pilots, so I'm going to reinstate you."

I responded by saying, "keep it." He knew it was normal for the duty crew to go to the base movie. Why couldn't he just admit that he was wrong and overreacted? Before the OINC could respond, Bill immediately jumped in and pulled me away. It was difficult for me to take crap from someone when I didn't do anything wrong. After a few minutes Bill convinced me that it was a stupid thing to say. I went back over to LCDR Martin and apologized. I still wasn't happy. I felt the OINC unnecessarily prejudged me, but Bill was right, at that point I was the most experienced FTL in the detachment. The next day I had my Fire Team back. I always had a tendency to self-destruct when I thought I was right. It wouldn't be long before we went at it again.

Another new pilot checked aboard, he was a lieutenant, and he couldn't fly an attack helicopter if his life depended on it. Memories of what happened on the *Bon Homme Richard* quickly came back. I was going to have to train him even though I knew Lt. Conlin was a little rank conscious. He didn't like the idea of being co-pilot to a junior officer. That coupled with his poor flying skills made me dread getting in the cockpit with him. It was going to be fun trying to teach this guy how to fly when he wouldn't listen to anything any junior officer had to say. That meant two more nuggets and a lieutenant that couldn't fly. The detachment definitely needed some experienced pilots.

Later that night we got called out in support of the SEALs. They were in contact with an unknown number of VC; they knew they were out numbered and needed some support to withdraw from the area. As the gunships arrived overhead the situation on the ground changed rapidly. Charlie hunkered down to wait for an opportunity, not wanting to expose their position to us, knowing they were too close to the SEALs for us to take any serious action from the air. I made contact with the OINC of the SEAL detachment. He came up over the radio in a very quiet whisper. They had been in contact and were in a defensive position. The enemy was so close, the next thing would be hand-to-hand combat if Charlie initiated an attack. I couldn't use the rockets; Charlie was too close. I had an idea on how to get them the support they needed to withdraw without taking heavy casualties.

Earlier that month we had experimented with a box of grenades. If we flew over the tree tops at two hundred feet and 85 knots, the grenades would explode right above the ground. Charlie was trying to maneuver to cut them off so we didn't have much time. The SEAL team leader talked us into his position and marked the perimeter with red lights. We had to be directly over their position because they had the lights covered so they would only reflect straight up. When I had a good idea of where they were, I made one last flight over the area to confirm my track over the ground. The SEALs agreed with my track and I was good to go.

As I came around I shut off all my lights and descended to 200 feet. I told them to get down as I rolled in. The wing ship stayed at altitude. As I reached the outer point slightly north of their position I told the door gunners to empty the box of grenades as quickly as they could without dropping any. I had complete confidence in these guys, they always performed flawlessly. It was a dark night and with my lights off, Charlie couldn't tell the direction or the altitude of the helicopter. There would be no muzzle flashes coming from the helicopter for them to shoot at. The maneuver with the exception of the live grenades was relatively safe compared to some of the other situations we had been in. Bill was orbiting at 1,000 feet ready to put suppression fire on anything that came up at the lead ship.

As we emptied the box of grenades on Charlie's position, I heard the SEAL team leader come up on the radio. "That's fantastic Seawolf 28. Charlie didn't know what hit him. We have them running in all directions." He then asked if we had enough fuel to stay on station until they got to their boats.

I told him, "We have 0+45 on station," and asked if that would be enough time.

"Roger that," replied the SEAL. I climbed back up to altitude and turned my running lights on for Bill to join on me. As the SEALs withdrew we continued to lay down machine gun fire between them and the VC until we were sure they completed the extraction. Once we were sure they were clear, we turned and emptied our rockets into the area. The SEALs were able to extract without any additional casualties and that's what it's all about.

The following night at the O'Club in Nha Be, the SEALs bought a few rounds of drinks and taught me the "Dance of the Flaming Asshole." It was something only the SEALs could dream up. The skill seemed to require twisting the toilet paper in to a tight rope that would burn slower than the others. As they climbed up on the bar in the O'Club they dropped their trousers and shorts down to their ankles and placed the rolled toilet paper up between the cheeks of their ass. In a coordinated effort the toilet paper was simultaneously set on fire. The winner was the one that was the last to drop the toilet paper as it burned its way up. I declined the challenge from the winner. Oh yes, it required large amounts of alcohol. It's amazing what you can come up with when you've had too much to drink and you're bored. The small O'Club at Nha Be was a place to let your hair down a little. We didn't have to worry about getting too drunk or being perfect gentlemen. The Navy had this desire that when you were in combat, they wanted you to be as fierce as needed, but when you're back in civilization you were to be a gentleman. Sometimes the two didn't necessarily go together. The Nha Be O'Club was a place to let off steam, and the CO of the base did not write down names. In fact the base CO should have been an aviator; he had the heart of one.

The days and nights went by quickly with a few mortar attacks to keep things lively. Things were pretty calm. Almost two weeks and not even a shipping attack. The typical mission was Charlie would hit and run and we would go and try to find them. Most of the time Charlie would not give his position away unless he was sure he could get a shot in at us without showing his hand. We would end up putting a strike in where we thought Charlie would be, or what exit route he might use to escape. It was not an exact science and luck had a lot to do with it.

The next day when I took over the duty I was told they had a problem. They were trying to make contact with the captain of an Army cargo ship that had anchored directly at the end of our runway during the night. They had been trying for several hours with no luck. Our runway ended right at the waters edge and the ship was anchored less than a hundred yards away. It made it almost impossible for us to launch at night. The nights were so dark most of the takeoffs were half on instruments and half visual. In a loaded gunship we didn't have the distance to get the altitude to fly over them. I went out to take a look.

A few minutes later I returned and told my crew I was going to take the lead bird out for a test hop. After we turned up I slid out on the runway and lined up with the cargo ship. I pulled in the power and headed right for the side of the ship. I kept the bird low over the water and just pulled in enough power to clear the ships deck by a few feet. We flew right between the two masts of the ship. I came back around and landed the lead ship in the revetment and walked into the hooch. As I entered the room I looked over at the OINC and said, "lets see what that does." Less than an hour later the ship had picked up its anchor and moved down stream.

They gave us a new toy to play with called a Star Light Scope. The scope allowed us to see much better in the dark and we caught Charlie on several occasions trying to sneak down the small canals. The only problem was the scope was a first generation, and if you used it for an extended period of time it would give you a tremendous headache. The crew chief used the scope most of the time. It took two hands to use it. It would be another fifteen to twenty years before they perfected it for pilots.

On our days off, it was pretty boring at times. I got a lot of workouts in, and there was a little paperwork to do. Most of my activity was conducting any maintenance test flights that needed to be done. Cribbage was the game of the hour. Somehow the SEALs had picked up a couple of water skies and asked me if I wanted to join them in a little water skiing. We used one of their high powered insertion boats to water ski down the river near Nha Be. We even rigged an American flag on the tow rope handle. We got about two days of skiing in, when the base CO found out about it and ended it abruptly. It was probably a dumb idea, but when you're young, you're invincible.

The following week, I was on the way back from Vung Tau after picking up a helicopter that just had an engine change. I had my co-pilot, crew chief and an extra pilot that was riding back to Nha Be in the back. We had climbed up to 8,500 feet to cool off. The heat on the deck was sweltering. It was a beautiful day; the sky was a brilliant blue with the afternoon thunderstorm clouds starting to build. As we approached Nha Be, I switched over to the command center and told them we were inbound. Just then I noticed the engine oil pressure dropping. I alerted the crew that we had a problem and to make sure they were strapped in. I called the center and told them our problem and started a slow descent toward the base, making sure that I had enough altitude to make it to the runway if we lost the engine. I practiced simulated engine failures (auto rotations) to the runway all the time and could do it in my sleep.

By the time we got to 6,500 feet the oil pressure was zero. I continued my descent into Nha Be. I knew that if the engine kept turning for a few more minutes I had a good chance of making it to the runway. Seconds later the engine quit with a loud grinding noise. We were passing through 5,500 feet. I immediately dropped the collective and started to adjust to max glide airspeed, we were still pretty far out from the runway but I thought I might have a chance. I checked the rotor RPMs and couldn't believe what I saw. As the engine started winding down the rotor RPMs were very slowly decaying along with it. I checked the collective, it was full down.

Just then the co-pilot came over the radio, "Shit, we're loosing rotor RPM!" I started a tight turn as we descended. The RPM hesitated then continued to drop off slowly. I made a turn the other way, same thing. By that time the RPM warning light flickered as I search for a solution. Each time I traded airspeed for the RPM. I wasn't about to sit there and wait to see how far the rotor RPM was going to decay. There would be a point where we would lose control and fall like a safe. I didn't know what that was and I wasn't going to wait around to see. I decided to get down as quickly as I could.

I rolled the helicopter over in a modified split S maneuver and dove for the water. I put us into one hell of a spiral, it was almost like a spin. We fell out of the sky, the vertical climb indicator went up to 3,000 feet per minute, and it was pegged. There was no way I was going to make it to the runway at Nha Be. The water was the only place left and that was fine with me. If we didn't have enough RPMs left to cushion the landing, maybe the water would absorb some of the impact. The maneuver was extremely violent. The co-pilot came up over the radio and said, "We're going to hit awful hard."

I replied with, "awful fucking hard." I didn't remember

what was said on the way down, but it was brought to our attention by two Army pilots that heard us over the radio as they monitored the emergency while they were sitting on the runway at Nha Be. Evidently, with the adrenalin and the violent maneuvers we must have transmitted over the UHF. If I couldn't use the airspeed to get some of my RPMs back at the bottom there would be nothing to break our decent when we reached the water.

The water was coming up fast, and we were in a steep nose dive. Timing the maneuver was critical. I pulled in hard on the cyclic and flared the shit out of the helicopter to lose the forward airspeed. It did just what I had hoped; the "G" forces caused the rotor system to cone, increasing the rotor RPMs. The increased air flow through the rotor system gave us enough RPMs to use the inertia to cushion the landing. I quickly dropped the nose of the helicopter over, and pulled in the collective. As the RPMs decayed the helicopter slowly settled into the water.

The ride down was enough to give anyone nightmares but I was too focused on what had to be done to let it interfere. I don't know if I can say the same for the crew. All they had to do was hold on and it must have been one hell of an experience. I firmly believe that if it wasn't for all the times I had taken the Huey to the edge of its flight envelope, I never would have had the skills to set it down like I did. My aggressive approach to flying also helped. If I had waited to see how low the RPMs were going to go we may have fallen out of the sky uncontrolled. The next thing I saw, would have been funny if it wasn't for the situation we were in. I held the helicopter steady as we settled in the water and the rotor RPMs slowed down. The co-pilot had already exited the helicopter and was moving across the front of the windscreen facing me.

This wasn't a good situation, the helicopter had settled so slowly it gave the co-pilot time to get out of the aircraft before the rotors had actually come in contact with the water. When rotor blades hit anything, they shatter. There was nothing

I could do about it as the helicopter rolled to one side and the blade hit the water. From that point on the helicopter was going to do what ever the impact forces caused it to do. I unbuckled and turned to climb into the crew compartment to check on the crew chief and the other pilot. As I climbed between the seats I could see them both moving around and they appeared to be okay. They seemed to be a little disoriented as the rotor blade hit; the force knocked the helicopter over to the other side and as the second rotor hit the cabin flipped back over to the other side again. The pilot that was riding in the back was standing in the doorway not sure what to do as the compartment started to fill with water. The rotor blades were gone. There was no shrapnel to worry about so I gave him a push out the door. We both surfaced and swam away from the helicopter as it continued to fill with water.

I wanted to get away from the helicopter so we wouldn't get sucked down with it. As I turned and looked back to see if everyone was clear, I saw we were about 10 feet from the helicopter. What I saw next I can't really explain. Petty Officer Heady was motionless, floating face up as the crew compartment filled full of water. He was fine as I climbed into the crew compartment to check on him. I pulled off my helmet and swam back to the helicopter. As I reached the helicopter I could hear my co-pilot say, "Don't go near the helicopter."

I reached the crew chief just as the compartment filled with water and the helicopter rolled upside down. I grabbed Heady just as the helicopter rolled inverted and started to look for a way out. The water was murky and I couldn't see a thing. I felt the side of the cargo door and gave Heady a pull and we were free from the helicopter. As we came to the surface we were a few feet from the helicopter. The current was very strong. After I inflated the crew chief's life vest, I checked to see if he was alright. I was able to get his helmet off and he started to respond to my questions. By this time the current was pushing the helicopter further away from us.

I then turned to see how the other two were doing. The co-pilot was more than 40 feet away by this time. As I turned around I saw the other pilot holding on to the skid of the helicopter as it sat in the water upside down. The helicopter was still completely intact with the exception of the rotor system. The helicopter was completely striped and there must have been some air in the fuel tank that was keeping the helicopter afloat.

I yelled at Clark. I couldn't believe he went back to the helicopter. "Get the hell away from the helicopter! That thing is going down!" The pilot did as I said, but as he started to move away, he hesitated and said in a very quiet voice, "I think I'm caught." There was no struggle, nothing, he just hung onto the skid!

I started toward the helicopter. I could hear my co-pilot say again, "Don't go near the helicopter! It's going to sink and pull you under." As usual I didn't think. I did a lot of things on instinct. There was too much drag with all my flight gear on. I had to fight to get back to him. It was exhausting but the adrenalin kept me going. I was able to reach the pilot just as the helicopter went under the surface of the water. It was strange, the pilot made no attempt to free himself, he just held onto the skid until I got there. I grabbed his back and pulled at him frantically as the helicopter went under. The pilot did not struggle or try to grab hold of me. I worked my way down the pilot's back and then down his right leg.

By this time the pressure was starting to build. My lungs were burning from pulling the crew chief out and fighting to get back to the helicopter again. Once the helicopter broke the surface of the water it started to quickly sink. I could not find where the pilot was caught. I worked my way down the other leg and got to just above his boot. The visibility was zero. He seemed to never let go of the skid. I could not find where he was caught. Still the pilot did not struggle or try to hold on to me or free himself.

The pressure was starting to worsen and I felt my lungs

were going to burst. I had no idea how far we were from the surface. I let go, something that has haunted me to this day, and started for the surface. With my wet flight suit, boots and .45 revolver I thought I was never going to make it. I couldn't hold my breath any longer but kept struggling for the surface. I took a breath but all I got was water. When I broke the surface, I could barely stay afloat. I was exhausted and gasping for air as I choked on the water I had swallowed. The patrol boats from Nha Be were already on scene and started pulling the crew out of the water. I was devastated. I had always promised myself that none of my crew would ever get killed or hurt if there was anything I could do about it. I made that promise when I lost my roommate, when they crashed off the *Bonnie Dick* in bad weather, and we couldn't save them. I've gone over it a thousand times in my head over the years and don't know what else I could have done. Maybe if I could have held my breath just a little longer...

A couple of days later they discovered the pilot's body. The flight suit was fully intact, not even a tear, and there were no marks on his body. One of the detachment junior pilots escorted the body to his family back in the States. It came out during the safety investigation that the pilot was uncomfortable in the water and almost didn't make it through pre-flight and swim quals. They never found the helicopter. I wanted that helicopter. That was my second engine failure in less than a month and we were flying over some pretty nasty areas everyday. If they found it, I was going to jam the engine up the MO's ass. I also wanted to know why the rotor RPMs started to decay.

I was down for a couple of days. Every muscle in my body was sore. I swallowed half of the river and it was extremely polluted. I had never been so sick in my entire life. It was something that would follow me for years after. It would hit me almost like malaria once or twice a year. The doctors said they had no idea what it was. Each time it only lasted about 24 hours, so I learned to live with it. Petty Officer Heady came by to thank me for saving his life and explained that he didn't know what happened. He remembered starting for the door when all he saw was a wall of water. He then turned and started to exit out the other side when the other blade hit and pushed the helicopter over to that side causing it to fill with water. It was the last thing he remembered until he saw me in front of him in the water, shaking him and asking him if he was alright.

The following day LCDR Aldridge, the squadron flight surgeon, and one other pilot flew up from Vung Tao to conduct the accident investigation. They had given me a physical the day before and treated me for a few scrapes and abrasions and given me something for the pain in my back, hip and knee. I didn't like Aldridge, but I wanted to get it out of the way so I could get back to flying. Aldridge had pulled some real crap just to advance himself and had spent a good part of his tour in Vung Tao instead of out on detachment where the action was.

The meeting lasted about an hour as we discussed what had happened. Then LCDR Aldridge spoke up and asked, "Are you sure you had an engine failure? I've been flying for 12 years and have never had an engine failure."

I lost it! I jumped up from the chair and started across the room toward Aldridge. "What do you mean you ignorant son of a bitch? A pilot lost his life and you're asking me if I really had an engine failure. I've had five fucking engine failures, two in the last month. I think I know when my fucking engine quits." The flight surgeon stepped in between us. Aldridge just glared back at me. I'm sure no junior officer had ever talked to him that way before.

I was in a self-destruct mode. Aldridge was the same ignorant son of a bitch that hid in the bunker while his crew was exposed out on the runway during a mortar attack waiting for the asshole to show up. He had to be humiliated into manning his aircraft by the off duty crew in the bunker. He later put himself in for a medal and a purple heart when he fell and scrapped his face running to the helicopter. He was the same SOB that almost got us shot down out of his stupidity and the one who quit flying the helicopter when the tear gas landed in the chin bubble and that was just in the few months I had known him. The self-promoting politician would eventually make captain.

I was emotionally drained. I had promised myself nobody would ever get hurt when I was flying the aircraft. I turned, threw open the door and walked out. I later heard that I was going to be put in for the Navy Marine Corps Medal for pulling the crew chief out, but Aldridge recommended that I not get it. I didn't give a shit; I was never there for medals. These men were the closest I had to a family.

I went back to flight status the next day and ended up with Lt. Conlin as my co-pilot for a couple of weeks. Conlin was a second tour pilot and had enough total flight time to quickly make HAC. I had mixed emotions about his flying. I knew he was an accident looking for a place to happen. As it came close to Conlin's HAC check, I put him in the pilot's seat to get him used to flying the helicopter from that right seat. I didn't know what to do with this guy. The *Bonnie Dick* kept haunting me; everyone looked away until it was too late and people lost their lives. Was I being overly critical? Was it that I just didn't like this guy's attitude? I would stay with him as long as I could until they forced me to either give him a HAC check, or put in writing why I didn't think he should be pilot in command. Maybe he would get it together. I was one of the youngest pilots in the detachment, would they even listen?

I loved being in the helicopter. If anything that engine failure gave me more confidence about my ability to fly. I took every opportunity to pass my experiences on to the co-pilots. Upon returning from a mission the door gunners would hold colored smokes out the doors as we made a low pass over the compound. I'd pull the nose up, roll into a vertical rotor over the way McCormick taught me, and add a roll in on the descent. There would be almost no G force's felt during the maneuver, including the recovery at the bottom. We would put on quite a show with the smokes and the crewmen loved it. I think the word is "Hotdog." I was always keeping the co-pilots on their guard. I would pull the helicopter up into an unusual attitude and then say, "I'm hit. You've got it." The co-pilot would have to take positive control of the helicopter and bring it back under control. It was good training for them. Most of the nuggets were very timid pilots. It gave them confidence that they could recover from almost any flight condition. Besides you never knew what type of a situation you'd be in if the pilot took a couple of rounds.

You were either up at altitude, away from the small arms, unless you were in a skirmish, or you were on the deck. I liked to low level and so did the crew. Sometimes the door gunners would have to use their gunner's belt to climb out on the mounts to clean the elephant grass off the skids, so we could return to home base.

Between getting scrambled in support of a unit in trouble, flying cover for an insertion, and H&I missions we periodically got called up to fly a medical team out to some of the small villages. When we stripped the ships, we could carry a couple of passengers. Usually it would be a doctor and a dentist and couple of corps men that would go down to the outlying villages. This particular trip happened to be a small fishing village right on the coast. When we arrived there was a very small landing pad built up of mud and dirt. The village was in the lower part of the Delta and it was the rainy season. I landed first, shut down and turned the blades for and aft so the wing ship could land. After the wing ship landed and shut down we started into the village surrounded by dozens of small children and villagers.

About half way up the trail they all started yelling and pointing back towards the helicopters. In order to make enough room for the wing ship I had moved the helicopter to the edge of the pad. As I turned to look, I couldn't believe what was happening. The lead ship was sinking into the ground and starting to roll over on one side. I took off on a dead run, we were about 100 yards away by this time. As I headed for the helicopter, I was thinking, how in the world will I explain this? The Petty Officer Heady was right behind me. As I ran, it was like watching a slow motion picture as the helicopter continued to very slowly roll on its side.

Nothing was said. We knew what had to be done. Heady grabbed the rotor blade and untied it, as I jumped in the helicopter and turned it up. By this time the helicopter was really leaning and as the blades started to turn, there was more than a little mast bumping as I tried to keep the blades from hitting the ground. I started pulling in collective as soon as I had enough RPMs to make a difference. Heady was on the other side trying to stop the rolling. By the time I got the helicopter turned up and we broke free from the ground, the tips of the rotor blades were missing the ground by about a foot. We picked up the helicopter and took it around. After finding a better spot we finally landed and shut down. Everyone was still halfway up the hill watching us land the helicopter. When we got out we climbed all over the helicopter to see if we did any damage to it. Luckily there was no structural damage to the helicopter and we avoided the embarrassment of being pulled out by the Army. We completed our visit and returned to Nha Be, and I hoped I would not have to listen to any heckling for the next couple of weeks.

The following duty day Lt. Conlin was my co-pilot. I was being pressured to give Conlin his final check flight for HAC. In this instance, I used poor judgment. My ability to handle the aircraft in any situation, caused me to put the lieutenant in a situation he couldn't handle. That day we were asked to fly cover for a large flotilla that was going into the "T-ten" area. They didn't expect much contact; it was more of a show of force. I had never seen so many river boats all in one place. There must have been twenty of them, not including the PBR's as escorts. They made it up to the point where they wanted to go without incident and were preparing to turn around and exit out the way they came in. We had just returned from refueling as they started back down. Lt. Conlin was in the pilot seat. If we got in a little fire fight, I was sure I could conduct the operation from the co-pilot seat.

Just as we arrived back overhead all hell broke loose. The flotilla was taking fire from the west bank. Charlie was lined up for what appeared to be several kilometers along the bank of the river just waiting for the flotilla to return. It was the only way out and Charlie knew it. I went hot and directed the fire team to roll in on the west side of the river parallel to the flotilla. I told them to make the rockets count. I immediately regretted my decision to put Conlin in the right seat. I had no choice now. The co-pilot seat had control of the four flex guns, and it took both hands to operate them. From the amount of fire down there, we were going to need everything we had.

As we circled I had never seen so many bullets flying through the air at one time before. The reverine forces had massive amounts of fire power. There were bullets flying in every direction. The bullets from the flotilla were hitting the banks and bouncing up everywhere. Lucky for us, Charlie was focusing on the boats, which helped, but their bullets were ricocheting everywhere. They were trying to cripple some of the lead boats to jam the others up. I looked over at Conlin, he was a little pale. I had to get him focused, "Let's get in there damn it, and give them some help."

What was about to happen next, no gunship pilot wants to experience. I was focusing on the flex guns and as we rolled in on our initial rocket run. We were about halfway through our first rocket run when I thought we had just had part of our rotor blade shot off. I immediately dropped the gun sight and grabbed for the controls as I came across the instruments to try to assess what was wrong. The aircraft was thrashing and bouncing all over the place. The rotor RPMs were below 6100 and the warning light was flickering,. Normal was 6600. The torque was indicating just above 41 lbs. of torque, and we still had almost a 1000 foot rate of descent. From what I could tell, the helicopter was falling out of the sky. The UH-1B tops out at 37.5 lbs. of torque. As I came across to Lt. Conlin, he had the collective pulled as high as it would go, with a surprised look on his face and his mouth dropped wide open.

I said, "I got it!" while I tried to assess the damage. Although things were happening in micro seconds, it seemed as if everything was in slow motion.

He was trying to pull out of a steep rocket run in a fully loaded gunship with power only. We were in blade stall, I hoped! As soon as I got the collective down the wild thrashing stopped and that was a good indication we may not have received severe damage from enemy fire. Now we were sitting ducks. We had lost a lot of altitude and were only couple of hundred feet over the tree tops with bullets flying everywhere. I made a 90 degree right turn to reduce our exposure to the gun fire and headed across the flotilla and river to the other side. If we went in, I hoped that Charlie was only on one side of the river. I kept the nose down and tried to keep as much airspeed as possible as we descended.

The aircraft was redlined and shaking all over the place. My gun sight was swinging back and forth and slamming up against my right arm as I maneuvered to get clear of the area. I dove for the trees hoping to shorten the time they would have to get their sights on us. When we cleared the other side, I used the airspeed to get back up to altitude as quickly as possible. Unfortunately I had no control over Conlin, as I made the right turn to cross the river, Conlin was in a trance and still firing his rockets, he was methodically launching one rocket after the other every few seconds as we pulled out on the other side. He was still trying to fire the rockets long after the pods were empty. Fortunately none of the rockets hit the flotilla. From that point on Lt. Conlin was almost useless., He just sat there not saying a word. I had to run the rest of the mission without the flex guns.

I checked the helicopter out and went over the instruments. The aircraft appeared to be in good flying condition. We didn't have any rockets left so I told my wingman I would provide cover with the door gunners while he went in for another run. We still had the 50 CAL and it could get anyone's attention. We continued providing suppressive fire on the enemy positions until the river forces were clear and we were out of ordinance. To this day I can't figure out how we didn't get shot out of the sky. Charlie must have been so focused on the flotilla that that they poured everything they had into them. When we returned to base to rearm and refuel, I switched seats with Conlin and returned to continue to put strikes into the enemy positions. Lt. Colin didn't say a word for the rest of the action. We returned and rearmed several times until we were sure the enemy was no longer in the area. I was frustrated; Conlin did very little right and I was not about to recommend him for HAC. That last dumb move was because I was getting pressure to make him an aircraft commander, he was way over due. My job as I saw it was to ensure the safety of the crew that flew with Conlin. Was I being too critical?

Later that day after we shut down, Colin had the guts to ask me if I thought we should put ourselves in for a citation for the action we were just in. I just looked at him in disbelief,. I didn't say anything, the son of a bitch almost killed us, and he wanted a medal. I walked away before I said what I really felt. I was mad for letting myself be pressured into trying to qualify this disaster as a pilot in command. Throughout the entire time I was Fire Team Leader I don't think I ever put in for any citations. I wasn't there for medals.

Over the next few weeks I continued to get pressure from the OINC to give Lt. Conlin another check ride. Every time we went up I would give him as much training as possible. At the end of the two weeks LCDR Martin took Lt. Conlin up for his check ride and gave him an up. From that point on, you could see it in the faces of some of the crewmen. Nobody wanted to fly with the lieutenant. Stories started to build on the stunts Conlin would pull during the missions. Out of spite, I thought that LCDR Martin had Lt. Conlin assigned as my wingman. On one mission the lieutenant tried to stay with me on a low level pop up attack, and he ran into a tree top and shattered his chin bubble. This guy could do nothing right and to add to the problem he was unwilling to take orders from a junior officer.

It was time for a break. Periodically the crews would get a chance to go into Saigon for a little liberty and dinner, and it was our turn to go. While we were in Saigon the last time, I had an oil painting made from a picture of two gunships flying cover for two PBR's. For a little more realism I asked the Vietnamese artist to have a couple of the rockets coming out of the helicopter rocket pods. When we returned that evening to pick up the picture, the artist had the rockets going the wrong direction. They were being fired at the helicopter, instead of coming from the helicopter. It was too late in the day to make any changes so I took the painting and we headed back to Nha Be.

The next day I had duty and decided to take the Fire Team back into the area were the Riverine Forces got shot up. Out of habit I always zig zagged even when we were up at a 1000 to 1500 feet when we were in a suspected hostile area, unless I was putting in a strike. As we patrolled the area looking for any signs of movement on the ground I made a slight turn to the left and just about that time two B-40 rockets were fired at my helicopter. The first just missing to the right and the second passed right in front of the helicopter. I immediately told my wing ship what I was doing as I completed a rotor over and dove for the spot the rockets came from. I could still see the smoke trails. I think Charlie was beginning to think it was a bad idea as the wing ship rolled right in behind me. We used up half our rockets on the first run and came around for a second run. As I lined up and fired off another rocket it stuck in the tube. If you've ever had a rocket stick in the tube it can really through you out of balanced flight. Consequently when I fired one out of the starboard side it missed the target. I tried again and another rocket stuck in the port tubes. I continued the attack until we were out of ordinance without anymore problems. From the explosions we were able to spot some hooches hidden in the thick triple canopy. I called the information into the command center and they set up a few air strikes into the area from the Air Force. When we returned to base we discovered we had taken a couple of rounds in the port tubes and it had jammed the rockets. For weeks we continued to put H&I strikes and slowly uncovered numerous hooches and bunkers in the area.

We would not be able to get any results of the attacks, the terrain was not that accessible and besides Charlie owned most of the area. I was sure we ruined their day and eventually kept them from operating from that location. On the way back to Nha Be I thought it was interesting. One day after I picked up the painting with two rockets being fired at a helicopter, I had two rockets fired at me. Maybe the artist knew something I didn't. I decided I wouldn't have any more paintings done. That's the way it was in Vietnam, just a matter of luck sometimes. A couple inches this way or that, or a wrong turn to the left or right. That's why everyone got a little edgy their last month in country.

Going against Squadron Policy

During my tour at Nha Be, my friendship with the SEALs continued to grow. The team leader and his second in command were two young JG's, full of life and totally unpredictable. I think we had a lot in common. I had duty one day when the SEALs came over to brief me on an operation they had that night. They were going into a village near the area where the river forces were attacked and wanted to make sure they had Seawolf cover. I told them that one of the helicopters was hard down and the squadron policy was not to fly any missions single ship. The SEALs told me they had to go in that night, the weather (no moon) and the tides were right. I understood and told them that I would be on standby if they got into trouble. They showed me the location and I told them I could be over head in 10 minutes, but I would only have the fire power of one gunship to provide cover.

Later that afternoon I called the OINC and told him the situation. The OINC told me that he wasn't going against squadron policy, and I would not be launching single ship. I acknowledged and hung up the phone. I think he knew if anything happened I was going and didn't want to know.

I waited until later that afternoon when everyone but my crew was out of the ready room. I called them all together and told them about the SEAL team's request and about squadron single ship policy. I was going to support the SEALs and if they got in trouble I would need three volunteers to go with me. Within seconds the entire crew volunteered to go. There was a code in the Seawolves that if someone needed help we would do everything we could to support them, despite any politics. I didn't want them to mention it to anyone until the following day. I left the discussion with the OINC to myself; nobody else needed to take the heat if anything went wrong.

At about 0230 that night, the SEAL team called into the command center for our support. They were pinned down by heavy fire with three wounded. The ready crew slept in their flight suits and boots, the longest part of the launch was getting to the helicopter in the dark. I loved this kind of shit! It was almost better than sex. Everything was multiplied tenfold. Your hearing, your sense of touch, your smell, everything was heightened. It was like you were on a high. I guess it was what they call an adrenalin rush. It was almost addictive. Anyway, I knew I never felt so alive as when I was scrambled in support of someone in trouble, on a moonless night where you couldn't see your hand in front of your face.

As we approached the SEAL team position I got an update on the situation. The team was receiving heavy fire from the tree line and the Viet Cong were trying to flank them to the north. I was trying to coordinate getting some Army slicks with the command center back in Nha Be. I didn't want to run out of ordinance and fuel before they arrived. The SEALs were cut off and couldn't make it back to their boats. The command center was trying to get a couple of Army slicks out to pick up the team, but they didn't have any estimated time of arrival (ETA) yet. After getting the enemy positions from the SEALs, they let me know their position with red lights. I turned off all my running lights and rolled in for the first attack. As we opened up on the enemy positions in the tree line we started receiving fire from several of the hooches on the edge of the small village.

I wasn't concerned. It was a dark moonless night. With our running lights off, all Charlie had to shoot at was the muzzle flashes and the sounds of the helicopter. We were maneuvering at 85-95 knots and 1,000 feet above the ground. All Charlie did when he fired at us was give away his positions to the door gunners. I smiled to myself when I heard the SEAL leader come up over the radio in an excited voice, telling us we were receiving heavy fire from a tree line again. It was typical of them. Pinned down with three wounded and after everything they had just gone through, they were concerned about the Seawolves. It said a lot about the caliber of people they were.

Charlie quickly realized he was in a no win situation. Every time they opened up on the gunship our response was lethal. The door gunners were deadly shots. After putting in a couple of rocket runs we would be circling at 1,000 feet at 85 to 95 knots in the dark of night and they would put the first round on target. The 50 CAL was even deadlier. It was remarkable to see what these young guys could do with these weapons. Although there wasn't much difference in our ages I felt much older than my years, and it was my job to bring them back safely.

When we stopped receiving fire from the tree line we turned our attention to the hooches in the village.

Fortunately I had not used many of the rockets because of the close proximity of the SEALs. This time there was plenty of separation so I rolled in and descended down to 500 feet and headed right down the main road to the village. I knew as soon as I opened up Charlie would get a fix on our position, so I told the crew to hold off until the first rocket was fired, then let everything go to keep their heads down. As I headed in, I lined up on the first hooch on the right and fired off two rockets, direct hit. Once that happened everything opened up, tracers were coming up at us from several of the hooches. I kicked the rudder peddle with a slight bank to the left and fired off two more rockets, hitting the hooch on the left. At that altitude they were hard to miss. By this time I guess we were silhouetted by the explosions and ensuing fires because the tracers seemed to be getting much closer. I broke off to the right and tried to put some distance between us and the village.

As we pulled off the run, the door gunners kept giving me updates on where the fire was coming from. As we exposed ourselves when we pulled off the target the door gunners kept laying down cover fire. They knew instinctively what to do without being asked. We had flown together so much it was like one person flying the aircraft. There were tracers coming from small pockets all over the village. I had a clearance on the whole village, if needed, but I wanted to make sure of the targets. As I turned back in for another run I could see the first couple of hooches were in flames. I decided to reverse the direction from the first run, knowing they would only be keying on the sound of the helicopter and betting that they wouldn't know it was a rocket run until I opened fire again. I took the gunship right down the center of town and dumped off the remaining rockets. That seemed to stop all the firing from the village.

As I climbed up to a 1,000 feet I orbited over the SEALs' position. You could hear the relief in the voice of the SEAL on the ground. I told the door gunners to conserve their ammo, pick their targets and not to make a continuous stream of fire. I didn't want Charlie to walk his fire in on our tracers. We continued this mode of operation hoping the Army slicks would arrive before we got low on ammo and fuel. About fifteen minutes went by while we continued to pick our targets as we circled looking for any movement. With no sign of the Army slicks I told the SEAL team leader that we were running low on ordinance and wanted to take this time to rearm before they could regroup. The SEAL team leader agreed.

I called into the command center and told them to have my crew ready for a quick turnaround, I needed a full load of ordinance and fuel, ETA 10 minutes. I also wanted to know if they were able to reach the Army slicks. The command center told me the Army slicks were about 30 minutes out. That gave me enough time to rearm and return. When we arrived back in Nha Be my wing ship crew had everything ready to go. I didn't even pull into the revetment. I slid right in next to where the fuel truck was and everyone jumped out and grabbed the ordinance.

If a safety officer would have seen us in those days he would have shut us down. I brought the throttle back to flight idle and everyone including me got out to arm the helicopter. We fueled and armed the helicopter as it sat there wobbling on its skids while the rotor blades turned and I chewed on my traditional cigar. We couldn't have been on the deck more than a few minutes before we were airborne again and heading back to the T-ten area. The longest part was the fueling. We didn't quite get a full bag, but I felt it was more important that we get back to the SEALs.

I called the SEAL team to let them know we were inbound and got an update on their status. Things were surprisingly quiet; they had not seen any movement since the last rocket run. Just about that time the Army slicks reported in. I briefed them on the situation and where the extraction point would be. As the Army slicks started their approach to the landing zone (LZ), they started receiving heavy fire from the tree line and waived off. Charlie must have been waiting for us to try to get the SEALs out. As the pilots waived off I came in right behind them and opened up with everything we had. As I pulled off the strike I called the Army helos and told them I would lead them in with another strike. They seemed to like that idea and rolled in behind me as they made their approach. I lead the slicks in and as soon as Charlie fired his first round I dumped several more rockets into their position. As I pulled off the target I immediately swung around to keep the 50 Cal on the area until the slicks took off. I had time to come around and lay down a few more rockets as the slicks picked up out of the LZ and departed. They were able to get out of the LZ without taking any hits. The night was really in our favor. It was so dark Charlie had a difficult time getting a good shot at us.

We emptied the rest of our ordinance into the area and then departed. On the way back to Nha Be, I was preparing myself for the wrath of the OINC. I was pleasantly surprised to find that the OINC was not there. I asked my wing ship pilot if the OINC had heard what went down. My wingman told me that he had not seen the OINC all night. I was sure I would have to deal with it in the morning. To my surprise I didn't hear a word from the OINC for two days. On the third day he received a call from the squadron CO. It seems the skipper got a call from the SEAL commander thanking him for the support. The OINC told me that he had briefed the CO on the incident and what had happened. He looked at me with disapproval and said, "The CO seems to think I should put you in for a medal. I told him you were a good pilot but you were a damn maverick and you should be reprimanded instead."

I commented by saying , "I'm sure you'll do what's right," and turned and walked away.

We were too much alike, and every time we got together, it was like two roosters clawing in the dirt looking for a fight. I was proud of myself for not saying something inflammatory. Maybe I was maturing. I had seen too much and decided that I would probably not stay in the Navy. At times I didn't bother to watch what I said, which was my problem. He was right about one thing, I was a damn good pilot. If going against squadron policy to cover for some of our buddies was arrogant, then I guess I was. To this day I don't know why I got away with some of the stunts I pulled. In the end, I was awarded the following citation.

Al Billings

COMMANDER IN CHIEF
UNITED STATES PACIFIC FLEET

The President of the United States takes pleasure in presenting the Distinguished Flying Cross to

Lieutenant (junior grade) Alan James BILLINGS
United States Naval Reserve

for service as set forth in the following:

<u>CITATION</u>

"For heroism and extraordinary achievement while participating in aerial flight in support of a U. S. Navy SEAL Unit on 11 October 1968. With one aircraft of his two plane light helicopter fire team in a down status, Lieutenant (junior grade) BILLINGS launched single ship into the moonless, overcast night to aid a SEAL Unit that was pinned down by heavy enemy automatic weapons fire. Once in the area, he located the friendly position by radio and a blinking red light and commenced his attack on three houses from which the SEALs were receiving fire. After two passes with rockets and machine guns, all three houses were destroyed. However, both the SEALs and the gunship then came under fire from a nearby wood line. Again, Lieutenant (junior grade) BILLINGS' precision attacks silenced the enemy. He continued the heavy suppressive fire long enough for a "Slick" helicopter to arrive on scene and evacuate the SEAL Unit. Lieutenant (junior grade) BILLINGS' selfless devotion to duty, courage under fire and outstanding professionalism were in keeping with the highest traditions of the United States Naval Service."

For the President

John J. Hyland
JOHN J. HYLAND
Admiral, U. S. Navy
Commander in Chief U. S. Pacific Fleet

They made a sweep of the area the next day and gave me credit for 27 KIA. It was a little bittersweet after the way the war finally ended. I was not proud of what I had to do, and I justified the action by helping to save the SEAL team. I was beginning to wonder if I was becoming too cynical at the ripe old age of 24. When I first got my commission I thought everyone above the rank of ensign had their act together. I even addressed most of the JG's as sir, instead of their first names. Now, I wouldn't give a rat's ass for some of them. Maybe it was a character flaw, but when I saw chicken shit things going on, I had a very low tolerance for it and usually spoke out. We were there to save lives if we could. I quickly learned it wasn't the rank that made the person, it was what they had inside.

I enjoyed the enlisted men, although we all had a few character flaws, they were hard working and most of them were straight up and didn't play games. All they asked for was a fair shake. When we flew together it was sheer music. The first thing you learn in your leadership training is to take care of your troops. Somewhere that got lost on some of the officers. Some of the officers always kept the enlisted men at a distance. It was that old Navy training, never let the men know any of your weaknesses. The crewmen worked around the clock on these helicopters just to keep them flying and then they got in them and flew the same missions as the pilots. We couldn't do our jobs without them.

The squadron continued to get top heavy. We had a commander visit the detachment for a few days. He was the Ops Officer down in Vung Tao and a squadron of the size of HA(L)-3 usually had a commander as the XO and CO. They were updating the tactics manual, and he wanted to fly with Det Two to get a feel for Fire Team Tactics. They scheduled me to take him out and get him some experience. The commander seemed like a nice guy but I didn't have any faith in what they were trying to do. Here you had a couple of senior officers who didn't have any Fire Team experience, writing the new tactics manual. Now that made a hell of a lot of sense. If he wanted to see some action I was going to try to find it for him.

I took the commander out on a mission. He wanted to pilot the wing ship and I had no problem with that. I knew the Rung Sat like the back of my hand by this time, so I took the Fire Team to an area where I had a good possibility of finding something. A few minutes into the flight we were called in support of an Army outpost that was under attack. When we arrived on scene there wasn't much action. The outpost had received some small arms fire from the northeast quadrant. We received clearance and put a couple of strikes in the area. I didn't know what to expect, so I approached it accordingly.

As I came around and prepared to put in the first strike, I noticed the commander was already out of position. I rolled in on the area and laid down some fire and dumped off a few rockets. As I came out, I rapped the helicopter into a tight turn so the door gunner could get his gun on the wing ship should they start receiving fire. The wing ship with the commander as pilot was just starting to roll in, that meant I didn't have the cover I was supposed to get from the wing ship. Great tactics! I was glad we were not under heavy fire. I could always rely on my door gunners. They always seemed to find a way to get some fire on anything that was coming up at us. Even if they had to lean out and shoot under the helicopter.

I held up so he could get on my wing again. This went on for about three passes before the wing ship got so far out of position, I broke it off. This guy must have been an old P-3 pilot. The whole time the commander was complaining that I was making the turns too tight and he couldn't keep up. The young JG's that flew with me never had a problem staying on my wing. It was rare to find a senior officer that could fly an attack helicopter the way it was supposed to be flown. The younger pilots always seemed to be more aggressive. I couldn't believe these guys were going to be writing the new tactics manual. I was sure it would be interesting reading.

We circled the area trying to get Charlie to return fire until we got low on fuel and then headed back to Nha Be. To make things worse, after we arrived back in Nha Be, I had to listen to the commander describe "good tactics" for 30 minutes. After all I was only a JG and I had a lot to learn. I was never good at hiding my emotions, even if I stood there quietly and listened, he could tell by the look on my face that I thought he was full of shit. I envied those guys that could disagree but make the individual think they had the greatest idea in the world. I guess you would call them politicians and that wasn't me. Fortunately he was only there for a short time and then he returned to Vung Tao.

On the night of my next duty day we were playing cribbage and waiting for something to happen. It was about 2245 when the windows were blown out and pieces of the ceiling fell in. I didn't wait, I knew the next round would hit somewhere close. I think I made it to the door in one step. I made the 50 feet to the revetment in record time. My crew was right there with me. They were always there. They took a great deal of pride in what they did. As I jumped in the pilot seat the rest of the crew took their positions. Everything was preset and all we had to do was hit the battery, fuel and the igniters, once we had 6600 RPMs, or close to it, we were pulling pitch. At night with the cool air we could get away with it. As I pulled out of the revetment the co-pilot was strapping into his seat, and switching on the radios and NAV aids.

There was usually enough time for me to get up to about a 1,000 feet before the co-pilot would tap me on the shoulder and take the controls. I would hold my hands out in front, to show I was giving control to the co-pilot, and then strap myself into my seat. By this time we were usually in contact with the command center getting an update on what had happened and directions to the suspected enemy position. Out of all the mortar attacks I never left any of my crew behind, sometimes they were at the helicopter before I was. It turned out that we were not responding to a mortar attack. It seems Charlie had floated a 500 lb mine up along side the base near our hooch. When it was spotted, they were in the process of trying to disarm the mine when it went off.

The mine disintegrated the three people who were working on it, damaged five trucks and injured several other personnel in the area, along with the damage it did to our building. I turned the team around and brought them back into Nha Be. When we returned one of the junior pilots told me that he had looked at his watch as we ran out the door and we had gotten airborne in 70 seconds. I know those who have been there might say that is bullshit, but you'll have to take it up with the officer who timed us. The next day everyone found that a little hard to believe, including me.

The days continued to go by and I spent much of the time training the newer pilots. We were preparing for a large operation in the Rung Sat. A while back we had been patrolling over the Rung Sat when I thought I saw the roof of a hooch in the jungle. It was a free fire zone so I decided to work over the area. As we proceeded to pour rockets into the area we spotted more and more hooches, wooden walkways, small bridges and much larger buildings. After we reported it, there were major air strikes placed into the area. By the time the triple canopy was blown away from all the bombs, they discovered an entire city in the middle of the Rung Sat. They even had a field hospital. I reflected over the fact that we flew over this area almost every duty day. I had already had two engine failures and if we ever lost one over this area, we could kiss our asses goodbye.

The following week they moved several hundred Mountain Yard troops into the area, (they were much better fighters than the ARVN soldiers). There were a couple of Marine advisors heading up the unit. They were going to sweep through the area and didn't know how long it was going to take. It could go late into the night. The Marine advisors felt a little better knowing they had Seawolf support. I was not a happy camper; I had LT. Conlin as my wing man, and if it went the way of the flotilla ambush, I could have my hands full. There was one thing positive, I think Lt. Conlin knew he was a bad pilot. Things went very smoothly during the daylight hours, but it was obvious that they would be there well into the night.

We flew several missions that day and were on standby. Unfortunately we only had two helicopters and there was nobody to relieve us on station. We could reach the Rung Sat in 10 minutes, and it was better to standby than have something happen when we were almost out of fuel. It was about 2230 when we got the call. Charlie had setup an ambush and was waiting for them as they extracted back toward the river. We made it there in record time. During some of the larger missions the Seawolf FTL became "On Scene Commander" out of default. The gunships were equipped with UHF, VHF, and FM radios. This meant I could talk with the troops on the ground with their FM radio, talk to any support aircraft and command center with our UHF radio and use our VHF radio to communicate with other support groups. In large operations it became quite a challenge to keep everything coordinated and also provide suppressive fire and coordinate the fire team. I seemed to enjoy it best when I got busy and I never had any trouble keeping things moving.

As the fighting got heavier they asked for air support and the command center also got the Air Force to bring an aircraft to drop some parachute flares to light up the area. This went on for several hours between breaks in rearming and refueling. I had my hands full trying to keep up with the movement of the ground troops and directing any support units that were being used. On a fire team the lead helicopter flies with his running lights on so that the wing ship can fly position on him. The wing ship flew with its lights off to give Charlie less of a target. In this instance all Lt. Conlin had to do was stay on my wing and provide cover support if necessary.

After we had returned for a third time I had everyone on the radios and was maneuvering in and out of the parachute flares while I was trying to maintain some type of visual contact with the Marines on the ground. The next thing I heard was the co-pilot holler, "Look out!" I looked up and there was my wing man headed straight for us between the parachute flares. He couldn't have been more than few hundred yards away, although it was hard to tell in the dark. I instinctively pushed the nose over and slid underneath the wing ship. Lt. Conlin never even saw the lead helicopter. I got his attention in very few words and told him to get his ass on my wing and stay there or return to base. I did not have time to deal with him.

It was a little distracting. I had to spend the rest of the mission wondering what he was going to do next. Because of our support, the Marines were able to make the extraction with very few casualties. The next night at the O'Club, I made some new friends. The two Marine advisors were 1st LT's, one had 27 years in the service and the other had 23 years in. You could tell by their rugged features they had lived a hard and full life. I thought these guys were great, right out of a John Wayne movie. Their stories and experiences were remarkable. They went all the way back to WW II. These guys were definitely characters and that's what I liked. Walking around in the jungle at night looking for Charlie, with a bunch of troops that didn't speak English, they had to be crazy.

It did no good to tell the OINC about another blunder that Lt. Conlin made, but it was my job, so I told LCDR Martin about the screw-up. I could not believe that he was allowed to keep his HAC paper's. Conlin was becoming a problem in the detachment and half of the crewmen just rolled their eyes when they found out they were flying with him. It was the OINC's job to make the tough decisions. Was this going to be another repeat of the *Bonnie Dick*?

Bill and I had the reputation among the troops as good pilots, even though we were two of the more junior officers. It didn't make a difference whether you had a 1,000 hours or 4,000, if you were good, the crew knew it. They were not in competition with you, and they counted on you to keep them out of trouble. If you were a natural pilot, it was obvious. Another second tour lieutenant arrived in the detachment. His first tour was flying SH-3G's in an ASW (Anti-Submarine Warfare) squadron. ASW's claim to fame was being able to hold a forty foot hover for hours at a time. He was a solid pilot but all he wanted to do was fly straight and level. Anything over a 15 degree angle of bank was too much. This was not going to work in an attack squadron.

I decided to break him in and take him out for a little low level flight and a few aerial maneuvers. I was sure I would get his attention. At the end of the flight, the lieutenant went in to the OINC and told him he would never fly with me again. It made me feel bad; I hadn't even shown him the things Mr. Combat SAR taught me. I still held Lt. McCormick as the ultimate Navy helicopter pilot, and I would never have a chance to see if I was as good as the he was. I heard that he got out of the Navy after his first tour.

That night we were called out in support of the PBR's. The river forces setup an ambush in the lower Rung Sat and caught a couple of large fishing boats trying to run the blockade in the dark. There were several dead and one seriously wounded. It was a young Vietnamese girl that was caught in the crossfire in the dark. They had to MEDEVAC her out of there, or she might die. The Army told them that if there was no landing zone, they couldn't land to pick her up. I overheard what was going on and told them I would give it a try. I hadn't seen anything that I couldn't do up to that point and really didn't think I had any limits. I told them that if they could clear some of the trees from the LZ big enough to get a helicopter into, I'd be there. I was just leaving Nha Be, so I turned back to lighten the load. The UH-1B gunship used by the Seawolves usually took off at 1,000 lbs, over the max gross weight with all of the ordinance we carried. At times during the hottest part of the year we had to bounce the gunship off the front of the skids to get into translational lift to get airborne. Even though it was night and the air was cool, I wanted to have as much available power as possible to maneuver in and out of a tight LZ.

After we lightened the helicopter we headed down to the mouth of the river. I made a slow pass over the tree tops with my landing light on to assess the situation. It was a very dark night with very little moon and stars. I never seemed to have the luck of a full moon. I guess Charlie preferred the darkness.

It was going to be a challenge. The area was really tight and there was a huge tree stump right in the middle of the LZ. I made a practice run first. I was going to have to make a high steep approach over the trees and then settle into the LZ in an almost vertical approach. I wanted to see how much power I had available if I got into trouble. I brought it in slow and started my initial descent at the angle I felt I needed. I then pulled in a handful of collective until the RPMs started to drop off. The helicopter stopped the rate of descent and climbed with no problem. I knew I had enough power to get in and out. My rate of descent had to be slow to avoid what they called settling with power. It was a term used when a helicopter made a steep descent and started flying into its own rotor wash turbulence. If the condition got too serious the aircraft would not have enough power to stop the descent. Now all I had to do was not hit anything!

I brought the helicopter in and set it right astride the large tree stump. The stump was so big the skids didn't touch the ground. I kept the collective pulled in to maintain control, as the helicopter wobbled on top of the tree stump. They brought the girl out along with one other wounded Vietnamese. I told the crew chief to double check for any weapons and we departed. We got out with no problem and headed towards the Army hospital in Saigon. I never heard if they made it, but we did what we could. The evacuation started me thinking. How would you pull someone off something like a PBR?

The next day I walked over to the Riverine forces area and

looked over their boats. With all the antennas most of the boats seemed to have, it would be difficult to make a transfer. They would have to somehow disconnect the antennas or fold them down to get them out of the way. Even with them out of the way, it would be a tricky maneuver. Nobody had ever attempted something like that, that I knew of, so it wasn't known if it could be done. I decided I could do it but it would be tricky. I always thought everything through. Would I someday exceed my capabilities by taking too many chances?

I'm going to see to it that you lose your wings for this.

As the weeks went on, the days tended to be pretty routine. The mortar attacks seemed to get further apart, the rocket attacks on the ships seemed to get even further apart, maybe we were winning. Every now and then there would be a sweep of an area to see if they could find Charlie. There were times that we had to support the ARVN. The joke was they picked an area where they knew Charlie would not be. We even had an opportunity to support the Royal Korean Marines (ROKs). They had a reputation of being so vicious, if Charlie even knew the Koreans were going to be in an area, they made sure they were someplace else.

I continued to work with the junior pilots to help them gain confidence. In some cases it was as simple as telling the co-pilot to sit down into the helicopter. One day I had noticed that one of my co-pilots always flew with his seat as far up as it would go and was constantly over controlling the aircraft. With his seat up that high he would have to reach down between his legs to hold the cyclic. I know it didn't make sense, but that's what we had to deal with. This reach made him over control the helicopter in a hover and almost any other maneuver other than straight and level flight. Actually anything that took a little finesse, like a shipboard landing, or even pulling into the revetment was clumsy at best. I told him to move his seat down and fit himself into the helicopter, like he was part of the aircraft. If he was uncomfortable while he was flying something was wrong. He tried it and on his very first hover it was as smooth as glass. He never had any problems over controlling the helicopter again. It was a start.

To break up some of the monotony we would look for most anything to keep us occupied. One day the SEALs brought by an Army jeep and asked us if we wanted it. It wasn't like they had taken it, they were government vehicles, and they said they had re-appropriated it. We didn't ask them what their definition of re-appropriation was. The problem was the Army painted their numbers all over it. So the jeep was painted a Navy green, with Navy numbers. When the squadron found out a detachment had its own jeep, they asked to use it down in Vung Tau. We couldn't tell them no, so the OINC agreed. We asked the Army if they would transport it down to Vung Tau for us. A few days later the Army came by with a CH-47 and carried it down to Vung Tau. The Army had a great group of guys, and they were very helpful.

My tour was coming to an end. I had accomplished what I wanted and found out a little more about myself. I had saved some lives, seen some combat, and made some friends. LCDR Martin had rotated through and now we had a new OINC, he was a nice guy, but not someone to lead the detachment. He should have been a Boy Scout master and probably was. He was definitely too timid to head up a fire team. He was a good pilot but was always adding a few hundred feet for his wife and kids, and I'm not saying that was wrong. He would come off the attacks early and start his runs way too high. He didn't have the heart to aggressively pursue Charlie when we had them on the run. Frankly, I had no idea why he volunteered for the Seawolves. Most of the pilots were pretty gung ho. This was an all volunteer unit and he didn't have to be here. I was very lucky. Even though I was one of the youngest pilots in the detachment, I had more experience than anyone else and nobody seemed to question what I did, or at least they didn't say anything.

Toward the end of my tour things seemed to be slowing

down. I was sitting in the Seawolf Hooch when the Ops Officer asked me where I wanted to sit on the next day's flight schedule. Since I had been there the longest, I got to pick with the exception of the new OINC what seat I wanted. The junior pilots were all getting their quals and were chomping at the bit to get some actual aircraft commander time. The new OINC had just made FTL, so I said I would take the nugget seat. That meant I would be flying in the most junior spot in the Fire Team, which didn't bother me. Although most the officers thought I had an ego, they were wrong. There is a difference between knowing what you can do and having confidence in your abilities, to me that was much different than someone with an over-inflated ego. My not being the FTL bothered the crewmen more than it did me. They enjoyed the way I handled the team and the way I flew. I was always able to find something to get us into.

That duty day as luck would have it, we had just taken off when two PBR's got ambushed up the T-ten area. As we headed inbound to provide support we could hear the gun fire when the petty officer keyed the radio desperately asking for help. He was a young sailor and you could tell by the tone and the excitement in his voice he was in a desperate situation. If you have ever been in a combat situation you understand that these situations can really get your heart racing. You're flying inbound to help, and some guy is on the radio pleading for someone to come in and help his wounded buddies that were dying right in front of him.

The young sailor had two seriously injured shipmates and the PBR commander was dead, the other two also had minor injuries. The Army was called to MEDIVAC the badly wounded sailors, but could not pick them up without a Landing Zone (LZ). The PBR was floating helplessly downstream with the current and could not get to an LZ. As we arrived overhead, the fire team leader cautiously stayed above 1500 feet over the spot of the attack. As he orbited overhead, apparently waiting for something to happen, the petty officer came up over the radio again with another gut wrenching plea for help. The other boat was making high speed gun runs trying to provide protection for the stricken PBR.

This was about all I needed, we were not going to sit there and do nothing while these guys bled to death. There was only one way to get them out, and if the Army wouldn't do it someone had to. I don't know what triggered my next reaction, maybe it was still the promise I made myself when I lost my roommate on the *Bon Homme Richard*. Or the pilot I tried my best to save. There was just something inside me, driving me. Nobody was going to die on my watch.

I grabbed the controls and took the helicopter away from the pilot and shouted, "I have the aircraft." He didn't hesitate to relinquish the controls; I had trained him since he arrived in country. I keyed the radio and told the FTL that we had to get down there and help them. The FTL said there was nothing we could do. I had heard that too many times before. That was it. I was going down to get them off the PBR and told the lead aircraft I was going in. The OINC came back over the radio in a defiant voice, "You're not going down there. It's too hot. That is an order." I don't remember what I said next. I was too busy assessing the situation and what my options were, but I was sure it was colorful. As a pilot I couldn't just circle overhead while I listened to someone tell me over the radio, his buddies were dying. Pilots are a different

breed; at times they have to make a conscious decision to go down into harm's way. There are always hundreds of reasons to justify why it can't be done. I had to try.

As I rolled in, I told the FTL to keep continuous fire on both banks. I radioed the other PBR and told him that I wanted him to make some coordinated high speed gun runs when I gave the word. I rolled the helicopter level and lined up on the right bank of the river and told the pilot to dump off half of the rockets along the bank where the other PBR was returning fire. I then rolled the helicopter up into a rotor over and told him to pickle the rest along the other side. The door gunner and the crew chief were focused and keyed into my every move. Not a word was said. They had flown with me on hundreds of missions and anticipated my every move. I told them to get rid of anything they didn't need and then pulled the helicopter up into a high turn and headed for the stricken PBR.

The adrenaline was beginning to peak. Everything was in a hypersensitive state. The bullets were flying through the air in every direction. I could feel every vibration of the helicopter as we maneuvered into position. We felt heavy. I told the crew again to get rid of anything we didn't need. I began to focus on the patrol boat. I could see where the winds were coming from by the smoke, but it eventually didn't make any difference. I told the fire team leader I needed him to keep a continuous stream of fire on the bank when I reached the PBR. He circled overhead and remained well above the skirmish but did what I said.

This was going to be a very tricky maneuver. The PBR was 31 feet long; the UH-1B was 53 feet long tip to tip and the fuselage was about 42 feet. The rotor down wash on the fiberglass PBR was going to be 80 knots plus in a loaded gunship. The damaged PBR was turning freely with the churning current of the stream. As I came around for my approach, I told the other PBR to start their runs and to make sure they kept Charlie's head down. Despite the renegade Seawolf, everyone did their job. The lead ship was circling overhead and the door gunners kept continuous fire on the banks. Power was going to be critical on this rescue, so I told the pilot (now co-pilot) to give me a continuous update on the power settings as I came into the hover. I placed the left skid of the helicopter on the bow of the PBR. The entire cabin area had been blown off along with the antennas. Those days we flew with the doors off. They weren't much good for anything and they cut down on the visibility. As the rotor wash from the helicopter started to blow the PBR around I had to somehow make sure I kept contact with the

PBR in order to make the transfer. The crew chief kept the twin 30 CAL's going continuously, keeping Charlie's head down. He could really make them sing, switching out one can at a time when the ammo ran out. He never stopped firing. I then instructed the door gunner to get down into the boat and grab the wounded.

I don't think the door gunner was ever given the credit that he truly deserved. This man, without hesitation climbed down into that stricken patrol boat with bullets flying everywhere with no concern for his own safety and picked those men up and put them into the helicopter. Not once did any crewman ever let me down, and he knew I would never leave without him.

I had to completely focus on maintaining contact with the PBR as it was being blown around in the water. I kept the skid on the side of the boat. It took total concentration; I could not move my eyes away to check the instruments. Too much pressure and I could sink or slide off the boat, too little and I would lose contact and have to chase the boat. The other PBR continued to make high speed gun runs with their 50 CAL's and M-60's blazing away, as the lead ship poured their machine gun fire into the banks. The amount of fire power that was poured in the jungle was impressive.

I had picked the right person to get the injured out. Smith was built like a tackle. Within seconds he had both the injured in the helicopter. The crew chief helped pull them in while he continued to fire the 30 CAL's. As the second one came aboard I hollered at the pilot to give me my power. I told him to give me continuous updates on my power setting and had not heard anything from him during the entire rescue attempt. I really needed to know what the power settings were. I yelled a second and a third time while I struggled to keep the helicopter steady. There was no way I could take my eyes off the front of the PBR. I was getting frustrated; I heard nothing. As the door gunner started to climb back into the helicopter I turned toward the pilot and as I did, I looked across the instrument panel at the power settings. We were at 6,100 RPMs, normal was 6,600 RPMs. The torque meter was reading over 41 lbs of torque, again well over the engine topping of 37.5. That meant we were well past the limits of what the engine had to offer.

As I came across the instruments toward the pilot, he seemed to be in a trance and was staring out the front of the cockpit. I knew we couldn't get out of there the way we were. If I tried to fly it out and we lost anymore RPMs we could stop flying at any minute, so I slid the helicopter down off the PBR holding in as much power as I dared to, hoping to get some help from the ground cushion off the surface of the water. It didn't help. We continued to settle right into the water before the ground cushion took effect.

In all fairness to the other pilot, there were an awful lot of bullets flying everywhere and he didn't have much to do. That allows the mind to do funny things. I had seen it happen on too many occasions. We were not going to stay there. I had no idea what Charlie was planning. He could be setting up for a better angle away from the current gun fire that was going into his position. I headed downriver with the current. The helicopter was sitting in the water and I was holding as much power as I could. The chin bubble quickly filled with water.

As we moved forward, water was sloshing around and inside the chin bubble mixing with blood from the wounded. I told the crew to get everything out of the helicopter they could. Just about that time I heard the pilot in the other seat come over the radio and order "Lighten ship! Lighten ship!"

As we emptied the helicopter I pulled in power and tried to pull the helicopter out of the water. It didn't work, with the additional weight of the water the RPMs dropped off too fast. We got rid of some more equipment. I pushed the nose forward to pick up as much ground speed as possible in hopes that I could get to transnational lift where the helicopter didn't require as much power. As I pulled in the collective I held the nose where it was, going with the current helped with the forward speed. I was able to break the suction from the water as the RPMs started to slowly decay 6500, 6400, 6300. I eased the nose slightly over and dropped the collective, in a slight milking action to hold my RPMs. I had done it hundreds of times, trying to get airborne off the short runway during the summer months, only this was a bit more challenging.

It worked; we were airborne and we were flying, the RPMs were at about 6,400 and slowly starting to build back. The helicopter wallowed out of the river as the water drained from the chin bubble. When we had enough airspeed and altitude, we headed directly to the Army field hospital near Saigon. The two sailors were badly wounded. The blood covered the floor of the cockpit and the chin bubbles. I hated that smell; it was something you would always remember. I could still smell it from the *Forestall* and my first rescue. We got both of the men to the hospital and I found out later they both lived, which made it all worth it. The door gunners performed flawlessly. I wouldn't have had a chance without them.

When we arrived back at the Seawolf compound the OINC had some words for me. For such a mild mannered person he could get pretty angry. He didn't like the idea of me going against his direct order. "Who the hell do you think you are? That was a direct order! I'm going to see to it that you lose your wings for this!"

I wasn't going to get into it with him, and as I tried to ignore him it just made him more irate. "When I give you a direct order lieutenant I expect you to obey it. You could have gotten everyone killed by that stunt."

I tried to walk away. I had heard it before, and besides I felt a little drained from the whole thing as the adrenalin wore off. He followed me so I stopped and stood there waiting until the OINC got it off his chest. As I stood there in my own thoughts I could hear his voice but not what he was saying. It bothered me. Why was he so pissed? Was it something he should have done and didn't? Was it just going against his direct order? Was it a crazy stunt? I didn't have an answer and honestly I didn't care. I don't think those two sailors would have lived if we waited. They had lost a tremendous amount of blood. The PBR recovered the other sailors down stream and got them out of the area. Frankly I was surprised to hear they both made it. Only I could pull off a rescue like that and get in trouble for it. It was something that would be repeated throughout my career. As the OINC seemed to run out of things to say I turned and walked into the hooch.

Later that evening a group of chiefs from the PBR detachment came over to the hooch. As they walked in, they wanted to know who Seawolf 28 was. I stood up to introduce myself and my crew. The chiefs held up a bottle of Jack Daniels and a box of cigars. "This is for you for being there. We understand that it was quite an exciting rescue."

The accolades went on for a few minutes and I started to feel very uncomfortable. I didn't like being praised for doing my job. It was like I had two personalities; one, I would stand toe to toe with anyone if I thought I was right, yet the other side of me did not know how to handle the praise being bestowed on me. After about an hour the chiefs left and gave me an open invitation to the NCO club. I would be an honorary member and would never have to buy another drink while I was in country. I thanked them and was glad to have all the attention go away.

The next day Bill had duty and I was sitting in the hooch playing cards with him while the duty crew waited to be called out on a mission. That morning a couple of reporters came into the hooch with some photographers. They started with, "We heard there was a daring rescue yesterday and we'd like to know more about it."

It just so happened that the OINC and my pilot were both in the hooch at that time. The OINC jumped up from his seat and said, "I was the Fire Team Leader in command of the rescue," as he walked toward the reporters. Right behind the OINC was the other pilot.

"I was the aircraft commander of the rescue helicopter," he stated. Both the OINC and the pilot escorted the reporters outside. As they walked toward the door I overheard the pilot say that he turned the helicopter over to his co-pilot because it was easier for me to make the rescue from my side. Go figure! Last time I looked the Huey had two sets of flight controls. I looked across the table at Bill as he sat back in his chair and rolled his eyes back. We continued to play cards without saying a word, there was no need to say what we really thought.

I never saw those reporters again, but I did hear that the OINC and the pilot of the rescue helicopter got their names in a few newspapers. As luck would have it one of the reporters was from the pilots hometown in Florida. I was a little disappointed in human nature but blew it off as I usually did when I saw things go against what I believed in. I was still struggling with whether I would stay in the Navy or get out. The following day a couple of the chiefs from the PBR detachment brought a *Navy Times* reporter over to talk with me. Fortunately that day nobody else was around. The reporters were very interested in what took place, but I continued to play it down as I always did. This was not the act of an arrogant egotistical young aviator, but then again few people would know who I really was.

Another day went by and I didn't hear anything more from the OINC about my losing my wings, which was fine with me. Maybe getting his name in the newspaper distracted him from going after me. Another day would pass before the OINC came into the hooch and told me the CO wanted to see me down in Vung Tao, immediately. I asked, "Do you know what it's about?"

The OINC answered , "He didn't say," but the seemingly personal look of satisfaction on his face left me with a knot in the pit of my stomach.

I didn't have duty that day, so I asked Bill to take me down to Vung Tao and drop me off. I had plenty of time to sit in the back of the helicopter and think about my fate. Bill dropped me off and said he was going on a patrol and would be back later to pick me up. I went over to the squadron spaces and was sent into the CO's office almost immediately. The CO was sitting behind his desk and looked up at me, as I stood at attention in front of his desk. "LTJG Billings reporting as ordered sir!"

I had never met the CO. He was a Navy captain, which was very unusual for an aviation squadron CO. Either he was deep selected or the Seawolves had high enough visibility to warrant a Navy captain. He was a big man with a stern face and looked to be in his late 40's., I figured my aviation career was about to end, but hoped there was a light at the end of the tunnel. The captain picked up a newspaper and handed it to me. It was the *Navy Times*. There was an article in the paper about a daring rescue of some wounded sailors off a stricken PBR. "Is this you?"

I looked at it briefly and replied, "Yes, sir, I believe so," my voice was scarcely audible.

The captain broke in, "Let me tell you something son. I don't ever want to read about my men in the newspaper without knowing about it first hand, is that understood?"

"Yes, sir!"

"You tell your OINC that I want to know about everything that goes on in that detachment."

"Yes, sir!"

After that, the captain seemed to settle down a little and asked me about the rescue. We had a good talk and he turned out to be a pretty decent guy. He was very complimentary and said they would make transfers from small boats part of their training. After a few more minutes of small talk he wished me luck and I left.

On my way back to Nha Be the tension in my body started to slacken. I was sure I had pushed it too far and I was going to lose my wings. When I arrived, the OINC was in the ready room area and asked me to step outside. He said the CO had just called and instructed him to put me in for a medal. He wanted to know what I thought I deserved.

I replied, "As far as I understand the process, I'm

not supposed to know about any awards that I'm being recommended for, but if you're asking me, I've never had a Navy Commendation Medal." What can I say, I was a genius with words. I turned and went back into the hooch. It was difficult for me to be nice to someone I didn't respect. The incident with the newspaper reporters ended any chance of my respecting anything but the rank he was wearing.

The Navy Commendation Medal came back in the following citation and is a perfect example of what really happened and what gets documented, very little was correct. I wasn't told but I found out later that the FTL and the pilot of the wing ship were both put in for medals so it couldn't go down as it actually happened. The Commendation Medal as I knew it was upgraded to a Silver Star:

COMMANDER IN CHIEF
UNITED STATES PACIFIC FLEET

The President of the United States takes pleasure in presenting the Silver Star Medal to

Lieutenant (junior grade) Alan James BILLINGS
United States Naval Reserve

for service as set forth in the following:

CITATION

"For conspicuous gallantry and intrepidity in action while engaged in aerial flight while attached to Helicopter Attack (Light) Squadron THREE on 8 November 1968. As co-pilot of a helicopter gunship, Lieutenant (junior grade) BILLINGS piloted the aircraft in an unprecedented medical evacuation of two seriously wounded men from a PBR in a hostile fire area. The helicopter fire team was scrambled from Nha Be to assist two PBR's that had come under heavy enemy rocket and automatic weapons fire from both banks of a small stream. The patrol officer had been killed and four crewmen were wounded, two seriously and in need of immediate medical attention. Since a MEDEVAC helicopter was still 20 minutes out and there was no helicopter landing site accessible to the PBR's, Lieutenant (junior grade) BILLINGS received permission from the fire team leader to attempt an underway pickup. The PBR's were still quite near the area they were when first hit. Lieutenant (junior grade) BILLINGS had the pilot put an attack into the enemy positions in order to discourage fire on his aircraft and also to jettison the bulk of his ammunition. To further lighten the aircraft he had the gunners jettison most of their ammunition. He then made his approach to the boat with only his gunners to protect his precarious position. He placed one skid on the boat's bow while the left door gunner pulled the two seriously wounded men to safety. He then flew directly to the hospital in Saigon. Lieutenant (junior grade) BILLINGS' courageous actions, sense of responsibility and devotion to duty were in keeping with the highest traditions of the United States Naval Service."

For the President

JOHN J. HYLAND
Admiral, U. S. Navy
Commander in Chief U. S. Pacific Fleet

I understand that the newspaper articles that were sent along with the citation carried more wait than the nomination did. I could get philosophical here and say that it didn't really matter, but as a young man and still to this day, the truth was very important to me. I never understood that telling the truth could be considered a character flaw in real life.

My tour with the Seawolves was coming to an end. The OINC asked me if I wanted to go down to Vung Tao my last week in country and I said no. I would just as soon stay in Nha Be with my crew. I was not a politician and there was no need to go down there other than to check out. I could do everything I needed in one day down in Vung Tao. At the end of the week, I went down to the squadron to check out and returned to Nha Be. I had one night left and after I tipped a few beers with some of the crew, I headed to the O'Club to spend some time with the two old salty Marines I had flown cover for. The SEALs had already rotated back to the States. We had one hell of a going away party when they left.

As the drinks went down, we talked about meeting in the States and doing the O'Club scene all over again. I really enjoyed them; they were real people and I could relate to them, they had character and grit and fell right into my John Wayne persona. As the night went on, they asked me how I was getting to Ton Son Nhut. I told them I was catching the Navy bus in the morning. I would have dinner in Saigon then head to the airport. My plane didn't leave until the following morning, but because of the curfew, I would have to spend the night in the airport. That was unacceptable to Steve. He said they would take me into Saigon and told me to be ready to go at 0900 in the morning and they would see that I got a proper send off. These guys were great; both of them had more time in the Marines than I had on the planet.

The next morning I was ready to leave. The Seawolves said their final goodbyes and I climbed into the jeep and headed to Saigon. When we arrived in Saigon it was about 1430 and we headed directly to the hotel room they operated out of when they were in the city. Steve, the older of the two Marines went to the refrigerator and pulled out a case of beer and set a bottle of Jack Daniels on the coffee table. The sea stories continued until about 1730, when a young soldier from Australia showed up. It seems the Marines let him use the hotel room when they were not in town. I wasn't familiar with the rank structure but he was an enlisted man and I figured him for an E-3 or 4. He was young, full of energy with a heavy accent and always had a smile on his face.

I laughed to myself. I was always calling people young back then. He was probably older than I was. I was finishing up my second tour in support of the Vietnam War at the ripe old age of 24. I didn't feel that young, what I had seen made me feel a lot older than my years. That evening we went out to a nice restaurant for dinner and returned to the hotel to continue our sea stories and finish the Jack Daniels and beer. About 2200 I had reached my limit. I could drink with the best of them, but these Marines could really put it away. I put my head back on the couch and the next thing I knew it was 0230 and they were waking me for the trip to the airport. I had to be at Ton Son Nhut three hours before my flight. It left at 0730 in the morning.

I was still feeling the effects of the alcohol. They grabbed my gear and put me in the back of the jeep. The young Australian drove while the Marines carried their favorite weapons for protection. The ride was memorable. All I heard was whistles and voices. They would start up one street and there would be a barricade, so they would turn around in the middle of the street and head in another direction. Just before we reached Ton Son Nhut, we ran across a checkpoint that was guarded by U.S. soldiers. After a few minutes they let us pass and on to the airport we went. As we reached the front entrance we all piled out of the jeep and shook hands. We said our goodbyes and said we'd see each other in the States and that was the way it went. Memories and friendships were made and then you went on to another assignment. These were good men. I would have gone anywhere with them. So many times people are judged by one action instead of the true character that is inside.

On the long flight back to the States, I had plenty of time to reflect on everything that I had seen and the people I met. The men in the Seawolves were dedicated. They never asked for a thing. They just did their jobs and when that was done they looked for more. When we flew together there was nothing better. They always had that extra cigar for good luck. At times I thought that I should have been a Marine aviator, instead of a Naval aviator. My personality seemed to fit the Marines profile much better than the Navy.

The Vietnam War was complicated and the Washington politicians and bureaucrats mismanaged everything. They were incompetent and got a lot of good men killed. They spent the next 25 years passing the blame off on anyone they could. As for me, I went over to do a job and I was good at it. I now understood who I was. Somewhere along the way I had changed. I wasn't the young carefree man that I used to be. Hopefully that change was for the better. Between the war and what I had seen on my last two tours I had decided the airlines looked a little more promising than the extra $165 I got each month for flight pay.

When I got home I was a little disappointed at how the movies and the news portrayed the Vietnam vets as dope smoking goof-offs, or crazed killers with irreparable psychological problems. I knew them as brave, loyal, honest, and patriotic men and that would never change. I could only feel sorry for the long-haired hippies that were holding the signs outside the bases calling us baby killers. They would never know what it was like to share the times we had both good and bad. The way the newspapers and the movies portrayed the soldiers and servicemen was unconscionable and difficult to understand. Their motivation was profit and sensationalism. It's understandable why so many of the returning servicemen had trouble adjusting when they came home. Many of those young men went over with high ideals and believing that what they were doing was right. To see your best buddy die right in front of you and then come home and get spit on and see yourself portrayed on the silver screen as a drug addict or someone that was too stupid to avoid serving was at best disheartening.

I was off for a new adventure with VRF-31, a Navy ferry squadron out of Norfolk, VA. Little did I know that there seemed to be no limit to the number of engine failures and emergencies in my future. Would I run out of luck before I gained the experience, or would the skills I had already learned carry me through?

Chapter SIX
Headed for Civilian Life

Navy Ferry Squadron

I didn't waste any time. I asked for VRF-31 and got it. I was back in the States only two weeks before I was in the air. I wanted to pick up as much flight time as possible in order to get into the airlines. This duty assignment would allow me to pick up some fixed wing time, as well as qualify in several different types of aircraft.

The mission of VRF-31 was to ferry aircraft for the Navy. This meant that you got a new aircraft out of the factory, one that was going to be overhauled, or went to the bone yard, for retirement of the aircraft. The assignment made for some exciting times. The aircraft that were going to be overhauled or to the bone yard would have the basic minimums to make them flyable. They usually had been stripped of anything that was working in order to use the parts to get the other aircraft in that squadron up and flying, any good maintenance officer would have done it. The new aircraft out of the factory could either be like the UH-2C, Sea Sprites I got out of the factory, or they would be in excellent condition, depending on the manufacturer.

The squadron had a new policy in that a pilot could only be qualified in six aircraft at one time. It wasn't so long ago the pilots could carry as many qualifications as they felt comfortable with. The sea stories about their flying experiences were unbelievable. I could sit in the ready room or operations and listen to them all day. Many of these pilots didn't have stellar Naval careers, but they were some of the best damn pilots I had ever seen. There were many reasons that these pilots were in VRF-31. Most of the younger pilots were there for the same reason as I, to build up flight time for the airlines. Some of the older pilots had made a career out of the Navy and were there for the love of flying. Others may have expressed their dissatisfaction with the incompetence of one or more senior Naval officers in their careers, or just didn't like the politics. Overall, the majority of them were exceptional aviators.

The best of all was Master Chief Carr. He was one of the last twelve enlisted pilots in the Navy. As the story goes, a few years before I arrived, the Master Chief got orders to a squadron up in Quonset Point, RI and he did not execute his orders and stayed in VRF-31. A couple of years later he got orders back to VFR-31 and nothing was said. I'm sure there had to be some agreement between the squadron CO's, but that's how sea stories go. Nobody was going to question the story; it was too good to be true. Most of the remaining twelve Chief AP's (enlisted pilots) in the Navy had enlisted at the tail end of WWII, and most were close to or already had their 30 years in. They only stayed around so they could have the distinction of being the last enlisted pilot in the Navy and pursue their love of flying. I got a chance to see a little of the Master Chief's independence when we had a dress white inspection and awards ceremony.

The Master Chief had seen too many inspections and did not enjoy them. The day of the awards ceremony the

Master Chief came into the squadron on crutches, with his foot wrapped up. The next day, the Master Chief was back in his flight suit ready to fly. Nothing was ever said, and that's no sea story. I was honored at the awards ceremony and was awarded a Distinguished Flying Cross for my single aircraft support of the SEAL team surrounded by a superior force. I was also promoted to lieutenant at the same time. During the Vietnam Conflict promotions came pretty fast. I had only been commissioned for 2 ½ years and was already a Navy lieutenant at the ripe old age of 24.

Several months later, my Navy Commendation Medal (Silver Star) came in and the squadron held another awards ceremony to give me the medal. I understand that the fire team leader and the pilot of the wing ship also received medals for their participation in the same action. It was nice to finally get the recognition, but I really didn't think the award would help me with the airlines, although I hoped one day that the truth would be told. The heroics of combat are fleeting moments in time and few will remember except those who were there. To those who were not, they will be just a few fascinating sentences in a book or citation and in some cases points of cynicism or envy. My crew chief and door gunner also got well-deserved medals for their unselfish devotion to duty, professionalism and courage under fire.

It was time to build up my flight time. As I learned about the squadron's operating procedures, I was able to get a few flights with the Master Chief. At times I couldn't tell if the Master Chief was just putting on a show or if that was the way he always flew. The number of hours the Master Chief had in his logbooks was staggering. He even got checked out in helicopters without gong through the training squadron. He had flown almost everything the Navy had, with the exception of some of the single seat jet fighters. The Master Chief had no interest in the fancy new stuff.

On my first trip with the Master Chief, we headed to NAS Glenview, in Illinois, with a Grumman, S-2 Tracker. I enjoyed flying with the Master Chief; I got most of the stick time. As we approached Glenview the weather was getting pretty bad and I believe he decided to make the approach just to show me what an old boy could do. As we headed inbound to the radio station, the Master Chief was cleaning his pipe and pouring another cup of coffee. He didn't miss a lick as we got station passage. He made his turn and started outbound. As we turned inbound for the final approach the Master Chief still had the map spread across the yoke blocking the instruments. I was glued to the instruments and was closely following the approach plate that sat between the two pilot seats. The Master Chief was right on. My adrenaline was building; I didn't have much actual instrument approach time and this was as good as it gets.

We were approaching minimums and the Master Chief was still screwing with the map and his pipe. I was just about to say something when we broke out at 300 feet. The Master Chief was right on target! He slid the map to the side, flared the aircraft and greased the landing. I could only hope that I would be that good someday. I was good with any aircraft as long as I flew by the seat of my pants and stayed VFR. Instruments were another matter. Time and experience would make the difference. I couldn't get enough. The winter months with the large massive frontal passages provided some of the best instrument flying you could get.

We were there to pick up a Douglas C-117. I couldn't wait. The C-117 was a passenger version of the old C-47. The C-47 was an upgraded version of the DC-3. The aircraft was originally built in 1925 and used extensively during WW II as a troop carrier. The airframe was most likely older than I was. When I first got into the cockpit I felt like Errol Flynn. This was pretty much what they had when they flew the paratroopers behind the lines in the Normandy invasion.

The flight was going to take us from NAS Glenview to Brownville in the southern most tip of Texas. It was at the maximum range for the C-117 and there was no room for error. The navigating would need to be right on and the winds would have to be in our favor to make it without refueling. The Master Chief was a very quiet person, but after what I just saw, if the Master Chief thought he could make it, I was sure he could. As the aircraft rolled down the runway the Master Chief had hardly raised the landing gear before he unbuckled and climbed out of the pilot seat and went aft. I was fixed on the instruments until we got above the overcast. I thought the Master Chief was going back to check something out, but when things settled down after climbing above the overcast I could see the Master Chief back in the passenger section with a cup of coffee, his pipe, and a newspaper. Obviously he had more confidence in me than I did.

Several hours went by and everything was going great. The engines were running smooth and the weather had cleared up and there was a magnificent blue sky ahead of us. It was a beautiful day to be alive. A few minutes later the Master Chief came forward and stood over my shoulder. A couple of minutes had passed when the starboard engine started to sputter. I looked out at the engine and came back in to check the engine gauges. As I did the Master Chief reached over and switched the fuel tanks and the engine was again running smoothly. This guy knew his aircraft; the Master Chief had run the centerline tank empty before switching tanks. He was getting every ounce of fuel out of it. He had only been standing there for a few minutes, so that meant he had it estimated right down to the last minute of fuel. From where he sat he couldn't see the gauges. I would never be as good as this guy. The amazing factor is that the ferry pilots didn't fly the same aircraft every day and had multiple qualifications in various types of aircraft. They had to know and understand all the systems and performance characteristics of the aircraft they flew. The only thing that frustrated me was the fact that he didn't pass on any of his knowledge. You had to ask all the questions and half the time he was sitting in the back.

We arrived in Brownville without any fuel problems. I

continued to build my flight time by staying on the road as much as I could. Over the next few months, I got flight time in P-2's, P-3's, C-2's, E-2's, and T-39's, qualifying in the H-1, H-2, H-53, H-46, S-2, and C-1. That's the way it was, if you loved flying it couldn't get any better than VRF-31. I could have made a career out of VRF-31. You were pretty much your own boss. You took an aircraft from A to B. You determined the route and as long as you got it there in a reasonable amount of time, nobody asked questions. There were no politics, just flying.

I remembered when I picked up my first CH-53D out of the factory. Again the meteorologist would be my nemesis. I needed to get out of Stratford, Connecticut to NAS Quonset Point, Rhode Island, to pick up another pilot who was bumming a ride back down to NAS Norfolk. Quonset Point was less than an hour away and the weather was miserable. I had to fly VFR; the CH-53D was a dual piloted aircraft and I was the only pilot. Many of our ferry flights were single pilot, unless we were bumming a ride to our next assignment. Being single pilot meant I was restricted from flying under instrument conditions in a dual piloted aircraft without another pilot. The meteorologist told me the weather eight miles to the east was great. I would have no problems and would not need an alternate.

I decided to go for it. I could stay overnight at Quonset and head out in the morning. When we picked up out of the factory, the ceiling was 500 feet, so I decided to head down the coastline, just off the beach, right into Quonset Point. At ten miles out the weather seemed to be deteriorating instead of getting better. I slowed to 80 knots, the CH-53D could easily do 185 knots. I continued to descend in order to stay below the overcast. We were down to 100 feet so I stayed out over the water to avoid any obstacles. I continued for 10 more minutes of flying in that crap. I was starting to weigh my options. It didn't take long before the decision was made for me. The visibility was easily less than a mile. Just then a huge sail boat with its large mast going up into the overcast popped up in front of me. I had no choice; I pulled in the power and raised the nose to avoid hitting it. The CH-53 could climb. It had more power than any helicopter I had ever flown.

I continued to climb and at 5,000 feet, I was still in the thick of it. I wanted to find the tops of the overcast to get VFR again. I was in a very busy part of the country with plenty of commercial traffic all around the Northeast. I had all of 10 hours in the aircraft and no co-pilot. I kept climbing and finally broke out at around 12,000 feet. The meteorologist didn't have anything right and I wanted to get my hands on him.

I switched over to Quonset Tower and told them the situation. Quonset replied by telling me the field was closed; the visibility was zero-zero. So much for the good visibility I was promised. I would really like to meet that weatherman, just one more time. I had used up almost one hour of fuel to that point. For tactical reasons and lift capability, the CH-53D held approximately 2 hours and 20 minutes of fuel before it was bone dry. I told the tower that I needed to land at Quonset Point and didn't have enough fuel to try to fly out of the weather. I got the old standard, "Wait one," and they went to get the base duty officer. I headed inbound to the Quonset TACAN (radio beacon) and orbited overhead in VFR conditions on top. I was already breaking the rules. The pilot in command has to be on oxygen above 10,000 feet. I started looking at the map and instrument approaches in the area to review my options. There weren't any. After about 20 minutes the duty officer came up over the tower frequency. I explained my situation again and told him I now had less than an hour of fuel onboard before the engines flamed out.

The duty officer replied "Roger, I understand, wait one." I didn't like the sound of that "wait one." What I needed was a duty officer with some brass balls that could make a command decision. The duty officer came back up over the radio, "Navy 326, I believe the field is starting to clear up a little. What I'm going to do is bring you in on a Ground Controlled Approach (GCA). The field is open. Navy 326, be careful on that final approach, there are still some patches of low clouds out there."

I replied. "Roger, tower, understood, and thanks". I had an idea that the visibility was still almost zero and that the duty officer was sticking his neck out in order to get me down. The radio communications were probably being recorded.

I flew the GCA down to about the last mile, backing off on the airspeed as I descended through 500 feet. By the time I reached the end of the runway I was in a 100 foot air taxi. The controller told me that I should be over the runway, so I started to slowly lower the helicopter down onto the runway. Between 50 and 75 feet I got a glimpse of the runway lights and called runway insight. The tower replied, "Roger, the field is closed." Needless to say I went to the O'Club that night and had a couple of beers. That kind of stuff is challenging enough if you have hundreds of hours in the aircraft.

The next day we headed out and after dropping off the other pilot at Norfolk, I turned towards San Diego, single pilot again. The days were long but I couldn't get enough of it. Outside of Tucson I lost an engine and took the 53 into Davis Monthan AFB. An engine failure in an empty CH-53D was a piece of cake. A CH-53 on one engine had more power than most twin engine helicopters. At least my engine failure was for real. One of the other helicopter pilots landed his CH-46 in the desert near Juarez, Mexico and walked across the border to get some tequila. When he got back to the helicopter and tried to start it, one of the engines wouldn't start. The pilot reported an engine failure and said he made a precautionary landing in the desert. The squadron CO gave him an "atta-boy" for good head work. I took my single engine into the Davis Monthan AFB so they could do the repairs there and didn't even get an acknowledgement.

The Marines out of Yuma had the 53 fixed in no time and I was back on the road in two days. On my way into San Diego

I decided to stop in at NALF Imperial Beach to see some of my old squadron mates. I filed the flight plan with a stop over and then a short leg into NAS North Island. As I approach Imperial Beach, I decided to wake up the place, so I called for a 300 foot right hand brake. The right hand break would put me right over the squadron spaces. The tower cleared me in for the break and I proceeded to rattle some windows. The CH-53 can be an impressive helicopter in a 180 knot brake at 300 feet. I taxied into base ops, shut down and told the crew chief to top her off, I'd be back in an hour.

After returning from a visit at my old squadron, I checked over the helicopter and turned it up. When I asked for a clearance to taxi the tower would not give me the clearance. I asked them what the problem was my flight plan was on file. Ground control told me the base operations officer wanted to speak with me. I shut down and went in to see the operations officer. The operations officer was livid. He could not believe a pilot would do a maneuver like that without authorization. I told him that I had asked for and received clearance for the break from the tower.

The ops officer, with his face beat red, growled, "There was no authorization. I checked with the tower, and they recorded all tower communications. There was no such thing."

I asked him if he listened to the recording. The ops officer told me to wait there and he would be right back. When he returned he was a little less aggressive than on our previous meeting. The tape was blank in that area and the personnel couldn't remember exactly what took place. I respectfully said, "Then you'll have to take my word for it." I turned to go out to the helicopter.

The ops officer was a commander and wasn't about to let a lieutenant get away with anything. "Wait a minute, Lieutenant. You're not leaving this base until you file a flight plan with me."

I at times didn't use good judgment, especially when I knew I was right. I didn't like a Navy Commander using his rank to be an asshole. I turned and said, "My flight plan is already on file, …. sir."

The commander replied by restating, "You will not leave my base without a signed flight plan."

After a few minutes of heated discussion, the commander said he would be in his office and that I could leave as soon as he saw the flight plan. I reviewed my options. None of them were good. I was getting out of the Navy in a few months so it really didn't matter if I was put on report, but I didn't want to get a flight violation. Just about then a lieutenant walked up. He was the assistant ops officer. He handed me a flight plan and asked me to sign it. I looked at it, signed it and thanked the lieutenant for his help. I then walked out to the helicopter and continued on to North Island.

The CH-53D was an awesome helicopter. I remember one trip from the factory to San Diego when I took off out of Greater Pittsburgh airport at the same time as a commercial 737. We were both headed for Raleigh Durham, NC. When I reached Raleigh I landed on the runway and taxied into the line to shut down. As I was securing the radios I overheard the pilot of the commercial 737 on final approach ask if I was the same Navy helicopter that just left Greater Pittsburgh. I came up over the radio and told the tower we were. When the 737 shutdown the whole crew including the stewardesses came over to look at the helicopter. They couldn't understand how we got there before they did and wanted to know more about the helicopter.

I led them on a little by telling them the performance characteristics were classified and I couldn't tell them. It was just an opportunity for a simple helicopter pilot to put one over on a jet pilot. I didn't want them to know it wasn't the performance as much as it was the route. They could figure it out for themselves. As they had to climb out to altitude to join the jet airways, I took off and headed direct, at treetop level, fast cruise. I had beaten them by about ten minutes. We refueled and walked inside to get a bite to eat.

When we departed the tower asked about the performance of the helicopter. I told him that it was just a standard Navy helicopter with nothing special in it. For fun I asked for a runway take-off and was cleared to the duty runway. I picked the helicopter up into a hover and held the nose a few feet off the runway until I reached 180 knots. At that point I pulled the nose almost straight up and started my climb. I reached 2,000 feet in a matter of seconds and was still climbing like there was no limit to the performance of the helicopter. The tower come up over the radio and said, "Man, that looks better than a Lear Jet!"

I replied, "It is," and headed west.

My next assignment was to take an H-34 out of North Island and fly it to the bone yard at Davis Monthan AFB. I met up with another pilot at North Island and because I had the most recent flight time in the H-34, I got to sign for the wreck. The H-34 had been around for a long time and I was sure if this thing was going to the bone yard, it had plenty of time on the airframe. We left early the next morning and were on our way to MCAS Yuma to refuel. We were over the mountains, in high wind conditions when we had a bad electrical fire. The smoke filled the cabin quickly before we could get everything electrical, shut down. With the winds like they were, and no stabilization, it was like trying to fly with a 2,000 lb. steel ball swinging 30 feet below the helicopter. All the stabilization equipment had been shut down and we were getting tossed around by the wind gusts. I kept the helicopter under control as the co-pilot and crew chief worked to get the fire out and bring the equipment back on line.

We were not that far from MCAS Yuma as they began bringing the equipment back on line. The in-flight procedure was to bring each piece of electrical gear back online one at a time until you found the equipment that was causing the problem. It ended up being some of the navigation equipment. We were VFR the whole way, so we just left the equipment off until we reached Yuma. We refueled and checked the helicopter out for any damage and decided to continue to Tucson, after all it was only going to the bone yard. We always made lots of allowances to try to get the aircraft to its destination. The day after we arrived I bummed a ride back to Norfolk in an S-2 and the other pilot headed for NAS Memphis. It was how we operated in the ferry squadron, but I was about to regret getting a ride in this S-2.

Everything went fine for the majority of the flight, but the pilot in command decided to push it all the way into NAS Norfolk. By pushing it we were due to arrive at 2230 in Norfolk. As we approached the East Coast the weather deteriorated. By the time we arrived, there was a heavy rain and the ceiling was about 1,500 feet. The weather in itself wasn't a problem until we tried to lower the landing gear for the final approach. The nose gear would not come down. We circled the airfield for the next 30 minutes trying to get the gear down, with no luck. I was not excited about making a gear up landing. I had heard stories about the starboard propeller shearing off and coming trough the right side of the aircraft on a gear up landing. As we looked for an answer, the heavy rain and high winds were relentless and continued to bounce the aircraft around as we circled the field.

I tried to talk the pilot into making a main gear landing, holding the nose off the runway until the airspeed dropped off and then lowering the nose to the deck. It made sense to me but the pilot didn't feel comfortable with it and decided to go in with the gear up. He didn't believe the prop would come off, and I didn't want to find out. God, I hated not being the pilot in command. At least if I screwed the pooch it would have been my fault. As the crash crew prepared the runway, the duty officer came up into the tower to talk with us. He was an old S-2 driver and had plenty of hours in the aircraft. He asked us to lower the gear and I did, the nose gear would not come down. He then said, "I want you to try it one more time, but this time raise the handle to the gear up position and as the indicators start to fluctuate, or cycle, snap the handle back down into the gear down position." I did it and I was one happy camper; the gear came down and locked in place. I was glad I didn't have to try my luck on a gear up landing. After a few days of rest in Norfolk I was on the road again.

That's Our Motto, "You start it for us and we'll fly it."

I continued to build my flight time and gain experience. We were on our way back from San Diego when we got diverted to an Army base in Texas to pick up a Huey (H-1) and take it up to NAS Quonset Point. I turned to the crew chief that was with me and asked him if he was qualified as crew chief in the H-1. The petty officer turned and replied, "Is that the one with the skids?"

I replied, "You're qualified." That's the way it went sometimes, you had to improvise. After we were dropped off, the petty officer and I walked toward the base operations building. In front was an Army Staff Sergeant on top of an H-1, training a group of what appeared to be plane captains.

As we approached the helicopter I hollered up at him. "Sergeant, is there a chance you can show my crew chief where to put the gas and oil in that thing?"

With a puzzled look on his face he looked down at me and said, "Sir?"

I replied, "We're picking up one of your helicopters and my crew chief needs to know where the gas and oil goes, can you help us?"

He grinned and said, "Yes, sir."

I left them and headed into the maintenance hangar to go over the log books and sign for the helicopter. As I walked down the passageway I spotted an old salty chief warrant officer (W-4) in a flight suit. I asked him where I could find the maintenance office. It just so happened the warrant was just the man I was looking for.

After I signed for the aircraft the warrant and I walked out to the helicopter, stopping by base ops first to file a flight plan. After inspecting the helicopter, I asked the warrant if he had an extra checklist. The warrant paused, the Huey was a pretty simple helicopter, but it was squadron policy to use a checklist. I wasn't supposed to pick up the Huey and I didn't have a checklist with me. Sometimes you would not see an aircraft for two or three months or more and it was always a good idea to use a checklist. The warrant, since it was the only helicopter he flew, he took it as though I was not familiar with the helicopter. I could tell by the expression on his face. I decided to play the old salt a little. The warrant replied, "No, but I can help you get it started."

I looked at him with a surprised look and said, "Really? That's great." I got in the helicopter.

As the warrant walked me through the checklist, I started to ham it up a little, looking in all the wrong places. When it came to starting the engine, I pretended I didn't know where the engine starter trigger was. When the warrant told me where it was, I reached under the collective and pulled the trigger, the engine started to turn. I looked over at the warrant with a big grin on my face, like a kid in a candy store and he just stood there watching me. I brought the RPMs up, turned on the radios and checked all the instruments, then looked over and gave the warrant a thumbs up. The warrant returned the thumbs up and reached through the window and patted me on the shoulder. I could see him mouth the words "good luck." I waited until the warrant had cleared the area. As I watched the warrant, I saw him walk around the corner of the hangar and then stick only his head back out to watch me take off. I picked up the helicopter in a nice smooth hover and taxied to the take off area chuckling to myself. I knew I had the old salt.

I headed out to fly up the eastern seaboard to Rhode Island and NAS Quonset Point. I only had a few months left in the Navy. I had received a letter from United Airlines that I was scheduled into their training class shortly after I got out. My last few months in the Navy were going to be fun flying. When we reached New York, I decided to fly up the

East River instead of going across the Long Island Sound. As I approached LaGuardia International, I called for a clearance through their air space. I could not get them to respond to my radio calls until I was right on top of their control zone. LaGuardia replied by clearing me into their controlled air space. As I flew up the East River, I could sea the end of the active runway right at the edge of the water. I called for a clearance across the approach end of the runway. LaGuardia cleared me and requested that I stay as low as possible until I was clear of the control zone.

I acknowledged and pushed the nose over to expedite my crossing. Right on the other side of the runway were the Whitestone and Throgsneck bridges. I had been instructed to stay as low as possible, so I went under both bridges. I had always wanted to fly under a bridge and it would most likely be my last opportunity. It just happened to be in one of the most populated places in the United States. I arrived at Quonset Point that day and called in to get my next assignment. As I closed out my flight plan, base operations asked me if I had seen any Army helicopters along the way. I had filed my flight plan as Navy, but the helicopter still had the Army markings on the side of the helicopter. Go figure! Another CH-53D going to San Diego was on the schedule. That afternoon while I was in the O'Club having a beer I was approached by the squadron maintenance officer. He wanted to know if I brought any transport wheels with the aircraft. The weather was turning bad and they needed to get it into the hangar. I told him if they couldn't find a way to get it in the hangar I would fly it into the hangar. The maintenance officer paused for a minute and then thought better of it. It was a big hangar; it would have been easy.

About five weeks passed bouncing around the countryside flying various aircraft before I returned the to Army base in Texas to pick up another Huey. As I walked down the passageway to the maintenance office, I saw the same salty old warrant officer walking down the passageway. As I passed, I said "hello."

The warrant stopped and stared at me, "You're the Navy pilot that was in here a few weeks ago."

"That's me," I replied.

The warrant said, "You really had me going. I thought you were going to turn that helicopter every which way but loose."

I replied, "That's our motto in the Navy. You start it for us, and we'll fly it."

We laughed and the warrant said, "I like the way you guys fly." We went in to sign for another helicopter so I could get underway that day.

I was beginning to regret my decision to leave the Navy. I enjoyed what I was doing and the crewmen that I flew with were great. They knew their jobs and never complained. I was beginning to feel I could fly anything with an engine on it. I received some bad news when I returned to Norfolk. United Airlines had cancelled the class that I was scheduled to go into. It seemed all the airlines were in a slump and cutting back. I had already submitted my resignation papers, and they were accepted. I was on my way out of the Navy and did not know what I was going to do. I weighed my options and decided to go back to school and finish my degree.

Civilian life and college

I returned to my old college in California and enrolled in their aeronautical engineering program. After the first two semesters were out of the way, I found out that the aerospace industry was also in a slump. I remembered one of the professor's telling me that when the industry started hiring again, I should be one of the first to be hired, with my aviation background and experience.

I had kept my flight time up by joining a P-2V reserve squadron. The squadron was a great group of guys, most of them were in the airlines. I remembered one of the inspections we had. When I showed up for the inspection without my medals or ribbons, the CO wanted to know why

I wasn't wearing them. I explained that I didn't want to draw any attention to myself. Now there's an ego for you. I had picked up over five rows of ribbons and medals in my short Navy career, in spite of my blistering, headstrong personality. Some people found that impressive; I didn't have a feeling one way or the other. The CO said that I was the only one in the squadron with any combat medals and made me return home to get them. After the inspection we retired to the O'Club and I didn't have to buy a drink the rest of the night. It was actually a very enjoyable experience and everyone seemed to want to hear the sea stories behind the medals. Even as the beers went down I had a tendency to play down the stories.

Another few weeks went by, the timing couldn't have been any better. It seemed the Navy had let out too many pilots and they sent me a letter asking me if I wanted to return to active duty. I didn't hesitate. I wasn't a civilian and I knew it. In 1970 the patriotism and sense of duty were just not there, especially at the university level. I called my detailer immediately. I had decided that if I went back in, I would make a career out of the Navy. That's if all the bridges I burned as a young officer didn't prevent it.

The call with my detailer was a little disappointing. The detailer told me that it would only be for two years and that I had a snowball's chance in hell of making a career out of the Navy. The Navy wanted career minded officers and broken service was like having a venereal disease on your medical record. I had been out less than 6 months but had made my own bed and accepted the consequences. We worked out a deal where I would return to Pensacola as a flight instructor and I could attend the university full time to complete my degree. I had decided that I would take it one step at a time and looked forward to being in uniform again.

Helicopter Training Squadron-Eight (HT-8)

Pensacola! What a great place. I looked forward to visiting all the places that started my career. Remembering all the excitement and high expectations of being a naval aviator. It felt good. It was like I was a cadet again. It's funny how some of the hardest times in your life become some of the fondest memories. The first thing I did, even before checking in for duty, was to return to NAS Pensacola and visit the old WW II barracks and the parade grounds where I spent many hours marching off demerits. Nothing had changed; it was like the place stood still in time. I could see the officer candidates marching around in formation, they looked so young even though some of them were my age (26). NAS Saufley and Whiting fields had not changed either. I thought back to some of the young cadets that didn't make it through the program and wondered what became of them.

I had been assigned to Helicopter Training Squadron Eight at NAS Ellyson Field. I was always eager to start a new assignment, so I checked in early. Patience was not my strong point. I had learned that a good friend of mine had been furloughed from the airlines and was a ground school instructor at Ellyson Field. It was going to be good to see him again. It turned out that several of my friends were scattered all over Pensacola. Most of them were from the airlines. There were quite a few pilots that came back on active duty. Most were only there until the economy got better and the airlines picked them back up. After that short return to civilian life I knew the Navy was for me.

After an initial indoctrination course I was told to report to the squadron standardization office. As I walked down the hall I saw the sign on the office door, "**Super Stan**". Standardization was a group of second tour pilots that trained the new instructors in the proper procedures and flight maneuvers that would be used in the student flight training syllabus. I knew I was in for a treat; the sign "Super Stan" meant that the office was filled with a bunch egotistical horses asses. I hated people that thought they were special or more important than the organization. Anyone that would allow a sign like that on the door would have to think they were superior aviators. I paused for a moment and reminded myself that I was going to try to make a career out of the Navy and I would have to pay homage to them. I just hoped I wouldn't have to put up with too much of their bullshit. I never learned how to deal with egocentrics and their condescending attitudes .

I breezed through the training with only one incident. Without my saying a word, standardization knew what I thought of them. My feelings were something I never learned to hide. Even If I didn't say anything, it was written on my face. The standardization pilots talked to the instructors like they were cadets. There definitely was a superiority complex that ran rampant in the office. I was finishing up one of my last flights with a Marine captain from standardization. He had less flight time than I did and was a mediocre pilot. His ego told him he was much better than he was. Toward the end of the flight the Marine told me that he was going to show me a few maneuvers that I wasn't allowed to do, to demonstrate what the TH-57 could do. Under no circumstances were instructors authorized to demonstrate these maneuvers to students. It was nothing more than a low level simulated engine failure with a quick flare to trade airspeed for altitude while you kept your RPMs under control as you made an engine off landing.

The Marine captain came around, shot the approach, over controlled the helicopter and made a sloppy, hard landing, but he did keep his RPMs under control. He tried to bullshit me by telling me that it was a good landing. Without saying another word the Marine captain signaled that I had the controls.

I brought the RPMs back up and picked the helicopter up into a hover and said "Do you mind if I show you something?"

The Marine shrugged and held out his hand, which I took as, "Go ahead." I took the helicopter around the field, came in faster and lower, cut the throttle, made a radical flare and dropped the skids so softly on the grass you couldn't feel us touch down. Oh yes, the RPMs did not move either. I then turned to the Marine captain and said, "I may not be able to do the maneuver, but I just wanted to show you what it looked like when it is done right." What can I say? I just didn't have any common sense.

I really knew how to make friends. I finished the flight, completing the syllabus. The Marine captain chose not to show me anymore maneuvers. My little stay with "Super Stan" would endear me to them for the rest of my tour in the training command. I was a better pilot than most of them and they knew it. Like most people with that type of personality they would never confront me. They would wait for me to make a mistake, then they would be all over me. With my personality it was just a matter of time. Nobody was supposed to challenge "Super Stan." I went to my flight and started training students. I also checked into the university and signed up for their undergraduate program. The schedule kept me pretty busy. I was a full-time student and a full-time flight instructor.

HT-8 had two types of helicopters: TH-57's and UH-1's. I had been assigned to the TH-57's. I was completing my first year as an instructor and really enjoyed my job. The Marine pilots were having their annual physical fitness test. I had always tried to stay in good shape, but had no idea how I compared with any rating system. The Marine instructors all had their tests on one day and I asked to participate. The Marine captain organizing the PT test told me in a very condescending way that I didn't know what I was getting into. The test was very difficult and I probably would not be able to finish it. I hated that. It just made me that much more determined.

I said, "That's fine. I'm always up to a challenge and would like to participate anyway."

The next day we took the test, so I didn't have time to prepare for it. Some of the Marines had been building up to the test for weeks. When the results came back I got a 96 out of a possible 100. The closest Marine got a 94 and the scores went down from there. The next day I was headed up the stairs as the Marine captain that organized the PT test was coming down. The Marine didn't say anything, so as I passed by, I coughed and blurted out 96! The Marine didn't say a word and kept walking.

I was glad I didn't fall for all the talk about how tough it was. I had already fallen for it two months prior when my best buddy talked me out of entering the iron man contest that the base sponsored. I always underestimated my ability and he knew the right buttons to push. He ended up winning the trophy and I knew I could have beaten him. The days turned into weeks and between school and flying the days flew by.

One day there was a heavy front moving through and the weather was turning pretty ugly, so they cancelled all flight ops. Dave and I decided to tip a few beers. We started early and by 1400 in the afternoon we were well on our way. We decided to go over to the O'Club and have a few more. As we sat in the O'Club, six Marines came in and ordered a round of drinks. Dave got a hair up his ass and decided he was going to start a fight with the Marines.

He leaned over to me and said, "See those Marines? I'm going kick their asses."

I replied, "Jesus Christ, Dave! You know I submitted my letter to go regular Navy. If you do that I can kiss any chances goodbye."

Dave was going back to the airlines, and he was in an ornery mood. He leaned over again and said, "Are you with me?"

I replied, "Do I have a choice?" I didn't.

You don't come across good friends like that very often. He was brash, outspoken, and wild. He was a complete opposite to some of those bureaucrats that I ran into in the Navy. He would have been perfect for the role Kurt Douglas played in the movie *In Harms Way*. Maybe we both should have been

Marines. Besides it seemed I was always watching my brother's back as he started a fight almost every weekend as we went through high school. That's all I knew.

I was pissed, but knew I had to help him if he got into trouble. Dave was a true friend and you don't find many of them as you travel through life. Dave got up and walked over to the Marines and called them just about every name in the book. I sat at the table watching what was going on, ready to move if I had to, which I hoped would not be the case. This went on for few minutes and the Marines didn't respond to David's insults. He finally tired of it and came back to the table and sat down. Which made me very happy.

We will never know why the Marines did not respond. Dave wanted to believe it was because,.... Actually, I don't know what he believed. Being a pragmatic person, I thought it was because they didn't want to deal with two drunks. In either case we must have made a good impression. There were many things that happened during my tour at Ellyson Field. This was one of only a few that I could mention. I was always teamed up with people and friends that were a little on the wild side and usually threw caution to the wind. They enjoyed life!

Recently there had been a couple of engine failures that resulted in two crashes of UH-1's. The CO was getting a little concerned. They changed some of the procedures to try to reduce the severity of the crashes, but nobody believed it would help much. Back then they were all single engine helicopters. When the engine quit, you landed where you could, or couldn't. I didn't think twice about it. I had plenty of time in the TH-57, it was a piece of cake to fly and I knew I could drop it down on a dime, if I had to. I had finished up my classes that day at the university and thought I would stop by the scheduling office to see if they needed any instructors. I was not on the schedule that day. I was soon going to learn what, "don't volunteer for anything," really meant.

The scheduling officer told me they needed some

instructors for the solo students. The weather was getting a little rough and the winds were too high for the students to go out by themselves, especially with the recent accidents. I told him, "no problem," and headed up to get my flight suit on. When I came back down, there was a student waiting to go on his first solo hop. As we headed out to preflight the helicopter, I told him that on my first solo flight I had a 150 lb. bag of sand in the other seat and to enjoy his hop and pretend I was a sand bag.

"No, sir," he replied, "I heard you were a good instructor, and I would appreciate you showing me anything you think I should know." I didn't reply.

We strapped in, the student went through the checklist and we got a clearance to taxi. We departed NAS Ellyson and headed down the highway that led to one of the outlying sites. The flight path took us right by a golf course where the instructors always pulled simulated engine failures. As we approached the golf course, I decided to give him a simulated engine failure. I cut the throttle back to flight idle, like I had done a hundred times before, and said, "You have a simulated engine failure." The student quickly got the collective down and kept the RPMs under control, but completely overshot the landing area by a wide margin, which was the golf course.

We were over the trees at 300 feet. I took control of the helicopter and brought the power back on just as it was written in the manual. Just then the engine quit. We were surrounded by tall pine trees and I was about to see if I was a good as I thought I was. I pushed the nose over and wrapped the helicopter up into a tight bank. We were too far out to make it over the trees. I had no choice; I found an opening and shot between two large pines, extending my glide as much as possible. When I cleared the trees, I had plenty of airspeed and no altitude so I kicked the helicopter into a sideslip, banked it almost 90 degrees, stopping my forward airspeed. I then snapped the helicopter back level, pulled in the collective and we settled onto a par four. When they repaired the helicopter and flew it off, there was nothing more than two small creases in the grass from the weight of the helicopter. I thought to myself, that ought to make the CO happy, he didn't lose another helicopter. As I said before, there is a difference between ego and having confidence in your ability to handle any situation. I don't know of anyone that could have pulled it off as well as I did.

While the maintenance crew checked over the helicopter we returned to the squadron in a Navy truck. The student couldn't shut up about what had happened and how I got the helicopter safely on the ground. I ignored the comments. It was Friday night and I was headed for happy hour to toast my flying skills. Friday happy hours were like a big party. The graduating class that week always bought all the drinks for everyone; it was a Navy tradition after getting your wings. People came from all over. The happy hour would start with the new naval aviators sitting on the bar with large glasses in their hands. It was the same tradition I had enjoyed when I got my wings and I never got tired of it. The excitement in the air and the aspirations of the new naval aviators was refreshing. They would put their newly earned wings in the glass and someone would ring the large brass bell at the end of the bar. At that point it was a race to see who could empty the glass first, catching their wings in their teeth, and the party would begin.

Would I really lose my wing's wings this time?

I was up in the locker room getting cleaned up to head for the O'Club. It was very quiet, and I felt the silence. Nobody came up to congratulate me on saving an aircraft, in fact it seemed like they avoided the issue. I shrugged it off and headed out. While I was at the O'Club, I sensed the same thing but didn't pay any attention to it. My buddy was there and we were going to tip a few beers and raise a little hell. Later that night the duty officer came into the O'Club and told me the CO wanted to see me first thing Monday morning. I didn't ask any questions. I knew what it was for, I was going to get an "Atta-Boy" for saving his helicopter. We finished the night and I headed home for the weekend.

Bright and early Monday morning I was outside the CO's office. As I sat there I saw the entire "Super Stan" office file into the CO's office. I sat outside for more than 30 minutes and the longer I sat, the more I felt the news was not going to be good. I was finally called into the CO's office, and when I walked in the room was full. All of "Super Stan" was sitting along one wall; the maintenance officer was there, the operations officer was there, and the executive officer was there. The first thing I thought was, "This looks like a lynching." I could almost see the rope with the noose draped across the laps of the "Super Stan" pilots. The CO told me to sit down, so I did. I listened to what they had to say.

I was devastated. I couldn't believe that naval officers would throw out such lies. Nothing they said was true. "Super Stan" had the lead and they were after my wings! They felt I had performed an unauthorized maneuver. Their case was the maneuver I did was in the syllabus on the A-12 and A-14 flights' instructional hops, but it was not authorized on a solo A-13. As if that wasn't pathetic enough, now the real trash started. I was young and naive and I had no idea that people would make up complete and utter lies in order to destroy someone.

At this point my John Wayne world of truth, justice and fair play was crumbling around me, and the real world was starting to show itself. They brought up over-inflated stories about the disrespect that I displayed while I was going through "Super Stan." They made up things I never even said. They alleged that it was overheard in the locker room that I said, "Screw the Navy. I'm only here to get a degree."

At this point, I was going into a self-destruct mode. I wasn't sure I wanted to stay in an organization that allowed these individuals to exist. Rarely do you get a chance to be confronted like this. These types of individuals usually keep you at arms' length and you never see the knife because it's always in your back. They never expose themselves to any risk or controversy. This time they must have felt they could carry the day.

The CO looked over at me and asked, "What do you have to say?"

Thank God the CO was a fair man and an independent thinker. Sometimes it was a toss of a coin on who you would be standing in front of. I didn't hold anything back. I was so angry I wanted to take a swing at someone. "This is a bunch of horse shit." I went down the list. "First, nowhere in the syllabus does it expressly prohibit a simulated engine failure on an A-13, if an instructor is in the aircraft. I've done that same maneuver hundreds of times throughout the year. In fact, the student is allowed to do a power recovery autorotation at the outlying sight on an A-13. Most likely the engine would have failed there, and the student would have rolled the helicopter up into a ball. You never would have found out why the engine failed and from what I understand you had 11 potential accidents sitting on the line."

The CO looked over at the maintenance officer and the MO moved his head in agreement.

The maintenance officer then spoke up and said they had determined what the problem was and they had found 11 other helicopters out of the 32 on the line with the same problem. They were putting in for an airframe change to eliminate the problem.

I continued, "Your so-called 'Super Stan' is a bunch of egotistical, mediocre pilots with marginal skills. I can out fly all of them on my worst day. Nothing they stated is in writing in the syllabus. They made this up after the fact to suit their own needs and hang my ass. As far as the disrespect shown to 'Super Stan,' that is total bullshit. In fact, I thought I demonstrated a great deal of restraint putting up with their egos and their condescending attitudes. I made one mistake and that was showing them I was a better pilot. Someone needs to look at their entire syllabus; it's full of holes.

"These other rumors about what I said in the locker room are trash, and I can't believe they are coming from Naval and Marine officers. Why would I say, 'Screw the Navy. I'm only here to get my degree?' I submitted my request to go regular Navy two months ago because I wanted to make a career out of the Navy. Now I'm not sure that I want to be in the same organization as these so called 'officers.' The only reason I'm standing here right now is I volunteered to come in on my own time to help get the backlog of students out."

I stood there disgusted. The CO asked me if I had anything else and I said, "No, sir." He asked me to step outside and wait in the hall. I turned and left.

A few minutes later the rest of the officers started filing out of the CO's office. I was still livid. I didn't want anything to do with this group of assholes. As I sat there I had time to reflect. I probably could have cleaned up my language a little. I didn't project the ultimate officer and gentlemen image. As they filed out the MO stopped and said, "Do you mind if I give you a bit of advice?" The MO was a mustang that worked his way up through the ranks. He was a Lt. Commander with 27 years in the service and as far as I knew was a straight shooter.

I said, "Sure, what is it?" as we stepped outside.

He came back with, "You need to show a little humility." I looked at him in total amazement.

"Humility? Those son-of-a-bitches were trying to hang my ass for saving a goddamn helicopter, and I'm supposed to go in there and beg forgiveness? I'd rather lose my wings than give in to those bastards."

The MO shrugged and said, "You did a good job on the landing," and then turned and walked away.

About 30 minutes later I was called back into the CO's office. "Sit down LT." The XO was in the room with the Skipper. He was a good man. The XO was also prior enlisted, and he didn't like bullshit any more than I did.

The CO started with, "I've talked it over with the XO

and what we would like to do is have you go over to the Standardization Office for a week. We would like you to go through their entire syllabus and point out any ambiguities or gray areas and make any recommendations you can think of to improve the syllabus."

I sat there down in the mouth and said, "Yes, sir." I felt he knew what was happening but needed to keep peace in the squadron. They excused me and I got up and walked out the door. As I walked back to the locker room, I thought I was the only one in the Navy that could save an aircraft and almost lose his wings over it.

Some of the other flight instructors who were supposedly my friends were back in the locker room. They were very interested in what took place. They seemed pleased when I told them the results of the meeting. What I wanted to know was, where were they when the shit was hitting the fan? Everyone knew what assholes "Super Stan" were. They were all friendly again and I wasn't sure I wanted their friendship. They avoided me until they found out the results of the incident. It was a trait in people that I would see far too often. I was not happy and decided to go home and cool off.

The experience left a bad taste in my mouth. I had decided to see what response I got back from my request to augment into the regular Navy before I decided what I would do. I had sent in the request with four other officers, all of whom had degrees except for me. When the response came back from the bureau, I was the only one of the five that was accepted. I didn't understand it; one of the officers even had a master's degree. I had calmed down while I was waiting for the results and decided to accept and go regular Navy. It was going to be my career, however bleak it may be. I would take whatever the Navy threw at me.

They changed the sign on "Super Stan's " door to "Standardization Office".

The XO took over as the new CO two months later. The XO had a personality more like mine. He joined Dave and I at happy hour and challenged us to an arm wrestling match. He was good but he never beat Dave, and I was too dumb to let him win. Nevertheless we got along well. He was straightforward, honest and a little rough around the edges, but that's what I liked about him. I completed my degree and was assigned as the Assistant Administration Officer and still continued to instruct. That was fine with me; I needed to pick up experience in administration if I was going to make a career out of the Navy.

I volunteered to represent the helicopter community and give presentations on the capabilities of helicopters to the new students in basic flight training at NAS Saufley Field. When the students left Saufley they were required to choose what pipeline they wanted. The choices were still the same: jets, multi-engine, or helicopter. Only in those days helicopter pilots were not third class citizens any longer. The Vietnam War had brought them to the forefront. The weapon systems were getting better and the versatility of the helicopter made it a challenging career path.

I was met with tremendous enthusiasm by the flight students. They couldn't seem to get enough of the sea stories and photos. After I had been giving the presentations for about six months I was called into the XO's office. As I stood in front of his desk, he looked up at me with a very solemn look on his face and said, "We have a problem."

I thought, "Oh shit, what now? I know I haven't told anyone off in months."

The XO continued, "I just received a call from one of the XO's of the jet training squadrons at NAS Memphis. He says you have to stop giving the helicopter presentations at Saufley." I stood there not knowing what to say, or understanding where the XO was coming from.

The XO then broke into a grin and said, "It seems there are more requests for helicopters than jets. The jet pipeline feels they have to get the best of the best, and they don't feel they're getting the best students anymore. I talked to the

Skipper about the situation. What we would like you to do is continue to give the presentations."

The XO leaned back in the chair and put his hands behind his head, and I started breathing again. He said, "We want you to keep doing what you're doing until you get your orders and then we want you to train your replacement." We talked for awhile and laughed about the complaint from the jet community. I liked giving the presentations and enjoyed the enthusiasm the young students showed when they listened to the sea stories. It reminded me of when I was a young cadet full of high ideals and looking for the excitement and adventure of naval aviation. I left the XO's office and headed for the flight line.

Along with my administrative duties, I continued to train students. One night I was out on a cross country in the TH-57. It only had basic instruments in the aircraft and was not considered a real instrument bird. The helicopter did not have a radar altimeter so if we lost an engine, the pilot would not know what altitude to flare at on a dark night. If we had to go in, we would be very lucky if we walked away from it. As we were flying from one checkpoint to the other my student asked me what I would do if the engine quit, right then. I pointed over to the freeway and said, "See that? I would take it right down there. If we took it into the trees, we'd never make it and the best case scenario we would only get busted up, a little."

The student said, "But what about the cars?"

I replied, "Son, if our engine quits, we have an emergency and I'm going to get my butt down as best I can. I could set this thing down on the roof of a car without denting it, if I had to. If we land in front of a car, then he has an emergency, and I hope he handles it as well as I would mine." It may have been a little self-centered, but I always had a strong survival instinct when it came to flying. It kept me alive.

I only had a few months left before I rotated to a new duty station. The lieutenant fitness reports came out and I was the number one lieutenant in the squadron out of 22. I even got a letter of commendation from the Skipper.

I hoped it would help me with my new assignment, but I was disappointed, the detailer was really negative. He told me that he didn't understand how I made regular Navy with my broken service. My career was going to be short-lived and he assured me I would not make Lt. Commander. The detailer offered me a job with Tactical Air Control Squadron Thirteen (TCARON 13) in San Diego. I accepted. It wasn't the best assignment, but I didn't have much choice. I said I would make the best of it. As I departed HT-8, the Skipper was very complimentary of my performance and wished me luck on my new assignment. I was going to miss him; he was a good man. I headed to San Diego as the top lieutenant who still had no future.

Tactical Air Control Squadron Thirteen (TACRON 13)

I headed for Tactical Air Control Squadron Thirteen (TACRON 13) and a staff position. The squadron's mission was to control and manage the airspace within an Amphibious Objective Area (AOA) in support of amphibious operations from the sea and/or on shore. They were also trained to provide forward air controllers, both in the air and on the ground for tactical aircraft within the AOA. The squadron was made up of Navy, Marine, and Army pilots. Because it was an inter-service assignment the Army and Marines sent some of their sharpest officers. It was not the same for the Navy. Although the senior Navy officers seemed to be pretty sharp, the junior officers were nothing but cannon fodder. The squadron would allow me to renew my qualifications in the C-1, S-2, and the T-28 and even get a little more time in the C-47.

The T-28 carried the rockets and gave us the ability to mark targets on the ground as forward air spotters. The T-28 would roll in low level and mark the targets so the tactical aircraft flying at 15 to 20 thousand feet could see where the bombs needed to go and roll in on the targets. It also gave me an opportunity to fly with a couple of Marine jet pilots to learn their tactics and get a feel for what it was like to be an attack pilot. The S-2 and C-1 were for flight time and moving personnel around.

After receiving training my first assignment was to return to Vietnam in support of the amphibious group off the coast. I was assigned as Assistant Officer in Charge for a small detachment. The Officer in Charge was a very senior lieutenant who had been passed over for Lt. Commander. I was briefed by the (Ops Officer) in a very delicate way before I deployed that I was to assist the OINC as much as I could. It seems he was having a difficult time communicating with the enlisted personnel. The rest of the squadron would be aboard the USS *Okinawa*, supporting the PHIBRON (Amphibious Squadron) staff.

When I arrived, I went over all the enlisted personnel training jackets. The enlisted personnel were all radiomen and air controllers. I was blown away by the suggested IQ's and test scores of these guys; they were some of the highest IQ's I'd ever seen. Traditionally the classification they were in required very sharp people for this type of assignment. I thought that it must be entertaining to these guys, watching some of these bozo officers and the stunts that they pulled. Especially the OINC, he was a real piece of work. The briefing that I got from the ops officer was not the whole story; this Lieutenant couldn't tie his shoes.

The enlisted personnel immediately took a liking to me. I was a straight shooter and could talk their language. It was an instantaneous mutual respect. Not that I was so dynamic, it was more that the enlisted men were so hungry for someone to represent and lead them, they would take anyone that was halfway decent. I could at least wear my uniform properly. They would have followed anyone that displayed common sense and had some semblance of military bearing. By default I became the OINC and the lieutenant was allowed to go off and do his thing, what ever that was. It was a short two months and I was grateful for that. We would be cross decking to the *Okinawa* in support of an amphibious operation off the coast of Vietnam, in the Gulf of Tonkin. I was eager to go; the staff bullshit was not for me. The squadron was split into two groups, the CO and his staff supporting CTF 76 and the majority of the senior officers and the XO with his staff supporting a smaller amphibious ready group.

We executed nine amphibious exercises, including five air lifts in support of the Republic of Vietnam and received a Meritorious Unit Commendation for our efforts. I was not happy; it seemed the Marines were having all the fun. I knew what it was like in country and wanted to get back. I missed the adrenaline rush and the excitement. The rest of the cruise was uneventful and a little boring. The only thing that made the cruise fun was an Army major from the First Air Cavalry. Where he got all of his energy I didn't know, but when we were in port, he could party late into the next morning and outperform everyone during the day. I enjoyed pulling liberty with him. He had a love for life and there was always something happening. He was brilliant; he could even play the concert piano. I enjoyed being around this caliber of person, especially when they also knew how to enjoy life. The XO didn't drink anything stronger than Coke and never left the ship. He had the personality of a mortician.

When we returned to the States the three west coast TACRON's were combined into one Tactical Air Control Group, ONE (TACGRU ONE). This created lots of problems because there were too many commanders and not enough meaningful positions for them. Some of the commanders had been ordered in as the XO and CO of the three squadrons, but now there were no positions for them. The TACGRU seemed to be very top heavy, more majors and Lt. Commanders than I had seen in one squadron. The scope of the mission expanded a little but the responsibilities for augmenting amphibious groups during amphibious/

expeditionary warfare operations remained pretty much the same. The TACGRU deployed throughout the Pacific Fleet, providing centralized planning, control, and integration of all air operations in support of amphibious operations, training, and transits. Additionally TACGRU personnel served on Joint Forces Air Component Commander (JFACC) staffs, providing air control and planning in a unified or allied theater of operation. TACGRU also maintained the capability of temporarily manning and operating a remote or existing control facility ashore, thus supporting amphibious or disaster relief operations.

While we were back in the States, I had one of the scariest engine failures I was ever involved in, and I couldn't even call it mine. We were working with the Marines off the coast of California when I was called into the beach for a briefing. When I returned to the ship, I was onboard a Marine CH-46 helicopter. About ten miles out from the ship the pilot lost an engine. I was riding in the back with some of the staff and could see the instruments and the pilot in command from where I was sitting. The pilot was a former student of mine. He was not one of my better students. All I could do was sit and watch the instruments for the next 15 minutes; it wasn't much fun. When he made his final approach to the ship, I held my breath. The pilot made an excellent single engine no hover landing. He must have had an outstanding flight instructor. I gave him a thumbs up as I departed the helicopter and said "good job."

I spent the majority of my time back in the States picking up as much flight time as possible, which wasn't much. I was always available for any flight or exercise that would get me some flight time. You would have thought after that many years, I would have learned not to trust meteorologists, but I guess I was gullible. I was getting in some of my night and instrument time in a T-28. I was flying by myself. It was hard to get someone to go with you late at night, while they were on shore duty. It was about 2330 when I returned to NAS

North Island. The meteorologist briefed me that the weather would be fine upon my return. Worst case was a 1,000 ceiling. I hadn't been in a T-28 in about 3 months and the total time I had that year in the T-28, you could count on one hand. I didn't like the T-28 for instruments; it was almost impossible to trim the aircraft up. It always wanted to fall off on one side or the other. You had to stay on top of it every second.

When I reported into San Diego approach control they were reporting a ceiling of 850 feet. No problem, this would be a piece of cake. I was cleared in for a Ground Controlled Approach (GCA). As I descended down into North Island I went into a solid overcast at about 4500 feet, which was pretty typical for that time of year. As I approached 850 feet I expected to see the approach lights. Nothing, I was still in the soup. At 600 feet I was still completely IFR. I went through 500 feet, which were minimums for that aircraft and equipment. I pushed it a little further, perhaps the altimeter was a little off. I descended further, 400 feet, still nothing. At 350 feet, still no approach lights.

I knew something was wrong. I had pushed my luck too far. I started to waive off. Just then I saw the approach lights. I had just leveled off at 300 feet getting ready to start my climb. I quickly cut the engine and dove for the runway. I had no problem with the landing but was a little aggravated with the meteorologist. One of these days his kind was going to kill me.

The one thing I liked about flying was there was always the unexpected, although I did seem to have more than my share of situations. About a month later I was getting some flight time in a C-1 on a round robin from North Island to NAF El Centro. On my way out to El Centro I noticed the engine oil pressure dropping off on the starboard engine. As I watched the oil pressure slowly dropping, I went over my options. I didn't want the engine to fail on final so I decided to pull the engine back to idle and trim the aircraft out for a single engine landing. I called El Centro tower and told them I was going to make a single engine approach. I was glad that I had practiced this in the past. Emergencies were something that I continued to practice throughout my flying career. Practicing emergencies was always more fun than grinding around in the sky straight and level.

On final I brought the gear down. The crew chief checked the gear and said the starboard wheel well was dripping with oil. The landing was uneventful. After we shut down I went over the aircraft with the mechanics at El Centro. I could not believe what had happened. It was entirely my fault. When you did a preflight on the aircraft, it was the pilot's responsibility to check the engine oil levels. When I got to the starboard engine the plane captain was just finishing up his inspection. I stood over his shoulder and asked him if the engine oil level was okay. The plane captain told me it was fine, and I watched him secure the oil dip stick and close the compartment. The C-1 had a small wire clip that went over the oil dip stick that kept it from being forced out from the pressure of the engine. I watched him do it but did not check after he was done. He must not have seated it properly. The pressure from the engine forced the dip stick out, and engine pressure pumped the oil over the side. I'm glad it was a short leg to El Centro. If it would have been any longer of a flight I would have lost the engine for sure. We had lost half of the engine oil but the mechanics felt it did not hurt the engine. The heat in El Centro made working on the aircraft difficult. They had recorded 133 degrees Fahrenheit on the duty runway. The metal on the aircraft was so hot you needed gloves just to touch it. Later that day I returned to North Island.

We had been back in the States for about five months when I was called into the CO's office. It seemed that I was going to get a chance to have my own detachment. It was not a good situation, the current OINC was a Navy commander and I was a lieutenant. The commander had hurt the TACGRU's reputation. He had even given away the TACGRU tactical communications' spaces aboard the ship, telling the ship's

CO and the PHIBRON Commander that he had no use for the spaces.

I wondered why I was being given this assignment. How was I supposed to go in as a young lieutenant and correct everything that a commander had screwed up? The CO wanted me to go out there and turn things around. There wasn't much I could do about the assignment. The only good news was the commander would be gone before I got there, and I wouldn't have to deal with him. It appeared the current OINC didn't want to be there. His career was at an end, so I guess he decided that if he made a big enough mess of things, they would bring him home, which they did. I wondered where the other senior officers were. We were definitely top heavy, why didn't they jump at it? I didn't ask. It was an opportunity and I took it.

Minesweeping in Hai Phong Harbor

Why did I always seem to be the lucky one? If there was a lousy assignment, I always seemed to be the first on the list. I flew over and met the *USS Okinawa*, LHP-3 at Subic Bay in the Philippines. I quickly got to know the detachment personnel and decided to put together a dog and pony show for the commodore and his staff. The CO of the ship, along with the Marine Amphibious Unit Commander, also decided to attend. It went well, and I got our spaces back and was able to show off our multi-tasking capabilities in preparation for our next exercise. In order to get a feel for what the detachment could do we spent the next few weeks running exercises.

I had been onboard the *USS Okinawa* for a little over two months when the word came in that we would be moving to the *USS Cleveland*, LPD-7, a much smaller ship. We would completely retrain our personnel and our new assignment was to be the controllers for the aerial minesweepers that would work in Hai Phong Harbor. This was a first for TACRON, and the men were looking forward to the challenge. The Vietnam War was coming to an end, and we would be part of the minesweeping unit and would be some of the first American ships into Hai Phong Harbor.

The minesweeping mission was designated "Operation ENDSWEEP." Planning for Operation ENDSWEEP had begun before the conclusion of the Paris Peace Talks. The mining of Hai Phong was having an impact on the North Vietnamese economy; the U.S. negotiating team had used an offer of removing the mines as a bargaining point to get the Prisoner's of War (POWs) out of Hanoi. Sweeping the harbor was a condition for the release of American prisoners . After the training, it became a waiting game, while they negotiated the release of the POWs. There was also a problem with the three commodores that were in charge of the respective organizations. It appeared they let their egos get in the way and they had a disagreement as to who was going to be in charge of the entire operation. As a young lieutenant I found this a little disappointing. The Admiral from CTF-78 finally had to step in and take charge in order to get things moving.

I had all the confidence in the world in my men; they were sharp. Most of them probably had a higher IQ than I did. In less than a month the detachment had all the procedures worked out, and we were ready to go. We had used Subic Bay as an actual training ground to simulate the environment that we would face in Hai Phong Harbor. We would be controlling all the aerial minesweepers in the operating area. The detachment's air controllers would use the ship's radar to maintain positive control over the helicopters that would be towing a sled (towed array) behind them. The sled was supposed to set off any mines that were placed in the harbor, if they got close enough. Our objective was to plot accurately each track of the helicopters to ensure proper coverage. It was time-consuming, tedious work that required the team to be in a dark room working on plotting tables for about 14 to 16 hours a day. We would go in before the sun came up and leave after sunset. We might get to see the sun on the way to the enlisted mess or the wardroom.

Shortly after the New Year we received word to embark for Hai Phong Harbor. A total of 10 ocean minesweepers, 9 amphibious ships, 6 fleet tugs, 3 salvage ships, and 19 destroyer types served with Task Force 78 and got underway. We arrived on January 6, 1973. The *USS Cleveland* was the second U.S. ship into Hai Phong. We didn't even get our anchor dropped before we were ordered to turn around and head back out to sea. The next day we entered the harbor again; this time we got to drop anchor. Then we sat for two days. The negotiations were still going on. On the third day we raised our anchor and steamed back out into open water.

Finally the negotiations were complete. We steamed back in and started to work. At the end of the first month the long hours were starting to take their toll on the flight deck personnel. I got word that the air department onboard one of the other LPD's went on strike. The air boss was a close friend and a classmate from Preflight. He was an up and coming naval officer with a bright future. It seems the air boss, ship's operations officer, and ship's executive officer tried to negotiate with the flight deck personnel. They had to suspend flight operations for several days while they tried to resolve the issues. In order to respond to the situation and most likely, save his own ass, the ship's CO, blamed the XO, ops officer, and the air boss. That ended George's brilliant career.

After it was all over, I was able to get a helicopter flight over to the LPD to see how my old friend was dealing with the situation. He told me what had happened and asked me what I would have done in his place. It was an unfair question. It was after the fact, and I detested people who would always second guess someone, especially when they were not at risk. He said he wanted to know, so I told him what I probably would have done in his situation. "This is the military, not a democracy, and the operation was critical to the successful return of the POWs. I would have asked who was in charge of the strike and when he stepped forward, I would have had him thrown in the ship's brig. Then I would have asked, now who is in charge? I would have asked him to return to his duties, and if he refused, he would have gone to the brig. It would be repeated until I found someone that was responsible enough to do the job they were sent out there to do." George quietly agreed, but it was too late for his career.

Would it have worked? Who knows? You always have those political individuals that come out after the fact to determine what should have been done. I hated to see what was happening to George. He was a dedicated naval officer with a fine record and bright future. To see his career end like that was disturbing. Life at times was unfair and didn't make any sense. Here I was, a wild card and hot head, with a career path that was full of holes, and I was headed for the Naval Postgraduate School to get my master's degree. To see someone I had a great deal of respect for have his career end over such ridiculous bullshit, made me doubt the wisdom of the Navy's senior officers. I know I didn't have the complete story, but he was a good friend, and he would be a loss to the Navy.

During the remaining weeks of the minesweeping operation the task force detonated one mine, lost one helicopter and lost a minesweeping ship. What the Vietnamese didn't know was the mines were set to self-destruct at a greater percentage, than we had the technology at that time, to accurately sweep the mines. We got the POWs back and that's what it was all about.

When we returned to Subic Bay I found out that a friend of mine was debriefing the returning prisoners at Clark AFB. He went into Navy intelligence because he had chronic sea sickness. I flew over to Clark the following day to spend the night and have dinner. The BOQ was full so I had to go out in town to one of the hotels. The hotels were packed with reporters. While we were having dinner that night I got the opportunity to see some of the top notch reporters that were staying at the hotel. I was curious to see what they were like, since they had done such a terrible job of reporting the war by twisting the facts. I was amazed at the egos and the self-promotion. Jet pilots are famous for having egos, but they couldn't hold a candle to the egos of some of these reporters. I was glad I got an opportunity to see them in action. I had prejudged them, and I never liked to do that, preferring to see how someone behaved in person. In this case I was right.

I returned to San Diego onboard the *USS Okinawa* and picked up my orders for the Naval Postgraduate School in Monterey, California. Before I left I was called into the CO's office and given my fitness report and a letter of appreciation for the work we did in support of Operation ENDSWEEP. He told me it was one of the best fitness reports he had ever given a junior officer and I deserved it. I was also selected for Lt. Commander and they pinned the oak leafs on in his office. Everyone in TACGRU ONE was almost happier than I was when I got selected. I was the first lieutenant that had been promoted while in the unit in recent history. In fact nobody could remember the last time someone was promoted. On top of it I was headed for the Naval Postgraduate School for which it was an honor for most naval officers to even be selected.

Naval Postgraduate School, Monterey, CA

After a short leave period I was on the way up the coast to Monterey California and the master's program. I thought about the turn of events. It was said that only the top five percent got to go to the Naval Postgraduate School. My career was supposed to end at TACGRU ONE in San Diego. The detailer had promised me I would never make Lt. Commander. I didn't care; it was another opportunity, and I was going to take it and run with it. I was not an academic; I was operationally oriented, and I thought on my feet, not spending hours and hours with my nose stuck in books. The idea of spending two years at a graduate school with such a tough reputation was not my cup of tea.

Many of the officers felt they were sent to Monterey

because they were being looked at for future flag rank. I knew this to be a fact because I had to listen to some of the officers and their wives as they continually reminded me. I knew that wasn't the case with me and it allowed me to be a little more objective. I enjoyed many of my classes but the competition was fierce. Many of the officers in my class studied seven days a week at a minimum of 12 hours a day; I didn't. If the professor asked for a 15 page paper, he got 50 pages. The professors used to laugh; no matter what they asked for, the student would overkill any assignment.

I enjoyed one class in particular more than the others, it was a management/leadership course. Back then I was outspoken, and it seemed I had a unique leadership style. In fact the professor found my approach so unusual he wanted to put some of it in a book he was writing. Because of my strong convictions he had the rest of the class compete against me. It seemed part of the book was about the ability of individuals and groups to analyze situations and take action. I think he felt this situation was unique enough to warrant a little further exploration.

The professor would setup a scenario that required immediate action in order to prevent a catastrophic or troubling situation. He had me sit facing the rest of the class that was broken up into separate groups of two to three throughout the room. In each case, I was able to come up with a solution long before the rest of the class that was equal to or better than the individual groups. Of course it was subjective, and it was the opinion of the professor that made the final determination. In some cases the different teams could not come up with a decision they could all agree on.

The lesson was: no decision was worse than a bad decision. Some people (many) lived their whole lives not making decisions and hoped that nothing would happen on their watch. If they were lucky, they went through their entire careers without anything remarkable happening. I had no problem taking action, and I was amazed at the indecision of the other groups. It seemed they were so concerned about the consequences of their actions, they lost focus on what really needed to be done.

I would find out as I progressed in my career that many of the senior officers used this cautious approach to ensure longevity. By my nature I would continually test them while I was in the fleet. By the end of the course the professor agreed with me on the majority of the situations. He told me that I helped make his book a little more interesting and that he would probably use some of the situations from the class. What I did was certainly different from anything he had seen in that course before. Everything always seemed so clear to me and I didn't understand why being decisive and direct was considered unorthodox or unusual. It was simple; if you took action, instead of waiting for something to respond to, you had better control over the situation. The key though, was you had to be ready to be held accountable for your actions and leave your own personal interests out of it. The threat of this threw many of the officers in a tail spin. Even at that early stage they were honing their political skills.

The professor was interested in knowing if I had used my approach out in the fleet and whether it proved successful. I told him that I was not senior enough to make much of an impact but I shared a few short stories about my experiences as an OINC while deployed. To my surprise he seemed interested in everything I had to say. I enjoyed having someone express an interest in my views. Up until that point I had found most people close- minded unless it directly impacted them. Maybe it was because in the world of academia you never got to see your theories deployed. I decided to tell the professor about a similar incident in a training environment during my Tactical Action Officer (TAO) course.

While I was in TACGRU ONE I tried to get every qualification I could. The TAO course was a classified six week course that trained junior officers as ship's Tactical Action Officers to respond to incoming immediate hostile threats. The number and speed of the tactical weapons of that day required that a new position be created to respond to these rapidly developing threats.

The course was very intense. All of the studying had to be done in the classified spaces. In order to respond, everything had to be committed to memory. We didn't have access to computers like we do today. For example, the TAO would stand his watch in the ship's Combat Information Center (CIC). If a missile was fired at his ship there would be no time to look up information or call the CO to determine the next step. This was a new concept in the late sixties and early seventies. The TAO was trained to determine the threat through various means: radio signal/frequency, trajectory, speed, profile, platform, and provide the appropriate response to protect the task group. The whole concept was to defend the ship or task group against any attack: subsurface, surface, or airborne.

In the final week of training they conducted an exercise in a large simulator at the Fleet Training Center in San Diego. The simulator was setup as a Combat Information Center (CIC). The team would consist of six officers, each with an assigned task within CIC. In order to graduate, each officer would have to take his team through a computerized scenario acting as the TAO. I drew slot number 6, which meant I would conduct the response to the last scenario in the exercises. The only problem was, in order to keep the playing field even they increased the threats after each exercise. The first TAO had one submarine as a threat and each TAO after that had the threats increase.

By the time it was my turn in the barrel they threw everything at me. The objective of the exercise was to protect the high value target, which was usually the aircraft carrier. I had watched each succeeding TAO as they went through the exercise and the mistakes they made. Some of the TAO's seemed timid and indecisive and in most cases they did poorly in the exercise or received unacceptable damages.

Very similar to some of the scenarios in the classroom. Taking action and following it through to completion had always worked for me in the past. As my scenario developed, the threats increased to three Russian Bear bombers, two submarines and numerous incoming missiles. I decided to aggressively attack with all available assets, including the high value target as we made an end sweep to flank them. The tactic was a huge success with almost no damage to any of the Task Group assets.

Later that afternoon the instructor would debrief the day's exercises and analyze the results of each event, walking through each step of the exercise. When it came to mine, the instructor reported to the class that it was the most unorthodox approach he had ever seen. He later qualified the comment by saying, "you cannot knock success," and it was the highest score that had been recorded for that particular scenario. The professor at Monterey seemed entertained with the approach and felt that the key to all good leaders was their analytical ability, decision making processes, determination, and of course, LUCK! Good leaders were authoritative, decisive and displayed conviction in their beliefs, and that confidence was passed down through the ranks. It seems pretty simple, so why then is it so difficult to do? Is it the individual that makes the difference, or is it the combination of uncontrolled factors that come together just at the right time? When you add in the insecurities and self-doubt, prejudices, self-promotion, and avoidance of accountability, the probability of success becomes even less likely.

It was time for orders. I couldn't believe the luck. I was looking forward to getting back into the cockpit. Many of the students opted for their pay back tours in the subspecialty they had just picked up. This usually meant they would be behind a desk someplace. I received a letter from the Naval Air Systems Command and was selected for the Navy Weapons Systems Acquisition Manager program. It may have been the wrong choice, but I turned it down. I wanted to get back to the fleet, not sit behind a desk in DC. I was returning to an operational squadron, and it would be Helicopter Combat Support Squadron ONE (HC-1), back where I started as an ensign.

I seemed to be entering a new phase in my life as I left Monterey. I was older, more mature and now I was considered educated by some standards, whatever that meant. My views on leadership, fair play, and integrity had not changed since I was a young man and would remain the core of my beliefs. I would be tested in the years to come and my ability to put the men and the mission first would prove to be the cornerstone for the noteworthy successes we would enjoy. My aggressive, uncompromising and relentless style would be judged as arrogance by some who preferred the comfort of anonymity and indecisiveness. Some of the biggest battles that lay ahead would be challenging senior officers to do the right thing, at the risk of my own career.

Chapter Seven
WESTPAC Trouble Shooter

I reported to the Replacement Air Group (RAG) squadron for training in the Sikorsky SH-3. It was good to be back in the cockpit even if it was the H-3. The SH-3 was a modern version of the H-34; it wasn't meant to fly, just hover. It was big, non-responsive and not particularly easy on the eyes. It looked like a large bug with a set of rotor blades on it. I always seemed to endear myself to instructors with my casual approach to flying. While flying the H-3 I tried to make it handle more like a gunship, which did not please the conservatively trained ASW instructors, and my apparent overconfidence didn't help either. I was even able to aggravate them while I was in the simulator. When I was asked to raise my arms after jokingly going through a simulator hop in the middle of a hot summer day, the instructor responded with, "You don't seem to be sweating much." My reply was, "It's not my nature to sweat things. Life's too short." The instructor was not thrilled with the answer, but gave me an up for the simulator anyway. I never understood why people got such superior attitudes. Was it the person or the job that made them that way? Maybe they felt they were supposed to be serious. I'm sure they were glad to see me complete the program. After finishing the RAG training, I reported directly to HC-1.

USS Coral Sea and Detachment Four

The day I arrived at the squadron I was asked to report to the CO's office as soon as possible. I hadn't even checked in when the CO told me they had a problem with one of the detachments overseas and needed someone to go sort it out. Unbeknownst to me he had observed me in a class at the Naval Postgraduate School and liked the way I handled myself. It seems the current OINC aboard the *USS Coral Sea* had reported that his life had been threatened by some of the personnel in the detachment. It probably didn't help that he caused a midair that almost resulted in the loss of two helicopters.

As I listened to the CO, it seemed to be all one sided. The CO was responding to the OINC's explanation of what took place. The OINC had explained that if it were not for him the entire detachment would crumble. I had heard it many times before, the self-importance of one individual always made me wonder how they processed actual events. It seems my luck hadn't changed. I hadn't even checked into the squadron and I was given a difficult assignment. Nevertheless, the decision had been made by the CO and CAG to replace the OINC, and I was the candidate. My reply was, "When do I leave?"

I did not understand what came next. It seemed the CO was apologetic about putting me in this position. It was pretty straight forward to me; it was a job and I would take it on like I had done with every other assignment I had been given. It was my experience, that if you treated people fairly and were straight with them, they usually responded in a positive manner.

I didn't see what the problem was, but I was concerned that I wasn't getting the complete story. The CO told me that I would need to leave immediately in order to meet the ship in the Philippines, and he wanted to sign my Helicopter

Aircraft Commander (HAC) papers before I left. I told him that I didn't need my HAC papers to run the detachment, my ego would be fine. I was going to be the OINC, not an aircraft commander. The worst thing I could do was go out there with my HAC papers and not have the proper amount of time in the aircraft to meet the squadron aircraft commander requirements. It would be setting the wrong example. I told the skipper that I would send a message when I felt I was qualified. He didn't understand but agreed.

As I left the office, the CO again apologized for putting me in this situation. The apologies bothered me. What was I not being told? I went home and packed for the deployment. I was eager to be operational again and couldn't wait to get there to see what the detachment was really like. The current OINC would already be gone; I wouldn't get the normal turnover and that was fine with me. I needed to make my own assessment of the situation. It bothered me that not once during the briefing with the skipper did he mention any discussions with the other personnel in the detachment. It seemed strange; the mindset of the men was an important part of the equation. Maybe he avoided it for a reason?

On the way over I had plenty of time to think about the assignment. The stories the previous OINC kept promoting about his life being threatened seemed a little melodramatic. I was about to find out if it was true. To go in there with preconceived ideas was wrong. I would assess the detachment when I got there and determine what needed to be done.

I flew into Manila International and the detachment sent a helicopter to pick me up. It was hot and humid. You could see the moisture rising up out of the jungle. It seemed to be even worse than anything I had experienced in Vietnam. Maybe I was getting older. When I arrived aboard the *USS Coral Sea*, I was met by the Assistant OINC and the operations officer. To say the least, the reception was a little cool. They were very reserved and were in a wait and see frame of mind.

Two days later the ship got underway for a 35 day at sea

period. While we were in port I talked with all the officers and senior enlisted individually, and on the second day I introduced myself to CAG and the CO of the *Coral Sea*. From what I could see the detachment was looking for an OINC that would support them instead of using them to make a name for himself. Now that sounded familiar! The maintenance control officer had lost 30 lbs. on the cruise, and most felt it was a direct result of the pressure from the previous OINC to look good and build flight hours so he could shine in the eyes of CAG.

I liked what I saw. The officers were young and enthusiastic, and the enlisted personnel were sharp and eager to show they could do the job. I had seen it before and it seemed so simple, the organization was the key. The people in the detachment made up the organization. The decisions that were to be made needed to be in the best interest of the detachment as a whole, not for the betterment of any one individual. If the detachment was a success, then everyone assigned to the detachment would be successful. It was not rocket science.

As far as I could see the detachment was fully functional, it just needed someone to bring it together. Someone that could make them feel like they mattered and get them to function as a cohesive unit. I had to break the negative environment they had been exposed to for the first half of the deployment. It wouldn't be easy, and I had to be positive in my approach. They had already developed enough mistrust to last the rest of the cruise.

On the first week out to sea, I was flying with the Assistant OINC. This gave me a chance to see what type of pilot he was and to get to know a little more about him and the detachment. One of our flights ended up being a very memorable one. It was a typical log run, transferring people and cargo to the accompanying ships. It was probably one of the more challenging tasks of the sometimes boring and routine missions. The weather was good and the seas relatively calm. We were hovering over a cruiser transferring mail and parts to the ship when I smelled hot oil. With all the emergencies and incidents I experienced over the years, I seemed to have picked up a second sense. I came up over the ICS and asked if there was a problem.

As I explained what I smelled, the crew chief hollered out, "Holy shit! We have a massive oil leak back here."

I dropped down to the instruments to see what was happening and saw the transmission oil pressure dropping off. At the same time the Assistant OINC, as aircraft commander, immediately started to break hover and depart. I grabbed the controls and held them in place, I asked, "Where are you going? Set it down right here." The lieutenant didn't say anything and held the hover right where we were.

I quickly explained our situation to him. We were 54 miles from the nearest platform that we could land on. The only chance we had was to set it down right where we were. I knew that we had at tops 15 minutes of flight time once the oil in the transmission was gone. At best, it was 45 minutes to the nearest authorized flight deck and the oil pressure was dropping quickly. The cruiser had been certified during the Vietnam War for certain types of helicopters but was not approved any longer for larger helicopters like the H-3. I called the bridge of the ship and told them we had an emergency and we had to set the helicopter down immediately. I got that old ominous "wait one."

I signaled to the flight deck crew that we were setting down. Everyone started diving for cover. As the Assistant OINC lowered the helicopter to the deck, the crew chief hung out the side of the helicopter clearing the tail wheel at the back of the platform. The assistant OINC was an excellent pilot; I could tell the first day I got into the cockpit with him. It was something about the way a pilot becomes a part of the aircraft when he takes the controls. We got the helicopter on the deck without hitting anything. As we quickly shut down the ship's crew climbed back out from behind the ship's structures. Just after we touched down, the bridge replied by telling us they were not certified for H-3's. After we got shut down we walked around the helicopter to check the clearances. The rotor blades were about a foot from the aft gun mount and the tail wheel was inches from the edge. Even though the weather was good the sea swells caused the deck to roll from side to side, dropping several feet. The pilot had done an outstanding job of getting the helicopter down. There was no room for error.

When we inspected the helicopter we discovered the main oil line to the transmission had become disconnected. They had made a new manifold out of aluminum and the line going into it was stainless steel. The continuous vibration from the helicopter had caused the stainless steel tube to strip the threads out of the aluminum manifold. The oil was under full pressure and getting pumped out an open line. We had only minutes of oil left in the transmission. While we checked the helicopter over, the CO of the ship came out and looked over the landing area. You could tell by the expression on his face he would not have authorized the landing if he had known how risky it was going to be. I could not blame him. His responsibility was the safety of his ship. We made the repairs, the transmission was still in good shape and we returned to the carrier the next day. I had them inspect the remaining helicopters and sent a message back to the squadron warning them of the potential problem. This did wonders for the detachment. Losing a helicopter after what had already happened in the detachment would have been devastating to the morale of the men. Most likely, they would be sending out another new OINC. That's the way it was; sometimes your career ended with a blink of an eye and you had no control over it and sometimes luck was with you.

A few days later I was finishing up with a few small deck landings that I wanted to get out of the way before I sent the CO a message telling him I was qualified as a HAC. On that flight I was with one of the more junior pilots in the detachment. I was pleased with the ability of all the HACs in the detachment. They were all professional and damn good pilots, unlike my first cruise on the *Bon Homme Richard*. We were practicing landings on one of the support ships when we started getting a tremendous vibration from the tail rotor. It was so bad you could not read the instruments. When the vibrations started I could feel it right through the rudder pedals and knew it was not good. The deck was small, but could easily handle an H-3. I had control of the helicopter and brought the helicopter around in a tight turn and expedited my approach to the deck. I landed without coming into a hover; I didn't want to put anymore strain on the tail rotor than I had to. After we shut down and inspected the tail rotor, we found that one of the tail rotor blades had failed. The trailing edge of the rotor blade had split causing the back portion of the blade to separate. The only thing that was holding it together was the thin spar on the leading edge and that was bent forward at about a 15 degree angle.

My luck still seemed to be holding, but I was beginning to wonder when it would end. If we had lost part of the tail rotor blade we would most certainly have lost the tail rotor gear box from the severe imbalance. The emergency procedure for losing a tail rotor gear box in an SH-3 was, don't lose one. If I had brought the helicopter into a hover the additional power requirements for the helicopter would have required the tail rotor to increase the angle of attack on the rotor blades, and I don't think it would have held together. If we had lost the tail rotor hovering over the deck we would have not only lost the helicopter but we could have put the ship in danger. It proved to be the right decision. We were also very lucky we were in the landing pattern and didn't have to travel a long distance. I'd had two potential helicopter loses in the first two weeks on the detachment. I wondered what was next. Was it a result of the previous OINC pushing the detachment too hard, or was it something deeper, or was it just plain bad luck? Needless to say I was slowly winning the confidence of the crew but there was one test that hadn't happened yet. The detachment had had some previous discipline problems that hadn't been addressed.

During my first week onboard I had received word from the ship's legal officer that he had two petty officers and one officer on report. The report chits had been sent to the ship's CO for action by the previous OINC. I was used to seeing this, it was pretty typical. The OINC would push the detachment beyond their limits for his own benefit, but when it came to disciplining the men, he passed it on to someone else rather than deal with it himself. The legal officer wanted to know if I needed to review them first before he took action. He felt they were a problem and that's why they were sent up to the captain for action. I thanked him for letting me know about the report chits and after looking at them, I told the legal officer I would handle the problems at my level. I could have passed it off as not happening on my watch but that wasn't the way I did things. Once I let it go to a higher authority it was out of my control.

The report chits were minor in nature but nevertheless they had to be dealt with to maintain good order and discipline. I took the petty officers to mast and fined them a half month's pay for one month, gave them a good ass chewing and told them I was going easy on them. The officer was a little different. He was young, bright and hot headed. I understood the hot headed part. The offense was being disrespectful to a superior officer (the previous OINC) and it couldn't be overlooked. I didn't want to ruin his career, and since I didn't have all the facts it was difficult to take the appropriate action. I had a feeling the previous OINC may have earned some of the disrespect. Nevertheless I couldn't let it go by and I needed to get his attention. I had a long talk with him and told him if there was any incident during the remainder of the cruise he would get a letter of reprimand to go in his personnel record. He said he understood and that he would show me that he was a good officer

It was perceived as fair and just by the majority of the detachment personnel. They knew I was for real and would not accept anything less than professionalism. The detachment continued to improve in statistics, operating time, and morale. We focused on mission support and not building flight hours. Our job was to support the AIRWING, the ship and its escorts and that's what we did. As it worked out we flew more hours than the first half of the cruise but when there were no support missions we used the time to work on the aircraft. Best of all the maintenance control officer started to gain his weight back.

While in port in Japan the detachment took over the spaces of Detachment Two, which was forward deployed at NAS Atsugi in support of the *USS Midway*. Detachment Two was out to sea and the *Coral Sea* was moored in Yokuska. I had to travel between the ship and the detachment on a daily basis. One evening the meeting with CAG went late so I decided to remain on the ship and return to Atsugi in the morning. When I arrived the duty officer met me at the helicopter. The detachment had a Chief Petty Officer and two petty officers on report along with another petty officer and two airmen on report for separate incidents. I learned a long time ago, that even some of the best sailors got into trouble. It was my job to see that they were dealt with fairly and good order and discipline was maintained. Sometimes it was a balancing act between motivation and discipline. In either case you had to be impartial and consistent to maintain morale within the unit. This may sound simplistic but it's amazing how leaders can let their insecurities or prejudices impact their decisions. It happens more often than you think.

I went to the base legal officer to find out what had happened. There must be more to it. I could have looked the other way and let the base CO handle it but I was a little overly protective of my men. They had performed well on the last at sea period and I knew of no troublemakers in the detachment. The legal officer was about ready to take the report chits and brief the base XO. We went over the report chits and I decided I needed to convince him that it was something that should to be handled at the detachment level.

We were heading back to sea in a few days and would not be returning to Atsugi. He would never see us again.

When I assured him that the matter would be dealt with he leaned back in his chair and paused for a long moment. He then stood up with a very serious look on his face and leaned across the table placing his hand on the stack of report chits. "This is what I'll do, I'm going to leave these chits on my desk. I have some other business I need to take care with the base CO. When I come back, if these report chits are missing, I know nothing about it, is that understood?" I reached over a picked up the chits and thanked him for understanding. I turned and followed him out the door of his office and headed back down to the hangar.

It was not over. The matter had to be addressed. The incidents were pure stupidity. How do you discipline someone for stupidity? I first called the Chief Petty Officer in. He was a new chief and had only held the grade for a few months. The chief was watching his whole career pass in front off his eyes. He was petrified. I wanted to make an impact so I played the part. I sat behind my desk with a stern face and lit a cigar. I thought the whole incident was ridiculous, but could not let it stand. It seems the chief was enjoying a little liberty at the club with two young petty officers when he decided to pat one of the waitresses on the ass as she passed by. It didn't create a problem with her, but the bartender was an off duty Marine and he got a little upset. It seems the waitress happened to be his girl friend. He also happened to be attached to the Marine detachment that ran the brig onboard the base.

As the Marine came around the bar to claim his territory, the chief and the Marine exchanged a few words. When the discussion got a little heated the petty officers jumped in to stick up for their chief. The Marine had called his on duty buddies at the brig and everything continued to escalate. It was a no win situation and alcohol contributed to their lack of good judgment. The Marines were a little heavy handed but the situation ended without getting out of control and they were put on report. They say I was very good at chewing ass; I had the chief at attention in front of my desk and chewed him up one side and down the other. His biggest problem was the lack of maturity that he displayed in dealing with the incident, especially involving the two young impressionable petty officers. They looked up to the chief, and he let them down by letting the situation get out of control, creating an incident that got them all into trouble.

After the ass chewing I told the chief that I did not want to ever see him in my office under these circumstances again. He would set the example for the rest of the men for the remainder of the cruise. I handed him the paper and told him to take the chit and tear it up, then said, "Now get the hell out of my office." The chief was frozen; I had to repeat myself, "You're dismissed."

He finally turned and headed for the door. When he reached it, he opened it slowly, then paused and turned toward me and said, "I owe you one sir!"

From that point on, that chief was there 24 hours a day, everything was done before it needed to be done. The two sailors got an ass chewing and the incidents ended there. I wondered what the shore patrol would do if someone really broke the rules.

From what I was putting together, the Marines were the ones that needed to be put on report. It seems the Marines that ran the brig and headed up the shore patrol were a little heavy handed some of the time. It was allowed because they had very few incidents on the base and the CO liked it that way. The other three also got off with only an ass chewing and restrictions. One was put on report for grabbing a woman's bottom while she was riding her bicycle as they drove by in the Navy truck. She was not wearing a uniform and it turned out that she was a Lt. Commander. I had seen the female officer, and I was about to fine the sailor for having such poor taste. Instead I restricted him to the ship for the rest of the in port period.

As the time passed a connection between the men and their new OINC continued to grow. Each day brought surprises and new challenges. The men seemed to enjoy the decisiveness with which I solved each situation and moved on to the next. It was something they hadn't seen much of in the past. My confidence seemed to be what they needed and it added to their own self-esteem while we were building a reputation as one of the better units aboard the ship. One day while walking over to the hangar in Atsugi, I happened to admire the Japanese Admiral's flag in front of the Admiral's headquarters on the base. I mention to several of the men how unique it was. When you are in a position of responsibility everything you say and do gets noticed. My comments would be remembered.

We were back at sea again and time passed quickly; it had been almost four months since I reported aboard. The detachment continued to improve and the men felt good about themselves and what they had accomplished. It was a good feeling to see men care about the organization they belonged to. When I arrived they were just going through the steps, now they seemed filled with pride about what they were doing. They had an OINC that actually seemed to care about them, and they felt it. The morale was at an all time high. The ship was due to return to the States in a few weeks. But then I got word from the squadron CO in San Diego. They had a problem with another detachment that was home ported at NAS Atsugi, Japan. It was Detachment Two. I had heard rumors while I was in Japan, but it wasn't my problem, so I ignored it. It soon would be.

To use the CO's words, "The detachment had failed three inspections in a row and the detachment was a disaster." The flag officer, Admiral P. A. Peck, Commander Carrier Group Three, and CAG were personally requesting that immediate action be taken to correct the problems with the detachment. He said he didn't have any choice and as always is the case he needed me there yesterday.

As usual, the CO was very apologetic and told me that it wasn't fair to send me to another detachment that was in more trouble than the first. I deserved to come home and I should be satisfied that I did a good job. I didn't find any problem with the assignment, I was happy when I was operational. Sitting back with the home guard was not my cup of tea. I did wonder where the other officers were. HC-1 was a large squadron with almost 500 enlisted personnel and more the 80 officers. They couldn't find another officer to take over Det. Two? Then I remembered my first tour in HC-1 and some of the dedicated officers that didn't want to leave mommy's side and go to sea. They would come up with every excuse in the world not to deploy.

It was high risk and most likely that's why none of them wanted to take the assignment. I didn't care, things were not good on the home front in San Diego. My wife and I had been at odds for several years and I had asked for a divorce. To me this was just another challenge and over the years I had gotten used to the excitement of taking on the unknown. Maybe I would have the same luck as I did with this detachment.

I went to CAG to tell him about my new assignment and that I needed to leave as soon as possible. The detachment was getting ready to leave for a long deployment to the Indian Ocean and every day I was delayed could mean the difference between success and failure. CAG said he would talk with the ship's CO and let me know what his answer was. When CAG returned he told me the CO did not want me to leave the ship. I could fly back from the States once they reached San Diego. I could understand the captain's position, but it put me in a no win situation. I told CAG that I needed to speak with the CO myself. CAG said it was a dead issue and that it was not a good idea to push my luck. It may even undo all the good that I had accomplished while I was there. I told CAG that I understood, but I felt I didn't have a choice. CAG said he would clear it with the captain.

CAG called me in the detachment ready room and told me

that the CO was available on his bridge and that he wanted to meet me in the wardroom after I spoke with the captain. On the bridge of a carrier, the CO is God. What a place to have a meeting. The captain had a reputation of biting off the heads of junior officers and discarding them over into the corner. It was a tactic that some CO's used to maintain good order and discipline. Every time they felt they needed to get the crew's attention they would grab a junior officer, chew his ass unmercifully and then discard the carcass. When I entered the bridge, the CO was sitting in his captain's chair looking out over the bow of the ship as it steamed through the open water. As I entered the bridge I said, "Good morning Captain," and gave him a quick solute.

The captain spun around in his chair and quickly said while he returned the salute, "Before you start, I don't want to hear it!" he had a very determined look on his face. He was a small man, very thin with eyes that could look right through you. He struck me as a person that could reach right in and tear your heart out if you screwed with him. The bridge was like a morgue; you could hear a pin drop if it weren't for the vibration of the ship moving through the water.

I jumped in with both feet, "I understand sir, but I don't have a choice," then preceded to explain my situation. By the time I finished, I had convinced the CO that the situation was serious and the detachment was not ready to deploy. I even threw in Admiral Peck's name for good measure. The CO thought I was crazy for accepting the assignment, but agreed to let me go. He would allow me to detach only after the *Coral Sea* pulled out of Subic and headed home. That would only give me ten days to try to solve any problems before the *Midway* deployed. It was suicide and the CO had just given me an out, what drove me to want the assignment, I can't tell you. I thanked the CO for his time and figured I had pushed my luck far enough. When I returned to the wardroom, CAG was waiting for me.

"What did he say," asked CAG?

"He said, I could leave from Subic."

CAG blurted out, "no shi.." but recovered before it all came out. CAG told me he was pleased with the detachment's performance and that it would be reflected in his evaluation. He said he hoped I knew what I was getting myself into, then wished me luck on my new assignment.

I shrugged and said, "It's another challenge." I really didn't have a good answer and was beginning to wonder if I had made the right decision.

As I left CAG and returned to the detachment, I was starting to get a sense that these people were taking these assignments more seriously than I was. They were acting like I was going to war the way they kept wishing me luck and apologizing for sending me in the first place. It was my job, and I had never been let down by the men I served with yet. I did not expect the response from the detachment when I announced my new assignment. The number of volunteers that offered to cross deck with me was overwhelming. I was taken aback, I must have had 20 to 25 sailors offer to go to the *Midway* with me, including the officer I reprimanded and the two sailors I took to mast. It meant a great deal to me. The fact that these sailors were willing to forgo their return home to stay with me on deployment demonstrated the bond that had grown between us in just a few short months. The decisions I had made were the correct ones and the men believed in what I was trying to do. What more could you ask for?

While in Subic the entire detachment threw a going away party for me. During the party they gave me the Japanese Admiral's flag I had admired. It seems it "fell off of the flag pole." They all signed it and put the detachment's motto on it, "**Service with pride through professionalism**." When I first arrived I had held a little contest to get them focused on pulling together as a cohesive unit and that was the winning slogan. It was a feeling that many OINC's would never know.

As I matured I had changed from trying to find out the man I was to believing in the men and what they could accomplish when they had the support they needed. To be honest I seemed to feed off of the men and their belief in what "Hollywood Al," which they now called me, could accomplish. The more I showed my human side, the more the men would relate to it. Above all I was honest with them and passionate about what we had to do.

I had another surprise. CAG called me into his office and gave me my fitness report. He was very complimentary and told me that I had a bright future in the Navy and that he ranked me as one of the top LCDR's in his AIRWING. It went something like this:

> DURING THIS BRIEF REPORTING PERIOD LCDR BILLINGS HAS CLEARLY DEMONSTRATED STRONG LEADERSHIP AS OFFICER IN CHARGE OF HELSUPPRON ONE DET FOUR. HAVING ASSUMED LEADERSHIP OF DET FOUR UNDER THE MOST DIFFICULT OF CIRCUMSTANCES ON THE EARLY RELIEF OF HIS PREDECESSOR, LCDR BILLINGS IMMEDIATELY AND FIRMLY TOOK CHARGE AND WITH OUTSTANDING RESULTS. THE DETACHMENT HAS SHOWN DEFINITE AND CONTINUING IMPROVEMENT BOTH IN AVAILABILITY AND ATTITUDE. LCDR BILLINGS IS A STRONG LEADER, PHYSICALLY FIT AND IMPRESSIVE IN APPEARANCE AND MANNER. DURING THIS REPORTING PERIOD, THERE HAS BEEN A DEFINITE AND OBVIOUS IMPROVEMENT IN THE DETECHMENT'S PRIDE AND MORALE AND A DRASTIC DECREASE IN DISCIPLINARY PROBLEMS. AN OUTSTANDING AVIATOR, HE SETS THE EXAMPLE AND ENSURES THAT HIS AIRCREWS COMPLY. LCDR BILLINGS IS MOST HIGHLY RECOMMENDED FOR EARLY PROMOTION TO COMMANDER AND SQUADRON COMMAND.

COMMANDER CARRIER AIRWING THREE

I was pleasantly surprised but didn't spend much time thinking about it. I was too focused on the new assignment. Rarely does a helicopter pilot get such a good fitness report while attached to a carrier AIRWING, especially for such a short period of time. I thanked the CAG for his support and hoped we would meet back in the States.

USS *Midway* and Detachment Two

As the *Coral Sea* pulled out of Subic, I boarded the COD (C-2 used for Carrier Onboard Delivery) and headed for NAS Atsugi, Japan. I had plenty of time to think about all the rumors that were running wild about DET Two while I watched the cargo door of the C-2 ice up as we headed north to Japan. I would wait and assess the situation when I got there. Every unit I had taken over to that point was completely different from the last and I was sure DET Two would have its own unique problems.

When I arrived, I received an entirely different welcome than I did with Detachment Four. It seems my reputation, whatever that was, started to precede me. The nickname of "Hollywood Al," seemed to also have preceded me to Japan. I think the sea stories about my hard charging no bullshit, gregarious style of leadership had the men expecting to see John Wayne step off of the aircraft. The cigars and sunglasses probably contributed to that exaggeration of the stories. Detachment Two welcomed me with open arms, with the exception of the current OINC, LCDR John Thompson. The aircraft were all hard down and we had less than ten days to get the detachment up and running before we deployed for a 128 day cruise to the Indian Ocean. Waiting for me were two additional HC-1 personnel from San Diego. A new maintenance officer, Lt. Richard Carter and Master Chief Bob Hayes. I set out to assess quickly the capabilities of the personnel assigned to the detachment and determine if any changes needed to be made. I knew that trying to restructure a detachment in less than ten days was crazy, let alone get the aircraft up and working before we went to sea. I didn't have any choice, the changes had to be made and they had to be made quickly.

The detachment was totally disorganized; the OINC had no clue of what was going on. I interviewed all the officers and chiefs in the detachment, they had been beaten down so badly that they actually believed they were worthless. They were crying for leadership and someone to get them out of this nightmare they were in. That I could provide and with a little style to boot. Within the first four days I had reassigned almost every critical position in the detachment, including some of the chiefs. I made it clear what I expected and let them know they would have my support, but I would also hold them accountable. I had no choice; there was no time for a smooth transition. I worked long days averaging about four hours of sleep each night. There was no time for sleep. The master chief and I spent every night until the early hours of the morning discussing the next day's events. I was lucky to have such a committed individual. We had to get the helicopters flying as soon as we could get them into the air. We pulled every trick in the book, including bribing the maintenance officer from the Admiral's detachment with a bottle of whisky for the loan of some helicopter parts. Our detachment didn't have the priority that the Admiral's detachment had for the critical parts that were needed. If we didn't get the parts we would have to leave an aircraft behind.

Early on while I was interviewing the detachment personnel, I picked up a feeling that something was wrong. Either the previous OINC didn't understand that I had replaced him, or he was deliberately trying to subvert what I was trying to do. I placed a call to the squadron CO back in San Diego. It was quickly very clear why the OINC was acting the way he was. The CO had not explained to LCDR Thompson that I was the new OINC and that I would have complete authority over the direction of the detachment. I was dumfounded, what possibly could have gone through the skipper's head? He throws me out here to sink or swim, and he doesn't tell Thompson he's relieved because he doesn't want to hurt his feelings? The skipper continued to meekly explain he was not sure if he made it clear to Thompson that I was in charge. It was more like I was sent up there to help out. What bullshit! It was unbelievable! I made it clear that I could not turn this detachment around if I had an assistant OINC wandering around thinking he was in charge and undermining my authority. The skipper apologized for the misunderstanding, and told me to do whatever was necessary to get the job done.

I hung up the phone and sat there for a minute; I couldn't believe the conversation just took place. The skipper would have more surprises for me when I returned to San Diego. I had a long talk with LCDR Thompson. I told him loud and clear that I was the OINC of the detachment and anything that went on in the detachment went through me. I would evaluate him to see if he was capable of taking over the detachment when I left. I was almost to the point of being brutal, but I didn't have time for any misunderstanding. The bullshit had to stop immediately! Fortunately his running around behind my back didn't have much impact. The men had very little respect for him.

By the end of the fourth day I called an all hands meeting and officially announced the new assignments throughout the detachment and also made it very clear who was in charge. Everyone seemed pleased. The right people were in the right places, they knew what was expected of them and they were eager to get to work. Most of them were already doing the job, this just made it official. I walked away thinking this was suicide; nobody reorganized an entire detachment in four days. I had to get them to start believing in themselves and the first test would be to get the aircraft back up and flying. We were running out of time and the odds were against us.

I went down to Yokuska that evening and had my first

meeting with CAG the following morning. That night I only slept a few hours. I kept wondering if I had missed anything. When I met with CAG, even I had to admit that I was a bit overbearing. At that point I was running on overdrive and trying to be everything to everyone on the detachment. I was trying to give the detachment the direction, confidence and the leadership they so desperately needed. When I realized that I hadn't switched from my aggressive hard charging detachment approach, I apologized to CAG for my bluntness. It was probably good that I did; he looked ready to throw me out of his office. I briefed CAG on what he could expect during the upcoming at sea period. I didn't hold anything back and told him we would need a little luck to succeed. What I had been asked to do was going to be difficult, if not impossible.

CAG understood but qualified it with, "We need those helicopters on this deployment and I've been told that you're the man for the job." The detachment would have one less helicopter than the standard deployment. The area of the world we were headed to required the ship to carry two additional CH-46's for vertical replenishment and that meant we would have to do the same job with less assets. Nothing seemed to be in my favor. I excused myself and prepared for the return to Atsugi. CAG was loud and clear. There was no room for failure. We would have to find a few more rabbits to pull out of the hat.

Upon my return I was met by the master chief and the MO. "We have a problem," they said. We don't have enough parts to go around.

Two of the helicopters were going into NIPPI; it was the Navy's version of an aircraft rework facility in Japan. The aircraft had to be up and in a flyable condition when they were turned over to NIPPI. That meant we would not have the parts we needed to get the other helicopters up and flying that were going on the cruise. NIPPI didn't care about our predicament; it was their policy. We decided to give NIPPI what they wanted, but the helicopters would be transferred just before we departed. After the acceptance flight, the detachment personnel would tow the helicopters over to NIPPI. While they were being towed, the maintenance personnel relieved the helicopters of the much needed parts. It was my call and I would take the heat for it.

The master chief was critical to the success of the detachment. He knew and understood what had to be done, and went about it in a tenacious way. He didn't know me from Adam, but supported me 150%. The master chief was an expert in repairing helicopters. He was also an excellent leader and knew how to motivate the men. We both knew we had one mission and that was to turn the detachment around. The master chief had an excellent understanding of human nature. At one point, when he got a little resistance from the maintenance crew, he told them that the only option he had left was to tell the OINC that it couldn't be done. They worked through the night and the helicopter was ready to fly by first light. It was fine with me, whatever worked, I was not there to coddle the men, I was there to motivate. The men worked long hours well into each night without a complaint. We were running out of time. It was asking a lot of them since they would be leaving their families for the next 4 ½ months. The only one that was able to spend time with his family was the new Assistant OINC, LCDR Thompson. He wasn't missed. He didn't know what to do with himself, so he stayed out of the way. I was very disappointed with Thompson and hoped he would show some interest in the detachment before I had to decide who would take over when I left.

The time came for us to deploy. The helicopters that were going aboard the *Midway* were up and half of the detachment was on its way to Yokuska to receive the helicopters. The next morning we flew aboard the ship and headed to the Indian Ocean.

During the first month at sea everything went well. The op ready status continued to improve and the men were starting to feel better about themselves. For the first time they were starting to see the results of their hard labor. CAG looked at the aircraft status reports with a bit of skepticism. I don't think he believed the detachment could have such a drastic turnaround so quickly. CAG called me into his office and handed me a message from COMFAIRWESTPAC. The message indicated that there were numerous parts missing from the aircraft that were given to NIPPI for overhaul.

"What do you have to say about this," he asked.

I responded with, "CAG, you asked me to do the impossible, I did it, and now you're questioning how I did it. I did what had to be done and I'm not apologizing for it. What we did was absolutely necessary. If NIPPI has a problem with it I'll personally deal them when we get back."

CAG stared back at me for a moment without a reply and then excused me.

The detachment continued to perform flawlessly and started to actually believe they were not losers. On the morning of the 63rd day we were about to be tested. We were one helicopter short and up to that point we had met every commitment by skillfully rotating the aircraft through their phased maintenance and required inspections. The helicopters were even looking better, which was a pet peeve of mine. When I first got there, I was embarrassed to have them parked in front of my hangar, but didn't want to say anything, they had been beaten down enough already.

It was the midpoint of the cruise. We were in port at Bondar Abbas, Iran. Both CH-46's were hard down. The supplies and parts that had been flown into the international airport in Bondar Abbas were sitting next to the runway. There was no way to get the supplies out to the ship within the time they had remaining in port. CAG came down to the flight deck and told me I was about to be tested, and that the operational readiness of my aircraft better not be just on paper. We had three days left in port and it would take the entire three days to move the cargo from the beach to the carrier and its escorts. I told CAG we would have the paper helicopters all ready to go at sunrise the next morning. Then I went down to brief the men.

It was all on the line. It reminded me of the high I got when we used to get scrambled in the middle of the night in Vietnam. It wasn't the same adrenaline rush but the excitement was definitely there. The men responded superbly and wanted the chance to show what they could do. The past years of being called the worst unit on the ship had eaten at their insides. The men worked through the night to ensure everything was double checked.

At sunrise that morning I went up to the bridge of the ship. CAG and the CO of the ship, Captain Felt, were looking down on the forward part of the flight deck. All three helicopters were turning and ready for a day of vertical replenishment (VERTREP). As I walked up beside them I said, "It's a beautiful sight, isn't it?"

CAG and the captain just turned and looked at me. I knew it wasn't a beautiful sight; the SH-3G's looked like flying dinosaurs sitting out on the flight deck. They were definitely not nice-looking, but they would do the work that needed to be done. The three helicopters flew continuously for the next three days from sunrise to sunset. The SH-3G had much less of a VERTREP capability than the CH-46. By the end of the third day all the escorts and the carrier had been supplied and there was nothing left on the beach. We never even shut down the helicopters. The relieving pilots would "hot seat" while the engines were still running.

This was a big morale boost for the detachment personnel, they had achieved something they had never thought possible. I was walking down the flight deck when I overheard a couple of my young sailors holler over at a jet pilot that was getting his picture taken by his F-4 Phantom Jet. "Hey lieutenant, why don't you come over and get your picture taken by a real aircraft?"

I chuckled to myself and knew we had turned a corner

and were headed in the right direction. The pride I felt was enormous, but even more than that, joy came from seeing the men feel good about themselves.

We were back at sea but the three days of continuous flying put us behind on the phased maintenance. We needed to swap out the ready aircraft and move it down to the hangar so we could work on it. I was in the ready room when maintenance control told the flight deck officer we needed to switch the duty aircraft for maintenance. A minute later a voice came back over the intercom. The flight deck officer accidentally left the intercom button on when he reported to the air boss. "Boss, those fucking helicopter pukes are screwing up my flight deck again. Those losers want to move the duty helicopter down to the hangar so they can do some maintenance on it. I'll be damned if they're going to move that helicopter."

I exploded! Without thinking, I jumped over one of the seats and grabbed the intercom switch and said, "This loser will be in flight deck control in 30 seconds and I'm going to clean the fucking floor up with you. Nobody calls my people losers."

I headed for flight deck control. I was out of control and had one thought in mind. I was going to put that flaming asshole in his place. As I reached the open hatch, the air boss was standing in the doorway with his hands braced at the sides of the bulkhead. I was amazed he'd gotten down from Pri-Fly so fast. I started through the door and the air boss held me back. He said, "Violence is not going to help anyone."

I replied, "It'll make me feel better," as I pushed his hand away and entered flight deck control.

I could see the flight deck officer over in the corner as the air boss grabbed for my arm. The flight deck officer looked like he had just lost his best friend. I started across the room toward him, as he stood frozen in the corner. The air boss blurted out as he pulled at me again, "I'm sure we can clear this up. What Roger said was uncalled for. I'm sure he would like to apologize for it."

I stopped and stared at the flight deck officer. That bastard always played the tough guy, he enjoyed being an asshole. I waited. In a quiet voice, staring down at the floor, he said, "The comments were uncalled for."

I looked at him for a minute, then said, "If you ever…, refer to any of my men that way again, the air boss will not be able to protect you, is that clear?"

He moved his head as if to meekly acknowledge my last statement and I turned and stormed out of flight deck control.

When I returned to the ready room the maintenance control chief said, "We were giving you 30 seconds more and then we were going to bring in the cavalry."

I looked at him and said, "The duty helicopter is down," and walked out of the ready room to get some fresh air. The negative comments did not hurt the morale of the detachment as I had feared. Instead the incident helped to boost the morale. From that point on, they knew they were not third class citizens and were not going to take shit from anyone. In fact they were feeling so good about themselves my next challenge was going to be keeping them from over-stepping the boundaries of correctness within the AIRWING. I can't say it was the "Esprit De Corps" you get from the Marines of God, Country, Honor, and Corps, but it was the closeness and brotherhood that only comes from serving in hard times and pulling together to defy all odds.

We spent a few more weeks at sea and then pulled into Karachi, Pakistan. The task group was in that region of the world to show the flag and port visits were part of it. Unfortunately this was not the Mediterranean. The ports were the armpits of the world. About the only liberty we had was a BBQ for the officers and chiefs at one of the villas the ship leased for the day. In my usual way and unintentionally, I did not endear myself to the fighter and attack community. The BBQ was held out on the large front lawn of the villa, only there was no grass, just sand and weeds. The villa was nothing more than a large house with a very large wall built around the property. As luck would have it, and when the beer started to flow, a chief from one of the fighter squadrons approached me and challenged me to an arm wrestling match. It seems that word had gone around that the helicopter OINC had done some arm wrestling. To this day I do not know how they found out about it.

I had never turned down a good challenge, especially when I had a few beers in me. It did not take long before I put the chief down. Between the beer, the testosterone, and the boredom the next ten minutes produced three more challenges. By the end of the picnic, I had defeated 22 challengers from the fighter and attack community. At one point my operations officer, Lt. Sutton was standing on a chair challenging everyone in the air wing. Lt. Sutton needed to stand on a chair; he was only 5'7" and weighed in at a hefty 145 lbs. I called him down off the chair just after he blurted out, "Come on, we'll take on anyone, all you jet jocks can do, is suck and blow." He was feeling no pain and unfortunately his choice of words was a little insulting to the rest of the AIRWING.

When we returned to sea I was asked by CAG to apologize to two of the jet squadron CO's for the insults and derogatory remarks during the picnic. It was quite a turnaround. The third class citizens were putting the jet jocks in their place. I apologized to them, but the apologies were not well-received. Jet pilots believed they were superior beings and the last thing they wanted to hear were insults from a bunch of rotor heads.

I had one more thing to take care of as we left Karachi. When I met with CAG he handed me a report chit. It seems I was put on report by my Assistant OINC. The ship's crew had a 2200 curfew in Karachi and all hands were to return to the ship. On the last night I remained in port with my maintenance officer and some of CAG's staff. The detachment MO was a good officer, but he had one continuous problem. He really enjoyed drinking. That night a few of us were having our last beers in a small hotel in Karachi before returning to sea. The MO was too drunk to get back to the ship and hearing that some of the staff officers were getting a room in the hotel, I decided to do the same thing. It would be easier than trying to get the MO back to the ship.

CAG asked me if I broke curfew that night. I replied, "Yes sir! I have no excuse. Whatever you think is fair, CAG."

The CAG broke in, "Al I can't have my OINC's and CO's breaking regulations."

"Yes, sir, I understand. Whatever you think is fair."

I knew that CAG was aware that some of his staff stayed in the hotel, but I didn't say anything. CAG handed the report chit to me and said, "Get the hell out of my office."

I took the chit, thanked CAG and returned to my ready room. When the time was right, I called LCDR Thompson to my stateroom. I didn't want anyone else to hear what I had to say. As I closed the door and turned toward Thompson I held up the report chit. "Don't ever...! Let me see anything like this again, is that clear?!"

All I got from Thompson was the blink of his eyes, which was about what I expected. He was never able to grasp the full picture and I'm not sure all of my yelling even got through. I went on for five minutes trying to tell him he was cutting his own throat. I had a decision to make at the end of this cruise and it would impact his career. He never said a word; he just sat there until I excused him.

We were back out to sea and headed towards Japan, but first we were scheduled for a "War at Sea" exercise off of Singapore. It would turn out to be one of the most significant events of the cruise and one of the biggest challenges some of the pilots would ever have to take on.

The air arm in Singapore was made up primarily of contract British pilots, and they were damn good. As the exercise started the weather went from bad to worse. During the daylight flight operations the British pilots handed the

Midway and its task group a significant bashing. They came in below the radar and popped up at the last minute, surprising the ships and avoiding any contact until it was too late for the ships to respond. The *Midway*'s reputation was getting tarnished. When night fell and the weather got worse, the Brits headed into the beach for a few beers at the O'Club and the *Midway* continued to operate around the clock.

The *Midway* was the forward deployed carrier. It had a reputation of being the best and the first to fight. It was something the whole ship's company took pride in. There were eleven officials onboard from Singapore to watch the exercise. In order to save face the *Midway* made the decision to continue operating through the night in some of the worst weather I had ever seen. It was 2200 and my turn to launch. It was raining so hard the wipers on the windscreen couldn't push the water away fast enough. It didn't make any difference, it was so dark, you couldn't see your hand if it was six inches in front of your face. It was going to be instruments no hover take-off, so we didn't need to see outside anyway. I was out for several hours while they launched and recovered aircraft to demonstrate their all weather capability.

This was a gung ho AIRWING; I expected lots of the aircraft to have mechanical problems, but not one reported in and downed their aircraft. At 0100, I was called aboard for refueling and a crew change. We decided to "hot seat" the helicopter and the crew changed while the helicopter was turning on deck. The ops officer, Lt. Sutton was the new pilot. I knew he was good and didn't worry about the weather conditions. He showed initiative; the ops officer has control of the flight schedule and nobody could overrule him accept me. I liked the idea that he assigned himself to the toughest part of the schedule. This detachment was showing its true worth; they had never missed a beat the entire cruise. I had been in maintenance control for about 10 minutes signing off the yellow sheets and letting the adrenaline burn off when I heard the general quarters alarm go off. One of the detachment flight deck crew came running in the door, we had an aircraft crash on the flight deck. I took off for Pri-Fly through the hangar. The flight deck was closed.

When I arrived in Pri-Fly they were replaying the video tape of the landing. It was an A-6 Intruder on final. The aircraft hit the round down and burst into flames. The entire aircraft was engulfed in the flames. As the fireball sailed down the angle deck you could see the two ejection seats shoot out of the ball of fire. There was a senior officer from Singapore standing in the back. He made the comment that we would never see those pilots again. I also had my doubts, the weather I had just come out of was as severe as I had ever seen. Extremely heavy rain with a minimum of 30 foot seas. Even if they spotted the pilots, which was doubtful, it would take a very skilled pilot to recover them. I listened to the radios intently to get the status of Lt. Sutton and his crew. The lieutenant was doing his standard search pattern behind the ship where they expected the pilots to be. He was calm and professional.

There was a stillness aboard the ship. You could tell by the communications between the bridge, the flag staff, and the air boss, careers were in the balance. Losing an aircraft is one thing, but losing the pilots on a decision to fly in this weather throughout the night meant heads would roll. The remainder of the fixed wing aircraft were diverted to the beach. Sutton and his crew spotted the first survivor and were preparing to go in for the rescue. As the helo went in for the approach the air boss tried to keep continuous voice communication with Sutton. Sutton did not respond. The air boss was excited and exaggerated as he asked why Sutton wasn't responding. I told him he was using every skill he had to keep his crew out of the water. A rescue during daylight in this weather would have been a challenge, but at night it would take a top notch pilot to pull it off.

Minutes seemed like hours. Finally Lt. Sutton reported back in, "We have one pilot in the aircraft and he seems to be okay."

They had lost their auto hover capability and were in the manual mode. When they opened the cargo door to lower the hoist a wall of water came in and shorted out some of the electronics that helped to stabilize the helicopter in a hover. In a calm voice Lt. Sutton reported "We've started our search for the other pilot."

They were in the right area and they needed to stay right on top of it. If they lost their position they may never find the other pilot with the sea state as high as it was. It was pure luck that they found the first pilot. I had been in situations when we spent days looking for a downed pilot in much better weather conditions than that and never found him.

A few minutes later Lt. Sutton reported sighting a strobe light and they were investigating it. Minutes passed with no word. Finally we heard, "We have the other pilot in sight and are going in for the pick up."

I couldn't believe the luck. What a fantastic piece of airmanship from Sutton, very few pilots could have done what he did. Everyone waited for the word. It took longer than normal. I knew Sutton had his hands full and was doing everything he could to make the rescue. A hover at night with all the equipment working was a challenge, doing it manually was remarkable.

The word finally came, "We have the second pilot aboard. He has an injured hand but appears to be in pretty good condition." There was a tremendous sigh of relief from everyone as the air boss reported to the bridge that the pilots were safe. I went down to the flight deck to meet the crew and tell them what an outstanding job they did.

The next day I was called up to the flag bridge to talk to the Admiral. The Admiral was very complimentary on the performance of the detachment. I told the Admiral what had happened to the helicopter and the outstanding job that Lt. Sutton and his crew did. I wanted to put Lt. Sutton in for an air medal, for his outstanding airmanship and the rest of the crew in for commendations. The Admiral agreed and parted by saying, "Keep up the good work."

I headed down to the ready room and started on the paperwork. It seems that DET Two was one of the highlights of the exercise. Nobody expected to see those pilots again. DET Two had gone from the goat to one of the stars of the cruise in just a little over four months.

After a short in port period in Singapore, the detachment was on their way home to Atsugi for Christmas. While in Singapore, I called in to HC-1 to talk with the skipper and report on the detachment's status. The skipper was pleased with the detachment's performance and said that he had received nothing but positive comments from the Admiral, CAG and Captain Felt. He asked me about LCDR Thompson and if I felt he was capable of taking over the detachment. I had to tell him the truth. I had put too much of myself into this detachment and could not turn it over to the Assistant OINC. I tried to bring him up to speed on everything I was trying to do, but Thompson didn't have a clue.

I told the skipper that he could not take over the detachment and that it was critical that I stay out here until the detachment recovered completely. It seemed that Thompson could not stop with the subversion. He had been writing the skipper and telling him his version of what was happening on the detachment. If it hadn't been for CAG and the Admiral, who knows what the skipper would have believed? We were not out of the woods yet. There had been talk about an inspection upon return from our deployment and there would be plenty of work to do when they got back to Atsugi. After we talked I went to CAG and suggested the inspection before we were told it was going to take place. CAG thought it was a fine idea and he would have it set up when we returned.

The Skipper was concerned about my being out to sea for so long. I had just completed the fourth month with DET Two and with the four months I spent with DET Four, the skipper felt that I had been deployed too long in a high stress, high tempo environment. I told him I was fine and the detachment needed me out here. It was the first time the men had believed in themselves, and I didn't want that taken away from them.

The skipper responded by saying, "Now I know you've been out there too long. You're losing touch with reality." He didn't understand I believed in these men and they believed what I was doing was right. It was something few people had a chance to experience.

I tried to relate the story of the 18 year old airman walking down the passage way at 0200 in the morning. When he approached me, he smiled and said "Don't worry Mr. B, we have you covered, we'll take care of everything."

With this type of attitude from the most junior man in the detachment, I couldn't lose. These young men would do whatever it took to make this detachment a success. They had pride, they believed in themselves for the first time, and it felt good. The skipper didn't understand, all he knew was the longer I spent out there in the fleet, the bigger the chance of something going wrong. Everything that I had earned up to that point would be destroyed. I didn't think that way, and never would. If something went wrong I wanted to be with them. I didn't plan my career; I lived it. I just played the cards that were dealt me.

We ended the conversation with the skipper saying he would be looking for a replacement and get back to me when we returned to Atsugi. He told me that he received a letter from Admiral Peck two months earlier and that he had forwarded a copy to me. It should arrive any day. The letter came in our last day in port and it read something like this.

Commander Carrier Group Three
FPO San Francisco 96601
8 October 1977

Dear Commander Hamilton,
Your forthright position and very accurate analysis of the problems existing in HC-1/DET-2 was like a fresh wind on a stale day. This kind of attitude is what allows the Navy to analyze its own difficulties and correct them expeditiously. I congratulate you.
In my opinion and in the view of both Captain Felt and CAG, the steps which have been taken to correct the deficiencies in DET-2 are beginning to show signs of effectiveness. I have talked with LCDR Billings, and he is a most impressive individual. The appearance of the aircraft has improved significantly and there are signs that the routine maintenance and preservation is also receiving substantially more attention than may have been given in the past. More importantly, availability has been excellent, although we need to look a little longer before setting any long term trend. In essence, I agree with your conclusion that progress is indeed being made, although I'll immediately caveat by saying that there is still a long way to go. We will continue to monitor the performance of the detachment, or more accurately I should say CAG will do so, but rest assured, all of us here realize that it will take some time before the detachment reaches desired standards. The best news I can give you at this time is, "so far. So good."
As time goes along, I will try to keep you advised. In any event, you may rest assured that we will certainly bring to your attention, any new problems which require assistance to correct. Again, I am very pleased with the help we have received from HC-1 and , in

particular, from you. The same can be said of CONFAIRWESTPAC and ASWINGSPAC.

In talking to LCDR Billings, I was impressed with his very positive and enthusiastic approach to this very demanding challenge. It is my intention to make note of this in a Concurrent Fitness Report. I know it has not been easy, but on the other hand, it may well get even tougher. My intent is to be at least as active in recognizing his performance as in citing problems. I hope that you will keep a close watch on Mr. Billings' future employment. He has been at sea since June, certainly not too long as yet, but it might be very easy to forget when it comes time to bring him back. While there are many considerations, and most of them are unknown to me, in determining the proper time to relieve him, I would suggest you think about the February time frame, perhaps following the inspection by your Executive Officer. Again, I only enjoin your best judgment.

Keep up the good fight and don't forget us. If there is anything to be gained from this drill, it is the lesson learned. We need HC-1's continuing surveillance of Det-2 to "keep us honest" out here in the hinterland.

All the best.
P. A. Peck

CDR R. F. Hamilton, USN
Commanding Officer
Helicopter Combat Support Squadron One
U.S. Naval Air Station, North Island
San Diego, CA 92135

Copy to:
RADM C. J. KEPF, USN, COMASWINGSPAC
CATT. D. L. Felt, USN, CO, USS MIDWAY (CV-41)
CDR W. B. KIRKCONNELL, USN, COMARAAIRWING FIVE

After reading the letter I knew where the motivation was coming from in wanting to get me home. As I returned to San Diego it would become more apparent how the skipper really felt about "Hollywood Al." We were getting visibility at the highest levels and the inspection back in Atsugi would be a very important milestone. The skipper had a lot riding on me and if I failed it could impact his making captain. Some of CAG's staff did not believe the detachment could be turned around as fast as it was and our readiness numbers were a little too good to be true. It was reflected in CAG's comment about the paper aircraft and some of the comments from his officers. The inspection was going to be tough and we needed to be prepared for anything. As in so many things in life the more successful you are the more people want to see you fail.

We had a few more days at sea and then a short stop in the Philippines, in Subic Bay, before returning to Atsugi. When we pulled into Subic, the detachment was headed to their favorite club for some liberty and asked me to stop by. Later that night I stopped in to see how the crew was doing and have a beer with them. In those days the bands in the clubs would play songs with "God Bless America" themes. To see these young men stand at attention and sing along with the band was something to behold. They were proud to be American sailors and wanted everyone to know. To me they were something special.

It was such a contrast from the days of Vietnam, when we had to listen to all the long-haired, dope smoking hippies and newspapers trash us. When I looked at the young men standing there, I felt a tremendous sense of pride and at the same time sorry for the hippies. They would never know what it was like to be an American serviceman. They had nothing but themselves and a few illegal drugs to prop up their false courage, knowing full well they would never be put in harm's way. They would never understand what we shared. These men had each other, the Navy and their country to believe in. God, I loved it!

Two days later it was back to sea and we were headed for

Japan. When we returned to Atsugi we had two weeks to prepare for the inspection. The detachment worked long hours and the men didn't complain. They had a taste of what it was like to be on top and they didn't want to lose that feeling. This was their home port. Their families were here and it was Christmas. They had just been deployed for 128 days and not one sailor asked for additional time off to spend with his family. Except for LCDR Thompson, who was noticeably absent from most of the efforts. I was impressed with this rag-tag outfit. A few months earlier they felt they could do nothing right. It always amazed me the response that I got from the men I served with, and I never wanted to lose that feeling.

As in most inspections there was no tension from the men, instead it was just the opposite. The men wanted the opportunity to show what they had done and what they could do. The following message was sent out after the inspection was completed.

```
      RTICZYUM   RUHGOFZ0014   0111363-CCCC-
RUH
      NZY CCCCC
      R 132336Z Jan 78
      FM CTG SEVEN SEVEN PT FOUR
      TO ZEN/USS MIDWAY
      INFO CTF SEVEN SEVEN
      COMFAIRWESTPAC ATSUGI JA
      COMASWWINGSPAC SAN DIEGO CA
      HELSUPRON ONE
      BT
      CONFIDENTIAL //N13000//
      HC-1 DET TWO MATERIAL READINESS (U)
         A.     COMFAIRWESTPAC INSP DEBRIEF
11 JAN 78
         1.     © RESULTS OF HC-1 DET TWO
```

MATERIAL READINESS INSPECTION REPORTED REF A NOTED WITH PLEASURE. THE FORMAL REPORT WILL INDICATE AN EVAL OF SATISFACTORY AND THE OUTSTANDING COMMENTS AND REMARKS BY THE INSPECTORS REFLECT THE EXEMPLARY EFFORT BY ALL HANDS TO CORRECT PREVIOUS DISCREPENACIES. THIS ALSO CONFIRMS THE EXCELLENT REPUTATION AND "CAN DO" SPIRIT WHICH WAS THE TRADEMARK OF HC-1 DET TWO DURING THE RECENT I.O. DEPLOYMENT.

2. (U) BRAVO ZULU FOR A JOB WELL DONE. RADM PECK.

GDS-S4
BT
#0114

After the inspection, the detachment had a couple of weeks to enjoy their accomplishments before heading out to sea again. The night before we were to deploy I was in the O'Club having a few last beers. We would fly aboard early the following morning. It was about 2230 when my duty officer came in and told me they had a problem at the barracks. We had three enlisted personnel at the dispensary, one on his way down to the Naval hospital in Yokuska and two in the base brig. We jumped into the duty truck and headed to the dispensary first as he brought me up to speed on what had happened. When we arrived, the young sailors were getting patched up from some minor cuts and scrapes and one black eye. After talking with the sailors it was clear the Marine detachment had over reacted and their heavy handed approach was uncalled for.

I put the sailors in the truck and took them by the barracks. After dropping them off, we headed for the brig.

As in so many cases, what initiated this event really took place long before I arrived at the detachment. There was a black airman in the detachment that had homosexual tendencies. He was put on report for making advances toward one of the younger sailors. The previous OINC passed the report chit on up the line to the former captain of the *Midway*. Because of the sensitivity of the problem it never got addressed other than a discussion about the lack of evidence.

That night while everyone was drinking their share of alcohol before they went to sea, the same black sailor came out of his room at the barracks and tried to pull the same young sailor into his room. Two young petty officers heard the commotion and intervened on the young sailor's behalf. They had seen enough and decided that if the Navy wasn't going to take care of the problem, they would. One of the petty officers asked the black sailor to step outside. Once outside the black sailor picked up a brick and struck the petty officer in the side of the head. Unfortunately he struck the wrong petty officer.

As the fight ensued someone called the base shore patrol. By this time there were a dozen or so sailors out watching the fight. When the base shore patrol called for reinforcements they announced over the loud hailer that there was a race riot. By this time more sailors started piling out of the barracks. In order to regain control the Marines overreacted by nailing anyone they could get their hands on. In those days everything was a racial incident, even if it was an Italian and a Pollock fighting. The three sailors in the dispensary obtained their injuries as a result of the Marines' overzealously performing crowd control.

When we arrived in front of the base brig, it could have been right out of a John Wayne movie. It was a small building constructed right after the end of WWII. I stepped out of the truck, straightened my uniform, took a few deep breaths and lit up one of my now famous cigars. As I stepped through the front door of the brig I could see a couple of Marines sitting at a desk across the room. On one side of the room there were three cells, each with a large heavy wooden door and a small one foot square window with metal bars in it. As I looked at the first cell I could see two sailors with their faces pressed together looking out the small window. Before I took another step they both said, "We're sorry Mr. B, we didn't mean to get you in any trouble. You're never going to get us out of this one."

I didn't say a thing; I looked back at the desk where the Marines were and headed directly for it. I had one card to play and hoped that it would work. The first thing I hit them with was the way they roughed up the other sailors and sent them to the dispensary. I could tell by the look in their eyes that I had hit a soft spot. I pushed a little further and demanded an explanation.

The Marines were hesitant. I had a feeling they realized the incident was not handled well, and I hoped they wanted it to go away. I pushed a little further. My goal was to get my men out of the brig, then I would deal with them. They were two of the hardest workers and some of the best maintenance personnel we had. We certainly couldn't go to sea without them. They say I can be pretty intimidating at times and this needed to be one of them. I told the Marines this whole damn thing had been blown out of proportion and that there would have to be an investigation into what really happened. Which I didn't want.

I had played my card and waited for the response. The Marines came back with a lame response and it gave me the opening I needed. I suggested that since all the personnel that were involved were in my detachment, it would be better if it was handled at my level. The Marines liked what they heard. I think they figured they were better off with me than dealing with the base CO. They agreed. I would take the report chits and the two sailors back with me. Five minutes later we were in the truck and on our way back to the barracks.

When we arrived back at the barracks, most of the detachment personnel that lived in the barracks were still in the lounge area waiting to find out what happened to their shipmates. Emotions were still running high and I knew from experience you didn't try to talk to a bunch of drunk sailors that were all worked up. I told them to turn in and I stayed there until some of the more ornery ones got tired and turned in. It was almost 0230 before everything settled down. I had a 0630 take off the next morning and needed to get a couple of hours sleep. We were only going to sea for a couple of weeks, so I told the duty officer that I wanted him to stay in Atsugi and make sure the sailor down in Yokuska was okay.

I wanted the duty officer to work with base legal to get the man transferred either out of the Navy or back to the States, I didn't care. The duty officer did not mind that assignment. It meant he got to stay home with his wife and new daughter. Later that week while at sea, I received a message from the duty officer that the sailor had submitted a letter saying he was a homosexual and they were processing him out of the Navy.

When we arrived overhead, the *Midway* was just leaving the pier. Once the ship departed the harbor we landed, unloaded the equipment and prepared for our at sea period. The first night out the ship had problems with the arresting gear and did not have the parts to fix it. The *Midway* only had three wires (arresting cables) instead of the standard four, now they were down to two. I was called into CAG's office and told that the captain wanted the helo to go back into the beach and pick up a part so they could continue to operate. I explained to CAG that we were too far out to sea and that it would be against regulations to send the helo that distance over water unescorted.

CAG was not pleased with my response. He didn't want to hear about regulations, he just wanted it done. He accused me of hiding behind the regulations. I told him the safety of the men came first and those restrictions were put in there for a reason. If I went against those regulations and some of my men got hurt or killed, the Navy would use those same regulations to hang me. CAG knew I was right but didn't want to accept my answer. He said he would get back to me.

I went back to the ready room and we went over the charts. We came up with a quick workable solution. I called CAG on the ship's phone and told him that if we could get within 175 miles of land the helo could head down the coast to Yokuska and pick up the parts. This in effect would give us what we needed to be legal as far as the regulations went. That would only take the ship slightly off of its current course and still keep them in the operating area. CAG said he would get back with me and to have the crew standing by. Later that evening we got the go ahead and launched the crew to the beach. Their expected return time was 0230 the next morning. We had no trouble getting volunteers for the flight. I thought about taking the flight myself but the squadron XO was flying out from the States with my replacement. I would be returning to the States in a few weeks and the detachment needed to know they could handle any situation.

I got a call at about 0130 from CIC that my crew was inbound, so I headed up to Pri-Fly to see how things were going. When I arrived the crew was still up on the CIC frequency and they were about 100 miles out. They were having a little problem with fluctuating oil pressure on the number one engine. They were almost at the halfway point and needed to make a decision. I told the pilot that he was the aircraft commander, the decision would be his and he would be supported. The pilot, Lt. Greer, was good but young, he decided to continue on toward the ship. I called maintenance control and told them to alert the standby helo crew and tell them to get to the ready room.

About 50 miles out they reported they had lost some oil pressure and the temperatures were starting to rise. I was kicking myself that I didn't take the flight. It was a tense situation for the next 25 minutes; those were my men out there and their well-being was my responsibility. I waited. They landed on deck without incident. The engine was replaced the next day and I figure I took a hit from CAG by standing by the regulations, but it paid off for the men in the long run. Was it still luck and if so when would it run out?

Timing was everything. The next day I was in the ready room when CAG called. He wanted me to come down and get my fitness report. I never paid attention to fitness reports, they were just something that happened. Getting a good fitness report was never a part of my decision process. CAG was leaving the AIRWING for a new assignment, and it was his detaching fitness report. It would go in as a concurrent fitness report along with the one from the CO of HC-1. I hated to see him go; he was a good man and I respected him, even though we did have our disagreements. I prepared myself for the worst. As I walked down the passageway, I told myself that if I was in the top 30 percentile, I did okay. In truth, I knew that if you were not in the top one percentile, you could kiss your chances for promotion goodbye. It was my way of easing the blow. I knocked on CAG's door and then went in.

CAG looked up from his desk and handed me the fitness report without saying a word. I read the report and could not think of any words to say, and I was never short of words. CAG had made me the number one LCDR in the

AIRWING. It was unconceivable. A helicopter pilot had never been ranked as the top officer in the AIRWING as far as I knew.

I didn't know what to say. I just stood there looking at the fitness report. It wasn't the ranking as much as the words he used to describe the accomplishments. CAG looked up at me and said, "We had our differences, but I admire the way you stick to your guns and look after your men."

I was still speechless. Operational CAG's were a rare breed, most of the desk jockeys would have found me a pain in the ass, and nailed me to the wall just out of principle. I would soon find out what the skipper thought of me when I returned to San Diego. CAG dismissed me and I turned and left. As I walked back down the passageway I was mentally kicking myself for being such a dumb ass. I should have said something, anything. I didn't even say thank you.

I must admit I was a bit overwhelmed by what was in the fitness report. I had received many good fitness reports before but none with the sincerity that this one was written and it was written by CAG. It went something like this:

> THIS REPORT ON THE FITNESS OF LCDR BILLINGS WARRANTS VERY SPECIAL CONSIDERATION. THIS OFFICER WAS HAND-PICKED BY HIS C.O. TO BE THE OINC OF HC-1 DET 2 FOR THE EXPRESS PURPOSE OF REBUILDING A BADLY SAGGING OUTFIT. SO LONG HAD THE DET BEEN OPERATING IN A STATE OF MEDIOCRITY THAT THIS ENDORSER, WHO WAS UNFAMILIAR WITH THE SH-3G HELICOPTER, BELIEVED THAT DEPENDABILITY WAS AN UNACHIEVABLE CHARACTERISTIC. LCDR BILLINGS HAS TOTALLY REVERSED THAT IMAGE AND HAS PROVEN WITHOUT QUESTION THAT A SH-3G HELICOPTER DETACHMENT CAN BE 100

PERCNET CAPABLE, BOTH MATERIALLY AS WELL AS OPERATIONALLY.

PRIOR TO HIS ARRIVAL ON THE SCENE, CONCERN EXISTED EVEN AT THE FLAG LEVEL THAT HC-1 DET 2 COULD NOT ADEQUATELY PERFORM DURING THE FORTHCOMING DEPLOYMENT TO THE INDIAN OCEAN. SERIOUS CONSIDERATION WAS BEING GIVEN TO REPLACE THE DETACHMENT IN TOTAL. HOWEVER THE PREVIOUS PERFORMANCE BY LCDR BILLINGS IN OTHER DETS LED TO THE DECISION TO PUT HIM IN CHARGE AND GIVE HIM THE AUTHORITY AND ACCOUNTABILITY TO UPGRADE THE DETACHMENT. THE WISDOM OF THE DECISION WAS IMMEDIATELY EVIDENT. ASSUMING LEADERSHIP ONLY 10 DAYS PRIOR TO SAILING, LCDR BILLINGS AGGRESSIVELY SET OUT TO ACCOMPLISH HIS TASKING. REPORTS OF MANAGEMENT CHANGES AND EFFECTIVENESS OFTEN REFER TO CLEAN SWEEPS AND REORGANIZATIONS AS THE KEY ITEMS PRODUCING POSITIVE PRODUCTIVITY IMPROVEMENTS. TO BE SURE, LCDR BILLINGS MADE CHANGES, HOWEVER CLEAR ANALYSIS OF THE PROBLEMS FOLLOWED BY POSITIVE DIRECTION AND ASSET MANAGEMENT WERE HIS BIG GUNS. THE RESULTS HAVE BEEN STARTLING. HC-1 DET 2 HAS BECOME PROBABLY THE FINEST HELICOPTER COMBAT SUPPORT DETACHMENT IN THE PACIFIC FLEET – IF NOT THE NAVY! AND IN ONLY FOUR MONTHS TIME.

LCDR BILLINGS IS SOLELY RESPONSIBLE FOR THIS OUTSTANDING ACHIEVEMENT. A MAN OF IMMENSE CONFIDENCE AND DESERVED EGO, LCDR BILLINGS IS NONETHELESS AS CONCERNED FOR THE PERSONAL AND PROFESSIONAL GROWTH OF HIS LOWEST RANKING ENLISTED MAN AS HE IS FOR HIS NUMBER ONE OFFICER. NEW AND STIMULATING PROFESSIONAL DEVELOPMENT PROGRAMS EXIST AT EVERY LEVEL IN THE UNIT. ATTENDANT PRIDE AND MORALE WITHIN THE DET IS AT AN OBVIOUS ALL-TIME HIGH. UNIT RETENTION RATES REFLECT THIS STRONG LEADERSHIP.

BY HIS PERFORMANCE AND OBSERVABLE ACHIEVEMENTS, LCDR BILLING HAS PROVED HIMSELF A LEADER WITHOUT PEER – UNMATCHED BY ANY OTHER LCDR I HAVE EVER OBSERVED. HE IS WITHOUT QUESTION QUALIFIED FOR COMMAND AND SHOULD BE PROMOTED TO THE GRADE OF COMMANDER AT THE EARLIEST POSSIBLE OPPORTUNITY WITH SUCH PROMOTION OCCURING WELL IN ADVANCE OF HIS CONTEMPORARIES,

COMMANDER AIRWING FIVE

My leadership instructor back in Pensacola could be justifiably proud that he passed me on my oral exam. At times I have a tendency to talk down my accomplishments and in most cases would rather have had the men get all the credit for what they did. Despite the perception that I had a strong ego, the men needed something or someone to believe in before they could start believing in themselves.

I was that vehicle and I played the part well. So that it does not get misconstrued as being egotistical again, these documents are only here for accuracy and to clarify the tenuous circumstances of the actual events. It will also act as a beacon when weighed against the political and bureaucratic approach my own squadron commanding officer demonstrated when he rewarded me for accepting the risks of the assignment and pulling his proverbial ass out of the fire.

The remainder of the at sea period was uneventful, everything ran smoothly. In fact everyone was doing their job so well, I was a little bored. I had been running so hard the past nine months, the slowdown seemed a little surreal to me. The men and the officers were dedicated professionals and they had tremendous pride in their detachment. They knew what was expected of them and the jobs were done with complete commitment. Maybe the skipper was right, maybe the detachment didn't need me any longer. They deserved to get the credit for their hard work, not me. I had received a message from the skipper that the executive officer (XO) would arrive at the end of February and he would be bringing the new OINC with him.

I called all hands together and told them my replacement would be arriving in Atsugi at the end of the month. Everyone was quiet. I couldn't tell how they felt. They knew it was going to happen; it was just a matter of time. We arrived in port a few days before the XO and the new OINC reached Atsugi. When the XO arrived it was an interesting meeting. The XO was a little distant and seemed very guarded. The new OINC was cheerful and upbeat but at times I felt he was a little too slapstick. I really didn't know the XO that well, since I was only in the squadron a couple of days before I left for WESTPAC. Most of that time was consumed with preparing for the assignment. I learned later it was the XO's way of presenting himself as an authoritative figure..

I spent many years watching the leadership styles of the various senior officers that I served under. It was interesting the different ways they projected their authority. Some of the officers like the XO had to perfect a style that suited them over the years. The smaller the physical stature, the tougher the personality seemed to have to be, almost like they were compensating for their size. The XO was Cuban born and later joined the U.S. Navy after the "Bay of Pigs." Every time he got in front of the men his voice deepened and his accent got heavier.

He seemed determined that he was going to tell me what to do. I didn't totally understand why he reacted the way he did, there was no question in my mind who was in charge, he was the XO. The stories that were getting back to the states about "Hollywood Al" probably didn't help either. The maintenance officer they sent over had already departed immediately after the IO cruise and returned to civilian life. That left the master chief, he was part of the HC-1 shore component and had been sent out here with me for six months. I owed him for his unwavering support, and he deserved to go home with me. I could not have done the job without him. The XO wanted to leave the master chief on the detachment.

The first thing that came to mind was, "This is the way you reward your people for doing a good job, you screw them." I explained to the XO that the master chief needed to get back to his family and it was my recommendation that he should return with us. At least we got through the first 60 minutes without a confrontation. We were at a stand-off; the XO did not want to give in so he deferred it to the new OINC. He said if I could get Jim to agree, then the master chief could come home. I was not satisfied with the response and headed into the office to talk with the relieving OINC. This was not the way I operated and I was determined to see that the master chief got fair treatment.

I sat down with the new OINC and went over every officer and chief in the detachment. These men were good, they just needed someone to give them support. I gave him a complete brief on their weak points and their strong points, then briefed him on why I thought the master chief deserved to go home. When I finished he told me he would give me his answer tomorrow after he talked with the XO. Was this a game of musical chairs we were playing? Why was it so difficult to make a decision, or were they waiting for me to back off so they could forget about it?

I was not about to back off. As we walked through the spaces I continued to brief him on the detachment and its relationship to NAS Atsugi. In response to one of my statements the new OINC made an off the wall comment that completely floored me. His response was, "Yes I know, I was briefed on the way over, you have to always keep the enemy off guard."

To my astonishment, he was referring to the detachment personnel as the enemy! I couldn't believe what I was hearing. It must have been some of that "command is lonely" bull shit! This detachment was not the enemy; it was the reason why he was here. They were going to make or break this guy and he had better start winning their respect. Was I doing the right thing leaving the detachment with this guy, or was it out of my hands?

The next day the new OINC told me that he thought it was best that the master chief stay in Atsugi. To say the least I was a little upset, this man deserved to return home, he earned the right. He was there when the squadron needed him and he never asked for a thing. He took as much pride in these men as I did. The detachment was a smooth running organization and it was able to stand on its own merits. I could not accept his answer.

I went over it again until the OINC agreed that the master chief could return. I wanted to seize the opportunity, so I walked him out into the hangar where the XO was. When we reached the XO I told him that the master chief was going home. The XO glared at me, he was not happy, and I was sure I was going to pay for it when I returned to the States. He gave me some bullshit about the new OINC having the toughest job, what I did was the easiest part. He had to maintain what the detachment had already achieved. The only place he could go was down.

I had heard that crap before and was tired of it. I was rapidly losing respect for these two. Jim had checked into the squadron the same day I did. I didn't see him jumping at the chance to take over Detachment Four when it was in trouble, and I didn't see him heading out to DET Two when they were at the bottom and had just failed three inspections. Now that Detachment Two was on top, he's the one that was going to have a tough time. The logic escaped me. I held back from telling them what I really thought. It was a done deal; the master chief was going back with us. That's how the XO and I started off our new relationship, and in a few months he would be taking over as CO. It was going to be an interesting relationship.

Two days later after returning from a briefing on the *USS Midway* the detachment put on one of the biggest and loudest farewell parties I had ever seen. Their spirits were high, even the XO was taken aback from all of the celebrating. There was something about the XO's demeanor that demonstrated he was not happy with my send off. Later it would come out that the XO did not like my popularity and relationship with the men, both officer and enlisted. He perceived my influence as a threat because I was headstrong and unpredictable. There was a tremendous sense of well-being and accomplishment in the detachment, and it all came out at once. The detachment was ready to move on to another chapter, and I was headed for the Sates and a new assignment.

Admiral Peck saw fit to give me a concurrent fitness report as I departed. Again I was taken aback by such a positive report. I don't want to drag you through the entire report but in order to understand the rest of the journey, I think it is important that an Admiral felt he should comment on a LCDR's performance even though I was not a direct report. It's also a reflection of the character of the men that served aboard the *USS Midway* in an operational environment and their sense of justice and fair play for a job well done. It would be several years before I came across the caliber of these individuals again.

LCDR BILLINGS HAS DEMONSTRATED SUPERB PERFORMANCE AND EXEMPLARY LEADERSHIP IN TURNING HC-1 DET 2 AROUND. HIS ABILITY TO EFFECTIVELY ORGANIZE AND INSTILL SELF PRIDE IN WORK ACCOMPLISHMENTS WAS A KEY FACTOR IN THE DETACHMENT'S IMMEDIATE RECORD OF IMPROVEMENT. THROUGHOUT THE DEPLOYMENT, LCDR BILLINGS' DETACHMENT HAS DEMONSTRATED OUTSTANDING PERFORMANCE IN A MOST DEMANDING AND VISIBLE ASSIGNMENT. HE IS A DYNAMIC, MATURE PERSONALITY AND EXHIBITS AGGRESSIVENESS AND INNOVATION IN PROBLEM SOLVING. THE DETACHMENT'S SUPERB PRODUCTIVITY DURING THIS DEPLOYMENT HAS BEEN VALIDATED STATISTICALLY BY THE FOLLOWING READINESS STATISTICS:

1) THE DETACHMENT AIRCRAFT AVERAGED 250 FLIGHT HOURS PER MONTH

OF OPERATIONS; THESE HOURS ARE MORE THAN DOUBLE THE FLEET AVERAGE. 2) THE AIRCRAFT READINESS RATES OF 97.2 PERCENT OPERATIONALLY READY AND 96.0 FULL SYSTEMS CAPABLE ARE UNSURPASSED BY ANY FLEET DETACHMENT. THESE STATISTICS ARE MOST IMPRESSIVE WHEN COMPARED WITH THE DETACHMENT RECORDS IMMEDIATELY BEFORE LCDR BILLINGS' ARRIVAL.

LCDR BILLINGS IS A MOST OUTSTANDING OFFICER, CLEARLY CAPABLE OF ACCEPTING THE MOST CHALLENGING RESPONSIBILITIES. HE IS A HIGHLY MOTIVATED OFFICER, ACTIVE IN ALL FACETS OF HIS PROFESSION. HE PRESENTS AN IMPRESSIVE MILITARY APPEARANCE. HE IS STRONGLY RECOMMENDED FOR ACCELERATED PROMOTION AND FOR COMMAND.

COMMANDER CARRIER GROUP THREE

Although I was there for only two short months with the new CAG, he was also very complimentary and insisted on giving me a departing glowing fitness report that also recommended me for accelerated promotion and command. It seemed that everyone who was forward deployed understood what we had gone through. I felt a little guilty for receiving so much of the credit. It was the men in Detachment Two, along with the master chief who really deserved the credit. They just needed something or someone to believe in. It would be different when I returned to San Diego. I had a few surprises waiting around the corner.

Chapter Eight
On the way to Command

I'm relieving you of your duties as Maintenance Officer, you're fired!

When I returned to San Diego, I took very little time off before going to work. I was never very good at vacationing and always had the maximum amount of leave on the books at the end of each year. With the constant turmoil at home it was best that I focus on my work. When I returned to HC-1, the skipper threw a squadron party in honor of my return. When I arrived at the party the skipper presented me with a case of champagne for a job well done. As the party progressed into the night, the skipper pulled me aside and seemed to have something he wanted to get off his chest. As he spoke it became more and more obvious that the champagne was a consolation prize. LCDR fitness reports had gone out and it seems the CO decided to give the number one and number two spots to two other LCDR's in his squadron. The skipper needed a few drinks before he had the guts to tell me. He knew it was horse shit and he knew I knew.

He tried to explain but it was lame. I had made quite a

reputation for myself while deployed and didn't need any help was his justification. The two LCDR's needed the extra boost, "BESIDES, THEY WERE NICE GUYS." I had gotten the brunt of it the first time. He was going to convince me before I left that night. I sat there and politely listened, holding back the rage from the bullshit I was hearing. Since he had such high regard for these two senior LCDR's, why didn't one of those two sons of bitches volunteer to do what I just went through?

I shook it off and told the skipper that I knew he had the best interests of the squadron at heart. Needless to say I didn't enjoy the rest of the night, or the champagne, especially when the skipper never let up on his rationale for screwing me. It was that age old tradition of promoting people who made you feel good, whether they were competent or not. It was the ones that played golf with the executives in the private sector, or those who always assured the CO he was doing the right thing, never putting themselves at risk. I was at a disadvantage; I was never any good at politics or making senior officers feel good. I did my job and I did it well.

I checked in and was assigned as the squadron maintenance officer. I would be relieving one of his top notch LCDR's. At that time the HC-1 maintenance department was one of the worst, if not the worst, maintenance department in the WING. During the skipper's briefing, he told me that I would not have the same luck as I did while deployed. The shore duty component didn't have as high a parts priority as forward deployed units and I would have to live with the poor operational readiness numbers.

I assured the skipper that what I did with the detachments was not luck and that I would like to take a look at the department before I gave him my opinion. I excused myself and took a quick tour through the maintenance area and then called a meeting with all the division officers and chiefs. Fortunately, or unfortunately, my reputation had preceded me, again. The men were expecting a flamboyant

"Hollywood Al" leadership style and were eager to see some positive changes. It seems the stories of my exploits overseas had been a little exaggerated. Nevertheless we had a job to do and we would see if my popularity would still be there when I was done.

The first thing I told them was, find someplace else to park the squadron helicopters, they were embarrassing to look at. They were so dirty you couldn't even see some of the markings. I did not want them sitting in front of the squadron spaces. Then the complaints came. The men were working long hours and weekends, they thought it was unfair, they were on shore duty and should be able to spend time with their families. They said they never knew when they would have to work weekends, until 1530 on Friday of that weekend. They couldn't make any plans. I quickly solved the problem and told them, "Until further notice, you will be working every weekend, so plan on it. We will work until these helicopters look like they belong to HC-1." I asked if they had any questions. There was dead silence in the room.

As was my standard practice, I brought every one of the officers and chiefs in to talk with me. It was clear before I got halfway through the interviews that some of the chiefs as well as some of the officers were in the wrong positions. Especially the old maintenance control officer. He was an LDO with 23 years in the Navy and appeared to be a stumbling block. The problem was the majority of the chiefs had a great deal of respect for him. He had tremendous knowledge but spent most of the time making excuses for why things couldn't be done. I made him Assistant MO and moved the master chief into maintenance control. I needed someone I could trust. I made several other moves. For example, the QA Chief, did not really have the personality or the training to be in quality assurance. The old philosophy was a Navy chief could do anything. That wasn't true in any business; everyone has their strengths and weaknesses. It wasn't rocket science. I made several other changes and made it clear that everyone would be responsible for their assigned duties.

When I was done, I went into the personnel office and got with the first class personnel man. Something was wrong and I wasn't sure what it was. I wanted to go over the squadron manning levels. It appeared we were undermanned in several key areas and additional personnel were getting orders out, with no replacements being ordered in. I confirmed my suspicions. It was apparent that nobody was minding the store. Where was the admin officer? Wasn't that part of his job description? I found out later, he was the other hot LCDR that got ranked above me.

I reported my findings to the CO and XO. They called the admin officer(AO) in and asked him what he thought of my observations. The AO said, "We're in fine shape skipper." This was my first real exposure to one of the skipper's top LCDR's other than seeing the fine results of the maintenance department. The other one had already departed the squadron.

I was not impressed. I knew this guy didn't have a clue about what was going on, but "HE WAS A NICE GUY." I told him I thought it would eventually lead to problems and if we didn't take action now we could be in serious trouble in the future. He assured the skipper the manning levels were fine and the meeting ended. I excused myself and returned to the maintenance office.

I always had the ability to see far into the future and project what was going to happen, as clearly as if it were tomorrow. It was frustrating to try to explain future problems to people when they were only interested in what was going to happen tomorrow. It was a problem that was inherent in the Navy, where you have personnel that rotate through every two years. If it is not going to happen on their watch, why make waves? The Navy was a big organization and it took time to correct things. Over the next few months I would work very closely with personnel to try to resolve some of the personnel shortages myself. The AO was no help; he seemed to have something to prove, and I didn't have time for games. If the maintenance department fell on its ass, it was of no concern to him. It would be Hollywood Al's problem.

I had one other problem. I had been in charge of every unit since I was a junior lieutenant. I was not good at politics, and I knew it. I seemed to be a little too direct for the skipper. They didn't seem to appreciate all the attention I got while I was deployed. From where they sat my resolve was a little intimidating. Maybe it was my fault; I had just spent the last year making things happen by brute force. It was my job to make the skipper understand, but he was leaving in a few months and didn't seem to have much interest. After all he was totally successful in straightening out the deployed detachments. My problem was I got too absorbed in the job and I should have spent a little more time telling the CO what a brilliant officer he was.

When I finished with the restructuring of the maintenance department I came up with a get well plan and presented it to the skipper. The maintenance department was in disastrous shape and the skipper had bought all the bullshit the last MO gave him. I told him that some drastic measures would have to be taken in order to clean up the aircraft. We needed to get the op ready status up to where it should be. I was blunt as usual. I didn't have time to wait and see if the CO and XO got the general idea of what I was trying to say. Traditionally the squadron operations officer always over schedules the aircraft in order to keep his portion of the flight hours and statistics up. This was done without any regard to the long term effects on the aircraft and maintenance personnel. This was well-documented in several studies, and I was surprised that nobody looked at the impact of chasing after flight hours. Again, it was not rocket science.

It came down to a test of wills, would the maintenance officer win or would the operations officer win? I handed the CO and XO the aircraft that were available for flights that day. They were more than enough to meet the squadron's commitments. As I placed the list on his desk, I said, "Here are your aircraft. Ops can do what they want with them, but if they go down, Ops will have to figure out a way to meet his commitments. The other aircraft will be hard down for some major maintenance."

The CO and XO looked at each other as if to say, "Can he do that?"

The CO said, "You're never going to get there, it's just a fact of life."

I replied, "I'd like to try; the aircraft are really embarrassing to look at."

It was really something. In many ways the aircraft in the shore component of the squadron were in as bad a condition as the aircraft in DET Two and they got hammered for it. I'm sure the CO and XO didn't appreciate my directness or the fact that I was telling them what to do, even though it was right. The maintenance department was working long hours and weekends primarily because nobody was managing the assets or seemed to care.

I went back to the maintenance department and took them on. After going through the maintenance reports it was obvious there was a lot of paper shuffling and padding of numbers going on. I told the division officers and chief that this was no longer acceptable and the true hours would be documented. I was able to get away with it because of the reputation I had for getting the job done and eliminating the bullshit. It was a "let's wait and see attitude," and they went to work. Within two weeks we were no longer working weekends and we were meeting the flight schedule. The aircraft started looking better and we were able to plan the maintenance, instead of spending every day reacting to the last minute assignments and emergencies from the operations department. I never heard a word from the operations officer.

The aircraft readiness and availability continued to improve. Within 2 ½ months, and the week before the CO departed for his new duty assignment, the aircraft readiness went from a mere 46% to 87%, which was slightly above the average for a shore duty component attached to ASWINGSPAC.

I took the report and put it on the skipper's desk. He was not happy. It was apparent that he had bought the excuses the previous maintenance officer had been giving him. I had proved that I was right and he was wrong, and he didn't like that. The aircraft looked better, the morale in the maintenance department was up and the statistics were a fact. The skipper acknowledged the numbers and made no comment. The previous maintenance officer was the top ranked LCDR in the squadron before he departed but.... "HE WAS A NICE GUY."

Before the skipper left he nominated me for Pilot of the Year at the Naval Helicopter Association (NHA) annual awards conference. No one had accomplished what I had in the past year, yet I did not receive the award. I didn't dwell on the outcome. There was too much to do. I was not a political animal and would most likely be disappointed in the rationale they used in selecting the winner. I told myself that I was sure the individual was deserving of the award and focused on the work to be done in the maintenance department. It was my mistake, even then I should have realized how political the WING was, it was peacetime and politics were the name of the game. I missed the *Midway* already.

The change of command took place and the XO fleeted up to skipper. His new XO was from the Anti Submarine Warfare (ASW) Community. The new XO, CDR Bruce Brown was a big boy scout. There is nothing wrong with that, but he was there to lead men. He did everything he could to please the new skipper. The more he tried to please him the less the skipper seemed to like him. I kept submitting the monthly maintenance report emphasizing the manpower shortages hoping that I would get ASWINGSPAC's attention and the skipper's support, without it we couldn't continue to operate safely.

The new skipper continued to ignore it and the situation continued to deteriorate. The mode of operation at the squadron seemed to be, "if we don't address it, maybe it will go away." The morale was starting to slide. The men didn't seem to relate to the XO and the CO was holding captain's mast every week for what seemed the slightest infraction. This continued for the new skipper's entire tour.

The previous skipper was right. I didn't need any help. I was screened for command and most assuredly would make commander. That still didn't make it right. Those two LCDR's he gave the boost to, were clearly dead wood, and only one would make commander. It was a waste of effort, at my expense. HC-1 was famous for screwing its own people. That's why half the squadron CO's were from another community, like the new XO. I vowed it would never happen under my watch.

After three months with the new skipper, I walked into his office with the monthly maintenance report, "It is my responsibility to inform you that we are borderline on safety. If we continue to lose personnel without replacements we will be an accident looking for a place to happen."

He responded with, "You tell me when we are unsafe and I'll do something about it."

My response was, "Skipper you know the only time they find you unsafe is after the accident. I don't want to wait until that happens."

The skipper replied by stating that he was not going to bother the WING with minor problems and besides, Stan (the admin officer) said we're fine. I left the report on his desk for his signature and returned to the maintenance department. It was clear the skipper did not want to make waves. Some people would rather choose to go through their whole tour hoping nothing would happen that they would need to respond to, or make a decision on.

Weeks passed by. The captain's masts continued and the squadron morale continued to go down the tubes. As I look back, it was the CO's way of maintaining good order and discipline and control. My department had the majority of the squadron personnel and I would deal with the men on my own, mostly by chewing ass and making them realize that it was in the best interest of the squadron and the men needed to pull together and make it work. I got so good at chewing ass and getting the most out of my men there were times when the men would ask to go directly to captain's mast rather than get chewed out by the MO. It was easier on them; when they went to mast they got busted or fined, and in their mind they were even, they didn't owe anybody anything. When they got their ass chewed by the MO they felt guilty for letting down their squadron mates.

Two months passed by. I thought long and hard about my next monthly report. I went over the numbers with the personnel department and it was unavoidable. I wouldn't be doing my job if I let it go any further. I added into the report the fact that the maintenance department could not continue to operate under the current manning levels, and in my opinion we were considered unsafe. The following immediate actions had to take place and I listed each step the WING and HC-1 would need to take to get the squadron back to the proper manning levels. I hand carried the report to the CO's office for his signature. The XO was in the office with the CO when I entered the room and handed him the report. After a few minutes of going over the report the skipper looked up at me and said, "Al you're forcing me to make a decision," and I replied, "Skipper, you asked me to tell you when I thought we were unsafe. I'm telling you we cannot go any longer without some replacements."

The skipper stood up with his face beat red and said, "You've forced me to make a decision, and my first decision is, you're fired. Consider yourself relieved of your duties."

It was useless to try to make him understand. After all, the admin officer assured him everything was fine. I replied with, "Yes sir," then turned and left the office.

I had become very popular in the squadron and that is probably why they tolerated my directness. I had turned around two detachments and made the squadron maintenance department one of the best in the WING, at 70% of my manning level and I did it with flare. We were even in the running for the Sikorsky maintenance trophy. The enlisted men loved my bravado and "Hollywood Al" no bullshit style. My weakness was I had very little patience and did not deal well with the lack of common sense and complacency I had observed. When I returned to the office, I called a meeting of the division officers and chiefs.

In minutes my office was full; everyone was quiet, nobody had a clue what was going on, but rumors were starting to fly. I was at my desk packing my briefcase when I turned to address them. "Gentlemen, there has been a misunderstanding between the Skipper and myself and I have been relieved of my duties as Maintenance Officer."

One of the chiefs blurted out, "Bullshit! We have enough on the Skipper to hang that son-of-a-bitch."

The office erupted into inflammatory statements and anger. I put a stop to it immediately, "There will be none of that! This is between the Skipper and myself. You will not tear apart this squadron. I am going to leave the maintenance office and you will give the Skipper your 100% support, is that clear?"

The room was quiet. Everyone seemed to be squirming around as if they wanted to say something but couldn't.

With my style of leadership I was much closer to the men than most officers. When I was relieved it became personal to them. It was critical that I make them understand that the squadron came first. They had worked too hard to get us where we were to let this hurt the squadron. The grumbling continued. I answered their questions and tried to put them at ease. I left them with, "No one man is worth hurting the reputation of this squadron, and if you do not support the Skipper, you will be letting me down. I am going to quietly leave and nothing is going to change. You will give your full support to who ever replaces me as MO."

I grabbed my briefcase, exited the office and headed to my car.

The skipper was concerned about my influence in the squadron and immediately sent out his people to see if he was going to be challenged. I have no idea what his people told him had taken place. I was at home for two days when I got a call from one of my division officers. The skipper had sent the WING the monthly maintenance report I had given him, which surprised me. The WING put together a team, led by the WING, MO to look at the HC-1 Maintenance Department. They should be finish the following day, and he would let me know what the results of the inspection were.

On the afternoon of the third day I got my call. The WING had recommended that my plan, which was now the skipper's plan, be implemented with the support of the WING. Later that evening I got a call from the XO. The CO wanted to see me in his office in the morning. I replied with, "Yes sir, I'll be there." There wasn't much dialogue; I don't think the XO ever knew how to deal with me.

Operations Officer, "If you break out into a grin or laughter, I'll fire you again."

The next morning the CO, XO and I met in the skipper's office. The CO started out with, "I have relieved you of your duties as Maintenance Officer, and I can't return you to that position. What I am going to do is make you Operations Officer."

I listened. The maintenance department was well on its way and with the support of the WING and with the new personnel they would be getting, they could do the job. My only concern was I wouldn't be able to protect them from any bullshit coming from the front office in the form of all the captain's masts. Up to that time I was able to focus on the maintenance department and provide them with the motivation they needed. The move to operations officer was actually a promotion.

The operations department was usually run by the third senior officer in the squadron and since I had already screened for command it was a logical progression. Besides, I had never held an operations billet, officially. There were ways I could still help the maintenance department. I could work with the maintenance department instead of against them, by trying to make a name for myself running the aircraft into the ground. I replied, "When do I start?"

"Now," said the skipper.

I went down and introduced myself to the personnel in operations. Over the next few weeks I went through every report and training record for all the officers, crew chiefs and rescue swimmers in the squadron, including the detachments. I actually should have been going to lunch with the skipper and telling him what a great leader he was.

There was an alarming trend. To confirm my suspicions I went to personnel again and went over the manning levels and personnel ordered in and out of the squadron. I could not believe what I was finding. I wondered what some of the department heads did while they were at work, obviously they were only interested in building flight time and sticking their nose up the skipper's ass. I sat on it for awhile; I wanted to be sure. Besides how could I tell him we were operating and barely able to maintain C-1 status on our operational readiness report. We could survive for now but we would be in trouble if any of the flight crews were to get injured. Besides, the skipper would go crazy if I told him we had another problem.

The squadron was a couple of weeks away from the annual Administration and Material Readiness (ADMAT) Inspection. We were busy putting together all of the squadron statistics for the skipper. A few days before the inspection the skipper wanted to have a dry run. I figured this would be a perfect time to let him know the potential problem. If I did not inform him I would be derelict in my duties. Back then we used butcher paper and an easel board to give formal briefings. When it came my turn, I stood up and walked over to the easel. I completed the first page, turned to the next and started with, "Skipper, here is where I think it's important that we tell the WING about our aircrew situation. We need to get their support. We are currently at C-1 but if we have a problem in any one of these areas," (and I went through the list) "or, if we have any of our aircrew hurt, we drop immediately to C-2, and if more than one, we go to C-3, which is unacceptable. We do not have the replacements coming in and we need the WING to give us priority. I have setup a new training program and as soon as we get the personnel, we can get started."

To my surprise the skipper looked over at the admin officer, "What do you think Stan?"

The AO looked at the skipper and said, "Sir, we're fine. Al is just trying to make a mountain out of a molehill again."

The skipper looked over at me, "Get rid of it."

I couldn't believe what I was hearing. This was the same idiot that told him the maintenance department was in fine shape. I ripped the page from the easel, wadded it up in a ball and sat back down in my chair. As far as I was concerned I did my job; it was the skipper's squadron and as long as it didn't cost lives, he could screw it up anyway he wanted. I was tired of fighting an up hill battle. I'm sure a psychologist would have a field day with this one. Why was it that the skipper took Stan's recommendation over mine? Stan had not been right once since I returned. Was it that the skipper just couldn't accept the answer because it came from me? It wouldn't be long before the truth came out.

The inspection with the WING went off without a hitch and the squadron continued to operate. Less than two weeks had gone by when I got called into the CO's office. When I entered I saw the XO sitting on the couch, neither of them looked very happy.

"Sit down Al," the skipper said as he glared at me. I knew what was going through his head from that look, if I broke out into a grin or laughter, he'd fire me again. I sat down.

"Al we've had an incident in Det Two and two of our aircrew men were injured. Since the DET is short of aircrew we have to send two of our aircrew from here. You need to send a message out to the WING to inform them of our op ready status."

I responded with, "Yes sir, what would you like in the message?"

"Basically we need to put what you had on the butcher paper you tore up."

I stood up and said, "Yes sir, I'll take care of it right away." I turned and left the office.

I was proud of myself for not saying anything. It would do no good to pour salt in the wound. The skipper was in a bind, just a short while ago we painted a rosy picture to the WING on our op ready status and now we had to tell them we were C-3. On my way down to the ops office, the safety officer stopped me in the passageway. He was a sharp young officer and everyone liked him. "Well Al, I guess you're the hero again."

"What do you mean?" I asked.

"What you told the skipper two weeks ago was right on."

I replied with, "I don't think you understand. When you tell the skipper something and he goes against you, then later you turn out to be right, you're the goat, not the hero." I turned and continued down to my office.

I worked with the personnel department and the WING to fill the billets that were left vacant. The admin officer continued to sit in his office and take up oxygen, but "HE WAS A NICE GUY." One good thing was about to happen; the AO was due to rotate in a few weeks. He had done enough damage and needed to move on. The changes in personnel would in the long run benefit me when I took over as CO. It would take months to get the billets filled and the men trained. By the time I took over, the squadron would be up to the proper manning levels. These preceding events probably sound like they were made up or impossible, but they actually happened. The ironic thing about it was, in their eyes, they were the victims and I was the bad guy.

As expected, I was picked up for commander on the next selection board and would be putting it on about the time I was due to take over as XO. Weeks went by and the skipper and I finally started to develop a relationship. It wasn't easy. One day the skipper came into the ops office and said "Let's go to lunch."

Without thinking, I replied, "No thanks skipper, I usually go over to the gym during lunch."

The skipper looked at me as his face got flushed, "You just let me know when you can work me into your busy schedule," and walked out the door.

I knew I had screwed up. I went down to the skipper's office and apologized. We went to lunch that day.

The skipper continued to win my confidence. I wasn't sure why he had changed his attitude toward me, but it was nice to be accepted into the fold. Several months went by and the reason for the friendship started to become apparent. It seemed the skipper did not like the XO's Boy Scout mentality. It was a shame; the XO was dedicated to the skipper, and followed his direction to the letter. I could understand the skipper's frustration; the XO had no leadership qualities. He was a follower and a politician. Every chance he got, he was over at the WING to get visibility.

The skipper told me that all I had to do was not make any waves over the next few years and I had captain made. With my combat experience and the reputation I made for myself as an operational trouble shooter, I was sure to be selected. Making captain hadn't even entered my mind, but probably should have. Then the skipper finally came out with his real intent, he did not want me to be CDR Brown's XO when he took over the squadron. He told me, "If you are Brown's XO, he will be a success as the CO and he doesn't deserve it."

I didn't say anything, I just listened. I couldn't believe what I was hearing. The CO owed him something for his loyalty, if only his silence. I wanted HC-1. I was scheduled to fleet up to CO of HC-1 and that's where I started as an ensign. What could be more fitting? I didn't give him an answer.

As department head, each morning the first thing I did was pickup the message traffic. One of the detachments lost an aircraft out in the Kawajalin Islands. The crew was able to make it to land but the aircraft burned to the ground. No one was hurt. There was very little left of the aircraft. Something kept bothering me. There were too many similarities to several other H-3 accidents that I had read about. I began doing a little research on the similar accidents and continued to monitor the message traffic to see if this was a trend. Unfortunately I didn't have enough information to help the deployed detachment. It was determined that it was a maintenance error, and the maintenance personnel and the pilots had their careers on the line.

I could not believe the way the situation was handled. I was appalled at the whole thing. Nobody questioned the investigation, which consisted primarily of one engineer that flew out from Pensacola to determine the cause. Something wasn't right. It was typical political bullshit; you never go up hill you always go down. These men were dedicated officers and enlisted personnel, nobody even considered there may have been another cause. The XO's comment about, "We need to show the WING we can take action," did not endear the XO to me. They were so eager to show the WING they could take action, I didn't feel they gave the men a fair shake. The XO and CO would do whatever it took to look good in the eyes of the Chief of Staff and Admiral. In my opinion the men were secondary to their personal goals.

Weeks went by and the skipper did not let up trying to get me to turn down the squadron. He kept building a case, "The XO will screw you, he's a politician, and he secretly doesn't like you."

I listened to it for months. The skipper finally told me that if I turned down HC-1, he could get me any squadron I wanted. I bought it; I was tired of the manipulation and innuendo. I wanted my XO and CO tour to be enjoyable. I finally agreed. The skipper was elated.

"I'll go to the WING tomorrow and we'll get you a new squadron," he said.

The following day I saw the skipper walking down the passageway, it didn't look good from the expression on his face.

"What did the Chief of Staff say?" I asked.

"The Chief of Staff said, not only will you be Brown's XO, you will be the best damn XO the WING has ever seen."

I'd been had! The skipper had not talked to anyone about this; it was a shot in the dark because he didn't like the XO. I was the pawn, and now I was on the WING's list of people with no allegiance. I kicked myself. I always had a weakness for wanting to believe in people, and now I had been setup by someone who pretended to be my friend. I had no idea of how it was presented to the Chief of Staff. I could only assume the skipper came away clean and only played the messenger. I was naïve when it came to the games that people played. If only they would have focused on what was best for the squadron, instead of their petty personal prejudices, everything would have been fine. I couldn't understand the logic of people and why they did the things they did. The impact of the stunt the CO pulled would follow me for the rest of my tour in HC-1.

Executive Officer, the men and the squadron come first.

There was about two months left before the change of command; the XO and I had developed a cautious relationship. I had no idea what the skipper had told the XO during his little game of manipulation. The squadron morale was at its lowest and the prospect of the XO taking over as commanding officer didn't help. They knew he would do whatever it took to promote himself over at the WING.

The only positive spot was, the men were looking forward to an exciting year as "Hollywood Al" took over as the new XO. CDR Brown was like a big teddy bear, none of the junior officers looked up to him. I had my biggest challenge ahead of me. It was going to be my job to make sure the new CO got the respect he deserved. But first we needed to have an understanding. The week before the change of command, I went into the XO's office and had a closed door session with him.

I was always straight and blunt and knew no other way. To me the men always came first and I wanted CDR Brown to understand that. The XO knew how the WING had responded, and we were stuck with each other for the duration. I had to make it work or the squadron would suffer. We talked for a long time. Most of it was insignificant; the XO was guarded. CDR Brown had no direction for the squadron and did not have any marching orders for me. To me that meant he didn't know what to do next. I think he was just holding on, hoping things would go well during his tour. I wanted to make one thing clear before I left. I told him I would support him 100% as his new executive officer, but if he ever sacrificed any of these men to promote his own career, or look good in the eyes of the Admiral, then we would have a problem. Other than that he would have the best XO the WING had ever seen. CDR Brown was in a difficult situation. I think he knew he wasn't very popular. It didn't help that his wife treated him like dirt in front of the junior officers during social functions. Could we make it work? Only time would tell.

I left the office. I knew it would not be an easy task, trying to run a squadron without overshadowing the commanding officer. The change of command went off without a hitch and it was my turn to see if I could shape the squadron. The morale was terrible. The junior officers had no focus, the chiefs did nothing but complain and pass all the problems up the line. The watch schedule was a disaster. Basically there had been no leadership just manipulation and mistrust, and plenty of captain's masts. I still had no marching orders from the new skipper. It was up to me to make the changes. When CDR Brown was the XO he was not allowed to make any decisions or changes without the CO's approval. I was fortunate in this respect. The new CO had no idea of how to run a squadron; he just wanted everyone to like him.

I called a meeting with the chiefs, and it wasn't to listen to their complaints. The approach was completely different from the detachments and the maintenance office. The moves had to be strategic, as they would affect the whole squadron. I made it a very short meeting, the communication was one way. I started out with, "Since the Zumwalt era, all I've heard, is the chiefs have lost all of their authority. Let me make this perfectly clear. In my opinion the chiefs have not lost their authority; they have given it away. The lack of demonstrated leadership is ludicrous. At 1630 you're in your car on the way home to pat mommy on the ass, like you were a bunch of damn civilians. This is the Navy; you will stay here until the job is done. A kid comes in late and you pass him up to captain's mast for disciplinary action, instead of handling it yourself. Just because you might have to stay late to set him straight. This is unacceptable and it will not continue.

"As XO I only want to see those cases that can't be handled at the division level. I don't care how you do it, but you will start demonstrating leadership. As long as you are fair and just, you will have my 100% support."

The room was quiet. I ended by saying, "That is all," and got up and walked out.

The chiefs must have stayed in the wardroom for over two hours. They were either going to try a mutiny or become the chiefs I wanted them to be. The word came back that the chiefs agreed with what I said and that I would not be disappointed.

The enlisted watch schedule was a disaster. The watch schedule may sound a little insignificant but it was critical to good order and discipline of any military organization. It was handled by the first class petty officers with the oversight of the squadron watch officer. I called a meeting with them and listened to some of the problems. Most of the complaints were petty bullshit, but it was obvious there was no ownership or accountability within the watch sections. The biggest problem was they did not get to contribute any input to the watch schedule or duties. I knew human nature, the petty officers were in that "it's your watch schedule you make it work mode."

I threw it back to the first class, "You will go over all the squadron guidelines and policies and make recommendations for a workable solution to the watch schedule and submit your recommendation to the watch officer and me by next week. Are there any questions?"

Again the room was quiet. I got up and said, "Next Tuesday at this time," and turned to walk toward the door. When I got to the door, I stopped and turned around. "One last thing, if we implement your recommendations, they'd better work."

The next week the first class presented their recommendations and the watch officer and I approved almost everyone of them. I knew I had them. It was now their watch schedule; if it failed they would lose control. Now they had to make it work. There were no more problems with the watch sections. The various meetings continued until the squadron understood that it would be, "the squadron comes first." There would be no more petty bullshit.

The officers were a different story. I had to get them motivated without overshadowing the skipper. It was my belief that the skipper was the squadron, while he was there he should be treated as such. Most of the department heads were older than I was, but it didn't make a difference. They knew how determined I was and what I had accomplished. Over anything else, they respected me for it. Most of the junior officers thought the stories of "Hollywood Al's" escapades in the fleet and ashore were some of the greatest stories they had ever heard. Unfortunately as the years went on the stories got a little exaggerated, at least that was my story. I would use that to my advantage. They needed something to focus on and motivate them.

I hadn't been the XO for very long when a reporter showed up on my doorstep and asked to write an article about me. I was a little skeptical and didn't know why he had selected me. Fortunately I told him I would only do it if I had a chance to review the article before it was printed. I was very glad that I did.

When he sent me the initial article, he made me sound like John Wayne. I quickly called him and asked him to eliminate some of the larger-than-life paragraphs. He said emphatically that he wanted to keep them in. He had never before had such a colorful character to write about and he thought it made great print. I had him take some of them out and still the article was quite colorful. A typical descriptive paragraph looked something like this after I had him take out the rest, so you can imagine what the original article was like:

> **"Mustachioed, tanned, trim but with arms like a blacksmith, Billings wants to identify... to relate to his subordinates. He sees it as the key to his success."**

I continued to make changes my way. It was the only way I knew to make things happen. Within weeks there were positive signs of improvement. The CO gave me a free hand; he realized that I made sure he was the CO and there would be no other way. There had been no mast cases, which was unheard of over the previous 18 months. The self-esteem of the men and the morale started to improve. The chiefs were leading their men, and it felt good to them. I had one last thing that needed attending to.

It was a new Navy, over the last year, the shore duty

component started getting females into their operational units. HC-1 had two of the first female helicopter pilots on the shore duty component. The other pilots, at times, didn't exactly know how to deal with them and I wasn't sure the female pilots knew exactly what was expected of them. Every time they turned around it seemed they were getting special treatment and their pictures in the paper. It was a sign of the times, nobody knew exactly what to do. It was going to take the Navy several years to sort it out. Everyone always knew exactly were I stood. I never left anything to doubt. I called the female pilots into my office to set the record straight.

When they arrived they stood at parade rest in front of my desk. As almost always, I had a cigar lit, and was enjoying the aroma. I looked up at them and said, "I know you're new to this environment, but I wanted to make one thing perfectly clear. I don't care if you two sit down to take a pee, or not. You will be treated like any other officer in this squadron and receive no special treatment. You will be given responsibility and promoted on your abilities, not your gender. Is that clear?" (If I had made that statement in today's environment, they would have both had me court martialed.)

They were both a little taken aback, but responded by saying, "Yes sir."

I sat there for a second with my XO's face on waiting for them to make a statement; they didn't. Sometimes I had that effect on people. I said, "That is all," and they turned and started to leave. As they left I mentioned that I didn't think it was fair to the other pilots to see their faces in the newspaper every month and to try to keep it to a minimum.

As the weeks and months went by the skipper continued not to interfere with the running of the squadron, and I continued to make sure it was understood that the skipper was in charge. It was November 5, 1979. Iranian militants had stormed the American embassy and taken 77 American hostages. The CO was in his office with the Chief of Staff on the phone. When I came in, he put the Chief of Staff on the speaker phone. The Admiral had received a message from CINCPACFLT. They wanted to know if the helicopters aboard the USS Midway were armed. They were reviewing all of their assets and wanted to know if HC-1 had any combat rescue helicopters aboard the *Midway*. If they didn't, could they be configured with what they had onboard the ship to go in and make a rescue attempt?

We informed the Chief of Staff that the helicopters had no armor plating but could most likely be configured with machine guns from the Marine detachment aboard the *Midway*. I knew it wasn't a good idea but as the conversation continued, it looked like it was a real consideration. I mentioned to the Chief of Staff that the flight crews had only basic combat rescue training from the exercises up in Fallon, Nevada.

I had been there before. I knew their chances of survival were not good, but I didn't have all the facts. I told the Chief of Staff that I could have my bags packed and be on a plane in a couple of hours. The skipper looked over at me and said, "You just want to go over there and get some more medals."

I was stunned; I couldn't believe what I just heard. Medals? What is he thinking? These were our men. The skipper himself had no combat experience and I should have known where the comment was coming from. It was what some people did; they judged you by their values, weaknesses, and insecurities.

I piped in, "Captain, those pilots over there have never seen a shot fired in anger. If I get over there and say it can't be done, at least I've saved some lives. Those kids would not know if they were in trouble until it was too late. I know what I'm talking about." The Chief of Staff said he would take it into consideration and the phone conversation ended.

Two days went by and it was decided that DET Two would not be used in the rescue attempt. I was glad. It made sense. The SH-3G did not have a carrying capacity big enough to handle all the hostages. They would need more assets than DET Two had to offer to make an attempt like that.

It was well into the sixth month of my XO tour and everything was going well. The CO continued to have confidence in me, and let me be the hammer in the squadron. We had not had one captain's mast since I took over as XO, although their had been a number of XO screenings. The screening is where the XO does a mini-mast to see if there are enough grounds to send the individual to mast.

I understood human nature, and in most cases worked it out beforehand with the division officers and chiefs. Most of the young sailors that got into trouble were good sailors, they just needed a little direction. In many cases they had never had anyone stick up for them, for any reason. Back then, their parents shipped them off to boot camp so they wouldn't have to deal with them. Or, they may have gotten in trouble with the law for a minor violation and the judge gave them the opportunity to go into the service or see what it was like in reform school.

When a young sailor goes to mast, in many cases, he has paid his debt and owes nobody anything. Usually he finds himself back in the same situation a few months later. I felt it was more important to keep them from hurting themselves and their careers while we waited for them to mature. If a sailor felt he owed someone for sticking up for him, he usually tried not to let that person down, if he respected him. The bad actors always came back and you could pick the time and place when you lowered the boom on them. This approach gave the men the feeling that someone really cared and when the hammer did fall it was well-deserved.

Leadership was a funny thing The differences ran the full gamut. Some would choose a method that suited their own insecurities or egos and some would overcompensate the other way. The bottom line should have been, "What is best for the organization and the men?" The CO started asking me why he didn't get any mast cases; he was dying to exercise his non-judicial punishment authority. That was no reason to justify a mast case. I put the skipper off as best I could. The morale and discipline were improving and I didn't want it to go back to the old way. We could maintain "good order and discipline" without holding a weekly captain's mast. I wanted the chiefs to exercise their leadership. The skipper didn't push for a mast case.

The scenario for the XO screening usually went something like this. I would get together with the division officer and/or chief and we would review the case. If we felt the sailor was worth saving, we would end it at the XO's screening, the first time. These were not the serious problems; they were the disciplinary problems or dumb-shit stunts that young sailors are so good at pulling. This covered the majority of mast cases. Nobody wanted to go to XO's screening. The XO's office had no windows and there was always a cigar available for screening. The chiefs and division officers would line up on one side and any witnesses on the other, the room was small, so everyone got to smoke the cigar, whether they wanted to or not.

As we went through the circumstances of the case, I would always wait for some indication that the sailor was taking this seriously. Usually it was a bead of sweat that started down the side of the sailor's face or the look in his eyes. Toward the end of the screening, I would constantly ask, "Is there anyone who would like to say something on the behalf of this sailor?"

In most cases it had already been worked out and the officer or chief would step forward and make a statement on the behalf of the young sailor. It worked well, the men pulled together and felt they were getting support rather than discarded, which to many of them had become part of their lives. The morale continued to climb because they knew someone cared. In some cases it almost backfired. Some of the young sailors were so taken at the fact that someone actually spoke up for them, they offered to wash their chief's car or cut his lawn. Some of the chiefs were surprised, I wasn't.

The CO was continually asking what the status of the disciplinary problems was. It finally happened. I went away for a week of training. When I came back the CO had taken two petty officers to mast and busted both of them to the next lower grade. One of the petty officers was one of the sharpest second classes in the squadron and the Navy needed people like him. He was wrong, but human. He lost his temper with one of the chiefs in his division and told him off in front of the crew, showing disrespect. Most of the squadron knew the senior chief was a bit of a bully, and at times had overstepped his authority.

I didn't feel the punishment was just, but I was in a bind. I could not circumvent the CO or usurp his authority. I was able to get the CO to agree that if the petty officer made a public apology in front of the crew, the skipper would reinstate him. The petty officer made such a strong appeal during his apology, it had a much greater impact on the men than the results of the mast ever would have. The other petty officer was a bad actor and deserved to be busted, he was due. The only problem was the skipper busted him for a dirty shower, instead of something that would set a better example for the men. Those were the only two mast cases during the skipper's entire tour. The discipline in the squadron was much better than it had ever been. The chiefs were handling the discipline at their level, and as long as it was done fairly, they gained the men's respect.

Over the months the working relationship the CO and I had developed seemed to be working. One day the CO returned from the Admiral's office with a big smile on his face. He couldn't wait to tell me. He received a rating on his fitness report as one of the top CO's in the WING. What happened next I didn't expect. The new admin officer had been given the task of making some organizational changes, which included the moving of a bunch of furniture to new office spaces. The skipper was so pleased with himself, he wanted to make a command decision, and so he took over the furniture move. I think that says it all. It took the AO two days to straighten out the mess after the skipper was done.

It wasn't long before the relationship between the skipper and me would finally be tested. One of the young pilots was operating off the small deck of one of the ships in the amphibious unit when he noticed the tire was low. The pilot asked the ship if they had any compressed air to inflate the tire, so they could continue their landing practice. The ship told them it would be no problem, and wheeled out a tank of compressed air. There was a problem; the tank didn't have a pressure gage on it, and it was pressurized much higher than the tire could withstand. When the petty officer applied the nozzle to the tire, the tire blew up and shattered the metal rim sending a piece of the rim through the sponson (wing strut) with such force that it could have killed someone, if it had hit him.

When the skipper found out about it, he immediately went to the WING to report the incident. When he came back he was all pumped up and called me into his office. He told me he needed to show the Admiral that he could take action. He wanted to make an example of the aircrew man and take him to mast. I sat down on the couch and held my anger in. I had seen this bullshit too many times before.

I responded by saying, "Skipper, this man almost lost his life doing his job, and you want to take him to mast because he made the assumption that the ship's compressed air canister was at the same pressure as the one he used in the squadron."

Things like malicious intent, culpability, negligence came to mind. I didn't see any of that. I saw a young, inexperienced sailor trying to do his job.

"I told you when I became your XO, I would support you 100%, but I would not allow one man to be sacrificed for political gain, or to look good in the eyes of the Admiral. You will not take this man to mast."

The skipper did not reply. He knew I was dead serious. He had had a free ride up until then and he knew it. I suggested that the aircrew man be assigned to operations for a week and then he would have to re-qualify as an aircrew man. I left him to think about it, but it had taken a toll on what relationship we had. He did not take the crewman to mast.

Commanding Officer, HC-1

The change of command was several weeks away and it had been smooth sailing for CDR Brown. It was my turn to be the commanding officer. I couldn't wait to be the skipper. Now I could walk around, shaking hands and patting people on the back and my new XO could be the disciplinarian.

It didn't happen. The new XO was not available when it was time for me to take the reins. I had to move my admin officer into the XO's office. He was a good man, but not a strong leader. He was selected for commander but did not screen for command. I would have to continue to be the motivator in the squadron. I was tired; I wanted to be the good guy for once. The WING saw fit to give CDR Brown a Navy Commendation Medal for his performance as CO of HC-1. I was glad for him. It must have been difficult putting up with me for 18 months. When the word got out, the men were unimpressed with the award and their displeasure would be demonstrated in the months to follow.

The day came for the change of command ceremony and everything went off without a hitch, except I got chewed out after the ceremony by the new Chief of Staff for wearing my sunglasses during the ceremony. At first I thought he was kidding, but when he came out with the comment, "Only third world dictators wear sunglasses during ceremonies," I got the message.

He also didn't like my mustache. I knew this was not going to be a marriage made in heaven. With important things like that to focus on, I knew the Chief of Staff must be a real intellectual. It was my turn to go to the WING for the monthly briefing with the Chief of Staff and Admiral. The reception was less than friendly, and the Chief of Staff was guarded. I had only met the man once, but he seemed to have it out for me. As in most cases they had interpreted my aggressive leadership style and confidence as arrogance. It was very political at the WING and I was not good at being subservient. Some senior officers enjoyed that elevated status. It may have been fallout from the incident with the previous CO's ploy to get me to switch to another squadron. There was nothing I could do about it, so I focused on running the squadron.

It had not been two weeks into my tour as CO when we lost a helicopter on its way up to NAS Fallen, Nevada. Timing is everything in life; CDR Brown had skipped through his CO tour with only one minor incident and I hadn't completed two weeks when this happened. What would the future hold? Ever since they lost the helicopter in Kawajalin, I had been monitoring the SH-3 accident reports. This accident had many of the same characteristics as the numerous SH-3's that were lost throughout the fleet over the past three years. I was not about to have my men take the blame for something if it was not their fault.

Although the majority of the helicopter burned to the ground we were able to recover what was left of the aircraft and stage it in the hangar for the accident investigation team. One of the first people at the crash site was the engineer from NAS Pensacola. It wasn't surprising that the next day a message came out from the Naval Air Rework Facility (NARF), Pensacola, that it was a maintenance error that caused the failure and subsequent loss of aircraft. I was furious; they had no right to go out with that message without the results of the accident investigation. This flight crew had performed superbly. The crew chief dove through a wall of fire to get to the fire extinguisher to fight the raging fire. The pilot was able to keep the helicopter under control long enough to get the aircraft on the ground, saving his crew. I was determined to get to the bottom of it.

On the third day a safety officer flew out from the aviation safety center on the East Coast to conduct the accident investigation. LCDR Robinson was a good man and wanted to cover every aspect of the accident. Several days went by and I was getting an update of their findings at the end of each day. With the message from NARF, Pensacola, the majority of the investigation focused on maintenance. It was a perfect setup, the message read:

"The bolts on the high speed shaft were tightened in an over torque condition and they sheared under the high speeds, which caused the shaft to come off, cutting the fuel and hydraulic lines and setting the helicopter on fire."

I couldn't believe what I was hearing from the accident board. It was a very touchy situation. The commanding officer was not supposed to interfere in an investigation of one of his own aircraft. I kept remembering what the previous CO told me. "Al, with your combat record and operational success, all you have to do is close your mouth for the next few years and you'll make captain."

I always had a tendency to put the men before my career. I couldn't look the other way; I needed to do what was right regardless of the consequences.

I had been over the wreckage several times, talked with the maintenance personnel and knew what caused the accident. I was tired of the bullshit. I was not going to see another flight crew get hurt, or killed. I grabbed the maintenance control officer and went back through the wreckage. After a few minutes we found the high speed shaft that failed; it was obvious to any layman it was a material failure and not a maintenance error. I grabbed the shaft and took it upstairs to where the accident board was meeting. I walked in the room and tossed the shaft in the middle of the table and said, "There is your cause of the accident. You're not leaving here until you find out the truth."

I looked across the table at the safety officer sitting there and said, "I want you to take this shaft across the street and have NARF, North Island take a look at it."

NARF North Island was the rework facility for the F/A-

18. The next day the safety officer came back with one of the engineers from NARF. Two of the F/A-18 engineers and one metallurgist were absolutely certain that it was a material failure and were willing to put it in writing. I asked them to put it out in message format to CO, HC-1 and info ASWWINGSPAC and NARF Pensacola. They agreed and the message came out the following day. The very next day I received a call from a CDR Rogers at the NARF facility in Pensacola. He was the department head that oversaw the rework of the SH-3G.

The CDR was very friendly and spent a great deal of time explaining their position. They had many years of experience on these types of accidents and were sure they were correct. The CDR assured me that they knew what they were doing. He went on until I had heard enough of his bullshit. I tore into the him, "Let me make one thing perfectly clear. The Navy assured me I would never make it past lieutenant. I am already two ranks higher than they promised. If it is the last thing I ever do, I am going to see that you son-of-a-bitch's are held accountable for your actions. You have killed or injured flight crews and ruined careers over the last three or four years that I know of, all to cover up your own incompetence. I will not let this go on any longer." I hung up the phone.

At home that night I received a call from a friend. He was on the ASWINGSPAC staff and had helped me before. He told me I was not very popular over at the WING. They were referring to me as a "maverick" and a loose cannon. They received a call from a CDR Rogers from NARF, Pensacola. He was very concerned about the actions I was taking and wanted to know if I was as crazy as I sounded over the phone. Everyone at the WING was taking a political, wait and see attitude. They would not involve themselves and if it blew up, it'd be my ass.

I said, "That's fine. This has gone on too long. I cannot look the other way and see another crew lost or hurt." I probably should have gone to the WING to ask permission, but I didn't think I would have gotten an answer if they were taking the political route. They were right; I was dangerous. I did not put my career ahead of the welfare of the men. They knew I would not look the other way and I could not be pressured into changing my mind.

When I returned to work the next morning one of the messages on the message board was from NARF, Pensacola. They withdrew their initial assessment, that it was a maintenance error, and declared that they were not sure what the cause was. They stated they may never know because of the lack of evidence at the crash site. I sat there contemplating my career. It was a cover up and they were not going to get away with it. They were attempting to confuse the issue so they could continue to operate. I got zero support from the WING; they kept themselves at a distance during the entire investigation.

I went into the wardroom where the accident board was meeting and spoke to the safety officer. "This is what I want done. I want you to call NARF, Pensacola and tell them we have a strong suspicion that it was a material failure and we would like to run a test to destruct. Let's see what their response is."

Later that day, the safety officer came into my office and told me that NARF, Pensacola wanted to conduct the tests in Pensacola since they had the capability in their facility. They also wanted to see the high speed shaft and do their own evaluation. I told the safety officer that was fine, but I did not want him to let that shaft out of his sight, even if he had to sleep with it. I didn't trust them. They had finally been exposed, and may try anything to continue the cover up. I was totally disappointed in the WING. They were true politicians. I never heard a thing from them. It was their duty to ensure the safety of the pilots and aircrew that served in their AIRWING, yet they did nothing but wait and see. The risk was all mine. If I was wrong, it would be a squadron CO meddling in an accident investigation of his own aircraft.

While we waited for the results of the testing, I put the pilot of the incident in for an air medal and the crew chief in for a commendation medal for their actions in getting the aircraft down safely and fighting the fire. It was worthy of some recognition. I didn't know how much support I would get from the WING, but it was the right thing to do. It was a first; for over five years they had only gone after the careers of the men that were just doing their jobs, just to show the Admiral they could take charge and also protect their careers. I guess that's why I was called a "maverick." It took six months but they did get their medals.

It was a couple of days before I got the results of the testing at NARF, Pensacola. They had put an engine on the test stand and were going to run it for 24 hours straight, to see what would happen to the high speed shaft. Three and one half hours into the test they had to shut it down. The coating on the high speed shaft was breaking down. It seems the shafts used to be sent out for a carbon hardening treatment. Several years ago, the process was brought in house. NARF, Pensacola did not have the capability to do carbon hardening, so they changed the process to a plasma treatment. The new treatment was not standing up to the high temperatures created by the high speed shaft and engine. The coating broke down in less than 7 hours of testing. It was done; they couldn't hide the problem any longer. I'm sure I made a few enemies but I felt I didn't have a choice.

I never heard a thing from the WING, and before Pensacola got a chance to send a formal message out, DET Two, out of Atsugi, put a helicopter in the water during a night rescue in high seas. After I read the message, I just sat there in my chair, looking at the wall. I couldn't believe what was happening. Four weeks into my CO's tour, I had two accidents and two lost aircraft. There was nothing I could do.

The results of the first investigation were overshadowed by the second accident. There was a job to do and I didn't want it to impact the morale of the squadron. The result of the second accident was pilot error. It was my responsibility and I would deal with it. I never heard anything from the WING and the squadron continued to focus on the mission. It was done and all I could do was put it behind us and move on.

I think one of the reasons I liked the military so much was there was always something knew and challenging, or maybe it was just me and the way I approached things. A few months had passed when I opened the message board and saw a message from VC-1 to ASWWINGSPAC, Info. HC-1. VC-1 was requesting that some of the helicopter maintenance personnel be transferred to VC-1 in support of the new CH-53E's that would be arriving next year. They also wanted part of HC-1's hangar space to perform maintenance on the 53's, since HC-1 had a much larger hangar. Again, I sat there in disbelief at what I was reading. I had no idea where this was coming from; nobody had ever mentioned anything to me. VC-1 was a fixed wing squadron, and they were getting helicopters. It didn't make any sense. I made a couple of calls to the WING; as far as they were concerned it was a done deal. The agreement had taken place several years before. I called the VC-1 CO and setup a meeting.

It was a short meeting. The CO of VC-1 was not excited about getting helicopters for Vertical Onboard Deliver (VOD). As far as he was concerned, helicopters were a maintenance nightmare and he didn't want to have anything to do with them. The VC-1 skipper told me that he understood it to be one of my predecessors that gave them to VC-1. He re-emphasized he didn't want the mission.

I thought that was lame. How could a HC-1 CO give up an opportunity for a new mission? It didn't make any sense. It solidified my theory that some CO's just passed through their squadron tours getting their ticket punched and couldn't have cared less about the squadron, mission, or people. I wish I would have known the logic behind this one. Maybe it was just politics and they didn't want to make waves. I couldn't think of any justification for the move. I asked the VC-1 skipper if he would mind if I talked to the WING to see if he could get this turned around. He said it was fine with him and he wished me luck.

It took several months of paperwork and message traffic, but HC-1 ended up with the new CH-53E's and the Vertical Onboard Deliver (VOD) mission. Unfortunately I would not get a chance to fly them. The first one was due to arrive two months after my departure.

It was time for LCDR fitness reports and it was one of the hardest things that I had ever done. I had two officers that performed well in the squadron. Unfortunately they had already been passed over once for commander. They were hard-working, excellent officers. I had to look to the future of HC-1 and there was nobody in the pipeline to come from HC-1 to take over the squadron. I didn't want outsiders coming in from other warfare areas to skipper the squadron. I needed to make them understand I had been in their shoes and knew how it felt. I had to do what was best for the squadron. The previous CO was from the ASW community and my new XO, who had not shown up yet, was from a CH-46 outfit. They passed through for a ticket punch and gave very little to the squadron. I didn't want it to continue.

I called the two officers into my office together. I told them it was probably the hardest thing I have had to do in my Navy career. "You are both fine officers. I can't say enough for the work you've done in this squadron. You both have been passed over for commander once, and one fitness report is not going to change things. I have to think of the future of this squadron and who will have a chance to make CO. Although I would like to, I cannot rank you up at the top." It was tough getting it out. I continued, "You both have supported me 100%, and you deserve an explanation of why I am ranking the officers the way I am." I continued to try to make the men understand, but they were only words and nothing I could say was going to ease the blow.

They both said they understood and that it made sense.

It was the first time anyone had been honest with them, and they appreciated the honesty. The fitness reports came out and the rankings were etched in stone. To my surprise, and a testament of the integrity of these two individuals, they performed superbly throughout the remainder of my tour as CO. They were the backbone; their years of experience and maturity ensured the success of the squadron.

It was our annual ADMAT inspection, and I had been CO for over six months and my XO had not reported in yet! It was fine with me. The new XO had a reputation of not liking paperwork. The next phone call says it all about his personality and dedication and fits him to a tee. When I answered the phone, he wanted to know if we had had the ADMAT inspection yet. I told him the ADMAT would take place next week, he said, "Good, I'll be checking aboard the week following the ADMAT."

I was not impressed, and to say the least, was a little disappointed in the lack of motivation displayed by my new XO. Maybe I was wrong. Everyone seemed to just be passing through HC-1, while I was living it. The current acting XO was doing a fine job administratively; he was very thorough and detail oriented. As far as I was concerned he could stay the entire tour.

The ADMAT went fine, HC-1 passed it with flying colors. The Chief of Staff seemed to still hold me in contempt for reasons I would never know. All he could ever talk about was my mustache and sunglasses, which led me to believe that he didn't have very much depth and seemed a little small-minded and petty, but that's my opinion. We were even awarded the coveted Sikorsky maintenance trophy during the inspection. The maintenance trophy was a first for HC-1. The HS community had always dominated the trophy in the past. It was a small accomplishment in the rather disastrous start to my CO tour. I could only hope that we would not have any more accidents before my tour was over. Sometimes you have no control over fate. The new XO checked aboard the following week.

The bombshells never stopped coming. Part of my squadron was the West Coast Search and Rescue (SAR) swim school. It was run by seven Navy SEALs. The master chief was in charge of the school; it was one of his shore duty assignments. I took pride in staying in shape and enjoyed working out with the aircrew and their instructors. There was no way I could keep up with the much younger men in the school, but I did enjoy the comradery of the SEALs. It was something about their personalities I enjoyed. Maybe it was their honesty and straightforwardness that I rarely saw anymore. I had just finished fighting for the CH-53E's when I got word from the WING. They were going to disestablish the West Coast SAR swim school and combine everything in Pensacola. I couldn't let it happen. HC-1 was the oldest combat search and rescue squadron in the Navy and the swim school was an integral part of the training.

We were due to go to the annual combat search and rescue conference and it was one of the conference agenda items. During the meeting I asked to present my case. Nobody could speak with the conviction and passion that I could when I really believed in something. Even the master chief said he was looking for an American flag to start waving in the background to go along with my speech. By the time I was done, they had agreed to postpone the decision until the following year. It was most likely so they would not have to deal with me because they knew I wouldn't give in.

When we returned to San Diego it was time for our annual swim quals. The master chief suggested we swim in from a mile out to sea just to add a little realism to the exercise. I liked the idea. We were scheduled to be flown out in three helicopters and they would drop us in the water a mile out to sea. Once in the water we would head for the beach. The master chief in charge of the swim school challenged me to a race. I knew there was no way I could beat a SEAL but I had been challenged and had to accept. I did have one thing in my favor; I had control of the helicopters. I put the master chief in the last helicopter and told them not to take off until I was in the water.

As we prepared for the exercise the master chief briefed the pilots and crew on how to exit the helicopter. Because of the number of participants we used a CH-46 for the third helo. The master chief told them about the danger of hitting your head when exiting from the rear of the CH-46. As luck would have it, the master chief was in the CH-46 when the swim commenced. When I hit the water I gave them a thumbs up and they let the last helicopter take off from North Island. In order to try to catch me the master chief jumped up as soon as the helicopter entered the hover and took off running out the back. As he reached the clam shell doors of the CH-46, he hit his forehead on the top door. He hit with such force, they said he exited the helicopter horizontally, feet first.

When he landed in the water he knew something was wrong. He swam over to the rescue boat and asked them how badly he was cut. The petty officer moved his finger across the full length of his forehead and said "From here to here." The master chief turned and headed for the beach. It was close, by my standards, but the master chief beat me fair and square, which again speaks to the special breed of the SEALs.

It was time for the annual safety stand down. The helicopter community always combined it with their Navy Helicopter Association (NHA) conference. The NHA was a three day conference held every year, and this year, it was in San Diego. It was the helicopter community's version of the "Tail Hook" conference held in Las Vegas, only much more conservative. During the three days they reserved one day for the annual safety review. The person they sent from the safety center to give the review was LCDR Robinson, the same officer that did the investigation on our H-3 accident. He spent about three hours going through the entire year of aircraft accidents in the safety review.

At one point he got to the SH-3G accidents including the subsequent SH-3 accidents prior to the one in the Owens

Valley. LCDR Robinson started by saying, "If it wasn't for the tenacity of one Navy CDR, we might never have known what was causing these accidents."

I thought that was an interesting way of making the statement without mentioning my name. He even avoided mentioning the squadron. Out of curiosity I pulled Robinson aside later that day. I mentioned that I was curious why he phrased the statement the way he did. He replied with, "CDR it was not my decision. I would not have phrased it that way, if it were left up to me."

I knew I didn't get an atta-boy from the WING for saving millions of dollars in equipment and who knows how many lives, but I didn't think they would begrudge me a little recognition. I was not going to worry about it and shook it off, as usual. I knew I was not going to get a break from the WING and what frustrated me was not knowing why. I followed what I believed and always tried to do what was right in spite of the consequences. They say making senior rank was all about politics and I didn't have that word in my vocabulary. If following what you believed was wrong, then I truly was a "maverick."

Back at the squadron the new XO proved to be completely useless. All he wanted to do was fly. When it came to running the squadron, it all landed in my lap. The XO had ten times more flight time than I did. At times I had to restrict the XO from the flight schedule, just to try to get him involved in running the squadron. It got to be a joke; the XO never touched any paperwork. He even told the AO to take the paperwork directly into my office, he didn't need to see it. All the XO did was walk around the squadron and shake hands. I was disappointed but I didn't want my disappointment to be known in the squadron, or have it be a focal point, so I let it remain a joke.

It was time for a new duty assignment and I made it through the remainder of the tour without another accident. I was a little surprised at my set of orders. It was to the *USS Belleau*

Wood, LHA-3 as air boss. I couldn't believe my luck; I had requested it, but didn't think I would get it. The assignment was the next step in the promotional ladder, and I would stay operational. I couldn't wait to start the new assignment. I was a little heavy hearted though. The men, women and officers of HC-1 meant a great deal to me. They had become an important part of my career. They had done everything I had asked of them and were as good as any unit in the Navy. I was proud of the squadron and what they had accomplished.

The going away parties and the plaques and memorabilia were overwhelming. I was taken aback at the sincerity with which they were given and the regard they showed for my leadership. I was truly a very lucky individual to share that time with such a fine group of men and women. I had spent the last five years in that squadron, and I was leaving part of myself behind.

As far as ASWWINGSPAC went, I don't remember even getting a fitness report from them. Maybe I didn't want to remember. I was satisfied with the job I had done and nobody could take that away. The speech I gave at the ceremony was filled with passion and emotion for the moments and successes we shared together. We had taken them all on during some of the worst of times and never failed. No one could take that away. The change of command went off without a hitch, and I was off to my new assignment. The squadron officers in their own way would try to set the record straight about who "Hollywood Al" really was with the WING.

Chapter Nine
USS Belleau Wood LHA-3

Air Boss

I checked aboard the *USS Belleau Wood*, LHA-3, after a short leave period. I wanted to stay busy, the long at sea periods had finally taken a toll on my family and I was going through a divorce. The turnover was very short. The air boss I was relieving could not wait to get off the ship. The turnover lasted two days and we were headed out to sea for a week. I couldn't believe the department; what a bunch of hard chargers. They were called Aviation Boatswain's Mates. They took pride in being the toughest sailors in the fleet. They worked long days, and the tougher it got the better they liked it. All of the officers were dedicated and ready to do whatever it took to get the job done. It was a smaller group than my squadron, but a completely different and dangerous operating environment.

Preparations for launch and recovery very much resembled a well-choreographed ballet. A flight deck was one of the most dangerous places in the world. Those involved in the evolution have specific, clearly defined roles, and if you don't know what you're doing, it very well could have severe consequences. These guys would stay out on that flight deck day in and day out through any type of weather. The chill factor alone with the wind blowing down that flight deck was enough to separate the men from the boys. I was happy to be part of the air department. My "Hollywood Al" personality fit right in with the Bos'n Mates. They related to me almost immediately.

While we were out to sea that week, we conducted night qualifications for the Marines out of the Marine Corps Air Station at Pendleton. To my surprise the on station rescue vehicle was from HC-1. The pilot was my old admin officer. He asked if he could land a little early and shut down for a few minutes. He had something he wanted to give to me. I told him that would be great, and asked if they needed any box lunches. It was going to be a long night. The pilot thanked me and gave me an ETA of 20 minutes.

When I met the pilot down in flight deck control, I wanted to hear how the squadron was doing. The admin officer walked in with a large envelope under his arm. After we greeted each other, he handed the envelop to me. "Here skipper, we thought you should have this."

"What is it?" I asked.

"The officers felt that CDR Brown got your Navy Commendation Medal, so we got together and put you in for one ourselves. Unfortunately the WING turned it down. We thought you should have the write-up anyway, because we didn't think it was right."

I thanked him and tried to blow it off by telling him the thought and effort was more important than the medal and that was the truth. What bothered me was why did the WING respond that way? It was probably a first for the WING, having a squadron put their own CO in for a medal.

I was pleased that the men thought enough of me to submit the write-up, but I felt I let them down. They would not understand why the WING turned down the award. I could only assume that it was because I was never subservient to the WING and that's what they wanted. It was a peacetime Navy and I was not part of their corporate club. I was unpredictable, and I didn't ask for permission for every move. I stood up for what I believed in, and the squadron and the men came first. I was a "maverick." HC-1 had turned into one of the best squadrons in the WING and they knew it. That was enough for me.

After a few minutes of small talk and an update on the squadron the AO went out to man his aircraft. We finished the night ops and returned to port that Friday. I was pleased with everything I saw. The men I would spend the next two years with were complete professionals. I was not going to change a thing. I would finally just enjoy this tour I thought. The *Belleau Wood* was getting a new CO in a week, and he would be an aviator. On the LHA's, they alternated surface line officers and aviators as captains of the ship. It was something about the surface line officers not having any deep draft commands, because the aviators got all the carriers. If it would have stayed that way I would have been the only aviator department head aboard a surface line officer run ship. I was looking forward to having an aviator as skipper, but I didn't know what was waiting for me around the corner.

The games people play.

The XO was a surface line officer deep selected for captain. He did not like aviators. Rumor had it he washed out of flight training and had a chip on his shoulder. His wife confirmed it one night at a wardroom party, and the XO was fit to be tied. The XO was going to make it an interesting tour. He was manipulative, sneaky, and always pulled the strings from behind the scenes, never exposing himself. Lacking in integrity, he set out to put a wall between me and the skipper. I would be no match for the XO. I didn't know how to be sneaky and refused to lower myself to his level. My entire career had been based on performance and that would continue to be my focus.

The XO used his manipulation as entertainment while we were at sea. He would start a story or situation and then sit back and watch it develop. He was so good at it, he must have done it for years. A simple trick in the XO's arsenal would go something like this. The captain would instruct the XO that he wanted to see each of his department heads at least once each day. The XO would forget to tell the air boss and would justify it to the captain as, "Maybe the air boss doesn't think he needs to report to you everyday." He would cover up the screw-ups of the surface line officers and go after the aviators every chance he got.

The new CO was a brilliant man. Aggressive and a strong leader, I could see he was flag material. I was impressed with how he came aboard and took charge immediately. I had not seen that before and enjoyed it. He was driven. This tour was going to make him an Admiral. I liked him. Regrettably after a very short period of time, the captain was convinced the XO was totally dedicated to supporting him and the ship's mission. Unfortunately it was just the opposite. The XO would continuously put down the skipper during morning meals. I would usually get disgusted and leave so I didn't have to listen to it. I avoided the other meals when I could. I could not tell the skipper; the thought of getting down to that level was disgusting. Besides, the XO was so good at it, the captain never would have believed me.

Several months of workups went by. When we completed refresher training the air department won the coveted Battle "E" for excellence. The other departments got nothing and at times marginally passed. The air department continued to shine throughout the next months, while the other departments continued to struggle. In fact before my tour was over, the air department would win another Battle "E" and secure a third. No other department got such a high rating. Even with all the manipulation that was going on, I was enjoying my tour. The air department personnel were a great group of dedicated sailors that loved life and took tremendous pride in their jobs. I couldn't believe how fortunate I was.

The ship's chaplain was so moved by what took place on the flight deck, he felt compelled to write a poem about the men and their work:

FLIGHT OPS
A WELL-ORCHESTRATED SYMPHONY OF MOTION
FLOWING INTO SMOOTH SEMBLANCE OF ORDER AND SYMMETRY;
REDS AND GREENS, PURPLES, YELLOWS AND WHITES,
EACH WITH A SPECIFIC TASK
FOLLOWING THE DIRECTION OF THE "VOICE ON HIGH"...
THE FLIGHT CONTROL TOWER (PRIMARY)
UNDER THE BATON OF THE AIR BOSS.
TO WATCH A TOTAL EVOLUTION
IS AN INSIGHT INTO AN ELOQUTION
OF COORDINATION EFFORTS WHICH BLEND INTO
A PRODUCTION MATCHING OR SURPASSING
ANY CECIL B. DEMILLE OR ANY BROADWAY THEATRE OFFERING AT ITS BEST.
MISSING ARE THE RAVE REVIEWS,
BUT VERY PRESENT IS THE SENSE OF PRIDE
AND ARTISTRY THAT ADD UP TO SAFETY AND SATISFACTION
OF A JOB WELL DONE.
"CHOCK AND BLOCK"
"CUT THE ENGINE"...
"WRAP IT UP"...
WORDS AND SIGN LANGUAGE ALL THEIR OWN
TO INDICATE A NEED FOR FUEL
OR THAT ALL SYSTEMS ARE <u>GO</u>.
PLUS A MYRIAD OF OTHER DIRECTIONS

*TO ENSURE THAT ALL IS DONE TO THE LETTER.
PURE ART FORM THIS SYMPHONY OF THE FLIGHT DECK, A HARMONY THAT BRINGS TO THE MOST DISCERNING OBSERVER
TEARS TO THE EYES...
OUT OF SENSE OF DUE RESPECT AND DEEP APPRECIATION OF SPINE-TINGLING AWE.
AS THE DRAMA UNFOLDS ON THE BELLEAU WOOD.
LISLE E. STEWART*
Navy Chaplain

I failed to develop a relationship with the captain and that was my fault. I justified it by telling myself that the skipper had his hands full with the other departments that were struggling to survive. Besides, I wasn't good at small talk, and since the air department was doing so well, the captain didn't need to be bothered with the little stuff. In effect, I played right into the XO's hands. It was time to deploy to the Western Pacific and Indian Ocean. I was to fly out a week early to Hawaii to train the Marine AIRWING before they flew aboard the ship. The training went off without a hitch and the Marines were excited about the challenges of shipboard operations. I would fly aboard on the first helicopter, and then bring the rest of the AIRWING aboard.

My mini boss (Assistant Air Boss) was a great person, but was not suited for high tempo air operations aboard a carrier. Most of the time I would just let him sit there and do his thing. He was probably one of the nicest individuals I had ever met, but nice I didn't need to operate in the department. There was many times during the work ups, that we started at 0400 in the morning. The mini boss wouldn't show up until 0900, even then he was wiping the sleep out of his eyes. It was fine with me; it was more trouble to drag him up there, than it was to operate without him. Besides, he was such a likeable guy, it was hard to stay mad at him all the time.

The *Belleau Wood* was off Hawaii and the AIRWING was preparing to fly out to the ship. I had flown out ahead of the ship to train the AIRWING and was in the first helicopter with a Marine captain. The helicopter went hard down and we had to shut it down. I immediately got into the second group of helicopters going out to the ship. As we were taxiing out to the runway, ground control called the pilot and told him his son fell out of a tree and was on his way to the hospital. We taxied back to the line and I quickly got out and into the next available helicopter that was going out to the ship.

We finally got airborne, and I was in the co-pilot seat in a Marine CH-46. As we approached the ship I could hear the chatter over the radio. The mini boss was not doing his job and that was not a surprise. The pilots were doing touch and gos to get their qualifications out of the way before they made a final landing. The pilots kept calling for a downwind leg, as they were taught. The mini boss for some reason wouldn't answer.

Sometimes they would have to call 3 or 4 times before they got a clearance. This strung them out for miles with more helicopters coming into the break every few minutes. I couldn't believe what was going on. It was an accident looking for a place to happen. The sequencing of the aircraft was critical aboard ship. All the mini boss had to do was clear a couple of helicopters for the downwind, out of sequence, and you had the potential for two helicopters occupying the same airspace. Not good!

The pilots could rightfully expect that the tower had positive control over all the aircraft in its airspace. It was the tower's primary responsibility. The mini boss had no idea of how many helicopters were in the pattern and what the sequencing was. I was livid as I listened to the situation deteriorate; the potential for an accident was mounting.

When we got within sight of the ship, I was blown away. While this cluster fuck was going on, they had an LPD (small amphibious ship) in their landing pattern conducting touch and go's, with two Marine helicopters on a completely separate frequency. As the two helicopters operated off the LPD, the helicopters in the *Belleau Wood* pattern, were flying over the top of them, on the final approach to the ship. This was madness! Meanwhile you could hear the mini boss over the radio. It was as if he was having a relaxed Sunday afternoon, with only one helicopter in the pattern.

I had seen enough. I came up over the radio and said, "All aircraft overhead 'Poor Boy' climb to 2,000 feet and remain in a left-hand orbit until further notice. Roger, tell HDC, I want them to get that damn ship out of our wake, they're conducting landing practice right under our landing pattern."

Just about that time, the captain of the ship came up over the radio. "Who is that giving orders to my aircraft?"

I replied, "It's the air boss! Roger, get me on deck immediately, I'm in '319.'"

I was cleared for a straight in and the Marine captain slid the helicopter into spot four. I jumped out before the helicopter shut down and headed up to primary. I was hot; I couldn't believe that adults could let something like this happen. When I reached Pri-Fly, the space was full of civilians and the mini boss was laughing and joking with them.

The first words out of my mouth were, "Everyone, get the hell out of my tower."

There was complete silence and everyone started to exit Pri-Fly, including the mini boss and the petty officer that kept the statistics. I pointed to Roger and the petty officer, "You and you, don't move." I know I could have used a little more finesse, but you needed to understand shipboard ops and how serious they can be. Everything we worked for was in the balance including the CO's next promotion. One accident and I doubt if he or anyone else involved would be promoted.

The civilians that were up in Pri-fly were part of the Navy league. Some of them were very influential men. Roger was spending more time entertaining them than he was with the aircraft. In fact when I entered Pri-Fly, he had his back to the flight deck.

It didn't matter, it was my job to ensure the safety of all aviation operations aboard that ship. I needed to get these helicopters on the deck before they had a mid-air or ran out of fuel. I had the helicopters overhead report in and get their sequencing. Then I called HDC to delay the second group coming out to the ship. When I got their initial landings out of the way I shut them down and had the flight deck clear the spots for the next group.

Just as the last helicopter from the first group landed the captain called from the bridge. "Boss, I want to see you up here, right now!" I was still hot. The CO had a volatile temper, and this wasn't a good situation. As I walked down the passageway, I still couldn't believe some of the craziness I had just observed. When I arrived on the bridge, the captain lit into me. "Boss you can't take charge like that on my ship. I ought to fire you right now!"

Where did I hear that before? As was my nature, I responded to the moment, and said, "That's fine with me skipper, just get me off the ship, this thing is heading in the wrong direction."

The CO looked shocked and responded by saying, "Boss, I want you in my at sea cabin, right now."

He turned and I followed the CO into his at sea cabin; the XO followed close behind. The XO wasn't about to miss this for the world. Once the door closed the captain turned around and in a much lower tone, said, "Boss, you can't talk that way to me on my bridge."

In a much more civil tone, I replied, "Captain, my job aboard this ship is to make sure that all flight ops are conducted safely. That was the biggest Chinese cluster fuck I have ever seen. It was an accident looking for a place to happen. If you want to relieve me, that's your call."

Things settled down quickly, and I was glad. I told him

exactly what I saw and he listened. He understood what had to be done. At the end I said, "Captain, if you'll excuse me, I have the rest of the AIRWING to bring aboard." The captain excused me and I headed back up to Pri-Fly.

Almost two hours had passed when the XO showed up in Pri-Fly. I was busy cycling the aircraft through their landings and take-offs; the XO stood between the two large chairs the mini boss and the air boss used during air operations. After watching the operations for a few minutes the XO leaned slightly towards my chair and said, quietly, "I think the captain has calmed down. He made a statement that, 'that air boss is the best damn air boss he has ever seen.'" I should have been flattered; the captain used to be the head of the safety center and did many of the air operations assessments aboard the carriers. If anyone knew who was a good air boss, he did.

I didn't comment. The op tempo of the flight deck and the helicopters in the air were demanding my full attention. The XO was not being nice to me, he knew I was good, "damn good," and I could get them through a successful cruise. He left after watching for a few minutes and we continued to operate into the evening hours. We needed to pick up a few night landings before we shut down for the day.

We pulled into Pearl the next morning and were able to get a few days of liberty in Hawaii. There were only three CDR's aboard the ship, engineering and operations were both surface line and me. The XO would only allow CDR's to act as the command duty officer; it was most likely a cover his six maneuver. If anything happened, he could always say he had the most senior qualified officers on the ship standing watch. What else could he do? There were plenty of qualified LCDR's that could have helped with the watch sections, including the mini boss who had just put on his CDR stripe. As it stood, that meant when we were in port, we would stand duty every third day.

We were delayed in Pearl for engineering reasons, and that was pretty typical. The engineering department always had problems, and the XO continued to cover for the engineer. I did have to admit, the engineer put in some long hours, but the situation didn't seem to improve. As the weeks went by the air department continued to shine and that always seemed to rub the XO the wrong way. He wanted us to be good, but not to shine. I got that age old phrase, "You have it easy." He had an agenda and it didn't include the air boss or the air department.

We continued to operate flawlessly throughout the weeks of deployment. Halfway through the cruise, commander fitness reports came out. The XO called me down to his stateroom and handed me the fitness report. It was not good, probably the worst fitness report I had ever received. I was ranked number three out of three onboard commanders. The XO had worked his magic.

After glancing at the fitness report, I looked over at the XO sitting at his desk with a silly smirk on his face and said, "You can tell the skipper for me, I don't kiss anyone's ass for a good fitness report. My department is the best department aboard this ship." I turned and walked out the door. As I walked down the passageway I was pissed. The XO had manipulated the entire situation, and I had helped him by not developing a stronger relationship with the captain. I did not want to be drawn into the he said, they said, bullshit. It was not my style. I did think the captain should know what the XO was doing behind his back, but didn't know how to approach it. The XO was starting to get overconfident with his ability to manipulate what was happening aboard the ship and about to step beyond those gray boundaries of manipulation. Would it be enough to convince the skipper of the XO's real agenda?

We were headed for the Indian Ocean, with a short stop in Diego Garcia and then Somalia. In all of my travels, I had never seen a country like Somalia. Nobody wanted to go ashore, not even the most diehard liberty hounds. Major J. R. Curtin and I had become friends during the work-ups and the initial part of the cruise and always pulled liberty together. We went ashore for a half day in Somalia and when we returned to the ship we wanted to throw our shoes away so we wouldn't bring anything back aboard the ship. I must say we did enjoy chasing the camels over the desert with the ship's helicopter. The stay in Somalia only lasted a few days and when we finished the exercise we headed for Perth, Australia.

While at sea the flight deck operations went so well we looked for things that would challenge us. The crew was one of the finest I had ever seen and there was nothing they couldn't do and do well. If the launch was to start at 0600, we would try to get the first helicopter to break the deck as the second hand passed through the 12. That meant you had to know the pilot in the lead helicopter in order to give him the lead time he needed to pick the helicopter up into a hover. Each pilot was different. We also broke up the long days by pulling small pranks.

I was down on the flight deck one day and took the place of one of the landing signal enlisted (LSE) men to land one of the helicopters. There was only one airborne. One of the petty officers in the fuels division brought up a bottle of bug juice (grape kool-aid) from the galley. It looked exactly like the JP-5 aboard the ship. As the helicopter landed, the tie downs went on and out came the fuels division to top off the helicopter. The procedure was to pour the first bit of fuel into a glass jar to check for contaminants and water, if it was clear they would fuel the helicopter.

I gave the pilots a hold signal as the fuels personnel connected the fuel line and checked the fuel. After a few minutes I signaled for the Bos'n to bring the fuel sample out to where I was. During this process, the fuels Bos'n had switched the fuel for the grape drink. As he ran out to where I was, he handed the bug juice to me so I could check the sample. I swirled it around and held it up in the air looking for sediment, then lifted it up to my lips and took a drink. I handed the jar back to the petty officer and gave the pilot a thumbs up.

The pilot remained frozen in his seat. When the pilot was given the signal to pick up into a hover, he just sat there for a few moments looking at me. He finally got airborne and I'm sure they spent the rest of the hop trying to sort out exactly what took place. The days at sea can be very long and it was good to break them up with a little humor once awhile. Life was good and the morale was some of the best I had ever seen.

We even made up a key with a large sign on it, "Ship's Helicopter Instrument Trainer." We assigned a room to it that didn't exist aboard the ship. We gave the key to the Marine AIRWING and told them they could use it while they were aboard the ship. If you've ever been aboard a ship as large as a carrier, you can spend weeks looking for a space if you're not familiar with the ship. There have even been stories of cutting through the bulkhead of some of the older carriers while in overhaul and finding spare parts for WWII fighters inside.

It was a great cruise in spite of the continued games from the XO. I did get an opportunity to let the skipper know about some of the games the XO was playing. Two of my men were trying out for the Olympic boxing team and I would spar with them to stay in shape. We worked out up in the forward part of the ship where they had a boxing ring. The ship's admin officer was an LDO and an ex-Navy boxer. We hit it off right away and the AO and I became good friends.

The AO didn't like some of the things he saw the XO doing and was a little upset with his lack of integrity. One day he showed me Major Curtin's fitness report. The major was an aviator and ran HDC, he was part of ship's company. The marks had obviously been changed by the XO after the skipper had signed the fitness report. The major was a friend of mine, and I wasn't about to see him get screwed like I did.

I took the fitness report up to the skipper. It was the first time I had something in black and white that could not be misinterpreted. When I showed the fitness report to the skipper he was stunned. He had truly believed that the

XO supported him 100%. He could not understand how something like that could have happened. There wasn't much the skipper could do but correct the fitness report. The XO had been deep selected and that meant he was on the fast track. The skipper was up for Admiral, and he didn't know how high the XO's connections went. Politics, I never really understood them, doing what was right always got in my way. It wasn't my place to say anything; I did what needed to be done. I brought it to his attention. At least the skipper knew the truth. The captain made the corrections and the major got what he rightfully deserved.

I went back down to my office. If I had to be like the XO to be deep selected it wasn't worth it. The Navy deserved better. I heard a few years later that the XO made Admiral. From that point on the relationship between me and the skipper started to improve. In fact, the very next time I brought the monthly report to the bridge the skipper said to me. "You know Boss, coming up and seeing me on the bridge is not kissing my ass."

I grinned and said "Yes sir." That broke the ice.

We were on the long leg home with stops in Singapore and the Philippines then on to the States. We had a very successful cruise and the skipper was sure to make Admiral. After a one month stand down we started short cruising again. While in port the XO was on leave and that left me as the acting XO since I was the third senior officer aboard the ship. During the week I went through several XO screenings for captain's mast. One of the young sailors, a black first class petty officer, failed a drug screening. The man vehemently protested the screening and said it was a mistake. I knew the drugs stayed in the individual's systems for a period of time. If the first class was found guilty his career would be ruined and he already had 12 years in. I had him retested and the test came back negative.

When the XO returned from leave he went ballistic. I had never seen him so mad; he never confronted anyone, he just marked it down and would get them later when they were not looking. He told me that he never wanted to see that happen again. "One man was not worth undermining the system." I felt I had done the right thing. Sacrificing one man's career when there was doubt was not the way I did business. In those days errors were not that common, but they happened far too often. I left the XO to stew in his own juices.

The *Belleau Wood* had a short stay in the shipyard up in Long Beach. It was a difficult time for me. During that short stay I lost three of my men to motorcycle accidents. One was dead, one was crippled, and one lay in the hospital in a coma. It was tough; you couldn't help but get close to these men when you spent all those days at sea sharing the successes, and the hard times, and long hours.

I found the shipyard interesting but was eager to get back to sea. The area that impacted the air department during the overhaul was the modification to the flight deck. They were adding a new landing spot directly in front of the bridge. As I monitored the progress of the work, it appeared they had marked the location wrong. I was a little concerned so I talked to the supervisor in charge of the work. The supervisor replied, "Commander this is the fifth flight deck we have done, I think we know what we're doing."

What is it with people? If someone had said that to me I would have double checked in a heartbeat. I decided to let the asshole deal with his own screw up. In order to put in the landing spot in, they had to cut holes in the flight deck for the lights and run electrical wiring for the entire area.

When they completed the work I went out and told them they had better check the drawings because I could not accept the new landing spot where it was located. The supervisor was livid and expressed his concerns to the XO. When he got the drawings out to show the XO the location of the spot, they realized it was in the wrong place. I could never understand why people labeled me the bad guy. All I asked was that he check the drawings. Two days later they tore up the deck, welded the holes closed and put the landing spot in the right place. It took them an additional two weeks.

By the time we returned to San Diego, it was time for the XO to leave the ship for a new duty station. I was not sorry to see him go. The ship's admin officer showed me his relieving letter to the new XO that would be relieving him. On it was a handwritten note at the bottom of the page, it said:

"The key to success onboard this ship is, never put yourself in a position where you can be held accountable for anything."

I couldn't believe the statement. What a snake. The XO had no balls and would slither through a successful career in the Navy manipulating people and ruining the careers of good men. I would see this philosophy of avoiding accountability again and again before I left the Navy. The new XO was the complete opposite, he was straightforward, honest and cared about the men and the ship. Timing is everything in life. If I would have served under the new XO, I'm sure it would have been an enjoyable tour. I looked forward to the change.

It was back out to sea for some refresher training. This time we would be working with AV-8B, Harriers, OV-10, Bronco's and 33 helicopters. Shortly after the XO's departure it was the skipper's time to rotate. His new assignment would be the senior aviation detailer back in Washington, DC. It was a good job, and he was sure to make Admiral. The skipper and I had finally understood each other and developed a good relationship during the last couple of months. His detaching fitness report on me was much better, but did not completely counter the earlier one. The skipper told me that when it was time for me to get a new assignment to contact him directly and he would see that I got the assignment I wanted. I had even heard from the ship's admin officer that the CO was thinking about changing the previous fitness report, but he never got around to it.

The new CO was a surface line officer. He was Irish Catholic and had eight children. He loved the Navy, loved sea duty and was an outstanding human being. The entire makeup of the ship had changed with the arrival of the new CO and XO. The new CO was not an aviator and gave complete aviation say-so to me. He told me that I was the aviation authority aboard the ship. As we continued with the refresher training off the coast, the mutual respect between the air boss and the CO continued to grow. On numerous occasions the skipper commented on the fine work of the department and the colorful leadership the air boss demonstrated.

Taking on the Commodore.

A few months had passed and we completed our work ups qualifying for another Battle "E." We were getting ready for a major two week exercise off the Southern California coast. It was a month away, and it would be my last major operation before moving on. It would be a 14 day, around the clock air, land, and sea exercise into the Camp Pendleton operating area. There was one little problem. They wanted the *Belleau Wood* to be the first ship to externally hoist the 155 howitzer and the tow vehicle into the beach. To add to the difficulty, they wanted it done at night. It had never been done before.

The 155 howitzer weighed 16,000 lbs., and the tow vehicle weighed in at around 20,000 lbs. I sent some of my flight deck crew into Camp Pendleton to work with the Marines on the beach. They needed to assess the capability of the CH-53E and determine the training and safety requirements for operating off the rolling deck of a carrier at night. After I received the briefing, I went to the CO with my assessment. I told him it could be done and done safely, but there was an element of risk involved. We had been asked to do the exercise and it wasn't right that he accept all the responsibility and risk for it. My recommendation was that we get the endorsement of the commodore to try this tactical exercise at night. The captain replied, "You're the air boss. I'll take it up with the commodore tomorrow."

Several days went by before the CO got back to me. The commodore did not want to know anything about the operation, and it definitely did not need his approval. My response was, "Skipper, it is my job to make sure that all aviation operations aboard this ship are done safely. There is an element of risk involved and it has never been done before, let alone at night. If any one of the pilots drops that howitzer or the tow vehicle on your flight deck it could very well keep you from making Admiral."

He replied, "You're the air boss, and I'm going with your judgment, but we need to explain it to the commodore."

The captain called the commodore and we headed for the staff briefing room. When we entered, the commodore was standing by the table with his chief of staff and several other officers. The commodore turned and acknowledged the captain as we approached the table, then looked at me. "Air Boss, I'm only going to say this one more time. I don't want to know anything about this exercise and I'm not going to authorize a damn thing. Just do it."

I had heard this bullshit too many times. I remembered the comments on the previous XO's relieving letter. The commodore was not going to be held accountable for this; it would fall on the shoulders of the CO and the air boss of the *Belleau Wood*. That would have been fine, if it was our idea, but we had been instructed to do this exercise. I replied with, "Commodore, I'm sorry. There is an element of risk, and I can't recommend that the captain put his career on the line for something that has never been done aboard ship before. I think it can be done and I think it can be done safely. What I need is authorization to go ahead and attempt the exercise."

The commodore looked at the captain with a contemptuous glare. "I'm sorry sir, I'm going to have to go along with the recommendation of my air boss."

The commodore came back with, "You two think it over and get back to me." He turned and glared angrily at me as if to say, "I'll remember this."

The skipper and I left and on the way back to the captain's in port cabin the skipper said, "It's your call, Boss, I'll support your decision." After several phone calls to the captain from the commodore's staff we had still not changed our position.

I could have rolled over and accepted the risk. That was what they wanted to see, that meant you put your career and the skipper's on the line and they stood by and watched. I remembered George's career ending with one small incident in Hai Phong Harbor. I already had a great career, but this wasn't right. The captain was in a different situation, he was a great human being, one of the finest naval officers I had met in my almost twenty years of service. I was not about to risk his career for an exercise someone else came up with. They would accept responsibility or it wouldn't happen. They couldn't even order us to do it, that would be accepting responsibility. It was sad to see senior officers in positions of responsibility without the guts to make a decision and accept the outcome. Maybe they knew something I didn't. At this point it was a test of wills and we would have to see how it played out.

As usual the air department performed superbly. The air department was so good at getting things to the beach, the new XO had difficulty keeping up. During an amphibious assault, the XO's duty station was directly behind primary and one deck down. His group's responsibility was to track and coordinate all of the assets and cargo that had to go to the beach. During the movement of men and equipment to the beach the XO came up into primary to determine what had gone to the beach. He asked if the smaller cannons had gone to the beach. I said "Yes." What about the shells for the cannons? I responded, "They can't use the cannons without the other ordinance. It's on the beach also." It went on, ………
….what about the water buffalos, jeeps, supplies,…… etc? Yes, yes, and yes.

He finally responded by saying, "Boss you can't keep doing that, my men can't track it that fast."

I replied with, "XO, if your troops put something on my flight deck, it's going to the beach. It's unsafe to have the flight deck cluttered like that. You need to get some people down there that can write a little faster." Frustrated, he left.

It was nearing the 14th day of the exercise and the skipper had not received approval from the commodore. The movement of the 155 howitzer and tow vehicle exercise was scheduled for the last day. The air department had anticipated the delay. We had completed all our training requirements while the crew was in Camp Pendleton. All that remained was the training of the pilots. We had set the requirements at 5 day external day lifts before they could attempt any night external loads, which took 3 to qualify. The last day of the exercise was rapidly approaching. The air department was at its best during high tempo operations as we waited for approval.

Life in the tower during these types of exercises usually consisted of a minimum of 16 hour days, with a very high tempo of operations. We were running out of time and had heard nothing from the commodore or his staff. As the day approached I had my crew stage all the assets that were necessary to complete the qualifications for the pilots. If we got the word, we would be ready. I knew the commodore would not forget this, and I would most likely pay for it one day. I was going to be the bad guy for making him do his job. I missed those days forward deployed aboard the *USS Midway*. CAG was tough, but at least he had the balls to do what was right. It was a peacetime Navy and I was dealing with politicians, not what I would call real naval officers. It was probably a good thing we were not at war.

It was the last 24 hours of the exercise; all we had left was the flight schedule for the remainder of the day, and a 0430 launch the next morning when the 155's were scheduled to go to the beach. The rest was cleanup. It was 0900 when I got the word that the commodore was flying to the beach to talk with the Admiral. My flight deck crew quickly pulled out the ship's helicopter and the commodore went to the beach with three of his staff.

After they departed I went to the bridge to brief the skipper on what needed to happen if we got the approval to complete the 155 exercise. The captain told me that he would get me whatever I needed. They had plenty of maneuvering room in the operating area. On my way back up to primary I stopped by the AIRWING ready room to tell them to have the pilots standing by and the aircraft ready to go.

At 1230, the captain received the approval to commence the exercise and the commodore followed it up with a message. I wondered if this was a tactic that the commodore used to have the air department fall on its sword. There was almost no time to complete the qualifications, but that was not going to stop us. I could feel the excitement building; it's what I thrived on. I never sat idly by and hoped things would go my way. The challenge was what it was all about. We were ready and the men were looking forward to the challenge. It was winter, the days were short. Sunset was 1722. That gave us about 4 hours to get four pilots qualified if we stretched it into the twilight hours. The first CH-53E broke the deck at 1320. The CH-53E was a huge helicopter and took up lots of room on the flight deck. We had the five AV-8B's and 33 helicopters onboard. We had gotten rid of the OV-10's, they had to land at Pendleton because we were not certified to land them. The men skillfully maneuvered the aircraft on the deck to give us the room we needed to position the payload.

Once we finished the day quals we worked into the night to get the pilots their night lifts. We alternated the 155 and the tow vehicle and were able to get three of the four pilots qualified. We finished at 2140 and I called the captain. "Skipper you can inform the commodore, we'll be ready to go at 0430, we have enough pilots qualified to complete the exercise."

It was exhilarating to see them work. The CH-53E was the largest free world helicopter in existence. We staged the 155 and the tow vehicle aft, near the ship's superstructure. When the Marines hovered over the equipment the rotor blades came within a few feet of the glass windows of the tower, just about eye level. They had to use a static discharge hook and line to keep from getting shocked. The static charge was so strong, that at night it looked like a bolt of lightning coming down from the helicopter. When you added the rolling deck to the situation, it took a highly skilled pilot to make the lift safely.

Again the air department performed superbly. I couldn't have been more proud of the men. They seemed to perform better under pressure. We again showed them that we could take on any challenge. The exercise was a complete success. In reflection I knew I had made an enemy of the commodore but I felt it was justified. Several months later, after I had left the ship I heard that they were trying the same exercise on the East Coast for the first time and they lost the tow vehicle full of cargo. Fortunately the helicopter had just cleared the deck before the truck broke loose. The captain later made Admiral and it was well-deserved; he was an outstanding naval officer.

When we got back to San Diego, it was my turn for orders. I called my previous CO and told him what I wanted. I needed to stay in San Diego. The captain told me that I would be ending my career if I took the orders I had requested. I told him I understood and thanked him for his support. I had been divorced for several years and at sea for most of that time. My ex-wife had gone off and married an alcoholic and drug user. I didn't feel I had a choice, and the captain didn't need to know the circumstances. It was a volatile situation for the kids and I needed to be there if they needed me.

With all of the time I spent at sea throughout my career they didn't really know their father. It was a chance I would have to take. The captain tried again to talk me out of it and offered me a job in DC, in the program office. I told him I understood, but I needed to spend some time with my children. For almost twenty years I had gone wherever the Navy sent me and done what they had asked me to do without question. This time the Navy would have to understand.

There were only a couple of weeks before the ship deployed

to WESTPAC. I had tried for several weeks to get the new air boss to take over and in each instance he declined. Maybe I was missing something. Why didn't he want to accept the responsibility? Finally, with the ship deploying, I told him he had no choice, it was time to take over. Leaving such a fine group of men was difficult. We had accomplished so much. Although this fitness report was written about me, it is really a testament to the men aboard the *USS Belleau Wood*. When we pulled together, we could not be stopped, or equaled.

> *Commander BILLINGS' professional performance as Air Officer during this reporting period has been <u>consistently outstanding</u> in all areas of responsibility, accountability, and leadership. Through his initiative and highly effective leadership style, the Aviation Department has met as well as exceeded requirements for all pre-deployment training readiness inspections and operational evolutions including:*
> - *The Training Readiness Evaluation (TRE) where Air Department received an <u>overall grade of "Outstanding</u>." The TRE-team was so impressed with individual training record jackets that they asked for copies of the forms used, to give to other ships.*
> - *The Annual PMS inspection. A <u>96% accomplishment factor</u> was received along with compliments from the inspection team on obtaining such a high grade and for an exceptionally well-qualified/organized department.*
> - *Modified refresher training where an <u>overall grade of "Outstanding"</u> was awarded the Air Department.*
> - *Amphibious Refresher Training where overall grades of "Excellent" were achieved. The inspection team was very favorably impressed; in fact, instead of making recommendations, they were taking notes on the way BELLEAU WOOD was organized.*

The Air Department in the BELLEAU WOOD is now widely recognized as the best in any LHA, due largely to the superior results achieved during Commander BILLINGS' tour of duty as Air Boss. The following additional accomplishments firmly support this claim and attest to the abilities of this superior Naval Officer:

- *The Air Battle Efficiency "E" was received for the 2nd consecutive competitive period. All Requirements for the 3rd consecutive efficiency "E" have been met as well.*

- *Air Department spaces are always a showplace! Visiting dignitaries always praise these spaces commenting that they are the best they have ever seen on any ship.*

- *During EASTPAC Exercise Kernel Usher 84-1, the Air Department performed superbly, working 16 to 22 hour days under an extremely high tempo of operations. The Air Department was safely and skillfully coordinated under the most arduous conditions and met all challenges with resourcefulness and ingenuity. Of particular note was the conduct of numerous external lifts of the Marine Corps M-198, 155 howitzer and the M-923 tow vehicle by the Ch-53E helicopter. Not only was this a first for this class ship, but the lifts were safely and efficiently completed at night under the most demanding of conditions.*

- *The ship has been twice nominated for the Admiral Flately Award for Aviation Safety. In the two years Commander BILLINGS has served in BELLEAU WOOD, including work-ups for the next deployment, not a single accident/incident or minor aviation mishap has occurred. This safety record, achieved during thousands of flight deck evolutions stands on its own merits as unequalled in the Pacific Fleet.*

Commander BILLINGS is, above all else,

*"people" oriented. He likes them, supports them and
encourages their personal and professional growth
and achievement. This particular trait has earned
him considerable admiration from all his assigned
Air Department personnel as well as contributed in a
most positive way toward high retention statistics and
unmatched esprit de corps. Commander BILLINGS
has my deepest appreciation for all his extensive
efforts devoted toward improved aviation operational
readiness in BELLEAU WOOD. Without his desire
to be the best, this ship would not enjoy the superb
reputation it does. His professional aptitude and
unlimited potential most certainly warrant accelerated
selection to the rank of Captain and for assignment to a
sequential command.*
   Commanding Officer USS BELLEAU WOOD

Again this is only to validate what actually took place and not the imagination or embellishment of an aging naval aviator. With write-ups such as this and the others in the previous chapters and there were others, along with the successful combat tours, making captain was not in doubt, or was it? Would it be blocked by those bureaucrats that detested the perceived arrogance and the way "Hollywood Al" openly took on any challenge and succeeded? Would it be my openness and honesty, or lack of political shrewdness that stopped it? Would I be loathed by those who never took a risk? Or would it be something deeper?

When I reflect back on those years, I realize that I was much better suited for sea duty. The demands of the operational environment fed the flame that was inside me. The more demanding the environment the better I was. The majority of the men I served with understood who I was and what I stood for. It was just the opposite when I went to shore duty. If the senior officer was a bureaucrat and politician, it would take less than a minute for me to rub him the wrong way. I didn't speak his language and I didn't kiss any rings. I was a little skeptical about my next assignment, it was shore duty.

Chapter Ten
A Matter of Trust.

Not made for shore duty.

The *USS Belleau Wood* enjoyed such a good reputation I was asked to develop a training program for new air officers for COMPIBGRU EASTPAC. I only had three weeks before I was due to report to my new duty station, so I came up with the idea of making a training video for the newly assigned air officers. The Admiral was very pleased with the results and said it would become an integral part of the indoctrination program and followed it up with a concurrent fitness report. Leaving the ship and the men in the air department was harder than I thought. It was going to be my last opportunity to work with a highly motivated operational unit. They were a great bunch and I would never see the passion and enthusiasm displayed by such an organization again. The two years I spent aboard the *Belleau Wood*, like HC-1, were some of the most memorable times in my career and now I was going to push papers.

I was recovering from an injury I had received from a fall down a ladder well aboard the *Belleau Wood*, or maybe it was just an accumulation of events over the years such as the crash off of Saigon in 1969. It had bothered me the last year I was aboard the ship but I learned to live with the pain. At times I was taking twenty-four aspirin a day because I wouldn't take anything stronger while we were operating. Over the next couple of years it would continue to worsen.

I was curious about the new assignment and wanted to see what it had to offer. It was the first time in over seven years that I had not been operational. I quickly learned that I wasn't meant to sit behind a desk all day. Program management could not compare to the high tempo of air operations and excitement aboard an LHA. As I did for almost 20 years, I took on the new assignment with enthusiasm and quickly made changes in the project review process and got the attention of the project officers. Many of the junior officers had little or no fleet sea duty experience and went through their duties without any dedication, doing only what was necessary. There was no passion for their work. I had four major civilian support contractors providing engineering services for my department. The only passion the contractors displayed was their zeal for the bottom line. God, country and "for the good of the services" were words you never heard. It was going to be an interesting tour. Through my whole career I had taken on every assignment with a passion and dedication for getting the job done. Now I was in an environment that you had to poke the people to see if they were awake. Let me add, there were some very good people there, it wouldn't be fair for me not to mention them, but there was no comparison between being operational and my new assignment.

The weeks turned into months and then before I knew it a year had passed. Even with my aggressive personality it was difficult to motivate some of the people. It was a completely different type of environment. After all, what could happen sitting behind a desk? The most dangerous thing you could have happen was to spill a hot cup of coffee in your lap. Many of the senior officers were already planning for their civilian lives. That meant the contractors got more attention than the mission.

As usual my disdain for politicians would culminate with one incident with the CO of the support activity. As I think back I probably could have tried a less direct approach. The skipper called me into his office to tell me about some problems that were occurring between the contractors and the data processing department for which I was responsible. It seems the contractors were not getting a fast enough turnaround on their work, and they wanted something done about it. It was a reoccurring theme.

As luck would have it the skipper was getting ready to retire and was looking at some of the contractors for a job when he got out into the civilian world. I had 176 men in the DP department and they were complete professionals and totally dedicated to getting the job done. I could feel my blood pressure starting to rise as I stood there listening to all the rhetoric. I had already checked into it, and the contractors were putting up a smoke screen because they were late on a delivery. I was supposed to go in and beat up my men because the contractors didn't have their act together, and the CO wanted to look good in their eyes. I had no problem holding people accountable but this continuous misuse of authority made me sick. It seemed the more senior I got the less I saw of the integrity that was supposed to be the foundation of a Navy officer. In my typical diplomatic approach I leaned across the desk and said, "There is no way in hell that I will put the contractors before my men. It might be more effective if we earned our paycheck and held the contractors accountable for their incompetence."

I may have been a little too aggressive as the executive officer felt obligated to grab my arm in an effort to protect the skipper. As I jerked my arm out of the XO's hand I said, "Nobody will come down on those men for something they didn't do while I'm their department head."

To my surprise the skipper seemed to have a better

understanding of where I was coming from than the XO did. Or maybe I just reminded him why he was there. The XO was ready to write me up, but the skipper said that we would all forget about the whole incident. He either understood or I would never see where the blow came from. My timing was always impeccable. I was up for captain and would have to wait for the results of the selection board. If the skipper chose to do something he had a perfect opportunity.

Was I missing the big picture? Should I have stepped aside? Using that old cliché of "live to fight another day," I'm sure the justifications would have been endless. Why was it that I felt so protective? Maybe it was a simple as I didn't like people stepping on others to get ahead. I didn't have an answer, and to this day I don't think I could explain the way I felt.

Later that month I had an opportunity to go to Washington, DC to get funding for one of my projects. While I was in DC, I stopped by the Bureau of Naval Personnel, BUPERS, to review my record before it went to the selection board. When I arrived at BUPERS, sitting at one of the desks was a young Navy commander. I introduced myself and told him why I was there. The commander invited me to sit down and pulled up my record on the computer.

The commander seemed very confident and sure of himself. He talked like he was carrying a few more stripes than he wore on his sleeve. I immediately went to a guarded response. When I met men with an ego and a little too much self-importance, I automatically mistrusted them. I had learned over the years that they would do most anything to promote themselves. Apparently he had been around DC for a while and felt he knew the system. He didn't have a command star so I knew he had not held an operational command and the ribbons on his chest showed he had no combat experience. To me that meant he was a pure Washington bureaucrat. The knees on his trousers were slightly worn and his lips had that permanent pucker from spending most of his time being politically correct. The position he held gave him a little too much power, and I'm not sure he had the right personality for the job. If this was what I had to contend with in DC I was glad I didn't take the assignment.

As he brought up my record and went through it, he sat back in his chair with a silly grin on his face and said, "Well, it looks like you're some type of a maverick."

I had heard that word before, and it wasn't a compliment. I replied with, "I always tried to do what I believed was right."

The commander's continued smug attitude was a little irritating. As he reviewed my record, it was apparent that I had only had a 50/50 chance for captain. My history was up and down, especially when I was a junior officer. Nobody had the write-ups that I did, but then again nobody had pissed as many people off as I had either. When I was operational, I could do very little wrong, besides they needed me. I always felt politics was a waste of time and I had very little respect for people who put themselves above everything else, and I always had trouble hiding it. My promotion would probably boil down to whether I had a champion on the screening board or not, and in my case I probably had more antagonists than champions. My current duty assignment would most certainly not help either; I was warned it was a dead end billet and would not stand well with the board. At that point in my life, I felt my children needed me more.

I was growing tired of those who simply stood in the shadows and waited for an opportunity without risking anything. They only promoted themselves, while doing very little to benefit the mission or the organization. If an individual was bold enough to seize the moment and he was successful, they would generally find fault in his methods in order to justify their own lack of initiative.

On my way back to San Diego I had time to reflect on my career and question the inevitable outcome. It was the universal question, does the end justify the means in getting that next promotion, or was fighting for what was right more important?

I always found it interesting the way people flocked to all the action movies in the theaters. In many cases they would be the most popular movies of that time. The lead characters would be bold, difficult, and would not hesitate to do what was right. It seemed people couldn't get enough of it. What was the draw? Was it that most people lived vicariously through the characters in the movies because they didn't want to risk it all themselves? Or was it that people saw so little of it in real life, the only place they could find it was on the silver screen?

It's ironic. If that same person they saw in the movie was sitting at a table in the same office, he would most likely be viewed as a maverick, or irresponsible, and in many cases they would just sit there quietly resentful and wait for him to make a mistake. Was it that the person in their office was too close to home, or a competitor? Was he a threat? Whereas the movies were impersonal, distant and not menacing?

There were many good officers out there, but there were also some that made senior rank by taking credit for something they didn't do, or avoiding responsibility and accountability, or in many cases, hoping that nothing would happen on their watch. As you go through your career you have to make those decisions for yourself. I chose not to live that way; everything I did I was passionate about. I would feed off the enthusiasm and dedication of the men. I knew the difference between right and wrong and I acted on it. Life is too short to sit on the sidelines. In this day and age we spend so much time trying to be politically correct, we've become impotent. If you're going to lead men and women you have to be decisive, not divisive The quickest way to destroy morale is to show them that you're only interested in what your seniors think, or your next promotion. These traits are not exclusive to the military, they're human nature and have no gender or racial barriers. It's just easier to spot them in the military because the risks can be much greater.

If you look back through history we have always seemed

to come up with the great leaders just at the right time. It is almost uncanny how close we have come to losing some very significant battles that may have turned the tide of the war against us. Decisions had to be made and they turned out to be the right ones. Where do these individuals come from? It's that age old question, is it the situation that makes a great leader or is it the individual that rises to meet the challenge because of who they are? If we do not continue to cultivate good leaders, and that means those who can make the right decisions and not put themselves first, the next time we may be wanting when it comes time to draw on our moral leadership to have the conviction to do what is right and just.

The results came back from the captain selection board, and I was not selected. It was not a surprise and there was nothing to be said. I had gone far beyond what the Navy told me I could ever expect, and I did because of the men who believed in me. I had the memories of the challenges and the respect of some of the men I served with, and that would never change. What bothered me was those junior officers that believed in me, might see me not making captain as a failure. I was afraid they may see it as a signal, that if they stood up for what they believed in, they could jeopardize their careers. I would never have a chance to explain to them that I would not change a thing. Although many may say I am wrong or crazy. To let down one young sailor that needed someone or something to believe in order to gain that extra stripe was just not in me.

I was extended another year at my current duty assignment while I got my second look. During that timeframe I aggravated that same injury again; it kept getting worse. Over the years I endured the pain and I learned to live with it. At times I had to use heavy medication to try to alleviate the pain. As the year went by I resigned myself to being a civilian, which didn't particularly appeal to me. It was a peacetime Navy and politics was the name of the game. I was able to spend more time with my children and it was worth it. When the results of the selection board came out I was a little disappointed. To be a little human, it did not help to see some of the names on the list of those who were promoted. If anyone was at fault it was me, for being so headstrong. My record of accomplishments will stand on its own.

I was told many times to bend with the wind, or go with the tide and when I made it I could change things. What I saw over the years was the individuals that spent so many years going with the flow didn't know how to change when they got to the point where they could do some good. In many cases they got so used to operating that way they couldn't tell the difference any longer. They had making excuses and justifying their actions down to a science.

As the time came closer to my leaving the Navy, it was standard procedure to get a retirement physical. When I went to the flight surgeon, the doctor seemed very concerned about the numbness and the lack of reflex response on my left side. I was sent to Balboa Naval Hospital for further evaluation. The rest of the story is not pretty but I believe it has to be told to complete the journey.

You're not an asset any longer, you're a liability.

When I arrived at the naval hospital I was treated like a third class citizen. I was a Navy commander, and I couldn't imagine how the more junior Navy personnel were treated. I assumed that this was how they treated retirees. You went from being an asset to a liability. The doctors in the orthopedics department insinuated that it was just another Naval officer trying to get a disability. They were abrupt, cold and irritated at the fact that they had to even see me. The physical was very short and they told me there was no real problem and that the pain would eventually go away. Disgusted with their attitude but accepting their evaluation I returned to my duty station.

The day finally came for my retirement. I had already told my commanding officer that I didn't want any formal ceremony and that I would like to retire quietly. My wishes were honored with a small ceremony in the CO's office and before I knew it, I was a civilian.

My condition continued to deteriorate. It had been less than seven days since my retirement when the pain reduced me to a point where I could not move. When my fiancée returned home I was lying on the floor unable to move. She called an ambulance and took me to Balboa Naval Hospital.

When we arrived I was again treated like a third class citizen. After listening to what had happened the doctor told my fiancée that it wasn't the Navy's problem and that she would have to take me to the VA hospital. When she expressed her concerns about what was happening, the doctor gave me something that would kill the pain. She tried to make him understand but was told that we could stay there until the drugs took effect and then we would have to leave. The doctor then turned and walked away.

The drugs were very strong and seemed to help mask the pain enough to make me partially mobile. She then took me to the VA where I laid on a gurney for almost four hours and was not seen. She tried everything to get their attention and was finally told to make an appointment and they would try to see me the following day. There was nothing she could do or say to convince them I needed to be looked at. The system in those days could take a proud person and make them feel worthless. I'm sure I would have gotten better treatment if I were a prisoner. The pain killer was still working and it was enough to get me back home.

The next morning the pain was gone. I couldn't believe it; after months and years of pain it was finally over. I was finally able to get a few hours of sleep. Almost 24 hours had gone by before I realized something was wrong. I discovered there was no feeling at all on the left side from the waist down. After the inhuman treatment from the Navy and the VA, I called a civilian doctor. After explaining my situation, the doctor told me to get to the hospital any way I could. They would be ready to admit me as soon as I arrived.

When I arrived they admitted me immediately and took me in for X-rays. When the doctor returned to my room, he went over the extent of the injury with me. The X-rays showed there was a free floating piece of disc that had lodged up against the spinal cord and appeared to be cutting off the nerve. He told me there had been too much nerve damage and it was beyond his capability to correct it. I would be turned over to a neurosurgeon as soon as he was available. He could not understand how it had gone this far and how I was able to deal with the pain. I told him what had happened and he was guarded but appalled at the treatment I had received from the naval hospital. He could not believe that any doctor would treat a patient that way. He told me the attending physician would be Dr. Shahhal and that he would be in later that day, then turned and left the room.

When Dr. Shahhal arrived that afternoon, he told me the prognosis did not look good and prepared me for what I could expect. They would not know the extent of the damage until they got me into surgery. I was scheduled for the operation the first thing in the morning, that was the earliest they could get me in. Later that afternoon, I had the nurse get me a phone and I called to talk with the CO of the Balboa Naval Hospital.

When the situation was explained to the CO of the hospital, he responded angrily. "You get down here to the naval hospital any way you can and we'll take a look at you. If you let the civilian doctors operate on you the Navy will have nothing to do with you. You can rest assured that the Navy will pay for nothing," then hung up. It was totally foreign to me; I had never met an individual like that in my entire Navy career.

I talked with Dr. Shahhal about my conversation with Balboa Hospital. Shahhal could not understand that a Navy doctor, any doctor, would even recommend something like that. Any movement may completely sever the nerve, if it was not already severed. He had never heard of a doctor acting with such callus disregard for the patient. We agreed that the operation should go forward as scheduled.

Early the next morning they wheeled me into the operating room and a few hours later I was in recovery. The operation went without incident. When Dr. Shahhal came in to talk with me about the operation he told me the nerve was almost severed. What was left of the nerve was less than a thread in diameter. If I would have tried to move down to the naval hospital, it would have most assuredly separated. He was guarded and told me the prognosis did not look good but that he had a wait and see attitude. I could understand why he didn't want to destroy any hopes of regaining the full use of my left leg. I had plenty of time that night to think about the future and reflect on what had just taken place.

I chose to focus on recovery.

On the morning of the second day, I grabbed a walker next to me and pulled myself out of the bed. I was concerned about the extent of the nerve damage and would not accept being any type of a cripple. As I slowly made my way out of my hospital room, two therapists were walking down the passageway towards me. "Mr. Billings?" they asked.

I said, "Yes."

"We were on our way up to show you how to get out of bed without putting too much stress on your back." She smiled and then said, "It looks like you don't need us, but we would like to go over the procedures anyway." We returned to the room to go over the best ways not to put stress on my back.

Later that morning Dr. Shahhal came in to examine his patient. After a short physical he told me that he was pleased with the results of the operation, but he was concerned about the lack of any response on my left side. There was a very good chance that the full use of my left leg would not return. At this point it looked like there was complete atrophy of the muscles. Time would tell and I would have to wait to see how much would return. Anytime the nerves are cut off more than 36 hours, they have very little chance of recovering. What I did have going for me was my previous physical conditioning and muscle tone.

He ended with, "You've had a very serious injury, and we'll just have to take one step at a time." I told him to just get me out of the hospital, and I would take care of the rest. He responded by saying, "If everything continues as it is, you could be out of the hospital tomorrow, but the recovery won't happen overnight and I was to take things slow at first."

I was surprised that afternoon by a few of my old Navy buddies and enjoyed their visits. One of the visitors was J. R. the Marine major from the old *USS Belleau Wood* who was now a Lt. Colonel. We had enjoyed a strong friendship during those two years aboard the ship and had kept in touch over the years. When he found out what Balboa did, he was disgusted and said the Marine Corps would never allow something like that to happen. Later that day without telling me, he contacted my former CO from the *Belleau Wood*, who had made admiral and was stationed in San Diego. After hearing how his old air boss was treated, the admiral requested an investigation of the Balboa Naval Hospital. The hospital responded to his request by starting a quality assurance investigation.

A week after I had returned home I was surprised by a call from Balboa Naval Hospital. It was a female Navy captain. She informed me that there had been a request for a quality assurance (QA) investigation and that she would be the point of contact. She assured me that the Navy would take care of their own and that they would get to the bottom of it. In any case, I did not need to contact a lawyer, the Navy would do what was right.

This would be a common theme during the investigation and it would be repeated during every meeting and phone conversation. When deception is not an inherent part of your character, it's difficult to see it when it's coming from another source. She asked me when I could come into the hospital and we agreed on an appointment at the end of that month.

When I met with the Navy captain, I was a little taken aback. She was very matronly looking. She could have been anyone's grandmother. Again the first thing that was mentioned was, "There is no need to get a lawyer. The Navy takes care of their own". It was a strange comment; up to this point there had been no mention of a lawyer, except from the Navy. "The Navy takes care of their own," is what I wanted to hear.

I was there because I thought they wanted to find out what went wrong and respond to the admiral's request. Contacting a lawyer was the last thing on my mind. At this point the CO of the hospital had said the Navy would not pay for anything and the medical bills were mounting quickly. As the conversation went forward the captain assured me that I would get a complete copy of any investigation when it was completed, and I needed to be as open as possible. At this point I still had no idea I was being manipulated. Trusting people was always my handicap throughout my entire career.

When we finished our conversation she escorted me over to the Orthopedics Department, where I was greeted with the same hostility as before. After almost an hour of physical examinations and questions they finished, and I was told that I would most likely have to come back for further testing. On my return home I thought about what had taken place. I was starting to mistrust the doctors and doubt their motives. My belief in the Navy enabled me to overcome my mistrust and I continued to respond to their requests. The idea of being sent to the same department that caused the problem for the evaluation seemed ludicrous. When the captain called back to ask me to come in for further evaluation, I asked if I could also be seen by a doctor from a different department. She agreed and said it would be set up at the same time.

Two weeks had passed before I returned to Balboa. The head of Orthopedics was even more hostile than the first visit. After a short physical and a series of additional questions the meeting was over. The Navy captain had set up another meeting with one of the Navy neurosurgeons, so I headed for his office. As I sat waiting to be seen by the neurosurgeon, I went through everything that had just happened and didn't like the direction it was going. I had complete atrophy from the waist down on the left side, and the size of my leg was less than half that of my right. I was able to get around using crutches and determination. There had been no improvement since the operation. To be treated the way I was by the head of the Orthopedics Department was personally insulting. If it wasn't for the respect I had for the admiral that had requested the investigation, I would have told them to shove it after the first meeting.

The neurosurgeon was finally able to see me. As the conversation progressed I felt a little more relaxed. The surgeon seemed sincerely concerned and thoroughly went through all the records. As he listened to what I had to say, he seemed to get more and more agitated. As I completed the story he responded with, "Let me tell you something Commander, what I've seen and heard is disgusting. The way this was handled makes me sick. After seeing these X-rays, you're lucky the Orthopedics Department didn't operate on you. If they did you would most likely be wearing a diaper for the rest of your life along with those crutches or worse. In fact this makes me so mad, I'm going to tell the CO exactly what I think of this entire incident. It's my guess that you have less than a 10% chance of recovery from your injuries." He stood up and said, "Let's go see if the CO is available right now." Finally, I had found someone that treated me as if I were still a human being.

As we reached the CO's office, the surgeon went to the assistant's desk and asked to see the captain. When the assistant came back out, the surgeon was told the captain would see him, but that CDR Billings would have to wait out here in the lobby. The surgeon went in to see the hospital CO and a few minutes later the female captain came over to where I sat and asked if I would come into her office. I followed her in and sat down; it was nothing but small talk.

She repeated her favorite phrase, "The Navy will take care of their own." I should have been smart enough to catch on; maybe I still wanted to believe they would do the right thing. At this point I was trying to rehabilitate myself with no direction from anyone. The CO's office door could be seen from where I was sitting and after a few minutes I saw a Navy CDR with a lawyer's insignia on his collar go into the CO's office. The small talk continued for a few more minutes, then I saw the surgeon being escorted out of the CO's office by the lawyer. In the next minute the captain received a short call and then hung up.

I expressed my concern over what had just taken place and the way I was treated by the head of Orthopedics. It was apparent that she wanted to end the discussion and displayed very little interest in my conversation with the neurosurgeon. Again she assured me, the Navy would take care of the matter and that they would get to the bottom of it. All that was left was for them to do was put all the facts together, and I should not be concerned about anything. They would be in contact with me when they completed the investigation. I asked to see the neurosurgeon again and was told that he wasn't available.

My whole life I had tried to stand up for what was right. I could not accept the fact that this was a cover up by the hospital. I was a victim of my own values and could not believe that naval officers could be this devious. There was still the matter of the almost $20,000 in civilian medical bills that were piling up. When I asked the captain about them, she showed very little interest and suggested that I might try to take it up with CHAMPUS, which was the medical insurance program for military personnel. I left and returned home to wait for the results of their investigation.

A month had passed and I had heard nothing. Out of frustration I called Balboa and the captain that had been handling my case. When I reached her, she had changed from her matronly demeanor to a more distant and unconcerned manner. When I asked about the results of the investigation, she didn't know what I was talking about. I got a little agitated; she had promised me a half dozen times that I would get a copy of the investigation when it was complete. Her response was, "I don't know what you're talking about. There has been no investigation, and I cannot discuss this matter with you any longer. You'll have to talk to our lawyers." Then she hung up the phone.

I was stunned. I could understand one person responding this way, but not the whole department. They were under the direction of the CO of the hospital and none of them seemed to have the backbone to do what was right. The entire Orthopedics Department seemed to be in collusion. Was there not one doctor that would put a stop to this conspiracy to cover up their incompetence? The disappearance of the neurosurgeon was a sample of how swiftly the CO dealt with those who tried to do what was right. It was a surreal situation; it was like I was the one that was wrong and they were standing up for their rights.

After I hung up the phone I sat there for awhile, not believing what had just happened. I couldn't believe I was so stupid, so gullible! Everything I believed in was turned upside down. A day would pass before I decided what to do. It was difficult for me to ask for help from anyone, I had too much pride. I decided to call the admiral and tell him what had just taken place. After all, he had requested the investigation.

When I reached him, we talked for a while and he said he would make a few phone calls to check into the matter. As the days passed my anger continued to build. I felt like I had been raped. What hurt most was it was the Navy that was doing this to me. I loved the Navy; the Navy could do no wrong. It was everything that I learned to believe in; I was sure the admiral would get to the bottom of it. A week had gone by before I got a call from the admiral's aide. The aide told me the admiral would like to talk to me and asked if I could come down to his office the following day. It would be great to see the admiral.

I hadn't seen him since the days aboard the *Belleau Wood*. I agreed.

When I arrived I was immediately shown into the admiral's office. The admiral motioned for me to sit down and we talked about the *Belleau Wood* and what had happened over the last three years. After all the small talk was done, the admiral turned serious. "Al, about this incident at Balboa. I've been instructed to stay out of it. I can't tell you how much this disturbs me. I wish there was something I could do or say, but it's out of my hands."

I sat there for a minute. I had a great deal of respect for the admiral and knew if there was anything he could do, he would have done it. The admiral saw the cane and asked me about the injury. I blew it off and told him I was rehabilitating myself. He didn't need to know the details. I told the admiral that I would work it out. The mood had quickly changed and there wasn't anything left to say. I thanked him for taking the time to see me and wished him luck in his new command.

I didn't understand. I never would have let this happen to one of my men. For almost 20 years I had fought for the rights of others and at the risk of my own career. I had gone against carrier air group commanders, commanding officers, and admirals to fight for what was right and for those who served with me. There was not one person in the position of authority that was willing to step up in on my behalf. I wanted to fight, but I was a civilian now and seemed to be getting blocked at every turn with lies and deception. I had gone from an asset to a liability and on my own I had to deal with a bureaucracy that was designed to defeat me.

When I returned home I decided to contact the lawyers at Balboa. There must be someone out there who was interested in the truth. Again it was my naïve understanding of what was right and wrong. After several calls I finally reached a Navy lawyer. The lawyer was familiar with what had happened. When I asked for a copy of the investigation, the lawyer told me there had been no investigation. When I tried to explain that I saw the written documentation the doctors had put together and that I was promised a copy when they were done, the lawyer cut me off and again assured me there was no investigation. I told the lawyer about the neurosurgeon, CDR Yansese, and what he said. I asked to see the neurosurgeon and was told he didn't work at Balboa any longer. At this point the lawyer got aggravated and said. "Look, CDR! There was no investigation. You have no rights. Don't call here again. You're the VA's problem now. If you have any complaints, see them," and hung up the phone.

Again I sat there staring at the wall. The Navy was all I knew. I was devastated at the thought that the Navy could do this to anyone. It was like getting kicked in the stomach a second time. Later when I made a request for my medical records I found out they didn't exist either. It was almost like I had never been in the Navy. I would have plenty of time to think about what had happened while I tried to rehabilitate myself. I'm not sure what was put into my file, but the Veteran's Administration (VA) didn't seem to want to have much to do with me either. I didn't know if the Navy had anything to do with it or it was the dismal apathy of the personnel who worked in the VA hospitals.

I would finally come to the conclusion that it was not the Navy. It couldn't be, not something that I had dedicated my entire adult life to, I couldn't accept that. The Navy had some of the finest men I had ever met and would ever hope to meet. One organization with a few sick individuals running it did not make the Navy. I needed to believe in that in order to try to put it to rest. What could possibly make these doctors respond in this manor? Didn't they take an oath to help people? What was driving them? I couldn't find an answer, my mind didn't work that way.

I later contacted the CHAMPUS office to see if I could get them to pick up some of the medical bills. When I explained what had happened, they were appalled, and suggested I contact one of the local TV news stations and tell them what had happened. It was not my way. I would not allow the Navy to get any bad publicity. Not an organization that I had respected for over 22 years. Back then the news still portrayed the military as a bunch of incompetent warmongers and enjoyed any opportunity to denigrate the military. It was Balboa and Captain Koenin, who was the CO of the naval hospital at that time. He orchestrated the whole thing. I had seen it too many times, career officers consumed by the idea of reaching the highest rank possible generally used poor judgment when it came to putting the men or the organization ahead of their own personal aspirations. What bothered me was it appeared that there was nothing I could do as a civilian. How many times had he gotten away with this and would he continue to treat servicemen like this? If I was still wearing a uniform I would have taken it as far as I needed to in order to get it stopped, that's what I did best. To this point I had been stopped at every attempt to resolve the issue. The VA was still keeping me at arms' length. It appeared they didn't want to get involved.

CHAMPUS was able to pick up most of the medical bills. The days turned into weeks and months as I struggled to recover. I exercised long hours everyday to try and build strength in my left side. I did not accept failure and pushed myself until my toes would bleed, trying to force the use of the leg. Over the next three and a half years, and without the help of the Navy or the VA, I would struggle to recover physically from the injuries. Finally I was able to walk without the use of a cane. I was even able to walk without the awkwardness of a noticeable limp. I had been given less than a 10% chance of recovering, but I never gave up, it was my nature.

The journey was complete, but it would take years before I would acknowledge what took place at the Navy hospital. It was too repulsive, too humiliating to think about. Unfortunately those doctors at the Balboa Naval Hospital never received any condemnation for what they did to many of the men that served their country without reservation.

Over the years I chose only to remember the goods things about the Navy and to honor the men I served with for what they accomplished. As an aging naval aviator I realized that I was in an environment where I was overmatched and out of my league when it came to the politics and manipulations of unprincipled men.

Duty, Honor, Country

Through my entire Navy career I was able to maintain my integrity and I did not compromise my beliefs or the men I served with. I met life head-on as I challenged those intrusions and aggressions of others. Above it all, I remember the loyalty and the comradery of the men who served. To this day those memories are some the most important in my life. Together we overcame enormous odds by believing in each other and nothing can ever change that. There will always be those people that are willing to standby and watch, while others make the decisions and take the chances. This in and of itself is not wrong. It's those individuals who are willing to run in after the risks are taken and try to claim credit for themselves, whom I find difficult to accept.

My Vietnam experience helped me to understand who I really was and hopefully become a better person. By the time the conflict ended I was old beyond my years and found that the truth about war was that it is not glamorous, or heroic, but complicated and at times morally messy. It was not glorious or noble deaths, but dead friends who never had a chance to experience life. I kept asking myself, where do we get these men of honor, patriotism and sense of duty that make the sacrifices that make our country so great? In their memory I feel obligated to revisit the Vietnam War one more time out of respect for those who made the sacrifices during a time when the military was treated like second class citizens. If we remember history as it truly happened, and not what the news chooses to portray, hopefully we will not repeat our mistakes.

The early chapters of the book bring to light the bureaucratic mismanagement of the war and the leadership ability and integrity required to lead the men and women of the armed services. These universal concepts have not changed in over 200 years of conflicts. I read an article published in the American Legend magazine, written by Fred Peck, a retired Marine Colonel, and in it he refutes some of the popular myths about the Vietnam veterans. I think it is important enough to paraphrase a few lines from it to help complete this journey and set the record straight:

The profit motivated, negative image shown on the silver screen in movies such as the *Deer Hunter, Born on the Fourth of July, Platoon* and *Full Metal Jacket*, to name a few, only portrayed the men as being from the lower rungs of society and those who were disproportionately young, poor, and minorities. They promoted the Vietnam War vets as cannon fodder who returned home addicted to drugs, suffering from Post Traumatic Stress Disorders (PSTD), and gave the impression that most are living in the streets as homeless derelicts today. What has been promoted though, comes almost totally from those who resisted, those who protested and from those who avoided the service. Is it any surprise that many of the news stations had their own version of the recent war in Iraq?

The real truth about the men who served in Vietnam comes from a 1980 Harris Poll. The poll showed that 91% of the Vietnam veterans were glad they'd served their country, 74% enjoyed their time in the service and 89% agreed with the statement that **"our troops were asked to fight in a war they were not allowed to win."** The politicians had screwed the war up so miserably there was no moral sense that played a part on the field of battle; it was survival and fighting for the man who stood next to you.

Nine million men and women served in the military during Vietnam, 3 million of whom went to Vietnam. Contrary to most beliefs, two-thirds of them were volunteers; only a third of them were draftees. Contrast this with the fact that two-thirds of those who served in World War II were drafted. Please don't misunderstand; this is not to criticize those brave men and women that served in WWII. We are only talking about statistics and the misrepresentation of the two myths by those who in many cases never served. The statistics show that the reverse of these myths is many times true. You need to consider the facts as reported by James Webb: In WWII, the average age of those who served was 25, of which 24% were high school graduates and 7% were college graduates. In Vietnam, the average age was 23, where 79% were high school graduates, and 20% were college graduates. Volunteers made up 67% of the forces in Vietnam but suffered 77% of the casualties and 73% of the deaths. Webb also debunks the myth repeated frequently today that minorities suffered a disproportionate level of casualties. In fact, Webb and many others have reported that African-Americans were 13.1% of the population during the Vietnam War, and they represented 12.6% of the Armed Forces. Contrary to conventional wisdom, they suffered 12.2% of those killed or wounded. Still, due to the efforts of the press and the film industry, the myths remain.

Today our servicemen and women return to parades, bands and people lining the streets waiving American flags in honor of their sacrifices. To a retired veteran it is heart warming to see that our military is finally receiving the recognition that they so richly deserve. As Vietnam veterans it is our duty to ensure that those we left behind and those that suffered the most are not forgotten.

That's one of the reasons I think I was driven to write this book. So many times our young men and women are motivated to take action by the manipulation of the actual events, or what someone chooses to remember and not what really happened. Unfortunately in this day and age of the "Spin Factor" it's difficult to really know what in actual fact is the truth. It seems we increasingly need to evaluate the source of the information and its seemingly hidden agenda before we can determine whether the information is based on fact or a convenient interpretation of what actually happened.

If any one group deserves the majority of the credit for the bad things that happened to the returning Vietnam veterans, it is the news media and the film industry. Both profited by misleading and maligning the men and women who served so gallantly. Any first year psychology student will tell you that if you tell someone they are a failure and a loser enough times they will eventually begin to believe it, and you may find them as a homeless person on the street.

It is also my belief that many of the returning Vets who sought help from the VA upon their return had their conditions and emotional state aggravated by the poor treatment and lack of interest demonstrated by the VA and the very government they swore to serve and protect. If they didn't have Post Traumatic Stress Disorder (PTSD) upon return, they got it from the feeling that their government had abandoned them. It's very simple. In combat you learn to trust each other and nothing is more important. In order to endure the sacrifices that are needed to make this country strong you must trust that your government will do what is right. There is nothing worse than having that feeling of trust taken away. Especially by a bunch of self-serving politicians that have assured that their own self-interests are taken care of first.

I went to Vietnam to find out who I was. What I found was the meaning of the words duty, honor, country, and I learned it from the men who served and the journey through my 22 years of military service. The unbelievers today will say they are but words, but a slogan, but a flamboyant phrase. Every scholar, every cynic, every hypocrite, every troublemaker, and, I am sorry to say, some others of an entirely different character, will try to downgrade them even to the extent of mockery and ridicule.

To me those words taught me to be proud and unbending in honest failure, and to be humble in success; not to substitute words for actions, and not to seek the path of least resistance. I learned to face each task head-on no matter how difficult the challenge and not to shirk from my responsibilities. I learned to stand up in the storm, but to have compassion for those who tried and failed. I learned to laugh at myself, yet never forgot how to weep for those who had fallen. I learned to be serious, yet never to take myself too seriously. If this is leadership, then this is what I learned.

I'm sure there were others that were there for some of the same reasons. To serve because they felt it was the right thing to do. We will always have those individuals that are willing to make the sacrifices that give us the freedoms we enjoy today no matter what their reasons. Thank God for those individuals. For those who choose not to go, they should have that right, but they should also respect the rights of those who served and honor their sacrifices. For above all they are the ones who must suffer the deepest scars of war.

Make no mistake, the military is truly different for those who believe in what they are doing, and few civilians will ever experience or understand it. The military is a profession of arms; you must have the will to fight, the sure knowledge that in war there is no substitute for victory, and trust that your government will do what is right. That if you fail, everyone, everything that is important to you may not enjoy life as they know it today. In order to endure the sacrifices of military service you must believe in duty, honor, and country.

Others will debate the controversial issues, national and international, which divide men's minds. Those that serve must remain unruffled, calm, and aloof, as they stand as the nation's guardians, as its lifeguards from the raging tides of international conflict. For almost two centuries the military has defended, guarded, and protected the traditions of liberty and freedom throughout the world without complaint. What could be more noble?

When you serve and if you should decide to make a career of the service you will have to standby while civilian voices argue the virtues of our processes of government. Whether our strength is being sapped by deficit spending indulged in too long, by Federal paternalism grown too strong, by power groups grown too arrogant, by politics grown too corrupt, by crime grown too rampant, by taxes grown too high, or by extremists grown too violent. You will have to standby while they argue whether our personal liberties are as thorough and complete as they should be. These great national problems are not for your participation or military solution. Such is the life of those who serve.

Although these stories center around the military and bring out the character and the politics of individuals that served, they are not meant to judge anyone, and I apologize to those who may have taken this story the wrong way or may be offended. It was a story that needed to be told to set the record straight, and it is my best recollection without prejudice of the actual events.

There will always be officers that get it backwards. They will never understand that we are responsible for our men, not the other way around. They will do whatever they need to in order to advance themselves or their agenda without taking any risks. The special operations forces have an aphorism of "Leave no man behind." It is my personal belief that it is the duty of every officer, including those in the medical field, to see that the men and women who serve our country are treated fairly and with dignity. There is only one reason you are serving, and that is to support those servicemen and women that make the daily sacrifices and stand as the guardians of freedom. If you do not perform these duties to the best of your abilities, and without prejudice, then you do not deserve to wear the uniform.

There is a trend today that the end justifies the means and anything goes when it comes to bending or manipulating the truth. When our children have to learn what integrity and honor means out of a book, then we are doing something wrong. It is our duty to show our children and grandchildren what integrity, God, country and family truly are, especially at a time when the world is so unpredictable.

Make no mistake that the loss of one of my grandsons in an armed conflict in the service of his country would be one of the most painful things I would ever have to endure. But to see them standby with indifference while they watched others defend this country would be just as painful. Freedom is not without sacrifice.

"Do it, learn from it, profit and move on."

Epilogue

When I retired from the Navy I had a 63 year old secretary, Ms. Thelma Munzer, working for me. In many ways she had better leadership qualities than some of the officers I met in my 22 years of service. The day I retired she brought a copy of her favorite song and said, "I don't know of anyone that this song fits better." This is for you Thelma.

"My Way"
FRANK SANATRA

And now, the end is near; And so I face the final curtain. My friend, I'll say it clear, I'll state my case, of which I'm certain.

I've lived a life that's full. I've traveled each and ev'ry highway; But more, much more than this, I did it my way.

Regrets, I've had a few; But then again, too few to mention. I did what I had to do and saw it through without exemption.

I planned each charted course; Each careful step along the byway, But more, much more than this, I did it my way.

Yes, there were times, I'm sure you knew, When I bit off more than I could chew. But through it all, when there was doubt, I ate it up and spit it out. I faced it all and I stood tall; And did it my way.

I've loved, I've laughed and cried. I've had my fill; my share of losing. And now, as tears subside, I find it all so amusing.

To think I did all that; And may I say - not in a shy way, "No, oh no not me, I did it my way."

For what is a man, what has he got? If not himself, then he has naught. To say the things he truly feels; And not the words of one who kneels. The record shows I took the blows - And did it my way!

If I had a regret, it is that I felt I let down those junior officers that believed what I was doing was right. When I didn't make captain, those junior officers may have seen it as a failure. That who or what they believed in at the time, was not the key to advancement. Because of events like those portrayed in this book, they may choose to bend to the political pressures, rather than hold fast to those beliefs that are so dear to them. If I had a chance to talk to them today, I would tell them that I would not have changed a thing. As the years go by and as each day ends I can reflect on the past and know that I did what was right and that I did not kneel to anyone. I did not compromise my beliefs for profit or personal gain. To be true to oneself and serve others is all the reward you need.